E–Adoption and Technologies for Empowering Developing Countries:

Global Advances

Sushil K. Sharma
Ball State University, USA

Managing Director:	Lindsay Johnston
Senior Editorial Director:	Heather Probst
Book Production Manager:	Sean Woznicki
Development Manager:	Joel Gamon
Development Editor:	Myla Harty
Acquisitions Editor:	Erika Gallagher
Typesetters:	Deanna Zombro
Print Coordinator:	Jamie Snavely
Cover Design:	Nick Newcomer, Greg Snader

Published in the United States of America by
Information Science Reference (an imprint of IGI Global)
701 E. Chocolate Avenue
Hershey PA 17033
Tel: 717-533-8845
Fax: 717-533-8661
E-mail: cust@igi-global.com
Web site: http://www.igi-global.com

Library of Congress Cataloging-in-Publication Data

Sharma, Sushil K.
  E-adoption and technologies for empowering developing countries : global advancements / Sushil K. Sharma, editor.
    p. cm.
  Includes bibliographical references and index.
  ISBN 978-1-4666-0041-6 (hardcover) -- ISBN 978-1-4666-0042-3 (ebook) -- ISBN 978-1-4666-0043-0 (print & perpetual access) 1. Distance education--Computer-assisted instruction. 2. Social networks--Developing countries. 3. Electronic commerce--Developing countries.
  LC5803.C65.E13 2012
  371.35'8--dc23
                                   2011044133

British Cataloguing in Publication Data
A Cataloguing in Publication record for this book is available from the British Library.

All work contributed to this book is new, previously-unpublished material. The views expressed in this book are those of the authors, but not necessarily of the publisher.

Table of Contents

Sushil K. Sharma, Ball State University, USA
Rui Chen, Ball State University, USA
Jeff Zhang, Ball State University, USA

Peter Woodhead, German Swiss International School, Hong Kong, China
David M. Kennedy, Lingnan University, China

Sibylle Mabry, Louisiana State University in Shreveport, USA

Nazim Ahmed, Ball State University, USA
Ray Montagno, Ball State University, USA
Sushil Sharma, Ball State University, USA

Olusegun Folorunso, University of Agriculture Abeokuta, Nigeria
Rebecca O. Vincent, University of Agriculture Abeokuta, Nigeria
Adewale Opeoluwa Ogunde, Redeemer's University (RUN), Nigeria
Benjamin Akintayo Agboola, University of Agriculture Abeokuta, Nigeria

Detailed Table of Contents

    Sushil K. Sharma, Ball State University, USA
    Rui Chen, Ball State University, USA
    Jeff Zhang, Ball State University, USA

The Internet and other Information and Communication Technologies (ICTs), in the form of e-adoption, have been used for social and economic development around the world. Information and Communication Technologies for Development is a growing research area and researchers worldwide have been conducting studies highlighting how the use of the Internet and ICTs are helping in socio-economic development in the fields of medicine, health, agriculture, education, and government. This chapter discusses the general impact e-adoption has on empowering developing countries for development.

Chapter 1
    Peter Woodhead, German Swiss International School, Hong Kong, China
    David M. Kennedy, Lingnan University, China

This paper examines what happens when young learners in a primary school in Hong Kong start from learning *about* information and communication technologies (ICTs) to learning *with* and *through* ICTs. The authors focus on how students used learning technologies when an H1N1 outbreak closed the school for three weeks and teachers were required to use ICTs to initiate at-home learning. This gave the researchers an opportunity to assess the capacity of young students using Web 2.0 technologies to support learning and the impact that these tools have on teacher views and practice. Data includes interviews with teachers and examples of students' work. Findings demonstrate how confident and comfortable young learners are with new technologies, raising questions about prevailing assumptions that young students have the capacity to easily use the existing school-based learning management system and Web 2.0 applications. The authors provide evidence that students can effectively engage with ICTs and demonstrate very high levels of skills. However, students did not do so automatically, and required assessment tasks were often key drivers for initiating student engagement and learning.

The spotlight on business innovation in growth-oriented organizations has never been hotter. Information systems (IS) innovation, in particular, has become the main focus for many businesses and their CIOs because of its potential for business agility and competitiveness. However, creating a culture that can effectively exploit the innovative forces of an organization is challenging, and no shared guidelines exist. The purpose here is to examine empirically how the competing forces of organizational cultures in tandem with senior executives constructively influence the innovative efforts of organizations. Central to this investigation is the adoption of an IS architecture (SOA) whose implementation may entail radical transformation of traditional business patterns. Data were collected from U.S. top IS executives, and the results suggest that the adopters of SOA (45%) are organizations whose executives embrace certain collaborative behavior, which, in people-oriented and progress-oriented cultures, seems to be a catalyst for change and adoption of transformational IS architecture..

The business environment of the 21st century require organizations to respond quickly to market demands and thus traditional organization structures and strategy are no longer capable of sustaining the needs of this relentless pace. New forms of organizations in the form of virtual organization (VO) hold promise in the network world. Several organizations worldwide have already been experimenting virtual organizations' structures and processes. These new virtual structures and processes, however, will require newer strategies to succeed. This paper attempts to highlight some strategy and structural issues of a VO. The study is conceptual in nature and inferences have been drawn from existing literature and practices.

Chapter 4

Knowledge Sharing Adoption Model called (KSAM) was developed in this paper using Artificial Neural Networks (ANN). It investigated students' Perceived Usefulness and Benefits (PUB) of Knowledge Sharing among students of higher learning in Nigeria. The study was based on the definition as well as on the consticts related to technology acceptance model (TAM). A survey was conducted using structured questionnaire administered among students and analysed with SPSS statistical tool; the results were evaluated using ANN. The KSAM includes six constucts that include Perceived Ease Of Sharing (PEOS),

Perceived Usefulness and Benefits (PUB), Perceived Barriers for Sharing (PBS), External Cues to Share (ECS), Attitude Towards Sharing (ATT), and Behavioral Intention to Share (BIS). The result showed that Students' PUB must be raised in order to effectively increase the adoption of Knowledge Sharing in this domain. The paper also identified a myriad of limitations in knowledge sharing and discovered that the utilization of KSAM using ANN is feasible. Findings from this study may form the bedrock on which further studies can be built.

Chapter 5

Location-based advertising (LBA) opens up new frontiers for marketers to place their advertisements in front of consumers. LBA is a new form of marketing communication that uses location-tracking technology in mobile networks to target consumers with location-specific advertising on their cell phones. It provides more targeted communication and interaction between the marketer and its potential customers. This paper reviews different aspects of LBA advertising and investigates the drivers of consumer acceptance toward it. Achieving this, a research framework is developed to explore the factors influencing consumer intention for using LBA in Iran. Individuals' responses to questions about intention to accept/use of LBA advertising were collected and analyzed with various factors modified from UTAUT with main constructs of utility expectancy, trust, effort expectancy, and control. While the model confirms the classical role of utility expectancy and effort expectancy as the key factors in technology acceptance, the results also show that users' behavioral intentions are influenced by trust and their control on ads flow.

Chapter 6

In this paper a Digital Terrestrial Television (DTT) based voting system is presented. This electronic voting technology allows disabled users to cast their vote from home by using common well-known devices. The needed equipment are a TV set, a Set Top Box (STB) with its remote control and a telephone line. The complete infrastructure consists of an MHP (Multimedia Home Platform) application that acts as a client application, a server application that acts as a network/counting server for e-voting, and a security protocol based on asymmetric key encryption to ensure authentication and secrecy of the vote. The MHP application is broadcasted by a certified (e.g., national) TV channel that grants its originality. The user needs a smart card issued by a national authority and to sign the encrypted ballot. The voter can browse the application by acting on the STB remote control. The server application is in charge to verify user identity, to gather and store user's encrypted ballots and finally to count votes. The communication between the client application and the server takes place by means of a secured channel (using HTTPS) while the voting operations are secured with the help of asymmetric keys encryption.

Chapter 7

The move toward Policy-Oriented Web is destined to provide support for policy expression and management in the core web layers. One of the most promising areas that can drive this new technology adoption is e-Society communities. With so much user-generated content being shared by these social networks, there is the real danger that the implicit sharing rules that communities have developed over time will be lost in translation in the new digital communities. This will lead to a corresponding loss in confidence in e-Society sites. The Policy-Oriented Web attempts to turn the implicit into the explicit with a common framework for policy language interoperability and awareness. This paper reports on the policy driving factors from the Social Networks experiences using real-world use cases and scenarios. In particular, the key functions of policy-awareness—for privacy, rights, and identity—will be the driving force that enables the e-Society to appreciate new interoperable policy regimes.

Chapter 8

E-voting increasingly gains interest in e-Democracy and e-Government movements. Not only the technical security issues of electronic voting systems are of paramount importance, but also the necessity of following an all-embracing approach is challenging and needs to be addressed. This paper discusses e-voting as being a supreme discipline of e-Government. It introduces an innovative e-voting concept using the Internet as the voting channel. The concept introduced is based on Austrian e-Government elements and the Austrian identity management concept in particular. This paper presents a novel approach of building an e-voting system relying on two core principles: strong end-to-end encryption and stringent identity domain separation.

Chapter 9

Electronic mailing systems are the dominant communication systems in private and business matters. Public administrations deliver documents to citizens and businesses—subpoenas, legal verdicts, notifications, administrative penalties, and so forth. However, official activities are more strongly bound to legal regulations than in civil law. Delivery of crucial and personal documents raises the demand for qualified identification and non-repudiation services as featured by registered and certified mail in the paper world. Legal requirements for electronic delivery carried out by public administrations (eDelivery) cannot be fulfilled by standard mailing systems. Although the requirements for eDelivery systems may differ due to national legal regulations, this paper discusses common requirements and properties on an abstract level. Moreover, the author shows how these requirements have been addressed by introducing the Austrian eDelivery system for eGovernment applications.

Chapter 10

Thamer Alhussain, Griffith University, Australia
Steve Drew, Griffith University, Australia

This paper discusses an exploratory study of government employees' perceptions of the introduction of biometric authentication at the workplace in the Kingdom of Saudi Arabia. The authors suggest that studying the factors affecting employees' acceptance of new technology will help ease the adoption of biometric technology in other e-government applications. A combination of survey and interviews was used to collect the required data. Interviews were conducted with managers and questionnaires were given to employees from two different government organisations in Saudi Arabia to investigate the employees' perceptions of using biometrics. The results of this study indicate a significant digital and cultural gap between the technological awareness of employees and the preferred authentication solutions promoted by management. A lack of trust in technology, its potential for misuse and management motives reflect the managers' need to consider their responsibilities for narrowing these gaps. It was apparent that overcoming employees' resistance is an essential issue facing biometric implementation. Based on the research the authors recommend that an awareness and orientation process about biometrics should take place before the technology is introduced into the organisation.

Chapter 11

Keith Thomas, The Chinese University of Hong Kong, China
Paul Lam, The Chinese University of Hong Kong, China
Annisa Ho, The Chinese University of Hong Kong, China

Successful knowledge transfer or diffusion of e-learning practice goes beyond precursor incentives and anticipated rewards for the individual lecturer. It also involves wider enabling of learning attributes and cultural capabilities in an organization. This paper examines how some of these attributes and capabilities play out in an educational institution in the context of web-enabled technology. An organizational-learning model is used to examine diffusion of practices after initial design and development. This paper is based on a case study of eight course-level e-learning projects in a university based in Hong Kong. The study illustrates a number of issues and challenges for the wider uptake of the initial idea from the individual course to the programme and wider institution.

Chapter 12

Zerrin Ayvaz Reis, Istanbul University, Turkey

The evolution of Internet has provided an opportunity for offering online learning. The old online learning models are getting replaced by new e-learning models. Many universities worldwide have started offering e-learning or online learning through a variety of online learning methods. In fact, the current e-learning models are revolutionizing the instructional content delivery, learning activities, and social communication. Although online learning environments are becoming popular, there is minimal research on learners' attitudes toward online learning environments. The purpose of this study is to explore learners' attitudes toward online learning. Over 300 participants participated. The findings of this study of students' perceptions and attitudes toward online learning not only will help assess pedagogical approach but also help university officials prepare Internet-based online education delivery.

Chapter 13

Fatih Gursul, Istanbul University, Turkey
Hafize Keser, Ankara University, Turkey
Sevinc Gulsecen, Istanbul University, Turkey

This study's aim is to find out student's perspectives on online and face-to-face problem-based learning approaches. The study was conducted at the Department of Computer Education and Instructional Technologies, Faculty of Education, Hacettepe University. Participants were 42 freshman students attending the department during fall of 2006-2007. These students were put into two groups—the online problem-based learning group and the face-to-face problem-based learning group. The research was conducted on Mathematics-I while implementing the topic of 'derivation'. The content analysis statistical technique is used, as well as a questionnaire consisting of open-ended questions, which perform as a data collection tool to find out the views of the students in context to the process.

Chapter 14

Wajeeh Daher, An-Najah National University, Palestine and Al-Qasemi Academic College
of Education, Israel

The constant comparative method (Lincoln & Guba, 1985) was used to analyze preservice teachers' discussions and interactions in wiki discussion sections regarding geometric lessons that were written by other preservice teachers in the year before. The data was compared for the following interaction aspects of knowledge building: dialogical actions, participants' roles, and discussion tracks. Research shows that building their content and pedagogic content knowledge, the preservice teachers together with the lecturer used mainly proposing, asking, requesting, arguing, presenting, and moving the discussion forward as dialogical actions. Proposing and asking were used for various goals such as proposing various ideas and actions, and asking about different issues concerned with geometric content and pedagogic content knowledge. The lecturer asked questions more than the preservice teachers, while the preservice teachers proposed more than the lecturer. The knowledge building was collaborative in nature, and one important aspect which enabled the collaboration is the topology of the wiki discussion section. This topology enables presenting the content of the messages; not just the titles, where the contents are presented as having the same level and thus the same importance.

Adeyinka Tella, University of Ilorin, Nigeria
S. M. Mutula, University of Botswana, Botswana
Athulang Mutshewa, University of Botswana, Botswana
Angelina Totolo, University of Botswana, Botswana

This study evaluated a WebCT course content management (CCMS) system at the University of Botswana. Survey methodology was used and questionnaires were distributed to 503 students selected from six faculties, and an in-depth interview were conducted involving (20) twenty lecturers who teach via the WebCT platform. Findings reveal that, generally, WebCT CCMS is doing well at the University of Botswana and that the system has been a success. The results also confirm the quality of course materials uploaded on the system, that is, service quality and the quality of the teaching and learning via the system. Furthermore, by learning through WebCT, students are able to self regulate their learning and, given the opportunity, they are ready to use and continue learning using the WebCT platform. Results also indicate that generally students are satisfied with the performance of WebCT and that there are many benefits associated with the system in context to teaching and learning at the university. Problems associated with WebCT CCMS that are experienced by staff and students of the University include access, network /server failure, lack of link between ITS and WebCT, lack of teaching expertise using WebCT, and failure to remove completed courses from the system.

Henk Eijkman, University of New South Wales at the Australian Defence Force Academy,
Australia
Allan Herrmann, Independent Researcher and Consultant, Australia
Kathy Savige, University of New South Wales at the Australian Defence Force Academy,
Australia

This paper explores the potentially powerful role e-assessment practices can have on culture change in learning and teaching. This paper demonstrates how new e-assessment practices can 'push back' through educational institutions. This is done by applying the work of Gibbs and Simpson (2004/5) to e-assessment practices. To illustrate the practical effects of this evidence-based framework, the authors use UNSW@ADFA to demonstrate the possibilities for new e-assessment practices and their potential to drive systemic change. The authors conclude that the incorporation of these structured, evidence-based e-assessment practices demonstrably improve learning outcomes and student engagement without increasing the workload of staff and students.

Christèle Joly, Chinese International School, Hong Kong, China
Nathalie Iseli-Chan, The University of Hong Kong, China

Growing use of information technology and communication (ICT) tools in language courses with communication at their core has brought opportunities as well as challenges in the predominantly conventional face-to-face context of the classroom. When the French programme in the Department of Linguistics and Modern Languages at The Chinese University of Hong Kong started to integrate an e-learning platform into all language courses, students as well as teachers showed reservations and even disbelief. However, it was unexpected to observe such an interdependent relationship between new technologies and the conventional teaching approach. In this paper, the broad implications of the e-adoption applied to learning French as a foreign language are investigated to highlight students' learning habits and learning process. The strategies used to make technology act as a facilitator across cultures, and various ways to *savoir-faire* diffusion are also discussed. The study shows how new technologies modify in-class teaching, while the traditional face-to-face teaching and learning approach can influence choices in the use of different web tools that lead to blended models of education.

The study focuses on 'horizontal' and 'vertical' adoption of e-learning strategies at The Chinese University of Hong Kong as revealed through computer log records in the centrally supported learning management systems. Horizontal diffusion refers to whether e-learning has spread to influence the practice of more teachers and students. In vertical diffusion, the authors examined whether or not teachers tend to adopt more varied online learning activities in successive years. The overall findings are that, while adoption of simple strategies is increasing, there is little evidence of horizontal and vertical diffusion of more complex strategies. Indeed, the use of some of the more complex strategies, which may relate to greater potential learning benefits, decreased. Results have led to discussions about new focuses and strategies for our institutional eLearning Service.

Preface

The emergence of the Internet and other information communication technologies (ICTs) has been changing the landscape of the business world and society. The Internet has become a new tool for boosting innovation, creativity and competitiveness of all industry and service sectors. It is widely believed that information and communication technology (ICT) has enabled organizations to decrease costs and increase capabilities and thus has enabled inter-organizational coordination. Facebook, Twitter, MySpace, blogs, wikis, collaborative tagging, and other Web 2.0 and social network websites are constantly changing lifestyles and businesses. The e-adoption revolution includes many new tools including social networking, blogs, syndication, folksonomy, wikis, rich media such as geo-localization, webcasts, webinars, virtual world events, interactive ads, applets, and widgets used for both personal interaction and business purposes. The e-adoption revolution is improving the productivity gains in our economies today. The gains stem from both the production of innovative high value ICT-based goods and services and improvements in business processes through the diffusion, adoption and use of ICTs throughout the economy. Literature suggests that e-adoption has improved quality of life, knowledge, and international competitiveness. The edited book, *"E-Adoption and Technologies for Empowering Developing Countries: Global Advancements,"* reports findings of some of the research studies that have been conducted regarding e-adoption.

This edited book, *"E-Adoption and Technologies for Empowering Developing Countries: Global Advancements,"* aims to present various aspects of e-adoption and its impact on empowering developing countries. Literature on e-adoption is growing in leaps and bounds.

This book certainly is not intended to cover every aspect of e-adoption. Rather, this edited book features the ongoing state-of-art research in the e-adoption domain. The book consists of nineteen chapters. The first chapter provides an overview of e-adoption and its impact for empowering developing countries.

The first three chapters in the book discuss how the Internet is becoming the game changer for bringing changes in society as well as in organizations. The Internet has become an instrument for connecting people and bringing change in communication. It is creating a revolution for disseminating useful information in a short period of time to bring changes. The first chapter discusses how students in Hong Kong used learning technologies during an H1N1 outbreak for continuation of their schooling.

The second chapter examines, empirically, how the competing forces of organizational cultures, in tandem with senior executives, constructively influence the innovative efforts of organizations. The results suggest that the adoption of transformational information system architectures, particularly service-oriented architectures, seems to catalyze innovation and change.

Several organizations worldwide have already been experimenting with virtual organizations' structures and processes. However, these new virtual structures and processes require newer strategies to succeed. The third chapter highlights some strategy and structural issues of virtual organizations.

The fourth chapter investigates students' Perceived Usefulness and Benefits (PUB) of Knowledge Sharing among students of higher learning in Nigeria. The study's results show that students' Perceived Usefulness and Benefits must be raised in order to effectively increase the adoption of knowledge sharing.

The literature suggests that marketing companies are using innovative location-tracking technology in mobile networks to target consumers with location-specific advertising on their cell phones. Consequently, location-based advertising is opening up new frontiers for marketers to place their advertisements in front of consumers. The fifth chapter reviews different aspects of location-based advertising and investigates the drivers of consumer acceptance toward it.

Chapters six through ten discuss e-adoption in the context of e-government. The literary evidence through these chapters indicate that an increasing number of countries worldwide have been offering e-government services to their citizens. E-government services are not only creating efficiencies in governmental systems, but also offering newer methods of participation for citizens through e-democracy. An increasing number of success stories of e-government experiments have been documented in the literature. Therefore, research on e-government would be of interest to practitioners, policy makers, and researchers around the world. The reported research in these chapters provides leads to government authorities in drawing up guidelines, approaches, and formulating more effective frameworks to promote e-government in developing countries.

Chapters eleven through eighteen highlight how the evolution of the Internet has provided an opportunity for offering online learning or e-learning. Many universities worldwide have already started offering e-learning or online learning through variety of methods. In fact, the current e-learning models are revolutionizing the traditional instructional content delivery, learning methods, and social communication. The research reported in these chapters indicates that e-learning is empowering the students for their educational opportunities.

The intended audience of this book consists mainly of researchers, research students, and practitioners in e-adoption. The book is also of interest to researchers and practitioners in areas such as e-learning, e-government, and e-adoption in general. I hope that the diverse and comprehensive coverage of e-adoption in this authoritative edited book will contribute to a better understanding of all topics, research, and discoveries as well as an expansion of knowledge in this evolving, significant field of study. It is my sincere hope that this publication and its vast amount of information and research will assist our research colleagues, faculty members, students, and organizational decision makers in enhancing their understanding of the current and emerging issues in e-adoption. Perhaps this publication will even inspire its readers to contribute to the current and future discoveries in this immense field.

The contents of most of the chapters included in this volume were originally published in various volumes of the International Journal of E-adoption. I am grateful to all authors who updated and enhanced their original papers to produce their current work. The whole process of writing, reviewing, rewriting, editing, and proofreading takes a lot of time; and we appreciate all the authors for their efforts and contributions in this project.

Sushil K. Sharma
Ball State University, USA

Acknowledgment

I would like to convey my appreciation to all contributors including the accepted chapters' authors, and many other invisible hands who helped to complete this book. In addition, I also appreciate all reviewers. I want to thank Myla Harty for her patience, encouragement, editorial skills and timely follow up with authors and me to put the book together in the editing, proofreading and layout of the various chapters. Myla regularly gave me a helping hand to complete this project in timely manner and her efforts are very much appreciated. I also thank and appreciate many invisible hands at IGI publications that might have played an active or facilitating role in the completion of this book. I dedicate this book to all the authors of this book for their professional contribution and support. Last but not least, I am grateful to my family who extended their full cooperation for expediting a timely completion of this book. In the end, our special thanks to Ms. Myla Harty for her kind support and great efforts in bringing the book to fruition.

Sushil K. Sharma
Ball State University, USA

Introduction:
E–Adoption and Technologies for Empowering Developing Countries

Sushil K. Sharma
Ball State University, USA

Rui Chen
Ball State University, USA

Jeff Zhang
Ball State University, USA

ABSTRACT

The Internet and other Information and Communication Technologies (ICTs), in the form of e-adoption, have been used for social and economic development around the world. Information and Communication Technologies for Development is a growing research area and researchers worldwide have been conducting studies highlighting how the use of the Internet and ICTs are helping in socio-economic development in the fields of medicine, health, agriculture, education, and government. This chapter discusses the general impact e-adoption has on empowering developing countries for development.

INTRODUCTION

The e-adoption in form of the Internet and other information and communication technologies (ICTs) applications have been delivering basic services in a wide range of sectors including health, agriculture, education, public administration, and commerce. The evidence from several research studies indicates that e-adoption has resulted in social and economic development in developing and least developed countries, worldwide (Bongo, 2005). Internet proliferation, wireless computers and other innovations are quietly eliminating huge barriers to development in poor parts of the world. The UNESCO 2010 report indicates that the e-adoption contributed to poverty reduction and improving health and education in several countries in South Asia (Asia Pacific Research Group, 2005, OECD, 2005, Tandon, 2004). The literature also suggest that Information and Communication

DOI: 10.4018/978-1-4666-0041-6.ch000

Technologies are helping developing countries to "leapfrog" to enhance public administration efficiency, increase access to information and knowledge, and reduce bureaucracy (UNESCO 2010 report, Ahmed et al., 2006, Bayes, et al., 1999, Baliamoune, 2002, Fong, 2009)

The Internet, through various satellite networks, has been linking remote villages to urban markets, bringing classroom education to communities too small or poor to support secondary schools, as well as connecting patients or doctors, or disparate family members for improving health standards. The Internet kiosks that access a global marketplace are used to access political information or organize grassroots campaigns in emerging democracies.

The e-adoption revolution has benefited all sections of society as well as small and large businesses and medium sized enterprises. All kinds of businesses use the Internet for advertising their products and services, exploring new markets for their products, investigating new sources for their supplies, and connecting with clients, partners, and suppliers.

ICTs are a forceful tool to improve government and strengthen democracy and citizen empowerment. It can help foster more transparent governance by enhancing interaction between government and citizens, promoting equity and equality, and empowering minorities (United Nations Economic and Social Council, 2010). It provides a voice to women who have been isolated and invisible. ICTs can contribute to increasing women's networking for social participation in the political process, supporting the work of elected women officials, and increasing women's access to government and its services (Daly, 2003, Martinez & Reilly, 2002).

In recent years, all around the world, e-governance has become a priority in delivering government services and promoting transparency and accountability. This is helping to strengthen the public voice to revitalize democratic processes, as well as improving capacity to deliver basic services.

The literature also suggests that e-adoption has created new opportunities for men and women for networking as well as for electronic commerce activities. Although in many developing nations, several reasons, such as poverty, lack of access and opportunities, illiteracy (including computer illiteracy), and language barriers, still prevent women from using ICTs, including the Internet. These developing nations must take steps to provide equal access to women for ICT-related education and training (Daly, 2003).

E-ADOPTION AND EMPOWERMENT

Various studies have confirmed the positive relationship between e-adoption and economic growth. These studies suggest that e-adoption has the potential in alleviating poverty, improving governmental services, improving health and education, and creating economic opportunities for underprivileged population groups in developing countries. Researchers worldwide are conducting studies on the impact of e-adoption for development and empowerment. The literature in this field is growing in leaps and bounds. Jensen's (2007) micro-level study on fishermen in Kerala, information economy through wireless networks in villages in Robib, Cambodia, (oneworld radio, 2006) for accessing medical and health services, and the global marketplace for their cottage industry are such examples where e-adoption has been exploited for sustainable development and empowerment (World Bank Report, 2006, United Nations Development report, 2010). Several successful e-adoption experiments, worldwide, have resulted not only in improving economic development, but also creating a new world of educational, social, and political opportunities.

A number of e-government initiatives enabling and assisting governments, citizens, and businesses to communicate efficiently, increased efficiency in government processes, delivery of government services to remote populations are found in the literature. For example, the e-government projects of Bhutan, Mongolia and Papua New Guinea, Democratic People's Republic of Korea, and the Palestinian Authority, improved communication amongst government officials and enhanced workflow. Facilitating access to government information services and online government transactions as well as empowering citizens and businesses through e-adoption to interact more efficiently with government are among the well-documented e-government project solutions in Azerbaijan, the Kyrgyz Republic, and Uzbekistan (Martinez & Reilly, 2002).

Mobile phones are quickly becoming an affordable and accessible tool to many poor communities around the world, not only for communication, but also to improve socio-economic opportunities. Several studies highlight the benefits of increased proliferation of Internet-enabled mobile phones among communities in developing countries. The studies indicate that Internet-enabled phones have certainly empowered citizens for their day-to-day business and other activities. For example, the Senegalese telephone company Sonatel, and Manobi, a French company, provided cell phones with Web Access Protocol (WAP) to rural women agricultural producers in Senegal, thereby extending their access to the Internet to obtain information about market prices of the inputs for their food processing activities and for the sale of their produce. Mobile phones for rural women in Senegal is also helping to improve education on gender equality, health and environmental issues, and strengthening poor women's rights and citizenship through the use of Internet radio (Goodman, 2005, Coyle, 2005, Hafkin & Odame, 2002, Holmes, 2004).

The Internet-enabled motorcycles project in Robib, Cambodia, has allowed villagers to get connected with their friends and businesses. The poor communities are getting medical advice from the world's best doctors and schoolchildren are getting their schooling from the best teachers. The Internet-enabled motorcycles project is fueling the village economy by letting local villagers sell their handmade silk scarves on the global market (http://www.prnewswire.com/news-releases/remote-cambodian-village-establishes-internet-telemedicine-link-aimed-at-closing-digital-divide-71328982.html).

Low literacy rates, diverse indigenous languages, limited electricity, strong oral traditions, and nomadic lifestyles or livelihoods are some of the contributing factors that make it difficult for communities in developing countries to e-adopt. The challenge also remains particularly for rural communities in developing countries, where building Internet infrastructures is not economically attractive due to the high cost of reaching users with low purchasing power. Rural tele-density in developing countries is still very low. The lack of good communications infrastructure in rural areas is exacerbated as a result of limited electricity, few fixed-line telephones, and low-income levels. Examining country data reveals a global digital divide between developed and developing nations and unless that digital divide is removed, the e-adoption revolution will not be able to remove income and spatial inequalities within countries (Rice & Katz, 2003).

The e-agriculture projects implemented in several developing countries, such as Honduras, Mauritania, Myanmar, Nicaragua, Kyrgyz Republic, and Samoa, enable rural farmers not only get latest real time market price information for their produce, but also help them to connect directly with buyers and markets (http://www.e-agriculture.org/blog/e-agriculture-rural-women-farmers-wougnet-experience). This has empowered the rural population in these countries for improving agriculture-based economy. In Africa, it was found that information available through the use of mobile phones enabled farmers in Senegal to double the prices of their crops and herders in Angola to locate their cattle through GPS (global positioning system) technology (oneworld radio,

2006, International telecommunication Union, 2004, Samuel et al., 2005).

Another example of empowerment is drawn from the Technology Access Community Centers (TACCs) project in Egypt. The TACCs project offers a unique delivery mechanism that empowers local communities to get a variety of services including telephony, fax machines, copiers, personal computers, software libraries, and Internet access. The TACCs project also provides training, seminars, workshops, roadshows, specialized training, and technical and technological expertise for professionals as well as for the general public. This has resulted in socio-economic development for many communities in Egypt (Hashem, 2001).

The Internet radio has opened a new vista for disseminating information, particularly in rural areas. In Zambia, a radio-based training system is now delivering primary education to out-of-school children, a third of which being orphans. The variety of radio programs covers not only schooling, but also health-related information like hygiene and nutrition. In Bolivia, a rural-based Internet radio helps farmers to deal with worms that devour the crops. Working online, the Swedish experts guide them to identify the worm and broadcast the information on pest control to the entire community http://unpan1.un.org/intradoc/groups/public/documents/unpan/unpan032690.pdf)

Cell phones have emerged as a leading form of leapfrog technology. The best-known example is Bangladesh's Grameen Phone, which has established a network of pay-per-use cell phones throughout the country. A similar network in South Africa has created a network of over 1,800 entrepreneurs, operating "phone shops" in over 4,400 locations across the country. Information that is gathered by cell phones allows farmers in Senegal double the price they get for their crops, and herders in Angola track their cattle via GPS (Ahmed et al., 2006, Bayes, et al., 1999, Fong, 2009, Samuel et al., 2005).

A project in the Mekong region of Thailand and Laos uses the Internet to educate young women and girls on immigration issues, employment alternatives, and health services. It's a way of helping a group that is often only semi-literate, and particularly vulnerable to HIV/AIDS, drug abuse, and sexual exploitation (http://www.policyproject.com/pubs/generalreport/ACF1B3.pdf)

In the post-Soviet country of Armenia, development teams are using the Internet for everything from teacher training to employment counseling. A fisherman, based in Singapore, learned of an earthquake and tsunami and transmitted the same information to Sri Lanka and Thailand through the Internet. This information was passed on to fellow villagers, who used the village's tele-centre to broadcast a community alarm. This resulted in the safety of lives and property (http://alexandrasamuel.com/writing/2005-01-17-TorontoStar-leapfrogging.pdf)

DISCUSSION AND SUMMARY

Several successful e-adoption examples described above, across the world, highlight the fact that e-adoption in form of the Internet and other information and communication technologies have been helping in empowering men, rural women, organizations, and citizens in the local government. The Internet and other ICTs are bolstering the unrestricted flow of information, freedom of expression, and protection of individual liberties. People around the world are using new technologies in unprecedented ways for networking, political participation, and advocacy. With the use of ICTs, women are empowered to promote women's rights. The ICTs have been acting as powerful catalysts for political and social empowerment of women and the promotion of gender equality (Ahmed, et al. 2006, Hafkin & Odame, 2002, Daly, 2003, Holmes, 2004).

The e-adoption revolution may help developing nations transition from the industrial era into the information age, taking the developing world directly from agrarian to post-industrial development. E-adoption also provides governments and businesses a tremendous opportunity to leapfrog. However, in spite of the significant growth in the use of information technology and the Internet, there are still several impediments including the absence of electricity/electricity interruption, lack of some ICTs in the villages/communities, lack of ICTs skills, high cost of ICTs, high cost of access charges, lack of awareness on some of the ICTs, absence of tele-center/information center/cyber café, and illiteracy. These identified impediments need to be taken care of in order to exploit the full potential of e-adoption (Fong, 2009).

REFERENCES

Ahmed, H., et al. (2006). *Measuring the impact of ICT on women in Bangladesh*. Retrieved August 8, 2011 from http://iec.cugo.edu.cn/WorldComp2006/EEE4168.pdf

Asia Pacific Research Group. (2005). *Philippines mobile and mobile data market – Outlook to 2010.* APRG, January 2005.

Baliamoune, M. N. (2002). The new economy and developing countries – Assessing the role of ICT diffusion. *United Nations University, WIDER (World Institute for Development Economics Research), 2002(77).* Retrieved September 9, 2010 from http://www.wider.unu.edu/publications/dps/dps2002/dp2002-77.pdf

Bayes, A., von Braun, J., & Akhter, R. (1999). *Village pay phones and poverty reduction: Insights from a Grameen bank initiative in Bangladesh.* Center for Development Research (AEF), Universitat Bonn. Retrieved August 12, 2011 from http://www.zef.de/publications.htm

Bongo, P. (2005). *The impact of ICT on economic growth.* Retrieved September 6, 2011, from http://129.3.20.41/eps/dev/papers/0501/0501008.pdf

Coyle, D. (2005). *Africa: The impact of mobile phones* (pp. 3–9). London, UK: Vodafone Group.

Daly, J. A. (2003). *ICT, gender equality and empowering women.* Retrieved September 3, 2011, http://old.developmentgateway.org/node/133831/sdm/blob?pid=5233

Economist Intelligence Unit. (2004). *Reaping the benefits of ICT: Europe's productivity challenge.* Report sponsored by Microsoft Euro monitor International, GMI Database. Retrieved September 5, 2011 from http://graphics.eiu.com/files/ad_pdfs/MICROSOFT_FINAL.pdf

Fong, M. (2009). Technology leapfrogging for developing countries. In Khosrow-Pour, M. (Ed.), *Encyclopedia of Information Science and Technology* (2nd ed., pp. 3707–3713). Hershey, PA: IGI Gobal.

Goodman, J. (2005). Linking mobile phone ownership and use to social capital in rural South Africa and Tanzania. In *Vodafone Policy Paper Series: Africa: The impact of mobile phones*, (2), 53-65.

Hafkin, N., & Odame, H. (2002). *Gender information technology and developing countries: an analytical study.* Washington DC: Academy for educational development. Retrieved April 4, 2007 from http://LearnLink.aed.org/Publications/GenderBook/Home.htm

Hashem, S. (2001) Community Telecentres in Egypt. *Journal of Development Communication: Special Issue on Telecenters, 12*(2). Online at http://ip.cals.cornell.edu/commdev/documents/jdc-hashem.doc

Holmes, R. (2004). *Advancing rural women's empowerment: information and communication technology (ICTs) in the service of good governance, democratic practice and development for rural women in Africa.* Background paper for the FAO Dimitra Network Workshop on Advancing Rural Women's Empowerment: ICTS in the Service of Good Governance, Democratic Practice, and Development for Rural Women in Africa, 23-25. Retrieved April 28, 2007 from http://womennet.org.za/dimitra-confereence/EmpowerinfRuralWomen.doc

International Telecommunication Union. (2004). *Africa: The world's fastest growing mobile market: Does mobile technology hold the key to widening access to ICTs in Africa?* Retrieved December 22, 2006 from http://www.itu.int/newsarchive/press_releases/2004/04.html

Jensen, R. (2007). The digital provide Information (technology) market performance, and welfare in the south Indian fisheries sector. *The Quarterly Journal of Economics, 227*(3), 879–924. doi:10.1162/qjec.122.3.879

Ling, R. (2002). *The social and cultural consequences of mobile telephony as seen in the Norwegian context.* Telenor R&D Report. Retrieved October 3, 2005 from http://www.telenor.com/rd/pub/rep02/R_9.pdf

Martinez, J., & Reilly, K. (2002). Looking behind the Internet: Empowering women for public policy advocacy in Central America. *UN/INSTRAW Virtual Series on Gender and ICTs, seminar four: ICTs as Tools for Bridging the Digital Divide Gap and Women's Empowerment.* Retrieved September 28, 2011 from http://www.uninstraw.org/docs/genderandICT/martinez.pdf

oneworld radio. (2006, December 18). *How radio, cell phones, wireless web are empowering developing nations.* Retrieved December 18, 2006 from http://radio.oneworld.net/article/view/78640/1/

Organization for Economic Co-operation and Development. (2005). *Good practice paper on ICTs economic growth and poverty reduction.* Retrieved December 27, 2006 from http://www.oecd.org/dataoecd/2/46/35284979.pdf

Rice, R., & Katz, J. (2003). Comparing internet and mobile phone usage: Digital divides of usage, adoption, and dropouts. *Telecommunications Policy, 27*(8-9), 597–63. doi:10.1016/S0308-5961(03)00068-5

Samuel, J. Shah, N. & Hadingham, W. (2005). Mobile communications in South Africa, Tanzania and Egypt: Results from community and business surveys. *Vodafone Policy Paper Series: Africa: The impact of mobile phones*, 44-53.

Tandon, N. (2004). *Information and communication technologies for poverty alleviation/development strategies and ICTs.*

The World Bank, Office of the Publisher. (2006). *Information and communications for development: global trends and policies.* doi: 10.1596/978-0-8213-6346-1

UNESCO (2010) *Development and Economic Growth Report.* Paris: Author.

UNESCO (2010). *United Nations Economic and Social Council Report.* Paris: Author.

Chapter 1
Digital Natives and H1N1:
How Adversity Can Drive Change

Peter Woodhead
German Swiss International School, Hong Kong, China

David M. Kennedy
Lingnan University, China

ABSTRACT

This paper examines what happens when young learners in a primary school in Hong Kong start from learning about information and communication technologies (ICTs) to learning with and through ICTs. The authors focus on how students used learning technologies when an H1N1 outbreak closed the school for three weeks and teachers were required to use ICTs to initiate at-home learning. This gave the researchers an opportunity to assess the capacity of young students using Web 2.0 technologies to support learning and the impact that these tools have on teacher views and practice. Data includes interviews with teachers and examples of students' work. Findings demonstrate how confident and comfortable young learners are with new technologies, raising questions about prevailing assumptions that young students have the capacity to easily use the existing school-based learning management system and Web 2.0 applications. The authors provide evidence that students can effectively engage with ICTs and demonstrate very high levels of skills. However, students did not do so automatically, and required assessment tasks were often key drivers for initiating student engagement and learning.

INTRODUCTION

This study examines the assumptions behind the notion of the 'digital native' (Prensky, 2001a, 2001b) and the claims that the learning needs of digital natives can only be met through radical reforms in educational design (pedagogy) and classroom practice. The opportunity for the study arose in a Hong Kong primary school when Web 2.0 technologies and a school-based learning management system (termed Learning Platform) became central to the learning environment due to an outbreak of H1N1 infection that led to closure

DOI: 10.4018/978-1-4666-0041-6.ch001

of the school. The paper focuses on two questions that arose from the response by the school, students and staff to this event. They are:

Q1: What is the impact on student learning behaviours when they move from learning *about* information and communication technologies (ICTs) to learning *with* and *through* ICTs?

Q2: What is the impact on teacher behaviour and attitudes when circumstances force changes in the way students' learning is facilitated and managed?

This is not a study that sets out to proclaim the technical agility of digital natives or the promises of 21st century learning; rather it is a story about a typical school with good internet connectivity and access, and committed teachers concerned about doing the best for their children, who begin a 'forced march to the digital frontier' because of circumstances. The study also attempts to offer some insights into the impact on professional responsibility and values when circumstances result in the adoption a new paradigm which leads to significant changes in the way learning technologies are perceived and valued by the school community (teachers, students and parents).

BACKGROUND AND CONTEXT

The study was situated in an established international primary school based in Hong Kong that has consistently enjoyed a strong reputation among the international and local communities for the quality of its education and excellent examination results. With the prior experience of Severe Acute Respiratory Syndrome (SARS) in 2003, the school developed a contingency plan to support online learning in the event of a school closure. This involved the use of material published on the school's website. All parents had access to these materials through a portal and a trial was conducted

in 2007 to familiarize students and parents with the platform. In September 2008 a full Learning Platform was deployed in the primary school section. While not an overarching or immediate priority, the senior management was keen to see greater integration between technology and learning based upon the availability of the Learning Platform in case of any future SARS-like event. The work reported in this study began initally as long-term research using design-based research methodology (Reeves, 2006) to generate data on students' learning behaviours, staff perceptions of technology and leadership expectations, with the aim of creating a 360-degree perspective on what actually happens when new technologies and new ways of teaching and learning are proposed and introduced. However, the arrival of H1N1 in June 2009 gave the researchers a unique opportunity to study learning behaviours of students and responses by staff when learning online became a necessity. Only the data from the period associated with the advent of H1N1 is reported here. During this time, the students were required to work at home and the teachers had to manage learning from school: both groups had to find creative ways to use the digital tools and resources available to them to create an engaging and meaningful learning environment.

LITERATURE REVIEW

Web 2.0 applications played an important role in this study. The affordances of Web 2.0 applications for student learning are usefully described in recent British Education Communication and Technology Association (BECTA) reports. For example, Luckin et al. (2008) cited Green and Hannon (2007) and Grunwald Associates (2007) in listing potential educational outcomes associated with the use of selected Web 2.0 applications. The outcomes claimed include "creativity, ideas generation, presentation, leadership, team-building, confidence, communication, innovation, initiative, criticality in information gathering and the ability to evaluate, question and prioritize information" (p. 24). However, Crook and Harrison (2008) provided a more conservative view and cautioned against more dramatic claims about the activities of digital natives, noting that "there is little evidence that uptake is happening to any significant degree. This is not helped by the fact that there remains very little research activity guiding the effective application of these new tools and practices" (p. 7). Green and Hannon (2007) noted that only 20% of 11 to 16 year-old students are active and productive users of technology. In other words, most digital natives are using Web 2.0 as an extension of Web 1.0 and only a few can be deemed to be taking part in activities such as creating content or rich forms of collaboration.

Social software makes up a significant component of Web 2.0 applications. McLoughlin and Lee (2007) identified four themes to articulate the affordances of social software – connectivity and rapport; collaboration and information discovery; content creation and knowledge aggregation. These themes are consistently echoed by other researchers, leading to the notion of Web 2.0 being associated with c-learning (as opposed to e-learning) characterized by *connectedness, collaboration, communication* and *creativity*. In this study these ideas informed the way in which these technologies were used to support teachers'

learning designs and student learning during the H1N1 outbreak.

METHODOLOGY

Schrader (2008) suggested that if researchers are to understand how students can learn with and through technology, then context is everything. Hence, the study adopted research methodology derived from the premises of an interpretive paradigm. The use to which the affordances of ICTs might be used in education were seen in this study as dependent on very pragmatic issues: the context and the tools available. Technological innovations need to be considered in the context of social interactions and the prevailing cultural norms (Crook et al., 2008). This study did not just focus on the interaction between users and computer, but instead examined in detail the contextual influences that impact on student learning behaviours. Table 1 lists the key data generated during the study and the data collected prior to the H1N1-induced school closure.

The data from three classes (one each of year 2, 4 and 5, with 25 students each) are reported in this study. Data from only these classes are included because the researchers had permission to access all of the data sets, especially student-generated digital material, associated with these groups.

Table 1. Project milestones

Date	Research activity
November 2008	Staff survey 'Teachers professional ICT attitudes' (n=10) *
December 2008	Online survey of staff about connectivity and access (n=13) *
May 2009	Structured interviews with staff on their perceptions of Web 2.0 (n=6) *
June 2009	1. Structured interviews with staff re perceptions about use of technology and impact on learning (n=5) * 2. H1N1 strikes. 3. Collection of data from student emails, forums, home pages and wikis
July 2009	4. Analysis of data from student emails, forums, home pages and wikis 5. Online survey to parents to measure their reactions to work@home (n=16; 61% return rate) **
* Background data not reported in this paper but which did influence the design of activities and support structures in this study. ** Not reported in this paper, though results of this survey do corroborate the student analysis reported here.	

DURING THE H1N1 CLOSURE

Within the first week of school closure it very quickly became apparent that merely sending worksheets home by email each day to be completed by students was not going to engage or interest students for very long; there were several parental and student complaints. The response by teachers (with the assistance of the first author) was to create learning activities which involved students using Web 2.0 applications within the Learning Platform to support their studies at home. Table 2 lists the activities students engaged with during the three-week school closure.

These activities and the associated correspondence from students, staff and parents generated additional data sets and these are summarized in Table 3.

In addition, it was realized from the data collected and communication with parents that the parental attitude to the use of technology influenced students' behaviours. It became clear that the school closure and the activities students were being asked to undertake were having a significant impact on parental perceptions and attitudes to the use of technology by their children. While this is not discussed in detail in this paper, parents were very supportive of the use of the Learning Platform and the activities the students were engaged in. Of course, these are parents who pay high school fees and so are not truly representative of Hong Kong parents in general.

DATA ANALYSIS

The Impact of the School Closure on Teachers' Perceptions of Web 2.0 Technologies

The suddenness of the school closure created a number of issues for teachers. The key issues were:

- That the old face-to-face models of common classroom activities could not work;
- How to make students learning more interesting, engaging and meaningful;
- How to provide better feedback to student activity;

Table 2. Learning activities used during the H1N1 closure

Activity	Comments
Daily diary	Forums were created on the Learning Platform for years 4 and 5 students inviting them to record and reflect on the work they were doing at home. Extracts from these forums were analysed to look for patterns and common themes. *The evidence gives a unique insight into how they felt about and responded to the challenges of using technology at home.*
Toy story	The year 4 students were also invited to design and build a toy that would float on water and write an explanation for other students about how to make the toy. The students were then invited to find ways of publishing their work using the technology available to them. *The results give some indication about the capacity of students to use technology to publish their work.*
Wikis on life in ancient Greece	Year 5 students were given the challenge of working in house teams to submit a joint assignment describing life in ancient Greece. They were expected to use a wiki from the Learning Platform for collaboration and knowledge sharing. *The results were used to evaluate their ability to use technology for knowledge building and collaboration.*
Home pages on student portfolios	All students were invited to use the opportunity to update and publish links to their work from their portfolio's home page (part of the Learning Platform) and publish their work to teachers, classmates or year mates. To support the use of multimedia, students were given access to school accounts for Slideshare and Motionbox, and were also encouraged to select an appropriate Web 2.0 application. Video tutorials about these applications were made available. *This activity provided evidence on how motivated and prepared students were to share their work.*
Technology challenge	This activity was specially designed to give some students in years 4 and 5 the opportunity to use technology to design, create and publish a multimedia show in which they describe what it was like to work at home. *This gave an indication of the ability of students to generate and publish online content.*

Table 3. Summary of data sources used during the H1N1 closure

Data Source	Type	Comments
Year page views from the Learning Platform for years 2, 4 and 5	Quantitative data	Presented as graph of views against date (Figure 1)
Email correspondence with ICT teacher	Text responses	NVivo analysis identified six strands (Figure 2)
Student posts on the daily diary forums in years 2, 4 and 5	Text, images and videos	Presented as charts of posts and views per year group (Figure 3)
Student-generated digital content from posts, digital portfolios and response to the technology challenge	Student-generated text, images, sound and video	Examples used to illustrate discussion as evidence of engagement and use of the technologies
Survey of all parents in the primary department	Text responses	Corroborated views about use of technology and using technology to support learning at home

- How to facilitate conversations between students, which the teachers valued highly in the face-to-face classrooms; and
- How the teachers could create learning activities that were not based entirely on text.

Before the school closure teachers and students had become familiar with the use of forums, creating a personal home page and use of selected Web 2.0 applications. However, the technologies and associated activities were generally not central to the normal teaching and learning activities. Teachers were happy to create opportunities for technology to be used to enhance students' learning, but not as core to the learning experience. The school closure quickly changed this relationship.

The school mandated a work@home plan, that required teachers to prepare resources on a daily basis. Teachers began to discuss in earnest how they might use the Learning Platform and array of Web 2.0 applications. In years 4 and 5 the work@home activities were managed from the Learning Platform because the teachers saw this as a better way of supporting their students' learning, allowing them to maintain a dialogue with their class using forums and provide students with feedback.

Literally overnight, teachers who, previously, had only watched their students using these tools became active users themselves. By week two, teachers quickly realized the need for multimedia resources if they were to keep their students en-

gaged, broaden activities, and elicit artifacts more likely to provide evidence of effective student learning. One group of students quickly became active users of Audacity (for creating and editing audio files) and Motionbox (which allowed them to stream video), publishing their work within the Learning Platform. A physical education teacher, when faced with the problem of how to celebrate the annual sports award evening (assemblies were forbidden), upgraded her PowerPoint skills and taught herself how to use Animoto (which allowed her to integrate photos, videos and text into a single video slide show), publishing her shows through the Learning Platform. Other teachers took the time to upgrade class home pages on the Learning Platform, adding forums for discussions and feedback, and links to learning activities

Analysis of Page Views

The page views created by each year group on the Learning Platform were analysed. Page views gave an indication of how frequently students logged onto their year page. The numbers represent a minimum as students may well have also visited the home page of the Learning Platform where page views averaged 85 accesses a day. Peaks and troughs of activity in Figure 1 reflect the most active times, for example after key assignments or information was transmitted to students. Figure 1 illustrates that year pages were not viewed by every family every day but, judging from the contribution to forums in years 4 and 5, it is likely that a large majority used the Learning Platform frequently during weeks 1 and 2. The variation in activity is significant and suggests that the children regarded the year pages as bulletin boards from which to get information. Their use of the forums was more intense, especially among the year 4 students, who saw this as a way of keeping in touch with each other; suggesting that the social aspect of the Learning Platform exerted a bigger pull on their attention. The Learning Platform was treated like a classroom online – listen to the teacher when you have to, but having conversations with your friends is more fun! Not surprisingly, activity decreased considerably in week 3 (the last week of term) but a small group of students continued to view and submit posts well into the summer holidays.

Analysis of Email Traffic

Analysis of the email traffic was carried out using NVivo. The data could be described by five strands, shown in Figure 2. This analysis provided evidence on the issues that caused the most concern to students and parents. Figure 2 demonstrates that different problems were experienced by different age groups. For example, a lost account was the major problem for year 2 students and how to upload files created challenges for the year 5 group. The data suggests that while year 2 students were motivated to use the Learning Platform, their capacity to understand personal accounts and security was, not surprisingly, less well developed. More significant were the numbers of year 5s who had problems publishing work via their portfolios and navigating through the Learning Platform. These students had enjoyed considerable exposure to Web 2.0 applications and activities prior to the school closure and it is surprising that they had difficulty uploading files. In the discussion section below we use this data to postulate that students in this study are still more comfortable surfing the web, than being producers of content. The nature of the problems experienced by students in this study suggest that they are not always in full control of their online world as has been suggested by others such as Prensky (2001a, 2001b, 2007) and Tapscot (1998).

Figure 1. Page views on the learning platform by students during school (Day 1 represents the first day of enforced school closure and day 21 is the last day of term.)

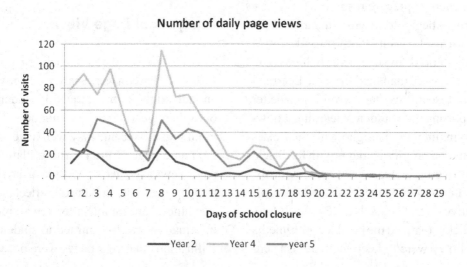

Figure 2. Analysis of email correspondence during H1N1 closure using NVIVO

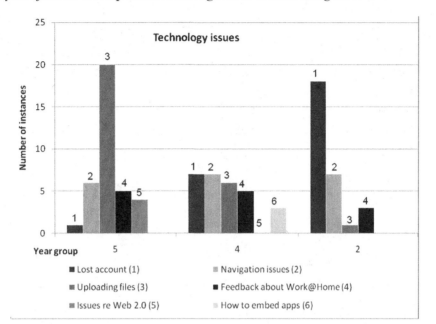

Analysis of Forum Posts

Forums were created in each of the year groups to support dialogue between students, and between students and their class teachers. The students were invited to post a daily diary about their working activities as well as correspond with their teachers.

The results, shown in Figure 3, reveal that, while many students enjoyed looking at each other's posts, only a minority made a contribution. The year 4 data shows that nearly all students were making regular posts on the daily diary but it was a 'hardcore' of four students who regularly took the lead in the forums. In year 5 the pattern was different with fewer posts on the daily diary and most posts appearing on the ancient Greeks wiki. Again there was a small hardcore of four active posters in year 5. Clearly, there were significant numbers of students in year 5 who did not take part. Significantly, it was the more able students who made the fewest contributions. There was no opportunity to elucidate the reasons for this information, but it raises an interesting opportunity for future research.

In year 2 a small group of four students made regular posts in response to the book-review activity but, given their age and possibly limited access to computers at home, the results indicate that year 2 students may have the potential to be more active. This data suggests that more analysis of student posting behaviour needs to be undertaken to better understand the behaviour of students when they participate in school-based forums, particularly for younger age groups.

From Figure 3, the data indicates that the number of posts as a percentage of visits to the website were 15% for year 2 students, 21% for year 4 students and 25% for year 5 students. Not surprisingly, the older students responded more as a percentage of visits and interacted more frequently as a result of a visit.

Analysis of All Digital Content from Years 2, 4 and 5

All year groups were comfortable using forums to exchange news about themselves and respond to posts. Even year 2 students were able to post

Figure 3. Total number of posts and views recorded by students in years 2, 4 and 5

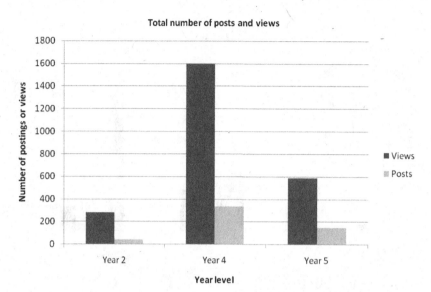

comments on their book reviews. Only a few posts reverted to 'SMS speak' and many were well-written, indicating that students had a good sense of audience. Many year 4s and 5s clearly wrote in a way that invited a response. They did not just make statements, but expressed opinions and feelings that were often responded to by peers. Some students even added sound files and images to illustrate an event or outing. The students' work seems to confirm at least some of the claims relating to digital natives: that this generation *can be* comfortable and literate when using these tools.

Students were less confident when it came to collaboration and this was particularly evident with year 5s who had been asked to use a wiki to complete a joint project on ancient Greece. A few students attempted to take the lead and set up Bubbl.us accounts for shared concept mapping, but no one succeeded in making the connection to a shared account. Only two of the four house teams created a wiki, and these were only partial successful. The students tended to use the wikis for sharing rather than for collaboration. These outcomes were unexpected because the students in years 4 and 5 had enjoyed significant exposure to Web 2.0 applications and had been shown how

to embed widgets into their home pages. Students had also been shown how to use wikis and other Web 2.0 applications (podcasting, Animoto, etc.), but only a few were able to remember how to use the applications and re-purpose for publication and collaboration.

The evidence suggests that students of all age groups can access information from a website but only a small minority can use digital tools such as Slideshare, Motionbox or wikis to publish, broadcast or collaborate about their work. This confirms the findings from the Green and Hannon (2007), noted earlier, that only 20% of young people are active content producers who can successfully use Web 2.0 technologies.

However, there were a small minority of students from years 2, 4, 5 and 6 who exhibited exceptional digital dexterity, perseverance and imagination in the way they took full advantage of Web 2.0 applications such as Motionbox, Slideshare (sharing PowerPoint presentations online), Powerzoom (a Facebook application that supports streaming video) and Zoho (document sharing and collaboration) to publish work to their audience of classmates.

These digitally dextrous students also made full use of the Learning Platform to ensure that they reached their audience. As one year 5 girl asked in an email to her ICT teacher:

I created a Zoho account and used the Zoho Show tool and embedded my PowerPoint, but then I tried to post the link on my Homepage and it didn't seem to work. You said something about an embed code... how do you find it? Thanks! Can you also tell me if I want my father to read my portfolio from overseas, is there a link I can send him without giving him my password to log on? Thanks again...

This email clearly demonstrates that she understood security and privacy issues associated with online publishing. The same student had also gone to great lengths to find a way of embedding her PowerPoint in her home page. Frequently, the published work was not directly related to the assignments set by the teacher. Other examples include a year 2 who extended her home page by embedding a photo gallery of her family along with sound files of her playing the violin. Another year 2 published her book review in Microsoft's Photostory3 onto her home page, and two year 4 students found out how to embed videos of the testing of their toy boat.

DISCUSSION

Changes in the Teachers' Perceptions of Web 2.0 Technologies

Before the school closure there was evidence, from the structured interviews undertaken with teachers, that the majority of teachers had positive attitudes towards their students using Web 2.0 and the Learning Platform, legitimizing these technologies as part of their learning culture. But there were significant differences between individual teachers with some very enthusiastic users

of technology and others who saw technology as useful, but better left to others more committed to its use. The teachers who did not use technology more frequently were not necessarily resisting the need for change. Rather, they were responding to their personal perceptions of what the technology had to offer, and felt they had limited opportunity or motivation to make sense of the new technologies for themselves, echoing the findings of Fullan and Stiegelbauer (1991) almost 20 years ago about the nature of change.

The introduction of Web 2.0 technologies into the face-to-face classroom prior to H1N1 in this study could have be expected to elicit significant changes in classroom dynamics, with the students acting as the harbingers of change by bringing their digital skills, behaviours and new learning styles into the classroom. However, this did not occur prior to the closure of the school for H1N1. This research has shown that students are not necessarily the drivers of change, but if given sufficient opportunity, support and meaningful activities, they can make significant changes to their learning practices.

H1N1 then, created the situation where teachers had to redirect their energies from face-to-face teaching and, most importantly, focus their time and motivation to prepare online resources and activities in order to meet the new priority of managing learning at home. Adopting new technologies became the solution, not the problem. Time was a key factor – the short time in which teachers had to respond, and the short time available to develop the new learning resources and new ways of accessing student activities and artifacts.

Several authors (e.g., Jeffries, Carsten-Stahl, & McRobb, 2007; MacFarlane, 2007) have referred to the underlying tensions associated with the introduction of technology into the classroom, commenting that learning technologies can undermine the legitimacy of the educational process. The potential for tension and dissonance from teachers who are not ICT-confident is obvious. Far from being seen as a solution, the introduction of Web

2.0 applications could have challenged teachers' beliefs and values about what is considered useful learning, resulting in the innovation bring rejected, used minimally, or possibily sidelined. On the other hand, if the dissonance is reduced, then the innovation is more likely to become embedded into practice. In terms of the impact on teacher behaviour and attitudes when circumstances forced changes in the way students' learning were facilitated and managed, the evidence was conclusive; teachers acted pragmatically, using the tools available.

The Students: What Can the Study Tell Us About Their Level of Digital Dexterity?

This study of primary school students shows that they are quick to learn how to use Web 2.0 applications, that they enjoy the medium and like to add Web 2.0-generated resources to their home pages but they were not at the cutting edge of technology. Only a small minority provided evidence of skills that enabled them to re-purpose these applications to publish their work in forms that demonstrated a sophisticated command of the opportunities offered by the tools to present their ideas and artifacts. While they were familiar with the process of publishing from their social-networking sites, the affordances of applications like Google Docs or Bubbl.us for collaboration had to be explained and demonstrated to them. Teachers had a key role to play in scaffolding these applications so they could benefit their students learning. This runs counter to the views of Tapscott (1998) who argued that teachers lack of skills and restricted connectivity in schools were holding back a whole generation of digital learners, or Mumtaz (2000) and Hayes (2007) who suggested that new pedagogies for teaching and changes to the 'core activities' are needed before teachers can successfully use new technologies.

This study also calls into question the idea that students enjoy a richer and more collabora-

tive environment out of school. From data in this study it would seem that for young learners the scaffolding provided when they are in school is a key factor in determining the way they use technology for communication and collaboration, and particularly content creation. Without their teachers, students would remain digital users – natives in the sense that they are happy to surf and play, but unaware of what else could be possible. In addition, their knowledge of the more educational examples of Web 2.0 was very limited and restricted to applications that were promoted as part of social-networking sites such as Xanga or Bebo.

Do Digital Natives Have New and Distinctive Learning Styles and Needs?

The study did confirm that students' exposure to multimedia from a young age does have an impact on their visual-spatial skills and non-verbal forms of intelligence. For example the year 2 students' capacity to visualize the construction of their home pages was striking. However, there was little evidence that they or their older peers, were able to re-purpose these digital tools to support higher-order thinking and processing skills. What this study does support is the research from Biggs (2003) and Ramsden (1992) that students' use of technology is very dependent on the task set by the teacher, a similar conclusion reached Cox et al. (2004). For example, there is no evidence that the students would have spontaneously collaborated through the wiki or forums in the Learning Platform unless these had been expressly required by their teachers. In the year 5 class the response rate on the daily diary was directly influenced by the engagement and encouragement of their class teacher.

Are Students Digitally Disconnected from the Schools and Education?

What happened initially in this school was probably similar to many other primary schools around the world and, if the views of Prensky (2007), Tapscott (1998), and Selwyn (2008) are to be accepted, then this school would not seem to support the learning needs of the digital native, and yet the evidence runs counter to these claims. Many students repeatedly posted messages about how much they missed schools and their friends; they repeatedly asked for help and support in use of ICTs with some complaining that connectivity and access at home was worse than at school. These were students of above-average ability who had been exposed to Web 2.0 applications and were used to engaging in learning dialogues on their forums. Indeed, many of these students had created quality digital portfolios, and yet they still needed the scaffolding and support from school. The evidence from this study suggests that if we left students to themselves, they would not automatically benefit from technology.

This study strongly supports the assertion that young learners need significant scaffolding if they are to make sense of the digital landscape in which they find themselves. It confirms that a significant number of young learners are digitally fluent but, if left to themselves, would use technology in ways not condusive for learning. It also challenges the view that schools need to undergo major transformations in their structure, management and the pedagogies implemented in their learning environment in order to accommodate new technologies such as Web 2.0.

The current study does suggest that if we are to have a better understanding of the digital native, then we need to look more closely at their differences. For example, the Green and Hannon (2007) survey of young technology users also points to the diversity of engagement among young users, again confirming that innovative use of technology among the digital natives is far from uniform.

The authors assert that more work needs to focus on the difference between digital natives in terms of their intellectual ability to engage and explore their virtual learning environments, and whether access in the home is a function of cultural and family dynamics, or a function of affluence.

The observations made in this study are supported by Bennett, Maton and Kervin (2008), who questioned the whole premise of the digital native by pointing out the lack of empirical data to support the claims about their unique learning styles and preferences. In their critical review of the digital-native debate they argued that there is little evidence to support the claims of Prensky. They suggested that research should focus more on the difference between digital natives in terms of their learning capacities and their technical capabilities. They also questioned the view that the digital divide is the reason for young people's sense of frustration and disaffection with school. This study implies that there is a gap between the hopes and aspirations for learning technologies as agents for change and reform on the one hand, supported by Prensky and others, and the growing evidence base that informs us about how young people actually use these technologies (see Kennedy, Judd, Churchward, Gray, & Krause, 2008). However, the current study also provides evidence that given the opportunity, students can become far more creative and productive users of technology as a result of changes in curriculum design and assessment.

CONCLUSION

The work from the students in the study group confirms their remarkable journey into the world of Web 2.0 and their fluency with the language of technology and their delight in being able to use technology to express their ideas. But, if left to themselves, only a few are able to re-purpose these technologies to support their learning effectively. Their engagement with social-networking sites like Facebook, Club Penquin and others, does not automatically transfer into productive learning behaviours that use technology. Perhaps we are in danger of underestimating the degree of scaffolding required if online learning is to be an integral part of the learning environment, benefiting all young learners who use such technologies. The data in the study supports the assertion that teachers have a key role to play in supporting the effective use of Web 2.0 technologies for, without this support, our digital natives will remain merely digital users or digital novices, with only a small minority emerging as digital innovators, creators or pioneers.

The teachers in this study have also made a remarkable journey towards the adoption and integration of Web 2.0 technologies, and developing learning activities and assessment practices within the Learning Platform. But their motivations were personal and practical. It was not the advocacy of 21st century learning, or the techno-romanticism of the early adopters that energized them to change; neither was it the desire to change their pedagogic practice. Instead their approach was to take rapid but small steps towards incorporating Web 2.0 applications into their existing schemes of work because they had a problem to solve. The school closure provided the impetus and, being pragmatists, teachers used the tools that were at hand. This study suggests that the 'moral panic' created by advocates of 21st century learning should not cloud our judgements or distract us from what teachers have always done well – which to continually adapt and modify. However the question still remains as to whether this event had a more permanent influence on their underlying attitudes and beliefs about the affordances of learning technologies. Or did the perceived benefits of the new ways of working exceed the investment required to adopt the new technologies? As a footnote it was interesting to observe that in the following term, when a new version of the Learning Platform was being introduced, there was a widespread acknowledgement that this

facility was necessary for both future closures, and ongoing teaching and learning.

More investigations will be required if we are to have a better and more accurate understanding of current students. Data about the differences between young people on how they use technology, and how educators need to scaffold learning to support the use of ICTs in general, and Web 2.0 applications in particular, are key areas for future study.

Finally, it is a concern of the authors whether the levels of interest, participation and engagement demonstrated by students in this study can be sustained in the long term once the use of Web 2.0 technologies becomes more ubiquitous and systemic in schools. Having 'been there' and 'done that', will the affordances, activities and current engagement offered by ICTs and Web 2.0 applications simply become another source of dreary activities to be accomplished by the student in search of good grades? Further work needs to be done to study how young people respond over time as more teachers use greater varieties of technologies, more of the time.

REFERENCES

Bennett, S., Marton, K., & Kervin, L. (2008). The 'Digital Natives' debate: A critical review of the evidence. *British Journal of Educational Technology, 39*(5), 775–786. doi:10.1111/j.1467-8535.2007.00793.x

Biggs, J. B. (2003). *Teaching for quality learning at university* (2nd ed.). Buckingham, UK: Society for Research into Higher Education & Open University Press.

British Education Communication and Technology Association (BECTA). (2004). *Self review framework for e-leadership. Coventry: BECTA.* Retrieved August 18, 2010, from http://schools.becta.org.uk/index.php?section=srf

Cox, M., Abbott, C., Blakeley, B., Beauchamp, T., & Rhodes, V. (2004). *ICT and pedagogy. A review of the research literature.* Coventry, UK: British Education Communication and Technology Association (BECTA). Retrieved August 18, 2010, from http://publications.becta.org.uk/download.cfm?resID=25813

Crook, C., Cummings, J., Fisher, T., Graber, R., Harrison, C., Lewin, C., et al. (2008). *Web 2.0 technologies for learning: The current landscape – opportunities, challenges and tensions.* Coventry, UK: British Education Communication and Technology Association (BECTA). Retrieved August 18, 2010, from http://partners.becta.org.uk/upload-dir/downloads/page_documents/research/web2_technologies_learning.pdf

Crook, C., & Harrison, C. (2008). *Report 5: Web 2.0 technologies for learning at Key Stage 3 and 4: Summary report* (No. 5). Coventry, UK: British Education Communication and Technology Association (BECTA). Retrieved August 19, 2010, from http://research.becta.org.uk/upload-dir/downloads/page_documents/research/web2_ks34_summary.pdf

Fullan, M., & Stiegelbauer, S. (1991). *The new meaning of educational change* (2nd ed.). New York: Teachers College Press.

Green, H., & Hannon, C. (2007). *TheirSpace: Education for a digital generation.* London: Demos. Retrieved August 15, 2010, from http://www.demos.co.uk/files/Their%20space%20-%20web.pdf?1240939425

Grunwald Associates. (2007). *Creating and connecting: Research and guidelines on social and educational networking.* Alexandria, VA: National School Boards Association. Retrieved August 15, 2010, from http://nsba.org/site/docs/41400/41340.pdf

Hayes, D. N. (2007). ICT and learning: Lessons from Australian classrooms. *Computers & Education, 49*(2), 385–395. doi:10.1016/j.compedu.2005.09.003

Jefferies, P., Carsten-Stahl, B., & McRobb, S. (2007). Exploring the relationships between pedagogy, ethics and technology: Building a framework for strategy development. *Technology, Pedagogy and Education, 16*(1), 111–126. doi:10.1080/14759390601168122

Kennedy, G. E., Judd, T. S., Churchward, A., Gray, K., & Krause, K.-L. (2008). First year students' experiences with technology: Are they really digital natives? *Australasian Journal of Educational Technology, 24*(1), 108–122.

Luckin, R., Logan, K., Clark, W., Graber, R., Oliver, M., & Mee, A. (2008). *Learners' use of Web 2.0 technologies in and out of school in Key Stages 3 and 4.* Coventry, UK: British Education Communication and Technology Association (BECTA). Retrieved February 27, 2010, from http://partners.becta.org.uk/upload-dir/downloads/page_documents/research/web2_technologies_ks3_4.pdf

MacFarlane, A. (2007). Online communities of learning: Lessons from the worlds of games and play. In *Proceedings of the Building Learning Communities 2007 Conference.* Retrieved August 18, 2010, from http://novemberlearning.com/professor-angela-mcfarlane-blc07-keynote/

McLoughlin, C., & Lee, M. J. W. (2007). Social software and participatory learning: Pedagogical choices with technology affordances in the Web 2.0 era. In *Proceedings of the Providing choices for learners and learning,* Singapore. Retrieved August 18, 2010, from http://www.ascilite.org.au/conferences/singapore07/procs/mcloughlin.pdf

Mumtaz, S. (2000). Factors affecting teachers' use of information and communications technology: a review of the literature. *Journal of Information Technology for Teacher Education, 9*(3), 319–342.

Prensky, M. (2001a). Digital natives, Digital immigrants. *On the Horizon, 9*(5). Retrieved August 18, 2010, from http://www.marcprensky.com/writing/Prensky%20-%20Digital%20Natives,%20Digital%20Immigrants%20-%20Part1.pdf

Prensky, M. (2001b). Digital natives, Digital immigrants, Part II: Do they really think differently? *On the Horizon, 9*(6). Retrieved August 18, 2010, from http://www.marcprensky.com/writing/Prensky%20-%20Digital%20Natives,%20Digital%20Immigrants%20-%20Part2.pdf

Prensky, M. (2007). *How to teach with technology: Keeping both teachers and students comfortable in an era of exponential change.* Coventry, UK: BECTA. Retrieved August 12, 2010, from http://partners.becta.org.uk/page_documents/research/emerging_technologies07_chapter4.pdf

Ramsden, P. (1992). *Learning to teach in higher education.* London: Routledge. doi:10.4324/9780203413937

Reeves, T. C. (2006). Design research from the technology perspective. In Akker, J. V., Gravemeijer, K., McKenney, S., & Nieveen, N. (Eds.), *Educational design research* (pp. 86–109). London: Routledge.

Schrader, P. (2008). Learning in Technology: Reconceptualising immersive environments. *Association for the Advancement of Computers in Education Journal, 16*(4), 457–475.

Selwyn, N. (2008). From state-of-the-art to state-of-the-actual? Introduction to a Special Issue. *Technology, Pedagogy and Education, 17*(2), 83–87. doi:10.1080/14759390802098573

Tapscott, D. (1998). *Growing up digital: The rise of the Net generation.* New York: McGraw-Hill.

This work was previously published in International Journal of E-Adoption, Volume 2, Issue 3, edited by Sushil K. Sharma, pp. 53-66, copyright 2010 by IGI Publishing (an imprint of IGI Global).

Chapter 2
Driving IT Architecture Innovation:
The Roles of Competing Organizational Cultures and Collaborating Upper Echelons

Sibylle Mabry
Louisiana State University in Shreveport, USA

ABSTRACT

The spotlight on business innovation in growth-oriented organizations has never been hotter. Information systems (IS) innovation, in particular, has become the main focus for many businesses and their CIOs because of its potential for business agility and competitiveness. However, creating a culture that can effectively exploit the innovative forces of an organization is challenging, and no shared guidelines exist. The purpose here is to examine empirically how the competing forces of organizational cultures in tandem with senior executives constructively influence the innovative efforts of organizations. Central to this investigation is the adoption of an IS architecture (SOA) whose implementation may entail radical transformation of traditional business patterns. Data were collected from U.S. top IS executives, and the results suggest that the adopters of SOA (45%) are organizations whose executives embrace certain collaborative behavior, which, in people-oriented and progress-oriented cultures, seems to be a catalyst for change and adoption of transformational IS architecture..

INTRODUCTION

Information systems (IS) innovation is vital to connecting information technology (IT) strategically to business processes and to enhancing an organization's responsiveness to business needs (Milburn, 2009; Prahalad & Krishnan, 2008; Wang et al., 2008). Not surprisingly, IS innovation has become the main agenda for many organizations and their CIOs (Leach, 2007; Merrifield et al., 2008). Particularly, the adoption of novel IT architectures and infrastructures that support a

DOI: 10.4018/978-1-4666-0041-6.ch002

process and network-oriented view of the business has been on top management's and academicians' radar for several years and has never been a hotter topic (e.g., Boni, Weingart, & Evanson, 2009; Merrifield et al., 2008; Swanson & Ramiller, 2004).

Innovation and the redefinition of the firm's strategic IT infrastructure is by no means a purely technical issue and essentially requires companies to rethink their business processes, understand their leadership challenges, and deal with their cultural forces (Jeyaraj et al., 2006; Wang & Ramiller, 2009). In other words, decisions involving the adoption of complex technology artifacts and infrastructure reflect the potentially strategic nature of the innovation; hence, organizational factors that contribute to a company's innovation adoption choice are on the forefront of managerial curiosity (Boni et al., 2009; Xiaotong, 2009).

Understanding the factors that lead to critical IT adoption decisions at the organizational level is vital for businesses because of the anticipated organizational benefits (e.g., Tellis et al., 2009). Various theories used in the IT-innovations adoption research have attempted to explain and predict information systems adoption from different viewpoints (Ramdani & Kawalek, 2007; Sabherwal et al., 2006; Wu & Lederer, 2009). But most of these adoption theories have been used to explain user acceptance and diffusion of information technology, and they focus mainly on end-user acceptance of already implemented systems (e.g., Jeyaraj et al., 2003). Hence, those theories do not seem to apply well to cases of strategic adoption and innovation regarding complex IT infrastructure. A more direct examination of the adoption practices of a company's cultural and managerial challenges may shed light on how firms can create an effective adoption process. By analyzing the organizational cultures of adopters versus non-adopters, this study examines how the dynamics between corporate culture and executives determine the adoption decisions regarding service-oriented architecture (SOA). Both academic and practitioner studies provide evidence of

the impact organizational culture has on innovation adoption decisions (Leidner & Kayworth, 2006; Todhunter, 2008). As there is less clarity on how executive leaders are typically involved with and dependent on organizational culture (see Schein, 2004), the current study examines the very relevant relationships.

Amazon, BMW, Cigna, Wal-Mart, Apple, and several other progressive organizations adopted service-oriented IT infrastructure early on (around 2006) to take advantage of the infrastructure's strong potential for business agility. Yet in 2008, the majority of Fortune 1000-type firms were still not ready to adopt SOA and with it an agile IS infrastructure (see Methods section). Demographic and organizational factors such as age, size, and area population do not adequately explain the differences in adoption behavior and do not necessarily have predictive power (see also Kennedy & Fiss, 2009). Alternatively, there is evidence that organizational culture factors can explain adoption motivation (Hofstede, 2001; Poskiene, 2006; Tellis et al., 2009). Information systems literature suggests that organizational culture influences the strategic innovation decisions of organizations (e.g., Chia & Koh, 2007; Schein, 2004; Smirich, 1983; Pandey & Sharma, 2009). However, the literature is vague in terms of the impact of competing cultures and in terms of the dynamics between culture and executive impact on organizational adoption decisions. Additionally, the literature has not yet explained how the interaction of these organizational forces affects the adoption of complex IT infrastructure.

To address these questions explicitly, I apply the upper echelons theory to the competing values model of organizational culture to differentiate between adopters and non-adopters and develop an understanding of how the interaction of organizational forces shapes strategic adoption decisions. I attempt to answer important questions concerning the strategic nature of infrastructural technology innovations, and try to explain why companies react differently to the uncertainty, ambiguity, and complexity that these innovations create. Answering these questions is relevant to gain insight into how cultural and individual forces affect adoption choices of innovative IT infrastructure that is said to drive value by increasing company flexibility and agility.

In this study, I develop a theoretical extension of the model of competing organizational cultural values which is useful in technology adoption situations because of (1) the considerable uncertainty surrounding complex technology artifacts, (2) the increasing emphasis on the role of organizational culture, (3) the importance of technology adoption decisions, and (4) the potential IT innovations to increase business agility and value. The model is used to develop new insights into situations in which organizational culture is a key component of IS adoption decisions and to make predictions about the impact of interactive organizational forces on adoption decisions.

IT INNOVATION: SERVICE-ORIENTED ARCHITECTURE

IT innovation is the adoption of an information technology that is perceived as new by the adopting organization (Rogers, 2003; Wang & Ramiller, 2009). Organizations innovate strategically with information technology by using the new technology to improve their business processes, enhance their customer service, and/or transform their business models. The innovation process involves the collection and interpretation of information about the technology, decisions about whether to adopt the innovation, and the implementation and assimilation of the innovation (Swanson & Ramiller, 2004; Wang & Ramiller, 2009). Central to this study is the adoption of service-oriented IT architecture (SOA) whose implementation may entail the radical transformation of traditional business patterns and models and intra/interorganizational network-orientation typically reinforced by IT architectures whose infrastructures reflect

the human, physical and logical aspect of the business (Erl, 2008).

SOA is not a *remove and replace* IT construct; its adoption can actually have a revolutionary effect on business processes and strategy because it encourages the network-oriented aspect and promotes the design of complex inter-organizational business processes via flexible, reusable software chunks (*services*) and web services (Erl, 2008). Spanning almost every aspect of IT infrastructure and computing technology, SOA has the potential to introduce a novel IT environment that supports the creation of business processes across and beyond the enterprise and is able to create a more agile business ecosystem (Erl, 2008; Aimi & Finley, 2007). Hence, SOA is a useful concept to examine organizational adoption behavior with respect to IT infrastructure innovation.

Many organizations have turned to SOA to use their existing IT assets in new ways. Since SOA makes application functionality available as a service, it is a key technology in business integration, and can support business agility and responsiveness. SOA, whose roots are in object orientation, represents a business strategy for creating interconnectivity by applying business process management (BPM), enterprise application integration (EAI), aspect-oriented programming (AOP), and web services (Erl, 2008; Leach, 2007). Companies embarking on service orientation aim at moving beyond proprietary applications and platform boundaries and attempt to create genuine, cross-enterprise federation and interconnectivity (Erl, 2008). The benefits of implementing SOA include increased vendor diversity, superior modification and extensibility options, free governance of services, and increased reusability of service logic (see Table 1).

The emphasis of SOA as an approach that supports a business process system, the reuse of services, and the governance of those services indicates that the adopting firms associate SOA with their long-term goals and the creation of transformative and competitive forces (Aimi &

Table 1. SOA business objectives, benefits, and risks

SOA Features	Objectives/Benefits	Opportunities & Risks
Modular Design • Based on object-orientation • Loosely coupled • Abstracted into business processes	**Increased ROI** • Support of network-oriented view of firm • Increased agility of the organization • Increased business/technology alignment	**Complexity** • Involves strategic aspect of business • Affects existing business processes
Web Services • Uses XML & WSDL • Facilitates point-to-point integration	**Increased Federation** • Vendor-neutral communications framework • Increased interoperability	**Business Risks** • Reorienting business strategies • Changing IT infrastructure
Service Orientation • BPM • EAI • Service inventory • Linked smoothly to other IT components	**Intrinsic Interoperability** • Business process visibility • Reuse of services • Creating new business models	**Requires Governance** • Intro of new resources, roles, & processes • Reliability & security concerns

Finley, 2007; McAfee & Brynjolfsson, 2008). Since organizations are looking for effective ways to gauge the impact of organizational drivers on long-term IT infrastructure innovation, research in this field is indispensable. The question here is if and how organizational culture and top executives interact to make effective SOA adoption choices. Another question is how organizational culture is related to innovation adoption choices. The present study responds to these challenges. Its aim is to focus on adoption decisions at the organizational level and to develop a unique account of adoption motivations.

To develop the framework, I drew on prior research that (1) relates top executives to organizational change and (2) organizational culture to innovation adoption. Empirically, I tested the theoretical argument, collecting data in 2008 from senior IT executives in Fortune 1000-equivalent U.S. organizations listed in the 2007 *Directory of Top Computer Executives*. The findings indicate that organizational culture type shapes the difference between adopters and non-adopters, and that the exchange of information among IT professionals, communication among executives, and collaboration within top management teams are strong drivers of pro-adoption decisions. In addition, the results show that if entrepreneurial and team cultures interact with collaborative-minded upper echelons, they drive pro-adoption decisions. The findings carry important implications for future research, specifically on sequential adoption and post-adoption behavior.

Framework of Organizational Culture and Top Management Characteristics

Although organizational culture has been used relatively frequently in innovation adoption studies, it has so far been tested mainly as an independent organizational force. Its dynamic and interaction with the individual executive forces within the organization has not been the focus of theoretical and empirical investigations. Defined as the joint programming of the corporate mind or the set of shared assumptions, beliefs, values, symbols, and behavior models developed and used by a given institution (Hofstede, 2001; Schein, 2004), organizational culture has been dubbed as vital to the research of organizational change issues because it plays a direct role in executive processes and has a direct impact on either corporate inertia or momentum (Huang et al., 2003; Iivari & Huisman, 2007; Leidner & Kayworth, 2006; Schein, 2004).

The effect of organizational culture on the degree of organizational agility, creativity, and innovation has been observed in a variety of disciplines (e.g., Dombrowski et al., 2007; McLean, 2005; Poskiene, 2006). Researchers found that aggressive, entrepreneurial cultures are able to encourage innovative processes, increase economic performance, and promote an entrepreneurial, global spirit (Feldman, 1988; Hitt, 1991; Jaskyte & Dressler, 2005; Jassawalla & Sashittal, 2002). Organizational culture also seems to have an impact on open-mindedness in human resources (McLean, 2005) and on participative management, risk taking, and decision making (Poskiene, 2006; Dombrowski et al., 2007). Diong and Cho (2008) emphasize that at firms like Walmart, Toyota, Tokia, and Starbucks, resourcefulness and innovation is an essential part of the corporate culture and almost a way of life. Not surprisingly, a recent study of the management literature on organizational culture across various disciplines and nations has suggested that the theories about the drivers of organizational agility point to organizational culture as the strongest driver of progression or inertia (Tellis et al., 2009).

The relationship between organizational culture and the degree of organizational agility has also been observed in various cases of IT innovation and adoption (e.g., Doherty & Doig, 2003; Nahm et al., 2004; Swanson & Ramiller, 2004). Numerous IS researchers have been intrigued by the multifaceted nature of organizational culture (see Leidner & Kayworth, 2006) and have found that understanding organizational culture is critical to the research of IS/IT management because it plays a direct role in innovation processes. Huang and his fellow researchers (2003), for example, found that opposing organizational cultures have prevented companies from effectively implementing integrative information technology, whereas homogenous, dynamic cultures have encouraged the adoption of transformative information systems (see also Merrifield et al., 2008). Other IS innovation studies suggest that rigid hierarchical settings may prevent independent thinking and self-directed work efforts among the organization's workforce, hindering the organization's

intention to introduce innovative information technology (Tolsby, 1998). Conversely, in team-oriented cultures, the attitude toward accepting innovative information technologies appears to be more positive (e.g., Nahm et al., 2004).

Although organizational culture is used widely in innovation adoption studies, it has so far been tested only as an independent organizational force, without taking its interaction with the organizational decision makers into account. Also, the focus in IS studies involving organizational culture is typically on the diffusion and implementation of an innovation among end users. Since culture appears to also play an important role during the innovation adoption phase (see Kennedy & Fiss, 2009) and has a strong impact on organizational adoption motivation, the current study focuses on these fundamental aspects neglected by the literature so far. To develop an assessment basis for this study, the competing values model (CVM) has been applied as a theoretical framework of organizational culture (Cameron & Quinn, 2006). The CVM (1) is parsimonious, (2) has a validated instrument, (3) is well reported in the management literature, and (4) lends itself well to being applied to IS research because of its opposing lenses (e.g., Iivari & Huisman, 2007). The model focuses on competing values (internal versus external and flexibility versus stability) as the cultural reflections of an organization (see Figure 1). The four cultural types based on the competing values are market, hierarchy, adhocracy, and group culture. Since the CVM is a theoretical model, it does not suggest that the opposing values cannot overlap in real systems, with some cultural types being more prevalent than others.

The *market culture* has an external focus, values short-term profit, and emphasizes stability, productivity, and goal setting. To be effective, the market culture needs a decisive authority figure whose task it is to establish rules and objectives and be personally productive. In the *hierarchy culture*, the focus is on internal stability, security, and routine. Employees assume well-defined

Figure 1. The competing values framework for organizational culture (adapted from Cameron & Quinn, 2006)

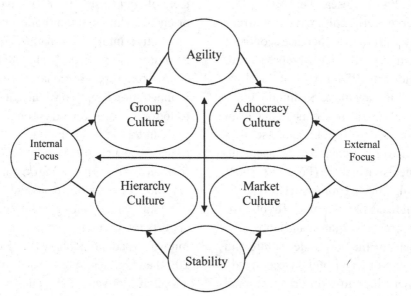

roles and are expected to follow the outlined regulations. Managers are expected to monitor and maintain the structure of the system. The *adhocracy* culture is diagonally opposed to the hierarchy culture. Innovation and growth make it effective. Doing completely new things and communicating effectively with the external environment are cherished values held by managers. The *group culture* is internally focused and emphasizes human relations, cohesion, and morale, but also change. This culture appreciates information sharing, trust and belonging, as well as participative decision making. Managers are expected to be mentors who encourage collaborative efforts and interpersonal relations (Cameron & Quinn, 2006). Connecting the CV model with IS research on IT architecture and infrastructure innovation (see SOA) suggests the following hypothesis:

Hypothesis 1: A nurturing people-oriented IT culture positively influences the organization's decision to adopt SOA.

Organizational culture as a framework within organizational theory has informed many IS researchers about the reasons some organizations are quicker to innovate than others and to adopt information technologies more successfully. Several studies have found that an organization whose culture is defined by a dynamic and flexible climate can use its agility to create competitive advantage (Diong & Choo, 2008). Creative, entrepreneurial cultures typically thrive on innovation and risk-taking (Cameron & Quinn, 2006) and are responsive to hyper-turbulent and fast-paced organizational conditions (Merrifield et al., 2008). Since implementing SOA can help the organization create new business models and move the strategic potential of its information technology beyond organizational borders (Erl, 2008), it can be expected that a change-oriented organizational culture most quickly responds to an IS/IT innovation such as SOA.

Hypothesis 2: An entrepreneurial adhocracy IT culture motivates the organization to adopt SOA.

Organizational culture has been linked to failures in innovation implementation. The IS literature suggests that conflict evolving from the differences among organizational cultures can be related to consequent IT adoption and implementation failures because it prevents the organization from collaborating (e.g., Huang et al., 2003; Von Meier, 1999). Yet organizational culture is not an isolated internal determinant of organizational innovation behavior. Managerial studies show that cultural factors are greatly influenced by the way top managers associate themselves with or distance themselves from the prevailing organizational culture (Schein, 2004), which in turn determines the extent to which they can be change agents (Hambrick, 2007; Liang et al., 2007). Organizational leaders play an important role in transforming organizational values. They are uniquely related to culture by developing, managing, and modifying values, as well as by disassociating themselves from the existing culture to create change processes toward adaptation (Schein, 2004).

Hambrick and Mason's (1984) upper echelons theory ties in with the notion that top organizational leaders can be change agents. Upper echelons act on their personalized understanding of the strategic situation they are confronted with. These personalized explanations of their environment are reflected in their personalities, values, experiences, and their role within the organizational culture. Therefore, the primary sources of organizational outcomes are not necessarily the inescapable and unpreventable situations confronting the organization, as theorized in the 1960s and 70s (see Hannan & Freeman, 1984), but top managers' choices based on their insights, seized opportunities, and good strategic management practices. Furthermore, external ambiguous conditions and internal uncertainty give top managers the discretionary opportunity to evaluate the environment and to use their analyses to pro-act and act appropriately (Hambrick, 2007). In the last two decades, only a few scholars have argued that the impact of top executives on organizational outcomes is minimal (e.g., Hannan & Freeman, 1984). Today most strategic leadership researchers suggest that senior managers influence organizational outcomes noticeably.

Very few of the recent information systems studies have reflected on senior managers' characteristics as critical factors for business process improvements; none has researched the adoption of service-oriented enterprise systems (see Jeyaraj et al., 2006). This study explains that to understand organizational adoption decisions, the personalities, biases, and moral fibers of the firms' most influential actors must be taken into account and are expected to influence the effects of organizational culture. Upper-echelons and strategic management research has recently focused on collaborative management, team behavior, and shared leadership. Much of the existing literature suggests that collaborative management practices enable the shift from traditional individualistic leadership practices to non-traditional, shared practices to achieve interdependent goals and make long-term goals and organizational agility more possible (Boerner, Eisenbeiss, & Griesser, 2007; Chen et al., 1998). This suggests the following hypothesis:

Hypothesis 3: A collaboration-oriented top management team positively influences the organization's adoption of SOA.

In the field of information systems research, a few scholars have found that traditional, individualistic leadership approaches are not adequate because they have hardly any relations to the interactive and participative approaches of the innovative organization (e.g., Moody, 2003). Collaborative behavior of senior managers is expected to strengthen the organization's entrepreneurial and team behavior by triggering discussions and encouraging innovative advances of the IT unit, and by creating knowledge to overcome short-term orientation. Hence, I propose:

Hypothesis 3a: Top managers who espouse collaborative behavior strengthen the positive relationship between a participative group culture environment and the organization's adoption of SOA.

Hypothesis 3b: Top managers who espouse collaborative behavior reverse the negative relationship between a short-term-oriented market culture environment and the adoption of SOA.

Assuming that managerial discretion is present, managerial characteristics such as attitude toward risk and innovation may also be reflected in the organizational strategy (Cho & Hambrick, 2006). Two attitudinal perceptions (a) *innovation propensity* (perceiving the innovation as an enhancement) and (b) *risk propensity* (perceiving risk as a positive force) have been discussed in the relatively recent management literature (Gilley et al., 2002; Pundziene & Duobiene, 2006) as characteristics that can determine an organization's behavior toward the adoption of innovative IT paradigms. Adopting a complex information system involves considerable financial and social risks for the organization, and typically, senior managers are confronted with the innovation risks. Research has shown that individual executives are different in their risk-propensity, and studies suggest that risk-propensity is relatively stable, even with changing situations (Pundziene & Duobiene, 2006). It can be concluded that risk-propensity is more associated with top management characteristics than with a concrete situation.

Hypothesis 4: Top managers who espouse a risk-taking position reverse the negative relationship between a hierarchical culture and the organization's adoption of SOA.

In an entrepreneurial adhocracy culture, organizations look outwardly and connect inter-organizationally to gain resources for their innovative and growth-oriented undertakings (Cameron & Quinn, 2006). Innovative IT tends to be adopted by organizations whose culture is entrepreneurial and whose leaders are visionary and transformational (Colbert et al., 2008).

Hypothesis 5: Top managers who espouse an innovative mindset strengthen the positive relationship between an entrepreneurial culture and the organization's adoption of SOA.

DATA AND METHODS

Sample and Data

The sampling frame was randomly drawn from the target population of 3000 senior IT executives in mid-size to large U.S. organizations listed in the *2007 Directory of IT Executives.* The companies were statistically equivalent to Fortune 1000 firms (their estimated total information technology budget was two percent or more of their total annual revenues), and as such they represented a reasonably homogenous population in terms of size and company characteristics, which reduces the risk of confounding variables such as size or revenues. The purpose was to gather information on how top IT managers view their organization's culture, how they assess senior management regarding entrepreneurialism, risk propensity, and collaboration, and whether they are adopters of service-oriented architecture. Top IT executives were chosen as the participants because they are expected to be involved in the strategic planning process and are familiar with the IT environment. Typically, not all departments in the participating organizations are directly affected by IT investment decisions; hence, the questionnaires focused on the IS/IT units (see Iivari & Huisman, 2007). Data were collected in 2008 via a mail survey with the option to fill out the survey on the web. Of the 750 targeted organizations, eighteen percent (121 executives) returned the completed survey. Given the level of management targeted, this response rate is appropriate and has been accepted in the academic IS literature (e.g., Newkirk & Lederer, 2007). Using Cohen's (1992) formula, I found that the study's sample size accommodates amply for statistical power with respect to hypotheses testing. The sample size was examined using Green's (1991) 50+8m rule suggested for linear regression and path analysis (where *m* represents the number of predictor variables in the regression equation). It is consistent with the minimum requirements for regression type equations; with a population of approximately 3000 and a returned sample size of 121, the required minimum of sample size was met (Bartlett et al., 2001).

Instrumentation and Variable Measurement

To test the study's research model (see Figure 2), I developed a survey instrument from existing questionnaires on competing cultural values and senior manager characteristics. The dependent variable of the study is the adoption of service-oriented architecture; the independent variables are the competing cultural values (Cameron & Quinn, 2006) and top management characteristics, specifically the propensity to collaborate, to innovate, and to take risks (Gilley et al., 2002; Liang et al., 2007; Simsek et al., 2007). To assess the responses to the items, I applied the 5-point Likert scales.

Data Analysis

Non-response bias was assessed via a time-trend extrapolation based on the logic that late respondents are very similar to non-respondents. No bias was identified. Common methods bias was not an issue either; it was assessed via principal component analysis. The following tables describe relevant sample characteristics. Table 2, Table 3, Table 4, and Table 5 summarize the main characteristics of company operations, participating industries, and top IT executives. The organizations are diverse in terms of their scope of operations (see Table 2). Over a third (42.1%) of the participating organizations was international/multinational; they were the main SOA adopters.

Figure 2. The research model: TM = top management; H = hypothesis

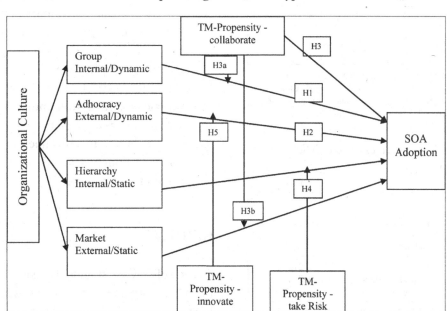

Table 2. Scope of company operations

Scope	N	Adopter/Non-Adopter	% of N
Local (city)	14	9/5	11.6
State	15	6/9	12.4
Regional (Multi-State)	21	4/17	17.4
National	20	12/8	16.5
International	35	15/20	28.9
Multinational	16	8/8	13.2

Table 3. Types of participating industries

Industry	N	Adopt/Not-Adopt	% of N
Banking/Financial	16	2/14	13
Education/Gov.	32	19/13	26
Health	22	9/13	18.2
Insurance	3	1/2	2.5
Manufacturing & Services	22	10/12	18.2
Retail	9	7/2	7.4
Transportation/Utilities	8	0/8	7
Other	9	4/5	7.4

Table 4. Company characteristics

Characteristics	Mean	SD
IS Employees	4.04	1.106
IS Budget	3.17	1.312
Annual Revenue	6.46	0.922

Note. A mean of 4.04 translates into an average of 150 to 200 IS employees per department. A mean of 3.17 translates into an IS Budget of about 3% of the annual revenue. A mean of 6.46 translates into an average of $900M in revenue per year.

Table 5. Top IT executive characteristics

Characteristics		N	Percent %
Gender	Male Female	103 18	85.1 14.9
Age	20 to 48 49 to 60+	45 76	37.2 62.8
Education	HS to BD Post Baccalaureate	33 88	27.3 72.7

Note. HS = High School; BD = Bachelor's Degree

Of the participating organizations sixty-four percent have been in existence for over fifty years, thirty percent between twenty and fifty years, and six percent for ten years or less. Controlling for age of the organization suggested that age did not affect SOA adoption behavior. With respect to the industries that participated in this study (see Table 3), the data collected reflect a relatively wide range of demographics.

On average, the participating organizations' IT departments had a relatively large staff (between 100 and 200 employees) and spent around 3 percent of their annual revenues on information technology (Table 4). Their top IT executives were highly experienced, very well educated, and had been employed by their current organizations for an average of twelve years (Table 5).

To uncover its latent structure and test for dimensionality, each construct that was measured via multi-item scales has been assessed via reliability assessment and factor analysis, specifically principal components analysis (PCA). Cronbach's alpha (see Table 6), was used to further determine internal consistency. The constructs show relatively strong internal consistency, with the exception of hierarchy culture.

Before testing the main constructs of the research model, I examined important demographic variables (annual revenue, number of IT employees, IT budget, and organizational scope) via *t* tests to make sure they would not confound the results and to determine if and how they might differentiate adopters from non-adopters. The results of the *t* tests were statistically non-significant, which implies that revenue, size, and scope of the organizations had no influence on the adoption of the IT architecture.

RESULTS

The results suggest that the adopters of SOA (45%) are organizations whose executives embrace certain collaborative behavior, which—in

Table 6. Principal component and reliability analysis

Constructs	Loadings	Cronbach's Alpha
Risk propensity	.827;.869;.679	.71
Propensity to **innovate**	.875;.870;.844;.862	.89
Propensity to collaborate	.736;.833;.780;.816	.80
Group culture	.727;.741;.814;.685	.73
Adhocracy culture	.740;.778;.864;.662;.771	.82
Hierarchy culture	.705;.804;.501;.628	.61
Market culture	.689;.671;.713;.770;.585	.71

people and progress-oriented cultures—seems to be a catalyst for change, particularly innovation adoption of transformational IS architecture. These results reflect in part the research model. To test the research model, I employed binomial (binary) logistic regression. Logistic regression belongs to a class of statistical models called generalized linear models (GLM). Binary logistic regression was the optimal choice because the dependent variable is a dichotomy and allows the researcher to predict a discrete outcome, such as group membership, from a collection of variables of any type. Logistic regression was also used to assess the interaction effects (see Jaccard, 2001) between organizational culture and top management characteristics. An initial model run showed that there is no significant difference between adopting and non-adopting organizations regarding both risk-taking behavior and attitude toward innovation.

Seven independent variables were simultaneously entered into the logistic regression model to test the hypotheses. The results of this particular regression model run showed four statistically significant predictors, (a) *propensity to collaborate* (p <.01), (b) *adhocracy culture* (p <.05), (c) *group culture* (p <.1), and (d) the interaction *group*collaborate* (p <.1). The other interaction terms did not yield significant results (see Table 7).

The Variables in Equation Statistics presents information about the importance and relative contribution of each of the independent variables. A primary conjecture of the study was that different IT cultures affect innovation adoption differently. The results indicate mixed support for the research model (see Table 8). In the case of team cultures (H1) and entrepreneurial cultures (H2), the statistical output corroborates that there is a difference between adopters and non-adopters,

Table 7. Variables in equation statistics

Variables	B	Wald	Sig.	Exp (B)
Propensity to collaborate	1.033	11.240	.002	2.810
Group *Culture	.997	3.328	.068	2.710
Adhocracy* Culture	1.273	5.720	.017	3.570
Group* Collaboration	1.034	3.450	.063	2.813
Adhocracy* Innovation	-.617	1355	.244	.540
Hierarchy* Risk	.399	1.122	.290	1.490
Market* Collaboration	-.041	.006	.940	.960
Constant	-12.146	25.084	.000	.000

Note. Interaction terms show asterisk between variables

Table 8. Summary of hypotheses results

Hypotheses	Result	Sig
H1 (GC Adopt)	Supported	p<.1
H2 (AC Adopt)	Supported	p<.01
H3 (C)	Supported	p<.001
H3a (C*GC-Adopt)	Supported	p<.1
H3b (C*MC-Adopt)	Not Supported	p>.1
H4 (R*HC-Adopt)	Not Supported	p>.1
H5 (I*AC-Adopt)	Not Supported	p>.1

Note. H=hypothesis; AC=adhocracy culture; GC=group culture; HC=hierarchical culture; MC=market culture; C=top management propensity to collaborate; I=top management propensity to innovate.

R=top management risk-taking propensity;

and thus the results suggest that creative, communicative organizational cultures motivate SOA adoption. Interestingly, of the three attitudinal management characteristics assessed in this paper, only *attitude toward collaboration* showed statistically significant results and thus confirms hypothesis 3 that collaborative top management behavior motivates the innovation adoption. The variables attitude toward risk and IT innovation did not suggest enough predictive power. Qualitative research may give us some interesting answers regarding the variables' statistical weakness.

Another central supposition was that attitudinal top management characteristics can strongly moderate the relationship between IT cultures and the organization's adoption of SOA. The conjecture was supported only in H3a; that is, top executives who advocate collaborative behavior motivate IT adoption in a people-oriented environment; surprisingly, the collaboration variable has no predictive power with respect to short-term-profit-oriented cultures (H3b). Remarkably too, the results do not support the supposition that senior managers who are risk-tolerant are able to influence the negative relationship between hierarchical cultures and IT innovation adoption (H4). Likewise, the regression results do not confirm that innovation-oriented executives can motivate entrepreneurial cultures to adopt service-oriented

architecture (H5). The findings have interesting implications for future research.

DISCUSSION AND IMPLICATIONS

Without understanding what drives a creative, innovative environment, it is difficult to create one. The main objectives of this study were (a) to expand the theoretical development in the area of IT adoption and innovation with respect to organizational culture and its interaction with top management and (b) to provide practitioners with guidelines to create innovative, integrative organizational IT cultures that support continuous innovation. Of the 121 participants, forty-five percent had adopted SOA in 2008. The empirical results of this study are important for top executives and support the theoretical premise that organizational culture is a primary driver of IT innovation and that a link exists between the idiosyncrasies of IT cultures, management characteristics, and SOA adoption in growth-oriented U.S. organizations. Specifically, we can see a positive link between external-dynamic as well as internal-participative IT cultures and positive organizational IT innovation strategies. Notably, the findings imply that senior managers who tend to promote a communicative environment also promote IT innovation adoption and strengthen creative and group-oriented cultures in their quest for IT infrastructure innovation. Yet, another interesting aspect of the results shows that collaboratively inclined managers who try to reverse the cultural impact toward IT innovation do not seem to be successful. Further studies could shed light on this ambiguous result.

Three broad drivers of IT innovation adoption emerge as important: (1) creative and communicative organizational cultures and (2) top management's propensity to collaborate, and (3) the interaction of collaborative top management with group and entrepreneurial cultures. Note that top management's risk propensity and attitude toward innovation do not seem to interact with cultural values regarding adoption motivation. Since this particular result is in part inconsistent with the existing IS literature, it may be worthwhile to find explanations via new case studies and grounded theory. But for the most part, these findings are consistent with the IS literature on organizational adoption research; values such as resourcefulness and effective communication help organizations to embrace innovative, long-term technologies (e.g., Kitchell, 1995). This study also corroborates that the aspects of agility, external orientation, and entrepreneurialism of the adhocracy culture are critical forces for organizations who strive for continuous innovation. Since SOA is an approach that crosses organizational and corporate domain boundaries, dynamic, externally oriented cultures offer more support for the adoption of a boundary-crossing IT strategy (e.g., McNeal et al., 2003). The strength of the construct *propensity to collaborate* is another of this study's critical statistical results. For top managers this driver refers to their inclination to include senior executives in the strategic business process and communicate across functional units. As such, senior management's openness to collaboration reflects both the inclusion in the decision-making process and the cooperation among team members. In addition, collaborative executives have a noticeable impact on people and entrepreneurial cultures and their innovation decisions.

CONCLUSION

Knowing how to relentlessly innovate information technology is crucial to organizational growth and agility and key to aligning IT/IS with business processes and strategy (e.g., Tellis et al., 2009; Oh & Pinsonneault, 2007). One of the key factors affecting organizational innovation endeavors is organizational culture (Tellis et al., 2009). This study has attempted both to explore and to explain if and how business culture affects the adoption of an IT infrastructure (based on service-oriented architecture) that is new and disruptive to the business environment. To examine how cultural values affect the organization's adoption decision, I analyzed the interaction impact of senior executive characteristics on competing cultural values. From the findings (only 45% adopters), we can conclude that (1) organizational culture is an essential driver of IT infrastructure innovation. But culture is an organizational factor that seems to be indefinable, unique, and sticky. Creative and communicative cultures, for example, are suggested to be perfect predictors of adoption decisions. However, hierarchical and short-term-profit-oriented cultures do not show significant enough differences between adopters and non-adopters to be accepted for explanation or prediction. Also, externally oriented cultures are better in explaining adoption decisions than internally oriented cultures. We can as well conclude that (2) senior executives who are open-minded toward collaboration and communication across top management teams and functional units have the ability to directly influence the organization's adoption decision and to interact with and shape the organizational culture. Since a collaboration/communication style is an important part of transformational leadership (Cox et al., 2003), one can infer that a transformational leadership style within top management teams may be conducive to radical innovation. However, a collaborative management style does not seem to have an impact on short-term and stability-oriented cultures. The explanatory power of the interaction between collaborative managers and inflexible cultures was non-significant. Finally, we can conclude that (3) certain upper echelons characteristics are uniquely able to drive, develop, and modify organizational culture to create change processes. Yet the findings show only one characteristic, collaborative management, which can drive change processes within the organizational culture. Also, tests showed that managers' attitude toward risk and innovation do not have significant predictive power to infer that, for instance, risk or innovation-averse executives would impede the adoption of SOA. An executive's attitude toward communication and sharing of leadership responsibilities, on the other hand, has strong predictive power and should be analyzed further by scholars and practitioners.

The findings have notable theoretical implications for IS scholars. First, this study is one of the few to empirically analyze the organization-centric view of IS/IT architecture adoption. The organization-centric view is resource-based and relates to the special roles that the social forces and human agents of the organizations play in the adoption outcome. Second, to approach the adoption issue from a more comprehensive viewpoint and to take the complexity of organizational decision-making into account, I examined an expanded set of possible predictors of IS/IT adoption. By testing top management characteristics, the paper expands existing IT adoption literature, which has rarely considered the dispositional aspects of executives. Third, strands of the organizational culture literature and the upper echelons literature bind the research framework. Interaction variables were particularly designed for application in this study and have shown to create additional insight into the prevailing adoption model than the main effects of focal variables.

The results of this study have valuable implications for top managers and IT practitioners. Due to the complexity and wide radius of action of integrative IT infrastructures that are based on service-oriented architecture, SOA adoption typically generates an immense domino effect throughout the organization and affects the majority of business processes and IT infrastructure (Erl, 2008). Yet, attempts by senior executives to manage or transform business processes in isolation may lead to less-than-optimal solutions or non-viable courses of action that may prevent the organization from achieving superior performance and creating competitive advantage (see Boni, 2009). Recent studies indicate that relentless innovation translates into financial value to the organization (e.g., Tellis et al., 2009). The results underscore the importance of information and responsibility exchange as one of the key behaviors executives need to adopt if they intend to shape their organizational culture and create a competitive, agile business. The results also highlight that specific attitudes and practices make innovative organizations special and foster innovation adoption. Organizations can use these findings as diagnostic tools to assess the appropriate dimensions of organizational culture and management characteristics. They will understand that it is essential to develop and manage a people and future-oriented culture in which external and internal communication is key.

LIMITATIONS AND FUTURE RESEARCH

This study identified several factors that can convincingly predict the adoption of integrative IT paradigms such as SOA. The study's limitations suggest several major research themes. An intriguing variation of this study's relationships would be to explore post-adoption and how the adoption and implementation of SOA affects and transforms the culture within the organization and within the IT function. For this kind of research, the study of causality and changes over time are essential.

Collective awareness and comprehension are said to be less malleable than leaders' aspirations (Ravasi & Schultz, 2006). Hence leaders need to be able to step outside the culture and perceive the limitations of their own culture to be able to begin change processes. Future IS studies could look closer at the diverse leader characteristics within top management teams to examine how certain dominating characteristics in the group alter organizational innovation behavior. This would expand findings from the latest studies about top manager personalities and organizational outcomes (Ling et al., 2008).

An organization's decision making is evidently influenced by the decision of others. When one organization adopts a particular IT infrastructure, another may pick the same. This kind of *herd* behavior is typical in the IT industry, and relevant research can be conducted—using informational cascades theory or sequential adoption theory (e.g., Walden & Browne, 2009)—on how particular organizational cultures are influenced by herd behavior or observational learning.

This study also suggests some methodological extensions. First, since data were obtained via a one-source survey, it would be important to conduct this study using a multi-source survey of members of the top management team, IT professionals, and the CEO. Second, hard measures (R&D expenditures, patents, financial returns) of organizational culture, although difficult to come by, may add credibility to self-reported measures (Tellis et al., 2009). Third, instead of employing a dichotomous dependent variable for SOA adoption (adopter/non-adopter), researchers may study causal processes of adoption decisions via structural equation modeling (SEM) or partial least squares (PLS). Fourth, this study's sample met all the statistical criteria, but in terms of generalizability it is restricted to larger, resource-rich U.S. organizations listed in the *2007 Directory of*

IT Executives. Examining smaller organizations should be intriguing.

Finally, the data employed in this study are purely quantitative. Further qualitative research may look into the intricacies and idiosyncrasies of why a company adopted SOA or not. Observing how organizational culture affects the pre-adoption and post-adoption behavior and performance within the organization would give the researcher important contextual information. Since qualitative studies are very powerful in terms of capturing organizational processes, the investigation of the SOA adoption, diffusion, and implementation process via qualitative research would be a very useful basis for further quantitative and longitudinal studies.

REFERENCES

Aimi, G., & Finley, I. (2007, May/June). SOA: The new value driver. *Supply Chain Management Review, 12-14.*

Bartlett, J. E., Kotrlik, J. W., & Higgins, C. C. (2001). Organizational research: Determining appropriate sample size in survey research. *Information Technology, Learning and Performance Journal, 19*(1), 43–50.

Boerner, S., Eisenbeiss, S., & Griesser, D. (2007). Follower behavior and organizational performance: The impact of transformational leaders. *Journal of Leadership & Organizational Studies, 13*(3), 15–28. doi:10.1177/1071791907013 0030201

Boni, A. A., Weingart, L. R., & Evenson, S. (2009). Innovation in an academic setting: Designing and leading a business through market-focused, interdisciplinary teams. *Academy of Management Learning & Education, 8*(3), 407–417.

Cameron, K. S., & Quinn, R. E. (2006). *Diagnosing and changing organizational culture.* San Francisco, CA: Jossey-Bass.

Chen, C. C., Chen, X., & Meindl, J. R. (1998). How can cooperation be fostered? The cultural effects of individualism-collectivism. *Academy of Management Review, 23*, 285–304. doi:10.2307/259375

Chia, Y. M., & Koh, H. C. (2007). Organizational culture and the adoption of management accounting practices in the public sector: A Singapore study. *Financial Accountability and Management, 23*(2), 189–213. doi:10.1111/j.1468-0408.2007.00425.x

Cho, T. S., & Hambrick, D. C. (2006). Attention as the mediator between top management team characteristics and strategic change: The case of airline deregulation. *Organization Science, 17*, 453–469. doi:10.1287/orsc.1060.0192

Cohen, J. (1992). A power primer. *Psychological Bulletin, 112*, 155–159. doi:10.1037/0033-2909.112.1.155

Colbert, A. E., Kristof-Brown, A. I., Bradley, B. H., & Barrick, M. R. (2008). CEO transformational leadership: The goal importance congruence in top management teams. *Academy of Management Journal, 51*(1), 81–96. doi:10.2307/20159495

Cox, J. F., Pearce, C. L., & Perry, M. L. (2003). Toward a model of shared leadership and distributed influence in the innovation process: How shared leadership can enhance new product development, team dynamics and effectiveness. In Pearce, C. L., & Conger, J. A. (Eds.), *Shared leadership: Reframing the hows and whys of leadership.* Thousand Oaks, CA: Sage.

Diong, A., & Choo, D. (2008). Transformative innovation for growth. *Industrial Management.* Retrieved May 4, 2009, from http://www.allbusiness.com/company-activities-management/company-structures/11463342-1.html

Doherty, F., & Doig, G. (2003). An analysis of the anticipated cultural impacts of the implementation of data warehouses. *IEEE Transactions on Engineering Management, 5*(1), 78–88. doi:10.1109/TEM.2002.808302

Dombrowski, C., Kim, J. Y., Desouza, K. C., Brganza, A., Papagari, S., Baloh, P., & Jha, S. (2007). Elements of innovative cultures. *Knowledge and Process Management, 14*(3), 190–202. doi:10.1002/kpm.279

Erl, T. (2008). *SOA Principles of service design.* Upper Saddle River, NJ: Prentice Hall.

Feldman, S. P. (1988). How organizational culture can affect innovation. *Organizational Dynamics, 17*(1), 57–68. doi:10.1016/0090-2616(88)90030-7

Gilley, K. M., Walters, B. A., & Olson, B. J. (2002). Top management team risk taking propensities and firm performance: Direct and moderating effects. *The Journal of Business Strategy, 19*(2), 95–114.

Green, S. B. (1991). How many subjects does it take to do a regression analysis? *Multivariate Behavioral Research, 26*, 499–510. doi:10.1207/s15327906mbr2603_7

Hambrick, D. C. (2007). Upper echelon's theory: An update. *Academy of Management Review, 32*(2), 334–343. doi:10.2307/20159303

Hambrick, D. C., & Mason, P. (1984). Upper echelons: The organization as a reflection of its top managers. *Academy of Management Review, 9*, 193–206. doi:10.2307/258434

Hannan, M., & Freeman, J. (1984). Structural inertia and organizational change. *American Sociological Review, 49*(2), 149–164. doi:10.2307/2095567

Hitt, M. A., Hoskisson, R. E., & Harrison, J. S. (1991). Strategic competitiveness in the 1990s: Challenges and opportunities for U.S. executives. *The Academy of Management Executive, 5*(2), 7–24.

Hofstede, G. (2001). *Culture's consequences: Comparing values, behaviors, institutions, and organizations across nations* (2nd ed.). Thousand Oaks, CA: Sage.

Huang, J. C., Newell, S., Galliers, R., & Pan, S. L. (2003). Dangerous liaisons? Component based development and organizational subcultures. *IEEE Transactions on Engineering Management, 50*(2), 89–99. doi:10.1109/TEM.2002.808297

Iivari, J., & Huisman, M. (2007). The relationship between organizational culture and the deployment of systems development methodologies. *Management Information Systems Quarterly, 31*(1), 35–58.

Jaccard, J. (2001). *Interaction effects in logistic regression*. Thousand Oaks, CA: Sage Publications.

Jaskyte, K., & Dressler, W. W. (2005). Organizational culture and innovation in nonprofit human services organizations. *Administration in Social Work, 29*(2), 23–43. doi:10.1300/J147v29n02_03

Jassawalla, A. R., & Sashittal, H. C. (2002). Cultures that support product-innovation Processes. *The Academy of Management Executive, 16*(3), 42–56.

Jeyaraj, A., Rottman, J. W., & Lacity, M. C. (2006). A review of the predictors, linkages, and biases in IT innovation adoption research. *Journal of Information Technology, 21*(1), 1–23. doi:10.1057/palgrave.jit.2000056

Kitchell, S. (1995). Corporate culture, environmental adaptation, and innovative adoption: A qualitative/quantitative approach. *Journal of the Academy of Marketing Science, 23*(3), 195–205. doi:10.1177/0092070395233004

Leach, J. (2007). The rise of service-oriented IT and the birth of infrastructure as a service. *CIO Research & Analysis*. Retrieved April 7, 2007, from http://www.cio.com/article/101100/The_Rise_of_Service_Oriented_IT

Leidner, D. E., & Kayworth, T. (2006). Review: A review of culture in information systems research: toward a theory of information technology conflict. *Management Information Systems Quarterly, 30*(2), 357–399.

Liang, H., Sharaf, N., Hu, Q., & Xue, Y. (2007). Assimilation of enterprise systems: The effect of institutional pressures and the mediating role of top management. *Management Information Systems Quarterly, 31*(1), 59–87.

Ling, Y., Simsek, Z., Lubatkin, M. H., & Veiga, J. F. (2008). Transformational leadership's role in promoting corporate entrepreneurship: Examining the CEO-TMT interface. *Academy of Management Journal, 51*(3), 557–576. doi:10.2307/20159526

McAfee, A., & Brynjolfsson, E. (2008). Investing in the IT that makes a competitive Difference. *Harvard Business Review, 86*(7/8), 98–107.

McLean, L. D. (2005). Organizational culture's influence on creativity and innovation: a review of the literature and implications for human resource development. *Advances in Developing Human Resources, 7*(2), 226–246. doi:10.1177/1523422305274528

McNeal, R., Tolbert, C., Mossberger, K., & Dotterweich, L. (2003). Innovating in digital government in the American states. *Social Science Quarterly, 84*(1), 52–70. doi:10.1111/1540-6237.00140

Merrifield, R., Calhoun, J., & Stevens, D. (2008, June). The next revolution in Productivity. *Harvard Business Review*, 73–80.

Milburn, R. (2009). IT's take on Web 2.0. *Enterprise Innovation, 4*(6), 31.

Moody, K. W. (2003). New meaning to IT alignment. *Information Systems Management, 20*(3), 30–35. doi:10.1201/1078/43647.20.4.20030901/77290.5

Nahm, A. Y., Vonderembse, M. A., & Koufteros, X. A. (2004). Impact of organizational culture on time-based manufacturing and performance. *Decision Sciences, 35*(4), 579–607. doi:10.1111/j.1540-5915.2004.02660.x

Newkirk, H. E., & Lederer, A. L. (2007). The effectiveness of SISP for technical resources, personnel resources, and data security in environments of heterogeneity and hostility. *Journal of Computer Information Systems*, 34–44.

Oh, W., & Pinsonneault, A. (2007). On the assessment of the strategic value of Information technologies: Conceptual and analytical approaches. *Management Information Systems Quarterly, 31*(2), 239–265.

Pandey, S., & Sharma, R. R. K. (2009). Organizational factors for exploration and exploitation. *Journal of Technology Management and Innovation, 4*(1), 48–58.

Poskiene, A. (2006). Organizational culture and innovations. *The Engineering Economist, 1*(26), 45–52.

Prahalad, C. K., & Krishnan, M. S. (2008). *The new age of innovation.* New York: McGraw-Hill.

Pundziene, A., & Duobiene, J. (2006). CEOs' entrepreneurship in relation to reaction to organizational change. *The Engineering Economist, 2*(47), 91–97.

Ramdani, B., & Kawalek, P. (2007). SMEs & IS innovations adoption: A review & assessment of previous research. *Academia, Revista. Latino Americana de Administracion, 39*, 47–70.

Ravasi, D., & Schultz, M. (2006). Responding to organizational identity threats: Exploring the role of organizational culture. *Academy of Management Journal, 49*(3), 433–458. doi:10.2307/20159775

Rogers, E. M. (2003). *Diffusion of Innovations.* New York: Free Press.

Sabherwal, R., Jeyaraj, A., & Chowa, C. (2006). Information system success: Individual and organizational determinants. *Management Science, 52*(12), 1849–1864. doi:10.1287/mnsc.1060.0583

Schein, E. H. (2004). *Organizational culture and leadership* (3rd ed.). San Francisco, CA: Jossey- Bass.

Simsek, Z., Veiga, J. F., Lubatkin, M. H., & Dino, R. N. (2005). Modeling the multilevel determinants of top management team behavioral integration. *Academy of Management Journal, 48*(1), 69–85. doi:10.2307/20159641

Smirich, L. (1983). Concepts of culture and organizational analysis. *Administrative Science Quarterly, 28*(3), 339–358. doi:10.2307/2392246

Swanson, E. B., & Ramiller, N. C. (2004). Innovating mindfully with information Technology. *Management Information Systems Quarterly, 28*(4), 553–583.

Tellis, G. H., Prabhu, J. C., & Chandy, R. K. (2009). Radical innovation across nations: The preeminence of corporate culture. *Journal of Marketing, 73*, 3–23. doi:10.1509/jmkg.73.1.3

Todhunter, J. (2008). Fostering innovation culture in an unpredictable economy. *CIO News.* Retrieved December 31, 2009, from http://advice.cio.com/james_todhunter/fostering_innovation_culture_in_an_unpredictable_economy?commentpage=1

Tolsby, J. (1998). Effects of organizational culture on a large scale IT introduction effort: A case study of the Norwegian army's EDBLF Project. *European Journal of Information Systems, 7*(2), 108–114. doi:10.1057/palgrave.ejis.3000295

Von Meier, A. (1999). Occupational cultures as a challenge to technological Innovations. *IEEE Transactions on Engineering Management, 46*(1), 101–114. doi:10.1109/17.740041

Walden, E. A., & Browne, G. J. (2009). Sequential adoption theory: A theory for understanding herding behavior in early adoption of novel technologies. *Journal of the Association for Information Systems, 10*(1), 31–62.

Wang, P., & Ramiller, N. C. (2009). Community learning in information technology innovation. *Management Information Systems Quarterly, 33*(4), 709–734.

Wang, W., Butler, J. E., Hsieh, J. J. P., & Hsu, S. (2008). Innovate with complex information technologies: A theoretical model and empirical examination. *Journal of Computer Information Systems, 49*(1), 27–36.

Wu, J., & Lederer, A. (2009). A meta-analysis of the role of environment-based voluntariness in information technology acceptance. *Management Information Systems Quarterly, 33*(2), 419–432.

Xiaotong, L. (2009). Managerial entrenchment with strategic information technology: A dynamic perspective. *Journal of Management Information Systems, 25*(4), 183–204. doi:10.2753/MIS0742-1222250406

Chapter 3
Strategy and Structure in a Virtual Organization

Nazim Ahmed
Ball State University, USA

Ray Montagno
Ball State University, USA

Sushil Sharma
Ball State University, USA

ABSTRACT

The business environment of the 21st century require organizations to respond quickly to market demands and thus traditional organization structures and strategy are no longer capable of sustaining the needs of this relentless pace. New forms of organizations in the form of virtual organization (VO) hold promise in the network world. Several organizations worldwide have already been experimenting virtual organizations' structures and processes. These new virtual structures and processes, however, will require newer strategies to succeed. This paper attempts to highlight some strategy and structural issues of a VO. The study is conceptual in nature and inferences have been drawn from existing literature and practices.

INTRODUCTION

Advances in internet and communication technologies are mandating organizations to experiment newer forms of organizations structures such as; distributed structures, network structures and virtual organizations for their business. A virtual organization is a network of companies which support each other around a product and or a service idea. The companies in the network should be seamlessly integrated by information and communication technologies so that to the customer it is not apparent that the different processes are handled by separate companies. With the availability of internet and other communication technologies a VO is a viable option for many innovative entrepreneurs. According to Lipnack and Stamps (1997), virtual team is "a group of people who interact through interdependent tasks guided by common purpose" that "works across space, time, and organizational boundaries with links strengthened by webs of communication

DOI: 10.4018/978-1-4666-0041-6.ch003

technologies" (p. 7). We are using the same definition for our study.

(Mowshowitz, 1986, 1994) used the term Virtual Organization for the first time in 1986. Since then, literature on virtual organizations has grown. There have been numerous definitions of virtual organizations (Dubinskas, 1993).

"In a virtual organization, complementary resources existing in a number of co-operating companies are left in place, but are integrated to support a particular product effort for as long as it is justifiable to do so." (Goldman et al., 1995)

"Virtual organizations are distributed 'business processes'. These processes may be 'owned' by one or more organizations acting in partnership. For a specific project, resources are assembled to perform a business process on behalf of the project owner(s), and then disassembled on completion of the contract." (Wolff, 1995)

A virtual organization (VO) is an alliance of companies formed for the purpose of delivering specific products and or services. According to Porter (1990) "A virtual organization is a collection of business units in which people and work processes from the business units interact intensively in order to perform work which benefits all" (Skyrme, 1999). The literature suggests that virtual organizations tend to be non-hierarchical (Beyerlein & Johnson, 1994; Goldman et al., 1995) and decentralized (Baker, 1992). The company who is responsible for the products and services may be called the "core" company. The core company is linked together by information and communication technologies (ICT) with other companies called "satellite" companies or VO partners. Core company and satellite companies share information, resources and skills in a seamless way so that the core company can deliver products and services to the customer and can create an impression to the customer that they have control over every aspect of the business process (Townsend et al.,

1998). With the availability and ubiquitous nature of networked based information technology, a company's business processes theoretically can span across the entire globe. Opportunity exists for organizations to deliver goods and services to the customer efficiently without the need to have physical control and ownership of many of the businesses processes. So the viability of VO's is a present reality rather than a distant possibility (Kotorov, 2000; Coulson & Kantamneni, 2000).

Nature of a VO varies in terms of its longevity and complexity. Table 1 depicts several types of VO from very transient to somewhat permanent. A virtual corporation may arise out of some interesting product and/or service idea. The originator of this product and/or service idea may succeed to actually market the product through entrepreneurial initiative using the virtual organization framework. Over time a successful VO may achieve some sort of permanency and may grow to be a traditional company (Pang, 2001).

The research on virtual companies can be categorized roughly into three broad categories: 1) the conceptual description and definition, 2) empirical studies, 3) issues related to managerial implications.

The concept of virtual organization was evolving in the early 90's as the internet and e-commerce was gaining momentum (Barnatt, 1995; Flaig, 1992). Davidow and Malone (1992) described virtual corporation as "edgeless, permeable and continuously changing interfaces, among company, supplier, and customer". Blau (1997) Concluded that virtual company has little need for physical capital and can be formed anywhere around a market opportunity by deploying intellectual capital and forming alliances based on core competencies of some existing companies. Goldman et al. (1995) defined VO's as one where, complementary resources exist in several companies which can be profitability utilized by sharing with others. Expert talent is recruited for the duration of the project and profit is shared among the companies.

Table 1. Typology of virtual organizations (Palmer & Speier, 1997, 2001)

	Virtual Team	**Virtual Project**	**Temporary VO**	**Permanent VO**
Range of Involvement	within one department	across functions and organizations	across organizations	across organizations
Membership	small, local	intermediate	typically large	smaller but scaleable
Mission	specific ongoing tasks	multiple organizational representative working on specific project	multiple functions responding to a market opportunity	all functions and full functionality as a working organization
Length of Project	membership varies, but form is permanent	temporary	temporary	permanent
Uses of IT	connectivity, sharing embedded knowledge (e-mail), groupware	repository of shared data (databases, groupware)	shared infrastructure (groupware, wans, remote computing)	channel for marketing and distribution, replacing physical infrastructure (web, groupware, wans)

Some recent empirical studies concluded that the many advantages of virtual organizations include flexibility, responsiveness, improved resource utilization in ever changing global business environment (Grabowski & Roberts, 1998; Jarvenpaa & Leidner, 1998; Cascio, 1999; McDonough, Kahn, & Barczak, 2001). Researchers also concluded there are several disadvantages such as low individual commitment, role overload, role ambiguity, absenteeism, customers find a lack of permanency, consistency and reliability in virtual firms (Jarvenpaa & Leidner, 1998; Cascio, 1999). Potocan and Dabic (2002) describe that virtual organizations enable organizations to bring their core competencies together to tightly coordinate the transactions and activities across a value chain. Snow et al. (1999) suggested that lack of influence and autonomy for the members may be a barrier to the functioning of virtual organizations. They also suggested that lack of human communication, inertia to change, and complexity of still evolving information and communication technologies and cultural differences can affect the performance of virtual organizations. Some authors suggest that virtual organizations may not be suitable for all businesses. Ahuja and Carley (1998) expertise and competence based tasks which is communication intensive can utilize distributed resources to form a virtual organization.

It may not be easy for the start-up virtual company to stay competitive in the market place. There are so many competitive forces working in a business environment, it is even hard for a regular company which has all the functional areas within itself to stay competitive. We see even big corporations becoming stagnant and losing market share for failing to come up with right product and services that will be competitive in the market place. The strategy of being competitive is an ongoing effort (McDonugh et al., 2001). As the product life-cycle shortens, it is imperative that a company must always be on its guard to bring out the right product at the right time to hold and build market share. So if a start up VO wants to mature to a permanent VO should focus on right strategy and structure and continuously update its strategy and structure. This paper investigates some structural and strategy related issues in a VO.

A virtual organization adopts different structures depending upon different internal and external uncertainties. Several studies have also supported the argument that the virtual organizations structure also depends upon level of adoption of technology (Ahuja & Carley, 1998). Baker (1992) suggests that all known virtual organizations structures evolved based on their needs. These structures vary by the nature of the task being performed. Few authors suggest that virtual organization structures evolve in three different stages known as establishment, virtualization and institutionalization (Hedberg et al., 1997).

Methodology

The literature study constitutes the major part of this study. The research examined a large sample of literature on virtual organization that has been published in information systems journals books, web pages between 1990 and 2006. The study is conceptual in nature and inferences have been drawn from existing literature and practices.

VO STRATEGY

In a traditional organization, strategy selection and formulation process involves first formulating the firm's corporate strategy by analyzing; customers, core competencies, which include workforce, facilities, market and financial know-how, systems and technology (Sharma et al., 2006). The firm also has to evaluate the changing nature of business environment especially the competitor's strength. After analyzing the above items the firm comes up with its corporate strategy. Then the corporate strategy is exploded into functional area strategies for functions such as operations, marketing, finance, and accounting. For example if an US auto company decides to go for Chinese market as a part of their corporate strategy, the operations function should design cars specific to that market. Also, they may have to find suppliers in China or setup plants there. Marketing department may have to find a Chinese auto dealership to market their car. Finance department may have to raise money from Chinese banks or investment companies.

For a VO which is usually resource constrained, strategy selection may not be that complicated. The basic strategy selection process for VO may be two step decisions. First and foremost, a VO to succeed must have a good product strategy. Then they have to also decide about their competitive priority. Once the product strategy and competitive priorities are decided, then the VO can deal with structure and infrastructure issues.

The firm also has to evaluate the changing nature of business environment especially the competitor's strength. For a VO, a traditional core competency may not exist in the sense that a VO may lack most of the functional components such as design, sales/marketing, manufacturing, distribution and so on. To setup their corporate strategy they have to rely on the core competencies of the companies in the network.

Product Strategy

Here in this article our focus is on a company which will actually come up with an actual product or service idea and then market and sell the product to the customers. There are a host of companies which sells products and services from other companies using internet. An example will be a phone card company which sells phone different phone cards through their websites. We would not consider them as VO for our purpose as they do not sell their own products.

Understanding customer demand is the first step in formulating the firm strategy. For an established traditional company the customer base is already there, however, for a VO the customers are usually new. A VO has to spend a lot of time trying to understand the nature of customer demand and also viability of the product. For developing a corporate strategy, a traditional firm will look at its core competencies in terms of workforce, facilities, market and financial know-how, systems and technology to evaluate whether a certain firm strategy is in line with its capabilities. For a VO, a traditional core competency may not exist in the sense that a VO may lack most of the functional components such as design, sales/marketing, manufacturing, distribution and so on. To setup their company strategy they have to rely on the core competencies of the companies in the network. So it is imperative that the Core company understands the relevant capabilities of the satellite companies. If the core company and the satellite companies do not have established relationship already then the core company should try to get as much information about them using whatever sources available.

The main impetus for a VO is the product idea. If one comes up with a brilliant product idea, the next thing is to make that idea succeed. If the product idea is promising, one may investigate into the possibility of using or forming a VO around the product idea. The product idea needs to be thoroughly evaluated analyzing all the related aspects. For a traditional company the feasibility of a product is evaluated by analyzing markets, competition, pricing etc. assuming that operational and supply chain issues will be handled by the organizations and its suppliers and distributors. However, for a VO, apart from analyzing marketability, competition etc., the operational issues such as marketing, manufacturing, sales, distribution issues should also have to be evaluated.

It may be advisable to come up with a product and or service idea which is not complex. For example, if one has to produce a new automobile or cell phone or a lawn mower, the degree of complexity in manufacturing, distributing and servicing the products could probably render a VO not an attractive option.

Here are some strategies for product selection for a startup VO:

1) Products/service itself should be innovative but not complex. The product should be such that there will be a demand for it and at the same time in terms of complexity, the manufacturing and after sales service etc. should be easy to manage. An example of this may be a VO which wants to sell tailor made clothing. They can setup a web-site where they may advertise different kinds of clothing products, including design, style, coloring etc. For each product, there should be clear-cut instructions as to how to make

measurements. The customers can select the design, color and give their measurements and find out the price. Once the order has been received, the order will go to a tailoring company in Thailand. When the order will be done it will be sent to a distribution company in U.S. The orders will be shipped by the distribution company to the customers. Complaints will be handled by a customer service company and if there is any re-do it will be handled by a tailoring company inside U.S.A.

2) Concurrent engineering approach should be used for product selection and the idea of concurrent engineering is that all the aspects of manufacturing, supplier issues, pricing, etc. should be resolved while the product is being designed. In a traditional company it is easy to team up with people from different functional area because they all belong to the same organization and all have stake in the company. However, concurrent engineering is not as easy in VO setting. Never the less it is very important to sort out details before the product is selected. It is important that the core company has interactions and communication with the entire all the satellite company's which will be ultimately involved in different processes in the supply chain for delivering the product to the customers.

Competitive Priorities

Competitive priorities are critical dimension that a process or value chain must focus on to satisfy both the current and future customers. There are four basic competitive priorities:

Cost

In most business environment cost is the important competitive priority as lowering price will facilitate gaining customers and increasing market share. To reduce cost, operations strategy should focus on achieving efficiency by redesigning the product, reengineering the processes, addressing supply chain issues and exploring global opportunities.

Quality

Competing on the basis of quality imply that company wants to sell products and services to a niche market. For example, a small private airline has a fleet of luxury planes to serve corporate CEOs. If a company uses quality as a competitive priority, then it should focus on two aspects of quality 1): Top quality and 2) Consistent quality. Top quality is those characteristics of a product and or service that create an impression of superiority. This may need superior product with grater tolerances, demanding requirements, high aesthetics and personal attention. Consistent quality is producing products and or services which meet customer requirement and expectations on continual basis. For example, a luxury private airline will be always punctual in picking up the clients, flying the plane and arriving at the destination.

Time

For many firms time is a competitive priority. Especially as the product life-cycle is becoming short it is imperative to bring out products and service ahead of your competition. There are three approaches to time-based competition, 1) delivery speed, 2) On-time delivery and 3) development speed. Delivery speed is how quick a customer's order can be filled. The time between the receipt of a customer's order and the filling it is called lead time. To compete on delivery speed one must try to design the order fulfillment process so that the lead time can be reduced. Sometimes companies may keep inventory or cushion or back-up capacities to compete on delivery speed. On-time delivery is meeting the promised schedule. This could be important for an airline. Also it is important for customers who are working on Just-in-time inven-

tory basis. Development speed is important for those companies where it is important to bring in new products or new version of products before the competition. For example Intel and AMD use this competitive priority. Whoever can introduce the newest computer chip in the market gains market share.

Flexibility

Competitive priority based on flexibility allows a company to react to changing customer needs quickly and efficiently. A company may compete based on flexibility using one or more of the following strategies, 1) customization, 2) Variety, 3) Volume flexibility. Customization is catering to individual customers needs. For example a custom home builder builds different houses for different customers. Customization generally implies that the products and or service are produced in low volume and has a higher degree of complexity. This requires that organization has people have higher skills and should be able to work closely with customers. Variety is producing products and or services with wide array of choices. Variety is different from customization, in the sense that customization is unique to each customer, while variety could entail different features in the product but the product is not unique. Volume flexibility is ability to produce in smaller or larger volumes within the confines of production parameters. The companies who use volume flexibility as a competitive priority must design their processes so that set-up cost is minimal.

Selecting Competitive Priority

Strategy selection process would dictate the firm strategy that will drive firm's effort in the areas of product design, process design, supply chain management and customer relationship process. Strategy selection would also include selecting a competitive priority which later is used design the structure of the VO. For example, if the VO wants to compete on the basis of cost, then all the satellite company strategy will have to use processes which will minimize cost at the same time providing implied quality. Or else, if the competitive priority selected is superior quality, then the companies in the VO network should gear their processes to provide superior quality and cost may not be the major consideration (Camillus, 1993).

STRUCTURAL DESIGN ISSUES

To be successful a VO should have all the responsibilities and attributes of a traditional company from customer point of view. For an ideal VO customer should not be able to know or at the very least feel inconvenienced by the fact that different processes such as order entry, billing, customer service and support are handled by different companies. So for a VO design seamless integration of the partner companies is very important. This integration has two major aspects. First, there is a need for technological integration so that all the companies in the network can work as one entity. Second, for management purposes there should be interaction among people from the companies in the network so that all the management issues can be handled effectively and promptly (Green & Inman, 2006). For a successful design of a VO, the following issues should be considered: 1) Selection of VO partners; 2) Understanding the nature of communication requirements; 3) Developing E- infrastructure; 4) Simulation and trial run

Selecting VO Partners

Once the core company has decided about the product and or service, and the competitive priority, the next step is to form the VO. It was mentioned earlier that, the product strategy should involve concurrent engineering, which means that the potential partners in the network should have input in the very beginning of the venture. However, it may be very much likely that, these relationships may be informal. Now is the time to select the partners in the network and design and work out the details of this partnership (Sommer, 2009).

One of the driving forces for selecting VO partners is the competitive priority of the core company. If the core company selects cost as it's core competency, the VO partners should have a similar competitive priority. That means that their processes should be geared towards providing cost savings maintaining expected quality. If the competitive priority is flexibility, the VO partners should have the similar competitive priority and their processes are developed to accommodate variety and customizations. Once, the issues of matching competitive priorities are resolved, a VO partner should be evaluated based on some other performance criteria such as: 1) capability; 2) reputation; 3) Reliability; 4) cost; 5) Technology integration; 6) Experience as a VO partner.

A VO partner should have the required capability in it's area of expertise. For example, a customer service company should have all the resources and people and expertise and technical know to provide customer support. Reputation of the company is very important. If the company does not have good reputation, which means one can expect trouble down the road. A VO partner should be reliable in the sense that it should repeatedly and consistently provide quality performance. For a new VO it is probably hard to judge the reliability of the partners. Some of the information may be obtained from secondary sources using internet resources. Cost can also be an important factor for selecting a VO partner, It is not true that one has to select the lowest cost partner, on the other hand negotiation for cost and prices should be done to the mutual benefits of the core company and the VO partners.

Technology integration is an important issue in selecting VO partners. It is imperative that most of the companies now have access to internet and e-mails. Apart from these basic technologies, A VO may need other knowledge management technologies such as: virtual reality, portals, Extensive markup language (XML), personal devices, intranets and extranets etc. It is also important that all the appropriate technologies are seamlessly integrated across the VO so the customer will not have any idea that the VO is a combination of several organizations (Davidrajuh, 2003). So it is important to understand the technology integration issues before selecting a VO partner. Last but not the least, if a company has already have experienced as a VO, then the implementation issues can be taken care of easily (Stough et al., 2000).

Understanding the Nature of Communication Requirements

To develop the e-infrastructure, it is important to understand the nature of communications between different entities in the VO. This not only includes the VO partners, but also the customer. Table 2 inventories the nature of communication between different entities such as customers, marketing

sales, production/operations, accounting and billing and maintenance and customer support. The core company is called the hub company. For, example the nature of communications between the customer and the hub company may be through phone, e-mail and company web-site. There will be probably no communication between customer and production and operations company. The nature of communications between hub company and marketing and sales company may be face-to-face, e-mail, video, work group and phone (Klueber et al., 1999).

Creating E-Infrastructure

Once communications requirements between the different entities in the network are established, the next step is to map appropriate information and communication technology to support those requirements. Table 3 shows the information and communication technologies required to support different communication interfaces. Communications between a customer and other customers

Table 2. Nature of communication

Entities	Customer	Hub Company	Marketing and Sales Company	Productions/ Operations Company	Accounting and Billing Company	Maintenance and Customer Support
Customer	Remote Information Exchange	Phone e-mail Portal	Phone e-mail mobile	No communication	Phone e-mail Mobile	Phone e-mail Mobile
Hub Company		E-mail Face-to Face Phone Work Group	Face-to face e-mail, Video, Work group Phone	Face-to face e-mail, Video, Work group Phone	Face-to face e-mail, Video, Work group Phone	Face-to face e-mail, Video, Work group Phone
Marketing and Sales Company			Phone E-mail	e-mail, Video, Work group Phone	E-mail Phone	E-mail Phone
Productions/Operations Company				Phone E-mail	Phone E-mail	Phone E-mail
Accounting and Billing Company					Phone E-mail	Phone E-mail
Maintenance and Customer Support Company						Phone E-mail

can be facilitated by online blog or company portal. Communications between hub company and the marketing and sales company can be accomplished by electronic meeting room, phone, internet, intranet, portal for both the companies. Apart from phone, many of the common information and communication technologies such as internet, intranet, video conferencing, portal may already exist among the VO partners. Some other technologies such as electronic meeting room and video conferencing may not be available to some of the partners. So it may be necessary to negotiate cost and other managerial and technical issues which are relevant for use of those technologies.

Simulation and Trial Run

To have a better understanding of how the whole VO works, a simulation may be performed incorporating all the processes starting from placing a customer order, billing process, communicating the information to the operations company, making a prototype, shipping the prototype to the distribution company, sending the product to the customer, handling customer complaints for billing, handling customer returns and so on. Before the trial run or simulation it is important to devise a performance matrix for all the important processes. Table 4 shows example of some of the performance criteria for different processes. All of the performance criteria may not be evaluated during the simulation. The ones which could evaluate, such as time between order and delivery, production lead time, time to answer customer complaint, time for refund etc. may generate valuable information which will help in redesigning the processes (Vakola & Wilson, 2004).

Table 3. Mapping information and communication technology

Entities	Customer	Hub Company	Marketing and Sales Company	Productions/ Operations Company	Accounting and Billing Company	Maintenance and Customer Support
Customer	Online Blog Portal	Portal Phone Mobile technology Internet	Phone Mobile technology Internet Portal	No communication	Phone Mobile technology Internet	Phone Mobile technology Internet
Hub Company		Electronic Meeting Room, Phone, Internet, Intranet	Electronic Meeting Room, Phone, Internet, Intranet, Portal	Electronic Meeting Room, Phone, Internet, Intranet, Portal	Electronic Meeting Room, Phone, Internet, Intranet, Portal	Electronic Meeting Room, Phone, Internet, Intranet, Portal
Marketing and Sales Company			Intranet Phone E-mail	Electronic Meeting Room, Phone, Internet, Intranet, Portal	Electronic Meeting Room, Phone, Internet, Intranet, Portal	Internet Phone
Productions/ Operations Company					Phone Internet	Phone Internet
Accounting and Billing Company					Phone Intranet	Phone Internet
Maintenance and Customer Support Company						Phone Intranet

Table 4. Performance criteria for important processes

Marketing and Sales and Customer relationship process	Percent of wrong orders Time between order and delivery Percent of delayed order Time to take an order Time to re-do
Productions and Operations	Production lead time Percent of returned order Percent of re-do
Accounting and Billing	Percent of wrong billing Time for refund
Maintenance and customer support	Time to answer customer complaints Percent of customers complaining Types of customer complaint

DISCUSSION AND SUMMARY

Rapid advancement, availability and affordability of internet-based technologies have changed the way the companies do business to stay competitive. Rapid growth of e-commerce and the disappearance of physical boundaries have enabled the emergence of virtual organizations from a "futuristic "concept to reality (Greiner & Metes, 1995). Virtual organizations consist of independent companies networked together for providing product and services to the customer on behalf of the core company. VO provides entrepreneurial opportunities for a company with limited resources. However, the implementation of a VO has a lot of challenges which must be overcome (Christie & Levary, 1998). This study augments the existing literature on virtual organizations. The literature research indicate that though virtual organizations suggest network structures in theory but in practice, structural dimensions have been of hierarchy and centralization nature (Black & Edwards, 2000). The relationship between task routineness and structure has been well established in the literature for virtual organizations (Stough et al., 2000). The study is limited to the number of information systems and management journals that were used for virtual organization literature search. The authors recommend that further studies need to be conducted widening the literature survey set on virtual organizations in larger set of journals. Also the conceptual framework needs to be tested for its empirical evidence.

In this paper we have discussed issues related to strategy and structure for a VO. Main focus of a VO should be the product strategy. Also, a product strategy should be established in conjunction with competitive priority such as cost, quality, time and flexibility. The competitive priority is important for designing important processes in the VO. For example, if a VO chooses to focus on the competitive priority of cost, then the VO partners should design their processes to be cost efficient at the same time maintaining expected quality.

Structural design issues for a VO includes selecting the VO partners, understanding the communication requirements, mapping the information and communication technology and simulating the processes. Simulation of the VO may resolve some technical and managerial issues before the actual operation and enable the company to achieve customer satisfaction from the very start (Vakola, & Wilson, 2004).

REFERENCES

Ahuja, M., & Carley, K. (1998). Network Structure in Virtual Organizations. *Journal of Computer-Mediated Communication, 3*(4), *10*(6), 741-757.

Baker, W. (1992). The network organization in theory and practice. In Nohria, N., & Eccles, R. (Eds.), *Networks and Organizations* (pp. 327–429). Cambridge, MA: Harvard Business School Press.

Barnatt, C. (1995). Office space, cyberspace and virtual organizations. *Journal of General Management, 21*(4), 78–91.

Beyerlein, M., & Johnson, D. (1994). *Theories of self-managing work teams*. Stamford, CT: JAI Press.

Black, J. A., & Edwards, S. (2000). Emergence of virtual or network organizations: fad or feature? *Journal of Organizational Change Management, 13*(6), 567–576. doi:10.1108/09534810010378588

Blau, J. (1997). Global networking process management challenges. *Technology Management, 40*(1), 4–5.

Camillus, J. (1993). Crafting the competitive corporation: Management systems for future organizations. In Lorange, P., Chakravarthy, B., Roos, J., & Van De Ven, A. (Eds.), *Implementing strategic process: Change, learning, and cooperation* (pp. 313–328). Oxford, UK: Blackwell.

Cascio, W. F. (1999). Virtual work places: Implications for organizational behavior. In Cooper, C. L., & Rousseau, D. M. (Eds.), *The Virtual Organization* (*Vol. 6*, pp. 1–14). Trends in Organizational Behavior.

Christie, P. M. J., & Levary, R. R. (1998). Virtual corporations: Recipe for success. *Industrial Management (Des Plaines), 40*(4), 7–11.

Coulson, K. R., & Kantamneni, S. P. (2000). *Virtual corporations: The promise and the peril*. Retrieved March 23, 2005, from http://www.dcpress.com/jmb/virtual.htm

Davidow, W. H., & Malone, M. S. (1992). *The Virtual Corporation: Structuring and Revitalizing the Corporation for the 21st Century*. New York: Harper Collins Publishers.

Davidrajuh, D. (2003). Realizing a new e-commerce tool for formation of a virtual enterprise. *Industrial Management & Data Systems, 103*(6), 434–445. doi:10.1108/02635570310480006

Dubinskas, F. A. (1993). Virtual Organizations: Computer Conferencing and Organizational Design. *Journal of Organizational Computing, 3*(4), 389–416. doi:10.1080/10919399309540210

Flaig, S. (1992). Virtual enterprise: Your new model for success. *Electronic Business*, 153-155.

Goldman, S., Nagel, R., & Preiss, K. (1995). *Agile Competitors and Virtual Organizations*. New York: Van Nostrand Reinhold.

Grabowski, M., & Roberts, K. H. (1998). Risk mitigation in virtual organizations. *Journal of Computer-Mediated Communication, 3*(4), 49–65.

Green, K., & Inman, R. (2006). Does implementation of a JIT-with-customers strategy change an organization's structure? *Industrial Management & Data Systems, 106*(8), 1077–1094. doi:10.1108/02635570610710764

Greiner, R., & Metes, G. (1995). *Going Virtual: Moving Your Organization into the 21st Century*. Upper Saddle River, NJ: Prentice Hall.

Hedberg, B., Dahlgren, G., Hansson, J., & Olve, N. (1997). *Virtual Organizations and Beyond*. New York: Wiley.

Jarvenpaa, S. L., & Leidner, D. E. (1998). Communication and trust in global teams. *Journal of Computer-Mediated Communication, 3*(4), 18–37.

Klueber, R., Alt, R., & Oesterle, H. (1999). Emerging electronic services for virtual organizations - concepts and framework. In P. Sieber & J. Griese (Eds.), *Workshop on Organizational Virtualness and Electronic Commerce* (pp. 183-204). Zurich, Switzerland: Simowa.

Kotorov, R. P. (2000). Virtual Organization: Conceptual Analysis of the Limits of its Decentralization. *Journal of Modern Business*. Retrieved from http://www.dcpress.com/jmb/jmb.htm

Lipnack, J., & Stamps, J. (1997). *Virtual Teams: Reaching Across Space, Time, and Organizations with Technology*. New York: John Wiley & Sons.

McDonugh, E. F. III, Kahn, K. B., & Barczak, G. (2001). An investigation of the use of global, virtual, and collocated new product development teams. *Journal of Product Innovation Management*, *18*(2), 110–120. doi:10.1016/S0737-6782(00)00073-4

Mowshowitz, A. (1986). *Social dimensions of office automation*. In Myovitz (Ed.), *Advances in computers* (pp. 335-404).

Mowshowitz, A. (1994). Virtual Organization: A Vision of Management in the Information Age. *The Information Society*, *10*, 267–288. doi:10.1080/01972243.1994.9960172

Palmer, J. W., & Speier, C. (1997). A Typology of Virtual Organizations: An Empirical Study. In *Proceedings of the Association for Information Systems 1997 Americas Conference*, Indianapolis, IN.

Palmer, J. W., & Speier, C. (2001). *A Typology Virtual Organizations: An Empirical Study*. Retrieved from http://hsb.baylor.edu/ramsower/ais.ac97/papers/palm_spe.htm

Pang, L. (2001). Understanding Virtual Organizations. *Information Systems Control Journal*, *6*, 42–47.

Porter, M. (1990). *Competitive Advantage of Nations*. New York: Free Press.

Potocan, V., & Dabic, M. (2002). The Virtual Organization from the Viewpoint of Informing. In *Proceedings of the Informing Science* (pp. 1267-1275).

Sharma, S. K., Chen, C., & Sundaram, S. (2006). Implementation Problems with ERP Systems in Virtual Enterprises/Virtual Organizations. *International Journal of Management and Enterprise Development*, *3*(5), 491–509. doi:10.1504/IJMED.2006.009572

Skyrme, D. (1999). Virtual Teaming and Virtual Organizations: 25 Principles of Proven Practice. In Lloyd, P., & Boyle, P. (Eds.), *Web-Weaving: intranets, extranets and strategic alliances*. Oxford, UK: Butterworth-Heinemann.

Snow, C. C., Lipnack, J., & Stamps, J. (1999). The virtual organization: promises and pay-offs, large and small. In Cooper, C. L., & Rousseau, D. M. (Eds.), *The Virtual Organization* (*Vol. 6*, pp. 15–30). Trends in Organizational Behavior.

Sommer, R. (2009). A planning solution for virtual business relationships. *Industrial Management & Data Systems*, *109*(4), 463–476. doi:10.1108/02635570910948614

Stough, S., Eom, S., & Buckenmyer, J. (2000). Virtual teaming: a strategy for moving your organization into the new millennium. *Industrial Management & Data Systems*, *100*(8), 370–378. doi:10.1108/02635570010353857

Townsend, A. M., DeMarie, S. M., & Hendrickson, A. R. (1998). Virtual teams: Technology and the workplace of the future. *The Academy of Management Executive*, *12*(3), 17–29.

Vakola, M., & Wilson, I. E. (2004). The Challenge of Virtual Organization: Critical Success Factors in Dealing with Constant Change. *Team Performance Management*, *10*(5-6), 112–120. doi:10.1108/13527590410556836

Wolff, M. (1995). *New Organizational Structures* for *Engineering Design Commissioned Report*. Retrieved from http://www.worldserver.pipex.com/ki-net/content.html

This work was previously published in International Journal of E-Adoption, Volume 2, Issue 4, edited by Sushil K. Sharma, pp. 48-60, copyright 2010 by IGI Publishing (an imprint of IGI Global).

Chapter 4
Knowledge Sharing Adoption Model Based on Artificial Neural Networks

Olusegun Folorunso
University of Agriculture Abeokuta, Nigeria

Rebecca O. Vincent
University of Agriculture Abeokuta, Nigeria

Adewale Opeoluwa Ogunde
Redeemer's University (RUN), Nigeria

Benjamin Akintayo Agboola
University of Agriculture Abeokuta, Nigeria

ABSTRACT

Knowledge Sharing Adoption Model called (KSAM) was developed in this paper using Artificial Neural Networks (ANN). It investigated students' Perceived Usefulness and Benefits (PUB) of Knowledge Sharing among students of higher learning in Nigeria. The study was based on the definition as well as on the constucts related to technology acceptance model (TAM). A survey was conducted using structured questionnaire administered among students and analysed with SPSS statistical tool; the results were evaluated using ANN. The KSAM includes six constucts that include Perceived Ease Of Sharing (PEOS), Perceived Usefulness and Benefits (PUB), Perceived Barriers for Sharing (PBS), External Cues to Share (ECS), Attitude Towards Sharing (ATT), and Behavioral Intention to Share (BIS). The result showed that Students' PUB must be raised in order to effectively increase the adoption of Knowledge Sharing in this domain. The paper also identified a myriad of limitations in knowledge sharing and discovered that the utilization of KSAM using ANN is feasible. Findings from this study may form the bedrock on which further studies can be built.

DOI: 10.4018/978-1-4666-0041-6.ch004

INTRODUCTION

Knowledge is defined as human understanding of a specialized field of interest that has been acquired through study and experience (Awad & Ghaziri, 2004). Hence, sharing this knowledge cannot be over emphasized. However, Knowledge sharing can be termed as the process where individuals mutually exchange their knowledge and jointly create new knowledge (Van den Hooff et al., 2003). It is defined as the process of exchanging knowledge (skills, experience, and understanding) among researchers, policymakers, and service providers (Lily Tsui et al., 2006). It is expected that increase in sharing of valuable knowledge would have a positive effect on the organization's performance. Unfortunately, people do not share their knowledge under all circumstances.

Knowledge sharing has been gaining attention among researchers and business managers (Kong et al., 2009; Kim & Ju, 2008; Van den Hoot & Huysman, 2009; Lu, Leung, & Koch, 2006; Han & Anantatmula, 2007). Numerous studies (Barson et al., 2000; Murray, 2003; Levina, 2001) have examined factors influencing knowledge sharing in an organizational context. However, a few studies have addressed knowledge sharing in a classroom context. Therefore, the purpose of this study is to investigate factors influencing knowledge sharing among university students in a classroom context. Few studies on knowledge sharing paid attention to the inhibiting factors that is likely to affect knowledge sharing (i.e., perceived ease, perceived usefullness and benefits and barriers affecting the behavioral intension of potential sharers). Most of the previous studies adopted simple statistic methods, or regression-based multivariate analysis, all of which are linear, only few studies used nonlinear structural models such as the nonlinear artificial neural network model. This paper utilizes ANN for generating an adoption model for knowledge sharing in a learning environment.

Neural networks, despite their empirically proven abilities, have been little used for the refinement of existing knowledge because the task requires a three step process. First, knowledge in some form must be inserted into a neural network. Second, the network must be refined. Third, knowledge must be extracted from the network. Artificial Neural Network (ANNs) has proven to be a powerful and general technique for knowledge sharing (Fisher & McKusick, 1989; Shavlik et al., 1991; Weiss & Kapouleas, 1989; Ng & Lippmann, 1990). We illuminate into the neural network black box by combining knowledge based reasoning with neural learning. Our approach is to form a three-link chain in which symbolic knowledge, in the form of propositional rules, is revised and corrected using neural networks. Thus, the approach we present makes possible the use of neural networks as the underlying algorithm of a rule-refinement system.

LITERATURE REVIEW

Technology acceptance model (TAM) and knowledge sharing adoption model (KSAM) are two models which are in some aspects, complementary. Therefore, it would be of great significance if they are integrated to investigate the adoption of knowledge sharing. The follwoing sections reviews these models.

Technology Acceptance Model (TAM)

In studying user acceptance and use of technology, the TAM is one of the most cited models. The Technology Acceptance Model (TAM) was developed by Davies (1989) to explain computer-usage behaviour. The theoretical basis of the model was Fishbein and Ajzen's Theory of Reasoned Action (TRA). The Technology Acceptance Model (TAM) is an information system (system consisting of the network of all communication channels used within an organization) theory that models how users come to accept and use a technology, The model suggests that when users are presented with a new software package or technology, a number of factors influence their decision on how, when and if it is necessary to use it. TAM posits that perceived ease of use, perceived usefulness predicts attitude toward use of a technology while attitude toward use predicts the behavioural intention to utilize it. However, intention predicts the actual use of the technology (Davies, 1989). A variety of applications have been used to validate the model (Ma & Liu, 2004). For example, the model was employed to study user acceptance of microcomputers (Igbara et al., 1995), the World Wide Web (Lederer et al., 2000), software, and decision support systems (Morris & Dillon, 1997). Figure 1 describes the model.

Perceived Usefulness (PU): This was defined by Davies (1989) as "the degree to which a person believes that using a particular system would enhance his or her job performance". That is, the prospective adopter's subjective probability that applying the new technology from outside sources will be beneficial to his personal and/or the adopting companies or user's well being.

Perceived Ease-of-Use (PEOU): Davis defined this as "the degree at which a person believes that using a particular system would be free from effort" (Davies, 1989). It is the degree to which the prospective adopter expects the new technology adopted to be free of effort regarding its transfer and utilization.

Attitude (ATT): Attitudes are made up of beliefs that a person accumulates over his lifetime.

Some beliefs are formed from direct experience, some are from outside information and others are inferred or self generated. These beliefs are called salient beliefs and they are said to be the intermediate determinant of a person's altitude. An attitude therefore is a person's salient belief about whether the outcome of his action will be positive or negative.

Behavioural Intention (BI): The possibility that a person will carry out a conduct defines its behavioural intention; it is made up of the attitudes and the subjective norms.

Relevant studies (Taylor & Todd, 1995; Venkatesh & Davis, 2000) suggested that TAM should integrate other theories of acceptance in order to incorporate relevant human and social factors and to facilitate its predictive and explanatory power. One of the areas of application is Lei-da Chen (2008), the author expanded the Technology Acceptance Model (TAM) and the Innovation Diffusion Theory (IDT), in which the study proposes a research model that examines the factors which determine consumer acceptance of m-payment. In addition, the number of studies on TAM in the field of knowledge sharing, particularly in learning environment, is rather limited. Besides, relevant studies on the application of TAM in knowledge sharing include: Nor et al. (2004) which suggested that knowledge sharing of other people's experience is perceived as more neutral and trustworthy and help to reduce tourist's perceived risks. The study of Jui-Chen Huang (2010) indicates that the utilization of the adoption model of remote health monitoring established by ANN based on

Figure 1. Technology acceptance model

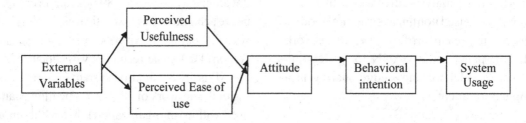

the health information adoption model (HIAM) is feasible. Therefore, this work opened up our interest in this work.

Knowledge Sharing Adoption Model (KSAM)

The components of KSAM mainly consist of six constructs perceived ease of sharing (PEOS), perceived usefullness and benefits (PUB), perceived barriers for sharing (PBS), external cues to share (ECS), Attitude towards sharing (ATT), Behavioral intention to share (BI). In KSAM, perceived ease of share and perceived usefullness are the primary motivational factors for knowledge sharing.

Perceived Ease Of Sharing (PEOS): is the perception about the degree of effort needed to share knowledge, In this case, 'ease' is conceptual as freedom from difficulty or great effort.

Perceived Usefulness and Benefits (PUB): Is the degree to which a person belive that sharing of knowledge will produce better outcome. Usefulness is the capability of being used to the advantage of the beneficiary.

Perceived Barriers for Sharing (PBS): are the challenges met when an individual is attempting to share his/her knowledge.

External Cues to Share (ECS): are the external factors that affects the reason to knowledge sharing.

Attitude Towards Sharing (ATT): An attitude therefore is a person's salient belief about whether the outcome of his action by sharing knowledge will be positive or negative.

Behavioral Intention to share knowledge (BI): Is a dependent variable to interpret the knowledge sharing adoption

As many previous theories and studies have indicated, the BI and the usage of technology share a strong and significant causal relationship, and can be used to predict the actual usage (Cheng, Lam, & Yeung, 2006; Davis et al., 1989; Mathieson, 1991; Sheppard, Hartwick, & Warshaw, 1988;

Venkatesh & Morris, 2000). Hence, it is justifiable to use BI as a dependent variable to interpret the knowledge sharing adoption. Agarwal and Prasad (1999) also argued that for a survey-based research design, behavioral intention is more appropriate than actual usage as "it is measured contemporaneously with beliefs."

On the other hand, Ajzen (1985) proposed the theory of planned behavior (TPB). He observed that BI is a prerequisite for action and that only the attitude toward using (ATT) cannot directly predict behavior. In contrast, only BI enables accurate predictions (Ajzen, 1985, 1989, 1991). Therefore, the research structure underlying this study is shown based on the theory of reasoned action (TRA) by Fishbein and Ajzen (1975), it is believed that if the attitude of an individual tend towards positive behavior, his/her BI is relatively stronger. On the contrary, when the attitude of an individual tend towards negative behavior, his/her BI is relatively weaker (Ajzen & Fishbein, 1980; Fishbein & Ajzen, 1975).

HYPOTHESIS

H1. An individual's ATT and BI with respect to knowledge sharing adoption are found to be positively associated.

H2a. PEOU has a direct effect on the ATT of knowledge sharing adoption.

As adopted in Jui-Chen Huang (2010), the stronger the PUB and PEOU the easier it would be to take action (Figure 2). On the other hand, negative perceptions pertaining to sharing, such as the considerable barrier to share, would also affect the possibility of action by functioning as PBS. Further, the stronger the PBS, the more difficult it would be for one to take action. Additionally, CUES, which act as triggers that stimulate people to take action, external cue (such as lecturers's advice, encouragement from friends and relatives,

Figure 2. Knowledge sharing adoption model (Adapted from Jui-Chen Huang, 2010)

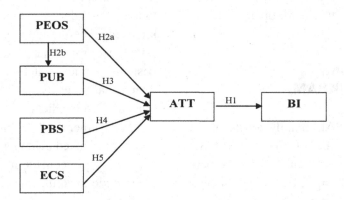

and media educators). This cues would positively affect the chances of action.

H2b. PEOU has a direct effect on PUB

H3. The stronger the PUB of knowledge sharing, the stronger is the ATT of remote knowledge sharing.

H4. The stronger is the PBS of remote health monitoring, the weaker is the ATT of the Knowledge sharing adoption.

H5. The stronger the ECUE, the stronger is the ATT of the Knowledge sharing adoption.

Artificial Neural Network (ANN)

An artificial neural network (ANN) has been widely used to examine the complex relationship between input variables and output variables (Nelson & Illingworth, 1994). Of the various ANN models, the back-probagation network (BPN) is the simplest model and the easiest to understand. Hence, it is the most commonly used model at present (Davies, Goode, Mazanec, & Moutinho, 1999).

The Backpropagation Algorithm

The back-propagation algorithm (Rumelhart & McClelland, 1986) is used in layered feed-forward ANNs. This means that the artificial neurons are organized in layers, and send their signals "for-ward", and then the errors are propagated backwards. The network receives inputs by neurons in the input layer, and the output of the network is given by the neurons on an output layer. There may be one or more intermediate hidden layers.

The back-propagation algorithm uses supervised learning, which means that we provide the algorithm with examples of the inputs and outputs we want the network to compute, and then the error (difference between actual and expected results) is calculated. The idea of the back-propagation algorithm is to reduce this error, until the ANN learns the experimatal data. The experiment begins with random weights, and the goal is to adjust them so that the error will be minimal.

Research Methodolgy

Sample Data

The attitude of students based on the fact that students could share any known knowledge among themselves was examined. To study how students share knowledge among themselves, we carried out a sample experiment with the students of the University of Agriculture, Abeokuta, Nigeria. The survey subject were mainly the registered students. 110 questionaires with 23 questions were administered to students out of which 105 questionaires were returned. Of these, 5 were not

Table 1. Profile of the respondent

Item	Fre-quency	Valid Per-cent	Cummula-tive Percent-age
Gender Male Female	71	71.0	71.0
	29	29.0	100.0
Age: Under 21 Years 21-25 26-30	14	14.0	14.0
	78	78.0	92.0
	8	8.0	100.0
College: COLNAS COLAMRUD COLANIM COLVET COLFEC COLENG	69	69.0	69.0
	2	2.0	71.0
	11	11.0	82.0
	2	2.0	84.0
	6	6.0	90.0
	10	10.0	100.0
Level 100 Level 200 Level 300 Level 400 Level Higher Levels	13	13.0	13.0
	10	10.0	23.0
	36	36.0	59.0
	27	27.0	86.0
	14	14.0	100.0
Total (%)	100	100.0	100.0

completely filled. Therefore, 100 questionaires were computed which is about 90.91%. The profile of the respondents is shown in Table 1.

Constructs and Validity Analysis

The knowledge sharing adoption model examined in this study consists of six constructs: Perceived Ease Of Sharing (PEOS), Perceived Usefullness and Benefits (PUB), Perceived Barriers for Sharing (PBS), External Cues to Share (ECS), Attitude Towards Sharing (ATT), Behavioral Intention to Share (BI). These constructs were studied based on the principle of TAM. The consistency of the constructs were assessed by using Cronbach's alpha. From Table 2, it was observed that the

alpha coefficients gotten from this approach ranges between 0.601 to 0.757 which are higher than the benchmark of 0.6 suggested by Bagozzi and Yi (1988). This shows the higher consistency displayed by our model and therefore is more reliable. Therefore, the questionnaires of this study have considerable content validity.

Methods of Analysis

The next section describes the methods used in the analysis.

Artificial Neural Network Framework

The first thing considered here is the feed-forward neural network (FFNN) which is regarded as a general architecture for our model. The feed-forward neural network in this case has n input and p output shown in Figure 2. The development procedure of ANN is divided into two processes: learning process, and recalling process. Here, it is recognised that large numbers of sample are required in both processing of the input and the output data, in order for the ANN operations to be completed at every stage. During the learning process, the errors of trained samples with targets were used to adjust the weigths of ANN by various efficient learning algorithms. The final weights were adjusted to meet the minimization of errors inteded while the trained weigths were stored in the network after learning is completed.

In the second stage, samples were used to verify the validity of the network. The neural network was utilized as a case study to get possible results. The knowledge sharing model for the sample is shown in Figure 3 while the ANN framework is given as Figure 4. In Figure 5, the relationship between perceived ease of share and perceived usefulness and benefit is displayed. It is expected that perceived ease of sharing will have great influence on perceived usefuleness and benefits because of the direct linked to the input and output layer (Figure 6).

Table 2. Cronbach's alpha for reliability and validity test

Constructs	Question	Cronbach's alpha
PEOS1	I find it easy to share course materials with my classmate.	0.703
PEOS2	I find it easy to discuss new ideas with my classmates.	
PEOS3	I am willing to share knowledge that I acquire with my classmates.	
PEOS4	I find it easy to put what I know into words.	
PEOS5	Overall,I find that sharing my knowledge is convinient.	
PUB1	I found that knowledge sharing increased my performance.	0.627
PUB2	Knowledge sharing can enhance my level of understanding.	
PUB3	Sharing my knowledge has a positive impact on my Friends.	
PUB4	Overall, I found that knowledge sharing is highly usefull.	
PBS1	Knowledge sharing is a waste of time.	0.662
PBS2	For me I feel knowledge sharing will violate my privacy.	
PBS3	I am concerned about the accuracy and reliability of external knowledge.	
PBS4	I feel that my classmates will perform better than me if I share my knowledge.	
ECS1	My lecturers support us in sharing knowledge with other classmates.	0.601
ECS2	My lecturers give us reward such as verbal praise and score when sharing knowledge with other classmates.	
ECS3	My friends praises me when i share Things I Know.	
ATT1	I like sharing my knowledge.	0.603
ATT2	I like using Ideas gotting from friends.	
ATT3	Overall I consider knowledge sharing to be just right.	
ATT4	In my current level I consider knowledge sharing to be Ideal.	
BI1	Overall,I am highly willing to share knowledge.	0.754
BI2	If possible I will be sharing my knowledge everytime.	
BI3	In my present level I recommend knowledge sharing for everybody.	

Figure 3. Feed-forward neural network (Adapted from Huang, 2010)

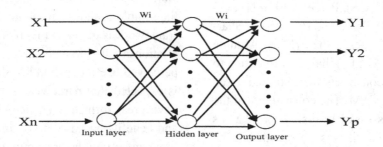

Figure 4. Knowledge sharing adoption model

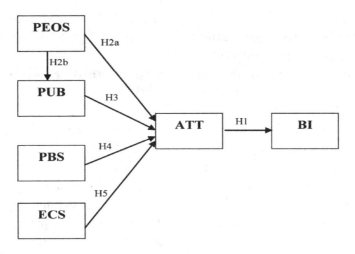

Figure 5. ANN framework for KSAM

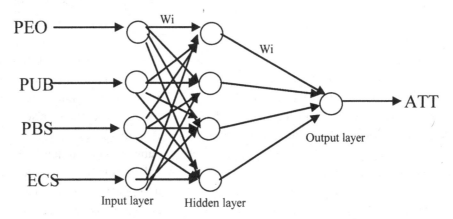

Legend	
PEO	Perceived Ease of Sharing
PUB	Perceived Usefullness and Benefits
PBS	Perceived Barriers for Sharing
ECS	External Cues to Share
ATT	Attitude Towards Sharing

Figure 6. ANN construct relationship

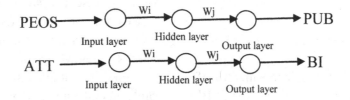

Data Analysis

Back-propagation algorithm is used to analysed the constructs. Since the back-propagation algorithm uses supervised learning, which means that we provide the algorithm with examples of the inputs for these constructs: PEOS, PUB, PBS, ECS, and for outputs ATT we want the network to compute, the error which is the difference between actual and expected results is calculated. The idea of the backpropagation algorithm is to reduce this error, until the ANN gets the sample data. The experiment begins with random weights, and the goal is to adjust them so that the error will be minimal. This is done as follows:

(i)   First experiment.

```
Inputs (PEOS)---- Output (PUB)
```

The neural network was trained with PEOS of mean value 4.144 and the expected value of PUB is a mean value of 4.508, so therefore we had an error of 0.364, which is needed as a feed back into the system to give our expected value.

(ii)   Second experiment

```
Inputs (PEOS,PUB,PBS,ECS)---Output
(ATT)
```

The neural network was trained with general average mean value of 3.985 for the four constructs and the expected mean value for ATT is 4.028 which means it had error of 0.0421,which is needed to be feed back into the system to give our expected value.

(iii)   Third Experiment

```
Inputs(ATT)----Output (BI)
```

The neural network was trained with ATT of mean value 4.028 and the expected value of BI is a mean value of 4.147, so therefore we had an error of.0119, which is needed to be feed back into the system to give our expected value.

Experimental Results and Discussions

The results obtained after testing of the four hypotheses indicated that; it is feasible to construct a knowledge sharing model with ANN, and to identify knowledge sharing by using ANN based on the knowledge sharing adoption model (KSAM). The findings of this paper have revealed that the utilization of the adoption model of knowledge sharing using ANN is feasible. Findings from this study may also form the bedrock on which further studies can be built. Tables for data analysis are presented in Table 3, Table 4 and Table 5.

The analysis done includes the Cronbach's alpha, which was as a measure of the internal consistency and reliability of a psychometric test score for a sample of examinees. Cronbach's alpha is a measure of internal consistency, which shows how closely related a set of items are as a group. A high value of alpha is often used along with substantive arguments and possibly other statistical measures) as evidence that the items measure an underlying construct. However, a high alpha does not imply that the measure is unidimensional. If, in addition to measuring internal consistency, you wish to provide evidence that the scale in question is unidimensional, additional analyses can be performed. Exploratory factor analysis is one method for checking dimensionality.

Limitations

ANNs have several well-known shortcomings; perhaps the most significant is that a trained ANN is essentially a "black box" determining exactly why an ANN for knowledge sharing makes a particular decision is all but impossible. Yet, without such ability, neural networks for our knowledge shar-

Table 3. Relationship of the four constructs that affects Attitude towards sharing (ATT)

Parameters	Mean	% impact on ATT	Mean value added to ATT	Expected Mean value for ATT	Total Error impact on ATT
Perceived ease of sharing(PEOS)	4.144	29.8	1.1601		
Perceived usefullness and benefits (PUB)	4.508	32.42	1.3058		
Perceived barries of sharing (PBS)	2.230	16.03	0.645		
External cues to sharing (ECS)	3.023	21.74	0.875		
TOTAL	13.905	100	3.9859	4.028	0.0421

Table 4. Results of the effect of construct relationship

Construct that Affects Attidute Towards Sharing				
Parameter	Mean	% Impact on PUB	Expected Mean Value for PUB	Total Error impact on PUB
Perceived Ease of Shasring (PEOS)	4.144	91.93	4.508	0.364
Perceived Ease of Sharing (PEOS) on Perceived Usefulness and Benefits (PUB)				
Parameter	Mean	% Impact on PUB	Expexted Mean Value for BI	Total Error impact on BI
Attitude Towards Sharing	4.028	91.93	4.147	0.119

ing research work cannot be used as the basis of a rule refinement system. Furthermore, it is hard to be confident in the reliability of a network that addresses a real-world problem. Also, the fruits of training knowledge sharing neural networks are difficult to transfer to other neural networks (Pratt & Kamm, 1991), much less non-neural learning systems. For example, the network tells that it has discovered something "wonderful", but then does not tell exactly what that something is. However, the testing is yet to be tested on a broad range of environment. It was tested in a university environment where tester's mind has been trained to appreciate the concept of knowledge sharing. We need to repeat same test on real environment where crude researches are done, findings are made and yet results are kept in the mind of the inventors till they die with it. Cultural factors are

considered a treat which can essentially inhibit knowledge transfers. They include lack of trust, different cultures and vocabularies, lack of time and meeting places, lack of absorptive capacities in recipients, belief that knowledge is prerogative of particular groups, etc. Cognitive and motivational limitations also interfere with people's ability to share and transfer their expertise. Cognitive limitations are related to the way experts store and process information, impeding them to share that expertise with others regardless of whether or not they are motivated to do so. The cognitive limitations faced by experts come partly from the way that they mentally represent the task, as expertise increases, mental representations become more abstract and simplified. Motivational limitations are related to the appraisal and reward systems of most companies, as well the internal competition between individuals, teams and units. Knowledge transfer requires resources of time and energy and the lack of company understanding and policy disturb the process as personnel need to be compensated for the invested time in knowledge sharing and conversations. Motivational barriers to sharing expertise are more easily addressed through changes in organizational practices. The motivational issues can be addressed by reducing competition between groups, allowing communities of practice to evolve, deemphasizing status hierarchies, and increasing incentives to share expertise with others.

CONCLUSION

A knowledge sharing adoption model called (KSAM) was developed in this study using artificial neural networks (ANN). We also investigated students' PUB of knowledge sharing among students of higher learning in Nigeria. The study was based on the definition as well as on the constructs related to technology acceptance model (TAM). Structured questionnaires were designed, analyzed with SPSS statistical tool and results were evaluated. The KSAM includes six constructs: PEOS, PUB, PBS, ECS, ATT, and BI. The results suggested that the most effective way to enhance the adoption of knowledge sharing among University students is to improve the PUB for the potential users which has 32.42% on ATT. Moreover, education of students on the importance of the ease of use of knowledge sharing PEOS for users appears specially paramount, which has a total percentage of 29.8% on ATT. Also, suggestions and encouragements which could serve as ECS should be sought from real sources for the potential users, such as the lecturers and friends. Furthermore, the intention of every potential user should be made known from the unset. Lastly, obstacles from action(s) (barriers of sharing (PBS)) also have to be cleared, which means that counseling has to be organized for

the students to encourage them about knowledge sharing adoption. The Knowledge Management (KM) and practical literature review emphasizes organizational learning and knowledge sharing as major factors for success of the KM initiatives within the organization. As the focus is put on human factors, the main limitations for effective collaboration are related to the human nature and lack of adequate motivation policy. In this context, communities of practice are appearing as an instrument for overcoming the behaviour constraints and manifesting the emergence of new organizational culture.

REFERENCES

Agarwal, R., & Prasad, J. (1999). Are individual differences germane to the acceptance of new information technologies? *Decision Sciences*, *30*, 361–391. doi:10.1111/j.1540-5915.1999.tb01614.x

Ajzen, I. (1985). *From intentions to actions: A theory of planned behavior. Actioncontrol: From cognition to behavior*. Heidelberg, Germany: Springer.

Ajzen, I. (1989). *Attitude, personality, and behavior*. Milton Keynes, UK: Open University Press.

Ajzen, I. (1991). The theory of planned behavior, organizational behavior and human. *Decision Processes*, *50*, 179–211. doi:10.1016/0749-5978(91)90020-T

Ajzen, I., & Fishbein, M. (1980). *Understanding attitudes and predicting social behavior*. Upper Saddle River, NJ: Prentice-Hall.

Awad, E. M., & Ghaziri, H. M. (2004). *Knowledge Management*. Upper Saddle River, NJ: Pearson Education.

Bagozzi, R. P., & Yi, Y. (1988). On the evaluation of structural equation models. *Journal of the Academy of Marketing Science, 16*(1), 74–94. doi:10.1007/BF02723327

Barson, R. J., Foster, G., Struck, T., Ratchev, S., Pawar, K., Weber, F., & Wunram, M. (2000). *Inter and Intra-organizational Barriers to Sharing Knowledge in the Extended Supply Chain.* Retrieved from www.corma.net

Cheng, T. C. E., Lam, D. Y. C., & Yeung, A. L. C. (2006). Adoption of internet banking: An empirical study in Hong Kong. *Decision Support Systems, 42*(3), 1558–1572. doi:10.1016/j.dss.2006.01.002

Davies, F., Goode, M., Mazanec, J., & Moutinho, L. (1999). LISREL and neural networks modeling: Two comparison studies. *Journal of Retailing and Consumer Services, 6*(4), 249–261. doi:10.1016/S0969-6989(98)00009-5

Davis, F. D. (1989). Perceived usefulness, perceived ease of use, and user acceptance of information technology. *Management Information Systems Quarterly, 13*(3), 319–333. doi:10.2307/249008

Davis, F. D., Bagozzi, R. P., & Warshaw, P. R. (1989). User acceptance of computer technology: A comparison of two theoretical models. *Management Science, 35*(8), 982–1003. doi:10.1287/mnsc.35.8.982

Fishbein, M., & Ajzen, I. (1975). *Belief attitude intention and behavior: An introduction to theory and research.* Reading, MA: Addison-Wesley.

Fisher, D. H., & McKusick, K. B. (1989). An empirical comparison of ID3 and back propagation. In *Proceedings of the Eleventh International Joint Conference on Artificial Intelligence*, Detroit, MI (pp. 788-793).

Han, B. M., & Anantatmula, V. S. (2007). Knowledge sharing in large IT organizations: A case study. *VINE: The Journal of Information and Knowledge Management Systems, 37*(4), 421–439.

Huang, J. (2010). Remote health monitoring adoption model based on artificial neural networks. *Expert Systems with Applications, 37*, 307–314. doi:10.1016/j.eswa.2009.05.063

Igbaria, M., Guimaraes, T., & Davis, G. B. (1995). Testing the determinants of microcomputer usage via a structural equation model. *Journal of Management Information Systems, 11*(4), 87–14.

Kim, S., & Ju, B. (2008). An analysis of faculty perceptions: Attitudes toward knowledge sharing and collaboration in an academic institution. *Library & Information Science Research, 30*(4), 282–290. doi:10.1016/j.lisr.2008.04.003

Kong, S., Ogata, H., Arnseth, H., Chan, C., Hirashima, T., Klett, F., et al. (Eds.). (2009). Factors Influencing Knowledge Sharing Among University Students. In *Proceedings of the 17th International Conference on Computers in Education* (CDROM), Hong Kong, China.

Lederer, A. L., Maupin, D. J., Sens, M. P., & Zhuang, Y. (2000). The technology acceptance model and the World Wide Web. *Decision Support Systems, 29*, 269–282. doi:10.1016/S0167-9236(00)00076-2

Lei-da, C. (2008). A model of consumer acceptance of mobile payment. *Int. J. Mobile Communications, 6*(1).

Levina, N. (2001). Sharing Knowledge in Heterogenous Environments. *Reflections: The SoL Journal, 2*(2), 32–42. doi:10.1162/15241730051091993

Lu, L., Leung, K., & Koch, P. T. (2006). Managerial knowledge sharing: The role of individual, interpersonal, and organizational factors. *Management and Organization Review, 2*(1), 15–41. doi:10.1111/j.1740-8784.2006.00029.x

Ma, Q., & Liu, L. (2004). The technology acceptance model: a meta-analysis of empirical findings. *Journal of Organizational and End User Computing, 16*(1), 59–74.

Mathieson, K. (1991). Predicting user intention: Comparing the technology acceptance model with the theory of planned behavior. *Information Systems Research, 2*, 173–191. doi:10.1287/isre.2.3.173

Morris, M. G., & Dillon, A. (1997). How user perceptions influence software use, decision support systems. *IEEE Software*, 58–65. doi:10.1109/52.595956

Murray, K. B. (1991). A Test of Service Marketing Theory: Consumer Information Acquisition Activities. *Journal of Marketing, 55*, 10–25. doi:10.2307/1252200

Nelson, M. M., & Illingworth, W. T. (1994). *Practical guide to neural nets*. Reading, MA: Addison Wesley.

Ng, K., & Lippmann, R. P. (1990). A comparative study of the practical characteristics of neural networks and conventional pattern classifiers. In *Proceedings of the advances in Neural Information Processing Systems*, Denver, CO (Vol. 3, pp. 970-976). San Francisco, CA: Morgan Kaufman.

Nor, L. M. N., Mardziah, H., Halilah, H., & Ariffin, S. (2004). *Community acceptance of knowledge sharing system in the travel and tourism websites: an Application of an extension of TAM.*

Pratt, L. Y., & Kamm, C. A. (1991). Direct transfer of learned information among neural networks. In *Proceedings of the Ninth National Conference on Artificial Intelligence*, Anaheim, CA (pp. 584-589).

Rumelhart, D., & McClelland, J. (1986). *Parallel Distributed Processing*. Cambridge, MA: MIT Press.

Shavlik, J. W., Mooney, R. J., & Towell, G. G. (1991). Symbolic a neural net learning algorithms; an empirical comparison. *Machine Learning, 6*, 111–143. doi:10.1007/BF00114160

Sheppard, B. H., Hartwick, J., & Warshaw, P. R. (1988). The theory of reasoned action: A meta-analysis of past research with recommendations for modifications and future research. *The Journal of Consumer Research, 15*, 325–343. doi:10.1086/209170

Taylor, S., & Todd, P. A. (1995). Understanding information technology usage: A test of competing models. *Information Systems Research, 6*(2), 144–176. doi:10.1287/isre.6.2.144

Tsui, L., Chapman, S. A., Schnirer, & Stewart, S. (2006). *A Handbook on Knowledge Sharing: Strategies and Recommendations for Researchers, Policymakers, and Service Providers.*

Van den Hooff, B., Elving, W., Meeuwsen, M., & Dumoulin, C. (2003). Knowledge sharing in knowledge communities. In Huysman, M., Wenger, E., & Wulf, V. (Eds.), *Communities and Technologies* (pp. 119–141). Dordrecht, The Netherlands: Kluwer.

Van den Hooff, B., & Huysman, M. (2009). Managing knowledge sharing: Emergent and engineering approaches. *Information & Management, 46*(1), 1–8. doi:10.1016/j.im.2008.09.002

Venkatesh, V., & Morris, M. G. (2000). Why don't men ever stop to ask for directions? Gender, social influence, and their role in technology acceptance and usage behavior. *Management Information Systems Quarterly, 24*, 115–139. doi:10.2307/3250981

Weiss, S. M., & Kapsuleas, I. (1989). An empirical comparison of pattern recognition, neural nets and machine learning classification methods. In *Proceedings of the Eleventh International Joint Conference on Artificial Intelligence*, Detroit, MI (pp. 688-693).

This work was previously published in International Journal of E-Adoption, Volume 2, Issue 4, edited by Sushil K. Sharma, pp. 1-14, copyright 2010 by IGI Publishing (an imprint of IGI Global).

Chapter 5
User Acceptance of Location-Based Mobile Advertising:
An Empirical Study in Iran

Kiyana Zolfaghar
K. N. Toosi University of Technology, Iran

Farid Khoshalhan
K. N. Toosi University of Technology, Iran

Mohammad Rabiei
K. N. Toosi University of Technology, Iran

ABSTRACT

Location-based advertising (LBA) opens up new frontiers for marketers to place their advertisements in front of consumers. LBA is a new form of marketing communication that uses location-tracking technology in mobile networks to target consumers with location-specific advertising on their cell phones. It provides more targeted communication and interaction between the marketer and its potential customers. This paper reviews different aspects of LBA advertising and investigates the drivers of consumer acceptance toward it. Achieving this, a research framework is developed to explore the factors influencing consumer intention for using LBA in Iran. Individuals' responses to questions about intention to accept/ use of LBA advertising were collected and analyzed with various factors modified from UTAUT with main constructs of utility expectancy, trust, effort expectancy, and control. While the model confirms the classical role of utility expectancy and effort expectancy as the key factors in technology acceptance, the results also show that users' behavioral intentions are influenced by trust and their control on ads flow.

DOI: 10.4018/978-1-4666-0041-6.ch005

INTRODUCTION

The high penetration rate of mobile phones has resulted in the increasing use of handheld devices to deliver advertisements for products and services. Mobile technologies imply many opportunities for marketing, in particular a direct communication with consumers without time or location barriers. In this regard, location-based advertising (LBA) can be considered as a new form of marketing communication that uses location-tracking technology in mobile networks to target consumers with location-specific advertising on their cell phones (Unni & Harmon, 2007). It provides more targeted communication and interaction between the marketer and its potential customers. As Okazaki (2004) notes, advanced technologies, such as FeliCa and Bluetooth, enhance the feasibility of applying GPS (Global Positioning System) technology that will allow advertisers to provide real-time offers to subscribers who are shopping in a specific store, or driving in close proximity to a retail outlet. Several forms of LBA have already been demonstrated using technologies enabling LBA such as GPS, Bluetooth, and RFID (Radio Frequency Identification) (Bruner & Kumar, 2007). Among the location proximity detection technologies for mobile devices, the obvious choice is Bluetooth which can be exploited in Iran to offer LBA messages.

As consumers are increasingly exposed to mobile advertising, their acceptance is also increasingly regarded as a critical success factor. Mobil marketing acceptance is of particular interest to the many researchers, and represents a fundamental managerial challenge in mobile marketing implementation (Merisavo & Kajalo, 2007). LBA is a very specific type of mobile marketing and it is therefore important to understand how consumers are likely to evaluate it. On one hand, consumers may see great benefits in receiving location specific advertising, while on the other hand privacy concerns and the intrusiveness of such marketing messages may turn consumers

away. With regard to LBA in particular, scholarly studies are still extremely rare. The few that have been done were more technically focused and/ or the consumer data were qualitative in nature (Bruner & Kumar, 2007).

The primary objective of this paper is trying to understand the acceptance of mobile location-based advertising from consumers' perspectives and to explore the factors that can influence their intention to use LBA in Iran society. The answers to these issues will inform marketing companies on how best to go about developing effective and appropriate m-marketing strategies that will have a positive impact on consumers.

In the following sections, we will first introduce a brief background into LBA, LBA characteristics and the associated "push" and "pull" strategies. Then, we briefly review acceptance research models and related work on location-aware mobile advertising. Next, we identify the constructs that may influence users' attitude toward LBA ads, and develop our hypotheses. After that the research model is presented and the empirical data is analyzed and results reported. Finally, the paper ends with discussion of the results in terms of the managerial and theoretical implications of the study's findings.

LOCATION-BASED ADVERTISING

With the emergence of high speed wireless network technologies and the increasing market penetration of mobile phones the global advertising industry's interest in using this medium as a means of marketing communication is rising. Mobile advertising can be more personalized and different forms such as permission-based, incentive-based, or location based (He & Lu, 2007). Researches related to mobile advertising have shown that this marketing instrument is very effective as a branding vehicle and in stimulating a response, thus increasing brand attitude and purchase intentions (Rettie, Grandcolas, & Deakin, 2005). In this regard, LBA refers to marketer-controlled information specially tailored for the place where users access an advertising medium (Bruner & Kumar, 2007). Marketers can entertain, inform, build brand awareness, create loyalty, and drive purchase decision among their target consumers through LBA. LBA can be defined as a subset of location-based marketing (LBM which includes all aspects of the marketing mix in the mobile location-based setting, whereas LBA is a narrower concept focused on the advertising strategy and communications elements of LBM.

Consistent with the classifications that are derived from general principles of direct marketing, there are two broad types or approaches in delivering LBA - pull and push (Okazaki & Taylor, 2008). Pull LBA is advertising specific to the location of the consumer delivered to the mobile device only when it is explicitly requested for. In this type of LBA, the consumer initiates the request for advertising or promotions for preferred product. While in push LBA, advertising messages are sent to a consumer's cell phone based on that consumer's location and often previously stated product preferences. In Iran, most of the LBA messages are using push strategy. This approach has a great impact on brand building and boosting sales in the short term. However, consumers can easily perceive push LBA as spam if done inappropriately. Thus, for LBA to be successful it needs to be analyzed user acceptance behavior. In the case of mobile advertising, very few studies discussed the effectiveness of LBA and the factors contributing to its success.

CONSUMER ACCEPTANCE MODELS

The acceptance of information technology has been studied actively already for a couple of decades. Acceptance research has provided important insights in explaining the success or failure of new products or services (Bauer, Reichardt, Barnes, & Neumann, 2005). Moreover, many authors have tried to identify acceptance determinants in order to better understand and somehow predict users' behavior. It is really a heterogeneous field mostly anchored in social psychology, sociology and Information System contexts. Acceptance models suggest that when users are presented with a new technology, a number of factors influence their decision about how and when they will use it. In this regard, Attitude is a key variable of consumer behavior and one of the most prerequisite of acceptance which is defined as a learned predisposition to respond in a consistently favorable or unfavorable manner toward advertising in general (MacKenzie, 1989). The positive attitude towards mobile advertising can leads to the behavioral intention to use mobile services.

Many attempts and theories have been made to study acceptance issues. Among the IT adoption theories, the most important and influential theories are TRA (Theory of Reasoned Action) (Fishbein & Ajzen, 1975), TAM (Technology Acceptance Model) (Davis, 1989), TPB (Theory of Planned Behavior) (Ajzen, 1991), and most recently, the UTAUT (the Unified Theory of Acceptance and Use of Technology) which was formulated based on conceptual and empirical similarities across eight technology acceptance models. The UTAUT aims to explain users' intention to use an information system and their subsequent usage behavior. The theory holds four key constructs (performance expectancy, effort expectancy, social influence, and facilitating conditions) which are direct determinants of usage intention and behavior and contains moderators, as gender, age, experience and voluntariness of use (Venkatesh & Morris, 2003). The evidence-based result shows that this new model's explanation strength for technology acceptance behavior is up to 70%, which is more effective than any known models from the past. In this paper, the UTAUT model will be used to extend the proposed research model. The modified UTAUT model will enable a better explanation of LBA acceptance and usage behavior.

RELATED WORK

The growth of mobile advertising specifically location-based advertising has opened a new area for research. A number of location-aware service studies list the mobile advertising as one of the future possibilities in the application area. Barnes (2003) introduced the concept of tempting nearby users into the stores and delivering geographic messaging related e.g. to security in particular area of a city. Varshney and Vetter (2002) suggested mobile advertising to be a very important class of mobile commerce. They augmented location information with the personalization of the delivery by obtaining the history of the user's purchases or consulting the user at an earlier stage. Unni and Harmon (2007) used an experimental study to test the effects of LBA characteristics on privacy concerns about location tracking, perceived benefits, value, and intentions to try LBA. Their study was an initial examination of issues to evaluate types and message content of LBA. Bruner (2007) were conducting an investigation of consumer attitudes towards LBA. Facilitating future studies by academic and industry researchers, they provide a multi-item scale for measuring attitude toward LBA messages. This scale, called Alba, is defined as a person's general predisposition toward commercial messages that are received on a personal mobile communication device and customized for one's geographic position.

RESEARCH MODEL
AND HYPOTHESES

In this section we develop our hypotheses and the proposed model based on constructs from UTAUT and additional relevant issues related to consumer acceptance of LBA in Iran and the specific na-

ture of the mobile phone as a medium. Although UTAUT is the most comprehensive model among models used in IT adoption but some of its factors may not be necessary or appropriate in the case of location-based advertising acceptance so we change it in a way that fits our situation in Iran. Figure 1 presents the proposed model for estimating users' acceptance toward LBA messages. The acceptance of LBA messages was evaluated using a UTAUT model modified from the one originally proposed by Venkatesh, Morris, and Davis (2003). The research model postulates four constructs (utility expectancy, Effort expectancy, trust, and control) that determine behavioral intent, and four demographic variables (age and gender Education, gadget lover) influencing both behavioral intention and user acceptance (usage behavior). The description and sources of every factor is described in the following Table 1.

Behavioral Intention

The best predictor of behavior is intention, which is the cognitive representation of a person's readiness to perform a given behavior, and it is considered to be the immediate antecedent of behavior (Fishbein & Ajzen, 1975). As we mentioned above, in our model, behavioral intention is determined by four dominant variables: utility expectancy, effort expectancy, consumer trust and control on ads flow. Relation of intention and use behavior (acceptance) has been heavily researched with a number of models being available (Venkatesh et al., 2003; Tsang et al., 2004). Proven is that the intention to use a system correlates to great extent with the actual use (Wakefield & Whitten, 2006). Therefore we hypothesize that:

H1. *Behavioral intention will have a positive influence on a location-base mobile advertising acceptance.*

Figure 1. Proposed research model

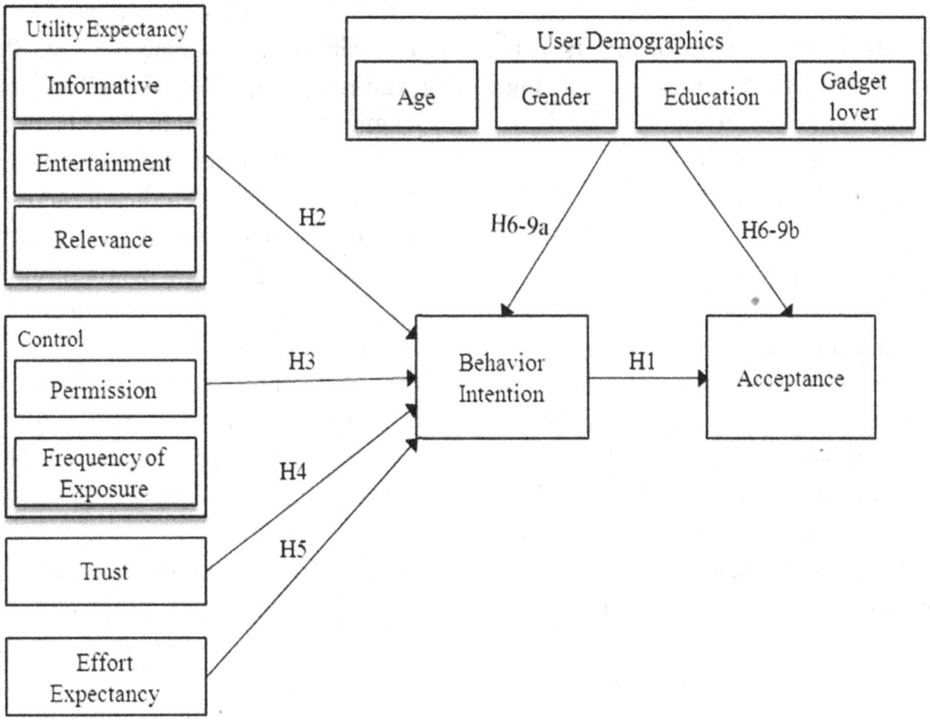

Table 1. Research variables summary

Model Constructs	Description	Sources
Utility expectancy	A subjective evaluation of the relative worth or utility of advertising to consumers.(include Relevance, informativeness and entertainment)	Venkatesh and Morris (2003); Ducoffe (1995); Tsang et al. (2004); Okazaki (2004); Nysveen and Pedersen (2005); Standing, Benson, and Karjaluoto (2005); Kajalo and Karjaluoto (2007)
Trust	amount of trust that users have to the service providers, mobile technology and its supporting protocols and regulation	Merisavo et al. (2007); Unni and Harmon (2007); Qingfei, Shaobo, and Gang (2008)
Control	Consumer perceptions of controlling on the flow of advertising massages. (include permission and frequency of exposure)	Standing et al. (2005); Barnes and Scornavacca (2004); He and Lu (2007)Haghirian and Madlberger (2005); Bruner and Kumar (2007)
Effort Expectancy	the degree to which a person believes that using a particular service will be free from effort	Venkatesh and Morris (2003); Standing, Benson, and Karjaluoto (2005)
Behavioral Intention	Cognitive representation of a person's readiness to perform a given behavior.	Venkatesh and Morris (2003); Standing, Benson, and Karjaluoto (2005); Tsang, Ho, and Liang (2004); Bauer et al. (2005)
User Demographics	Demographic characteristic which can impact on acceptance behavior.(include age, gender, Education level and being gadget lover)	Venkatesh and Morris (2003); Okazaki (2004); Haghirian and Madlberger (2005)

Utility Expectancy

Many of studies are shown that consumers usually have a negative attitude toward advertising unless these ads have a perceived value for them (Tsang, Ho, & Liang, 2004). This value can be defined as "a subjective evaluation of the relative worth or utility of advertising to consumers" (Ducoffe, 1995). According to the studies, usefulness, relevance, and monetary incentives, as well as entertainment and information value identified as important factors affecting consumer acceptance of mobile advertising (Kajalo & Karjaluoto, 2007; Okazaki, 2004; Nysveen, Pedersen, & Thorbjornsen, 2005). All of these factors together form the total utility that consumers perceive in mobile marketing. Reflecting these considerations the following hypothesis can be formulated:

H2. *Utility expectancy is positively related to behavior intention toward location-base mobile advertisement.*

Control

Given the negative perceptions and reactions to spam as well as regulatory pressures on mobile advertising, there is general agreement that LBA would be permission-based (Barnes & Scornavacca, 2004). The term permission marketing is closely linked to the concept of m-marketing as it is assumed that granting of permission to receive m-marketing communication is pivotal to its success (Barnes & Scornavacca, 2004). The benefits of permission marketing have been seen as reducing clutter and search costs for consumers whilst improving targeting precision for marketers. The problems of SPAM with email have significantly impacted on the potential of the channel for marketing, at least for the time being. The fear is that if consumers see the same happening to marketing then it too will be damaged a marketing channel (Standing, Benson, & Karjaluoto, 2005). As mobile phones are very

personal devices, consumer perceptions of controlling that permission as related to the mobile advertising (e.g., how many messages they receive in a given period) are considered important factors that might affect consumer acceptance of mobile location-based advertising (Nysveen, Pedersen, & Thorbjørnsen, 2005). Studies are shown that even if consumers have opted-in with several marketers whom they do not mind hearing from, receiving messages from all of them in a short period of time could be overwhelming (Bruner & Kumar, 2007). According to these studies, the attitude of the individual towards the mobile ads worsens as the quantity of these messages rises (Haghirian & Madlberger, 2005). Thus we expect that:

H3. *Consumers' perceived control of mobile advertising is positively related to users' behavior intention toward location-base mobile advertising.*

Trust

Clearly, the establishment of a well-founded basis of trust for mobile marketing as a generic form of marketing communication has to be a major goal for all advertising companies (Bauer, Barnes, Reichardt, & Neumann, 2005). Trust is conceptualized as an expectation of the mobile carrier's dependability, reliability, and integrity to deliver on its promises (Sirdeshmukh, Singh, & Sabol, 2002). This is the prime prerequisite for consumers' willingness to permit the reception of advertising messages on their mobile phones and to provide personal data for the personalization of those messages (Barnes & Scornavacca, 2004). Although consumers may see great benefits in receiving location-based advertising, privacy concerns and the intrusiveness of such marketing messages may turn consumers away. According to Unni (2007), consumers are worried about their privacy and risk of being monitored without being aware of it. They are also very sensitive about receiving messages from unknown persons or organizations (Haghirian & Madlberger, 2005). One of the important factors that can relieve these privacy concerns is the amount of trust that users have to the service providers, mobile technology and its supporting protocols and regulation (Qingfei, Shaobo, & Gang, 2008). Extending the privacy issue, consumers' trust in the use of their personal data and the laws protecting them might affect their acceptance of mobile advertising (Merisavo & Kajalo, 2007). So it is necessary to introduce privacy and trust issues in LBA user acceptance and their behavioral intentions to receive messages. Therefore we hypothesize that:

H4. *Consumers' trust in privacy and the laws of location-base mobile advertising is positively related to their behavioral intention to accept location-base advertisement.*

Effort Expectancy

Effort expectancy in UTAUT model is similar to TAM's perceived usefulness (Qingfei, Shaobo, & Gang, 2008). This determinant is defined as "the degree to which a person believes that using a particular system will be free from effort" (Venkatesh & Morris, 2003). In particular, effort expectancy as a construct is aimed at systems that involve a certain amount of learning and where usability is an issue. However, in terms of m-marketing this can be replaced constructs that test the cognitive load on users through length, readability and number of messages received. People preference is for short and easy to process messages. It is proved that people will have more attitudes toward mobile marketing if they believe that receiving advertising messages and the processing of them is easy and free of effort (Standing, Benson, & Karjaluoto, 2005). Therefore we hypothesize that:

H5. *Effort expectancy is positively related to the behavioral intention to participate in location-based advertising.*

User's Demographic Variables

Different types of users take different attitudes and acceptance behaviors toward m commerce (Qingfei, Shaobo, & Gang, 2008). Okazaki (2004) indicated that demographics characteristics, such as gender, age, profession, income, marital status, and family structure, affect m-commerce's user acceptance in the case of Japan. Reflecting these considerations, we cannot neglect the effects of users' demographic variables on their behavioral intention and acceptance toward location-based mobile advertising.

Age has been an important personal characteristic within the category of demographic variables. In practical terms, the identification of age groups within a population allows for market segmentation. According to studies Younger consumers show more favorable attitude toward advertising (Haghirian & Madlberger, 2005).It may originate from this fact that young people consider mobile devices as much as a fashion accessory as they are a communication device. So we assume that:

H6a. *The behavioral intention toward location-based advertising differs according to the age of the consumers.*

H6b. *Acceptance toward location-based mobile advertising differs according to the age of the consumers.*

Gender is another demographic characteristic that its' impact on adoption behavior has attracted some research interest (Ha, Yoon, & Choi, 2007). In mobile context, Attitudes toward advertising differ between men and women (Haghirian & Madlberger, 2005). On the whole, male consumers show a more favorable attitude toward ads than female consumers (Shavitt, Lowrey, & Haefner, 1998). So according to the literature, we conclude that gender as a demographic variable can also affect Behavioral intention and acceptance toward LBA messages.

H7a: *The behavioral intention toward location-based mobile advertising differs between men and women.*

H7b: *Users' Acceptance of location-based mobile advertising differs between men and women.*

Education is also one of the demographic factors that can moderate users' attitude and acceptance toward advertising (Haghirian & Madlberger, 2005; He & Lu, 2007). According to studies, users' attitude toward advertising decreases as their education level increases (Sarker & Wells, 2003). In other words, People with less education and lower income generally report a more favorable attitude toward advertising in general (Shavitt, Lowrey, & Haefner, 1998). So we expect that this factor can have a similar effect on location-based advertising too.

H8a: *The behavioral intention toward location-based advertising differs according to level of education.*

H8b: *Users' acceptance toward location-based mobile advertising differs according to level of education.*

The cell phone is by far the most popular personal communications device for consumers. They carry their mobile phones almost everywhere and use them frequently as these devices are becoming part of them. Marshall McLuhan (1964) was referring to this factor in his book and coined the phrase gadget lovers for describing it. Some people are so dependent on the devices that they may feel they cannot function well without them. Mobile devices have become a fashion statement for many with their usage being related to personality (Love & Kewley, 2005) and becoming "addictive" for some people, which means that they have an unusually high dependency on this medium and satisfy the needs through habitual use and to pass time (Park, 2005).these group of people seem to have a greater motivation than others toward advertising (Bruner, Gordon, &

Kumar, 2007). So we expect to be also a positive relationship with being a gadget lover and attitude toward location-based advertising.

H9a. *Being a gadget lover is positively related to the behavioral intention toward location-based advertising via mobile devices.*

H9b. *Being a gadget lover is positively related to the users' acceptance toward location-based mobile advertising.*

ANALYSIS AND RESULTS

In order to understand the consumers' acceptance toward LBA messages, the survey utilized the questionnaire method to test the hypothesized model. The questionnaire was developed and distributed to subjects in person and by e-mail in Iran. A total of 240 questionnaires were handed out. Of the returned questionnaires, 19 were excluded because of incomplete answers or obvious self-contradiction. Apart from the demographic attributes, all other measures were assessed via a 5-point Likert-type scale ranging from "strongly

Table 2. Demographic profile of respondent

Item	Range Frequently		Percent
Gender			
	Male	129	58.4%
	Female	92	41.6%
Education			
	high school and Lower	44	19.9%
	Undergraduate	125	56.6%
	Graduate	32	14.5%
	Masters/doctorate	20	9.0%
Age			
	<20	75	33.9%
	20-25	82	37.1%
	25-30	51	23.1%
	>30	13	5.9%

agree" to "strongly disagree." The demographic profile of the respondents is described in Table 2.

We used SPSS15 to analyze the data. It allows the researcher to specify the relationships among both the conceptual factors of interest and the measures underlying each construct, which may result in analysis of how well the measures relate to each construct and whether the hypothesized relationships at the theoretical level are empirically true or not. In the first stage, the measurement model is tested by assessing the validity and the reliability on each of the measures to ensure that only reliable and valid measures of the constructs are used before drawing conclusions about the nature of the construct relationships. The reliability of the scale variables was established by calculating Cranach's alpha to measure internal consistency. The overall Cranach's coefficient of the factors= 0.805 was obtained which is above the acceptable level (above 0.70). The variables in this study, derived from the existing literature, exhibited strong content validity. Table 3 summarized Descriptive Statistics of the constructs.

In the second stage, the structural model is tested by estimating the paths between the constructs in the model and their statistical significance. To achieve this, the Pearson Correlation is used to measure variables association. According to the result shown in Table 4, five main hypotheses were all supported in this stage.

In the third stage, we investigate the impact of demographic variables such as age and gender on behavioural intention and acceptance toward location based advertising. Based on the type and distribution these variables, the most appropriate test were exploited for each variable to investigate demographic effects on LBA use/acceptance. The results are reported and depicted in Table 5.

DISCUSSION

The purpose of this paper has been to describe an innovative new medium, location-based advertising (LBA) and propose an integrated model based on the UTAUT model to explore the factors that can influence consumers' intention to use location-based mobile advertising in Iran. Table 3 shows the total effects of the model constructs on the target variable. According to result, all the hypotheses were significantly supported. The quantitative analysis of the effects of each construct on "behavioral intention" reveals that "utility expectancy", with a total effect of 0.45, is the central driver of the consumer acceptance of LBA marketing, which indicated a same result with the prior literatures investigating web advertising and mobile ads (Bauer et al., 2005; Ducoffe, 1996). It means that the more informatory, more

Table 3. Construct reliability

Construct	Items	Mean	Variance	Standard Deviation
Utility Expectancy	3	2.65	1.331	1.145
Control	2	2.98	1.480	1.208
Trust	4	2.90	1.259	1.122
Effort Expectancy	1	2.90	0.881	0.939
Behavioral intention	3	2.64	1.197	1.094
Acceptance	3	3.53	1.500	1.225

Table 4. Results of correlation analyze

The Relationship of Variables	P-Value	Testing Result
H1: Behavioral intention Acceptance	0.500**	Supported
H2: Utility Expectancy Behavioral intention	0.454**	Supported
H3: Control Behavioral intention	0.412**	Supported
H4: Trust Behavioral intention	0.327**	Supported
H5: Effort Expectancy Behavioral intention	0.424**	Supported

** Correlation is significant at the 0.01 level.

Table 5. The results of demographic variables

Demographic Variable	Behavior Intention	Acceptance	Test
Age	**H6a:** F=-0.73, sig=0.227	**H6b:** F=-0.160, sig=0.017*	Correlation Analysis
Gender	**H7a:** F=0.064, sig=0.040*	**H7b:** F=0.377, sig=0.037*	Independent T- Sample Test
Education	**H8a:** F=0.934, sig=0.445	**H8b:**F=2.843, sig=0.025*	One-Way ANOVA
Gadget lover	**H9a:**F=0.355, sig=0.00**	**H9b:**F=0.307, sig=0.00**	Correlation Analysis

** Correlation is significant at the 0.01 level.
* Correlation is significant at the 0.05 level.

entertainment and more relevance LBA messages will gain more consumers' interests and favors.

The test of H3 hypothesis (user's control on LBA messages affect behavior intention positively) was supported which indicated a same result with the prior literatures. This result shows that the reaction to permission based marketing is much more positive, whilst unauthorized LBA has a negative impact on intention. If people provide permission to receive the LBA messages via their cell phones then the intention to participate improves markedly. This sends a clear signal to companies thinking of employing LBA as part of their m-marketing approach. Consumers want to be in control of the types and volume of information they receive. A high frequency of exposure seems to decrease the value of LBA advertising. This result is also supported by scientific literature (Ducoffe, 1995; Gordon & Kumar, 2007) which assumes that consumers who are confronted with ads repeatedly are less informed since they are already familiar with the content. Likewise the behavioral intention is positively influenced by trust Construct (H4, 0.327). It means that consumers' trust in the use of their personal data and the laws protecting them positively affect their intention of using LBA advertising. In other word, Hypothesis H4 suggests that customers who consider privacy very valuable are less likely to have a positive attitude towards LBA via mobile devices. Other studies have indicated similar results. According to Ackerman, Darrel and Weitzner (2001), a trade-off between perceived privacy and user benefit is also possible. They assume that consumers accept a certain degree of privacy loss if benefit is considered being sufficient and satisfying (Ackerman, Darrel, & Weitzner, 2001).

The Effort expectancy factor also affected behavior intention Directly (H5, 0.424).This shows that people preferred messages that were quick to read and did not take up a lot of time. Hypotheses 6 to 9 dealt with relevant demographic variables of the consumer. Hypotheses 6a and 6b state that the age of the LBA recipient reflects on their behavior intention and on their acceptance of LBA via mobile devices. According to result age influence the advertising recipients' perception of mobile marketing significantly in a way that younger people have higher rate of acceptance than other segments. Hypotheses 7a and 7b indicated that gender influences both of the dependent variables. The results are similar to those of Bracket and Carr (2001) who also report gender to be relevant for consumers' attitude toward the advertising. Hypotheses 8a and 8b proposed that a higher education level is positively associated with the dependent variables. Only hypothesis 8b could be supported. Interviewees with higher education did not show more acceptances toward LBA via mobile devices. Hypotheses 9a and 9b indicated that being gadget lover influences both of the dependent variables strongly. Based on this result, LBA acceptance has a positive relationship with being a gadget lover since cutting-edge technology plays a key role in making LBA a reality.

CONCLUSION

This study measure the influence of the user's experience towards each potential determinant of behavioral intention for Location-based advertising via mobile devices. Several managerial implications can be drawn from the study considering whether to use LBA ads. It appears that the trend is towards greater acceptance of LBA and therefore managers should find that it an increasingly effective channel for marketing. However, for LBA to gain acceptance among consumers, marketers have to allay privacy concerns and effectively convey the value proposition of timely, personalized, location-specific marketing delivered to cell phones. Only if LBA marketing messages are designed creatively and are entertaining, or if they provide a high information value, will consumers develop a positive attitude towards it leading to the behavioral intention to use LBA marketing services. Moreover, the establishment of a well-founded basis of trust for LBA as a form of marketing communication has to be a major goal. This is the prime prerequisite for consumers' willingness to permit the reception of LBA messages on their mobile phones and to provide personal data for the personalization of those messages. Thus, it is a prerequisite for the consumer acceptance of LBA messages. These factors indicate a generally positive future for LBA if organizations can make their marketing focused to the individual.

REFERENCES

Ajzen, I. (1991). The theory of planned behavior. *Organizational Behavior and Human Decision Processes*, *50*(2), 179–211. doi:10.1016/0749-5978(91)90020-T

Barnes, S., & Scornavacca, E. (2004). Mobile Marketing: The Role of Permission and Acceptance. *International Journal of Mobile Communications*, *2*(2), 128–139. doi:10.1504/IJMC.2004.004663

Barnes, S. J. B. (2003). Known by the Network: The Emergence of Location-Based Mobile Commerce. In Lim, E. S. (Ed.), *Advances in Mobile Commerce Technologies* (pp. 171–189). Hershey, PA: IGI Global.

Bauer, H., Reichardt, T., Barnes, S., & Neumann, M. (2005). Driving Consumer Acceptance of Mobile Marketing: A Theoretical Framework and Empirical Study. *Journal of Electronic Commerce Research*, *6*(3), 181–192.

Bruner, C., & Kumar, A. (2007). Attitude toward Location-Based Advertising. *Journal of Interactive Marketing*, *7*(2), 3–15.

Bruner, I., Gordon, C., & Kumar, A. (2007). Gadget Lovers. *Journal of the Academy of Marketing Science*, *35*(2), 329–339. doi:10.1007/s11747-007-0051-3

Davis, F. (1989). Perceived usefulness, perceived ease of use, and user acceptance of information technology. *Management Information Systems Quarterly*, *13*(3), 319–340. doi:10.2307/249008

Ducoffe, R. (1995). How Consumers Assess the Value of Advertising. *Journal of Current Issues and Research in Advertising*, *17*(1), 1–18.

Fishbein, M., & Ajzen, I. (1975). *Belief, Attitude, Intention and Behavior: An Introduction to Theory and Research*. Reading, MA: Addison-Wesley.

Ha, I., Yoon, Y., & Choi, M. (2007). Determinants of adoption of mobile games under mobile broadband wireless access environment. *Information & Management*, *44*(3), 276–286. doi:10.1016/j.im.2007.01.001

Haghirian, P., & Madlberger, M. (2005). Consumer Attitude Toward Advertising Via Mobile Devices - An Empirical Investigation Among Austrian Users. In *Proceedings of the European Conference on Information Systems*, Regensburg, Germany (pp. 44-56).

He, D., & Lu, Y. (2007). Consumers Perceptions and Acceptances towards Mobile Advertising: An Empirical Study in China. In *Proceedings of the International Conference on Wireless Communications, Networking and Mobile Computing*, Shanghai, China (pp. 3775-3778).

Love, S., & Kewley, J. (2005). Does Personality Affect Peoples' Attitude Towards Mobile Phone Use in Public Places? In Ling, R., & Pederson, P. E. (Eds.), *Mobile Communications* (pp. 273–284). London: Springer. doi:10.1007/1-84628-248-9_18

MacKenzie, S., & Lutz, R. (1998). An Empirical Examination of the Structural Antecedents of Attitude Toward the Ad in an Advertising Pretesting Context. *Journal of Marketing*, *53*(1), 48–65.

McLuhan, M. (1964). *Understanding Media*. New York: McGraw-Hill Book Company.

Merisavo, M., Kajalo, S., Karjaluoto, H., Virtanen, V., Salmenkivi, S., & Raulas, M. (2007). An empirical study of the drivers of consumer acceptance of mobile advertising. *Journal of Interactive Advertising*, *7*(2), 41–50.

Nysveen, H., Pedersen, P., & Thorbjørnsen, H. (2005). Intentions to use Mobile Services: Antecedents and Cross-Service Comparisons. *Journal of the Academy of Marketing Science*, *33*(3), 330–346. doi:10.1177/0092070305276149

Okazaki, S. (2004). How do japanese consumers perceive wireless ads? A multivariate analysis. *International Journal of Advertising*, *23*(4), 429–454.

Okazaki, S., & Taylor, C. (2008). What is SMS advertising and why do multinationals adopt it? Answers from an empirical study in European markets. *Journal of Business Research*, *61*(8), 4–12. doi:10.1016/j.jbusres.2006.05.003

Park, W. (2005). Mobile Phone Addiction. In Ling, R. (Ed.), *Mobile Communications: Renegotiation of the Social Sphere* (pp. 253–272). London: Springer.

Qingfei, M., Shaobo, J., & Gang, Q. (2008). Mobile Commerce User Acceptance Study in China: A Revised UTAUT Model. *Tsinghua Science and Technology*, *13*(3), 257–264. doi:10.1016/S1007-0214(08)70042-7

Rettie, R., Grandcolas, U., & Deakins, B. (2005). Text message advertising: response rates and branding effects. *Journal of Targeting. Measurement and Analysis for Marketing*, *13*(4), 304–312. doi:10.1057/palgrave.jt.5740158

Sarker, S., & Wells, J. (2003). Understanding Mobile. *Communications of the ACM*, *46*(12), 35–40. doi:10.1145/953460.953484

Shavitt, S., Lowrey, P., & Haefner, J. (1998). Public Attitudes Towards Advertising: More Favourable Than You Might Think. *Journal of Advertising Research*, *38*(4), 7–22.

Sirdeshmukh, D., Singh, S., & Sabol, B. (2002). Consumer Trust, Value, and Loyalty in Relational Exchanges. *Journal of Marketing*, *66*(2), 15–37. doi:10.1509/jmkg.66.1.15.18449

Standing, C., Benson, S., & Karjaluoto, H. (2005). Consumer perspectives on mobile advertising and marketing. In *Proceedings of the Australian & New Zealand Marketing Academy Conference (ANZMAC)*, Perth, Australia (pp. 135-141).

Tsang, M., Ho, S., & Liang, T. (2004). Consumer Attitudes toward Mobile Advertising: An Empirical Study. *International Journal of Electronic Commerce*, *8*(3), 65–78.

Unni, R., & Harmon, R. (2007). Perceived effectiveness of push vs. pull mobile location-based advertising. *Journal of Interactive Advertising, 7*(2), 28–40.

Varshney, U., & Vetter, R. (2002). Mobile commerce: framework, applications and networking support. *Journal of Mobile Networks and Applications, 7*(3), 185–198. doi:10.1023/A:1014570512129

Venkatesh, V., Morris, M. G., & Davis, G. B. (2003). User acceptance of information technology: Towards a unified view. *Management Information Systems Quarterly, 27*(3), 425–478.

Wakefield, R., & Whitten, D. (2006). Mobile computing: a user study on hedonic/utilitarian mobile device usage. *European Journal of Information Systems, 15*(1), 292–300. doi:10.1057/palgrave. ejis.3000619

This work was previously published in International Journal of E-Adoption, Volume 2, Issue 2, edited by Sushil K. Sharma, pp. 35-47, copyright 2010 by IGI Publishing (an imprint of IGI Global).

Chapter 6

Electronic Voting by Means of Digital Terrestrial Television:
The Infrastructure, Security Issues and a Real Test-Bed

Roberto Caldelli
University of Florence, Italy

Rudy Becarelli
University of Florence, Italy

Francesco Filippini
University of Florence, Italy

Francesco Picchioni
University of Florence, Italy

Riccardo Giorgetti
University of Florence, Italy

ABSTRACT

In this paper a Digital Terrestrial Television (DTT) based voting system is presented. This electronic voting technology allows disabled users to cast their vote from home by using common well-known devices. The needed equipment are a TV set, a Set Top Box (STB) with its remote control and a telephone line. The complete infrastructure consists of an MHP (Multimedia Home Platform) application that acts as a client application, a server application that acts as a network/counting server for e-voting, and a security protocol based on asymmetric key encryption to ensure authentication and secrecy of the vote. The MHP application is broadcasted by a certified (e.g., national) TV channel that grants its originality. The user needs a smart card issued by a national authority and to sign the encrypted ballot. The voter can browse the application by acting on the STB remote control. The server application is in charge to verify user identity, to gather and store user's encrypted ballots and finally to count votes. The communication between the client application and the server takes place by means of a secured channel (using HTTPS) while the voting operations are secured with the help of asymmetric keys encryption.

DOI: 10.4018/978-1-4666-0041-6.ch006

1 INTRODUCTION

Electronic, mechanical, or electromechanical voting are nowadays form of voting commonly accepted in various countries worldwide. Despite of this diffusion, these voting techniques have been always criticized for many reasons. Typical critics are related to the possibility, for the voter, to audit his vote or have some kind of control on the underlying mechanism during the polling phase that is when the vote is cast. This kind of frights arise naturally from the intrinsic complexity and/ or from the opacity of the mechanism itself and can be amplified by a justified sense of caution. These critics highlight that one of the most important open issues is security and in particular how to achieve or, eventually, increase it with respect to a traditional voting scenario. Electronic voting can, besides, enhance the accessibility to vote even for people living outside the country of origin or for disabled persons. Electronic voting, that is widely exploited, offers mainly two different approaches to solve both security and accessibility issues. The first approach aims to substitute traditional voting form in the polling stations with electronic machines trying to match the requirements for accessibility and security. The second tries to solve the accessibility issue by making people vote through web based or broadcasted applications, not disregarding the security of the communication channel that must be used in this case. Electronic voting machines in polling stations, named DRE (Direct Recording Electronic) voting systems (Federal Election Commision, 2001)(Federal Election Commision, 2001a), have been widely used especially after US presidential elections in 2000 when mechanical punching machines led to a large number of invalid ballots. Actually, despite of the confidence given by citizens to such a solution, DRE machines are very sensitive to various kind of attacks, as detailed in (Fisher & Coleman, 2005)(Kohno et al., 2007). In order to improve the security of DREs in terms of capability of performing an audit by the user,

secrecy of vote, and relative independence from technical flaws the receipt approach has been proposed. As explained in (Chaum et al., 2008) (Chaum, 2004)(Essex et al., 2007) (Garera & Rubin, 2007) (Chaum et al., 2008), the central idea is to give the user an encrypted receipt which can be used to audit the vote as an evidence that the vote has been cast and that can be seen like the ballot itself, since the user's choice is encrypted. Typically these systems, implemented as electronic or manual, give as a result of the voting operation two distinct ballots. After the voting phase (this is part of the security mechanism) the user is asked to destroy one of these ballot, chosen by himself, and scan the other one. The scanned ballots are sent to a server that acts like a ballot repository. Since both the ballots are encrypted and only the combination of the two can give some chance of recovering the vote, at the end of the operation the voter owns an encrypted receipt. The actual ballot is readable only with the help of some codes owned by the trusted authority that controls the voting operation (e.g., the Ministry of Internal Affairs). To allow the user to audit his vote, every encrypted ballot is identified by a readable unique number. The number, that is decoupled from the user's identity, can be used to audit the ballot via web with the help of a specific web application.

Recently electronic voting has proposed a new approach based on web applications allowing user to vote from worldwide. One of the first experiment in this direction has been SERVE (Secure Electronic Registration and Voting Experiment) (Jefferson et al., 2007a), a web based application developed for military personnel deployed overseas. Its security is mostly based upon asymmetric key encryption and HTTPS connection. An analysis of possible security flaws can be read in (Jefferson et al., 2007). Other similar systems have been developed starting from the SERVE experience, as for the Estonian e-voting system used during political elections in 2005 (Mägi, 2007). The SERVE security architecture and the Estonian experiment have been used as a reference for the implementation described in the proposed work. This paper is not aimed at presenting a new technology for voting security, but a new architecture whose purpose is to provide an usable voting system in order to allow, in particular, people with mobility problems to vote.

The architecture presented is based on the DTT (Digital Terrestrial Television) infrastructure and on the use of Java interactive applications running on a common television by means of a simple decoder (Set-Top-Box, STB). DTT is worldwide spread as a family of different standards for digital TV (DVB in Europe, Australia and Asia (http://www.dvb.org); ATSC in North America (http://www.atsc.org); ISDB in Japan and Brazil (http://www.dibeg.org)). Specifically the proposed architecture is built upon DVB-T/MHP (Multimedia Home Platform) (http://www.mhp.org) technology but it could be extended to the other standards. MHP applications, named Xlets, are similar to Applets for the web, both in structure and life-cycle; they are broadcasted by multiplexing them with the digital TV transport stream and can be accessed on the television screen. Such application, through the STB and a return channel (e.g., the telephone line), can allow a one-to-one interaction between the user and the server side.

The proposed system is based on two applications: an MHP application running on the client side and a server application running on the server side. The first, broadcasted by the authorized TV channel (trusted authority), when downloaded on the STB, permits to authenticate the user, and to send the digital ballot to the server application. On the other side the server application is in charge to check the user ID and eventually allows the user to vote. Then the server application manages the secret ballot and decouple the vote from the voter.

The whole system has been tested in laboratory emulating a real world situation by broadcasting the TV signal and checking the functionalities provided by various kinds of STBs present on the market.

During the phase of development an usability study has been performed to make on interface easy to use and understand even for users subject to "digital divide". Also the entire architecture, in an ad-hoc setup, has been presented and tested, as a demonstration, on 4th *of* November 2008 during the latest USA Presidential Election. A convention, organized by the TAA (Tuscan American Association) (http://www.toscanausa.org/Election_EN.asp), was held in Florence (Italy) to wait for the actual result of the elections.

The paper is organized as follows: an exhaustive description of the system is given in section 2. Security issues are debated in section 3, while usability aspects are discussed in section 4. The experience faced during the "Election Night Event" is presented in section 5 and section 6 concludes the paper.

2 SYSTEM DESCRIPTION

This architecture for electronic voting was basically designed as an aid to people with mobility problems and not only. The idea behind this infrastructure is to provide the chance to vote remotely by using very well-known devices, like a television and a remote control, in a domestic environment. In addition to that, the simplicity of the required equipment (i.e., a STB for DTT, a telephone line connection and a TV screen) allows to easy access to vote not only persons with computer science skills but also people without a personal computer, living in needy areas of the country.

The infrastructure is based on the DTT (Digital Terrestrial Television) platform and on the use of Java interactive applications called Xlets. Such applications run on common television through the use of a simple decoder called Set-Top-Box (STB). The standard that in Europe rules this architecture is based on DVB-T/MHP (Multimedia Home Platform) technology. DVB-T defines the caracteristics of the signal transmission, while MHP covers the part related to the interactive applications. MHP applications in DTT are similar to Java Applet for the web; they are broadcasted by multiplexing them with the digital TV transport stream and loaded in the STB where runs a Java Virtual Machine with MHP stack.

The whole platform is reported in Figure 1. The MHP application certified by the authority which is responsible for voting operations (e.g., the Ministry of Internal Affairs) is broadcasted by the TV channel/channels authorized to distribute the service (e.g. the national TV broadcaster like RAI in Italy, BBC in UK, CNN in USA, etc.). The user by selecting the channel can download the application and watch it on the television screen. Being equipped with the appropriate smart card (e.g., Electronic Identity Card - EIC), he can proceed to the authentication phase and then to the vote by using the return channel on the PSTN connection. It is easy to understand that the structure for this kind of electronic vote is basically composed by two main parts: the " Client" (MHP application) and the " Server" (Server-side application) which communicate each other through an HTTPS connection over the Return Channel. Decoders on

the market have to types of network interface: modem 56k or Ethernet.

The Client application is a Xlet (Java Application) broadcasted together with TV transport stream that a voting user can launch from the remote control of STB. STBs have a slot for electronic cards, typically used for pay TV or other interactive services, where user can insert his EIC to be authenticated by the system. Each smartcard has a secret numerical PIN that the user must enter by using the Remote Control. Through the remote control it is possible to easily navigate the application; instructions are provided on the screen too. When the user sends his vote, the application activates the Return Channel and establishes a secure connection with the server via HTTPS protocol.

The Server application has two principal roles: user authentication and vote registration. Authentication is done by receiving the identifying data contained in the Smart-Card by the return channel, validating the public certificate (X.509) and verifying if the user has already voted. When the user has been authenticated, he can select his

Figure 1. System infrastructure

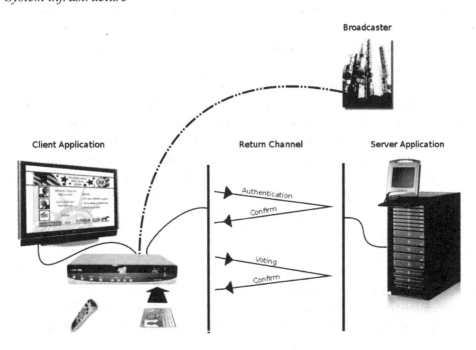

favorite candidate or party and his vote is sent to the server that records user's preference.

The following paragraphs illustrate in detail each part of the proposed system.

2.1 Set-Top-Box, Smart Card and Client Application

The client side is essentially composed by four parts: STB (Set-Top-Box) and its remote control, Smart Card (like Electronic Identity Card), Return Channel and MHP application (Java Xlet). Let's see in detail these components. STB is a decoder that transcodes the broadcasted digital television signal into a classical analog one by following the standard DVB-T (Digital Video Broadcasting - Terrestrial). It is essential that these devices implement the MHP stack with the appropriate Java virtual machine, without that Java applications can not be executed (common STBs on the market satisfy that). The user can launch the application by the remote control, generally clicking on the APP button (it depends on models). Another prerequisite is that the STBs are equipped with the SATSA (Security And Trust Services API) (http://java.sun.com/products/satsa) libraries to interact with this type of smart card (again common STBs on the market satisfy that). Once launched, the application needs to authenticate the user and at this stage the smart card plays an essential role. There are many types of cards used for pay-TV such as Irdeto® (http://www.irdeto.com) and Nagravision® (http://www.nagravision.com). This application supports all SmartCards that refers to ISO 7816 standard (http://www.iso.org/iso/search.htm?qt=7816 searchSubmit=Search sort=rel type=simp le published=on) like EIC (Electronic Identity Card) and NCS (National Services Card). Application is able to authenticate the user after he has introduced his card in the slot of the decoder. For security two checks are performed: one directly with the request of the PIN (Personal Identification Number), the other, once typed the code, using a secure cable connection with the server side exchanging the certificate (X.509) of the card using a system of asymmetric key encryption. Once the user has chosen his candidate, the digital ballot is encrypted and sent to the server following a protocol described in section 3. Consumer electronic STBs can access the Internet or a local network. Usually they have two types of interface: 56k modem or Ethernet. In the first case the connection is made using an ISP (Internet Service Provider) which the modem connects to. The parameters for the connection (i.e., ISP telephone number, user name, password) can be passed in two ways: either directly by setting the STB through its communication interface, or embedded inside the MHP application itself. After opening the return channel, the application can make requests to the normal internet network through protocols like http, ftp, https, pop etc. For save of conciseness, the MHP application features are not described here but in Section 4.

2.2 Server Application

On the server side, a server application (Servlet) exists which is in charge for the authentication phase and for vote storaging. It receives the public certificate of the smart card, extracts the personal data (i.e., an unique Revenue Service Code) and verifies that the user has not already voted. If the user has already voted the server returns a message stating that the session is going to be closed. On the contrary if voting is admitted it gets and records the user's encrypted ballot decoupling it from the voter. As previously mentioned, all transactions between client and server are made using the return channel within a HTTPS connection (Hypertext Transfer Protocol over Secure Socket Layer).

3 SECURITY ISSUES

In this section an implementation of the security protocol used to hide sensible data and authenticate the user is drawn. The architecture presented in the section 2 consists of two applications (a client-side and a server-side one) that exchange data along a secure channel using HTTPS and asymmetrical key encryption. In this scenario two main security issues arise: application security and communication security.

Application security is easily achievable by trusting two main authorities: the broadcaster of the MHP application and the server side application warrantor. The broadcaster must ensure that the application, acting like a client, is the original one. The server application instead must ensure that votes coming from the client are sent by a certain person and that, above all, the vote is decoupled from the voter. The adopted model of communication security, instead, makes use of an encrypted channel and two pairs of asymmetrical keys, one for the server and one for the client. The first necessary step is to build a secure channel between the client and the server. In order to do that an encrypted HTTPS connection is established adopting SSL (Secure Socket Layer) and TLS (Transport Layer Security) technologies. Typical attacks to the secure channel (e.g., Man-In-The-Middle attacks operated by poisoning the ARP - Address Resolution Protocol etc.) can be neutralized with an appropriate double check of the SSL certificate. Once the secure connection is established, the protocol makes use of the client and the server keys to encrypt the user's vote. The Server pair of keys are *PKS* (public) and *SKS* (secret). This pair is used to encrypt and make anonymous the vote of the user. In particular *SKS* is exclusively owned by the authority which is responsible for voting operations and will be used only during the scrutiny phase (see below). The Client instead has a pair of keys addressed as *PKC* and *SKC*. These keys are used to authenticate the user and sign the data exchanged along the secure channel. The exchange of public keys is done as follows: *PKS* is broadcasted directly with the MHP application, *PKC* is sent from the client through the SmartCard certificate.

The encryption mechanism used in a voting session is pictured in Figure 2 and detailed hereafter. The user logs into the client application by inserting his smartcard into the slot and by entering the secure PIN code to unlock the card. After this client side authentication, the user digital certificate is sent via HTTPS to the server that checks whether the user is allowed to cast the vote or not by extracting from the digital certificate the unique public data for identifying the voter (e.g. the Revenue Service Code). If the user is allowed to vote, the *PKC* key is extracted from the digital certificate and stored in a session object ready to be used for further operations. A message, containing the positive or negative acknowledgement, is sent back to the client through the established HTTPS channel. The message is signed with *PKS* in order to ensure the user that the message sender is the server. If a positive acknowledgement is sent, the user is invited by the client application to cast his vote. Once his choice has been expressed, the client application generates a random number r, encrypts the message with the server public key (*PKS*) and signs it with the private user key (*SKC*) as follows: $SIGN_{SKC}(ENC_{PKS}(v; r))$, where v is a unique identifier for the user's choice and r is the random number. Random number r is concatenated with the vote in order to generate each time a different encrypted ballot to improve security, otherwise the types of encrypted ballots would be as much as the number of eligible candidates/parties. $ENC_{PKS}(v; r)$, the encrypted ballot, is also stored as a receipt for checking back the server answer while the entire message is sent to the server. The client application stands by for a positive acknowledgement that will close the transaction. When the server gets the message it is confident that the message comes from the user that is granted by the signature. The server, verified the sender identity, obtains an encrypted ballot $ENC_{PKS}(v; r)$ containing the user's choice. The encrypted ballot is then stored in a common repository, ready to be successively balloted. In this phase the voter's identity is decoupled from the ballot as it happens in mail voting systems. The security model implemented is then, at least, the one granted with mail voting. If all these phases terminate with success, the server sends back to the client a signed answer containing the encrypted ballot. The answer is signed with the server secret key *SKS*. Once the client receives this message is able to recover the anonymous envelope and compares it with the previously stored copy. If the comparison is positive the transaction closes. Once the whole voting operations are closed, the server side authority, who is responsible to manage the votes, can disclose every single encrypted ballot

using the private server key (which is made available only in this phase) and taking into account r the random number, since r is separated from vote by a sequence of known characters. Then votes are computed and the final results are published.

4 SYSTEM CHARACTERISTICS: AN ANALYSIS

In this section an usability analysis and an explanation of some of the advantages and drawbacks of the presented system is carried out.

Figure 2. Security mechanism

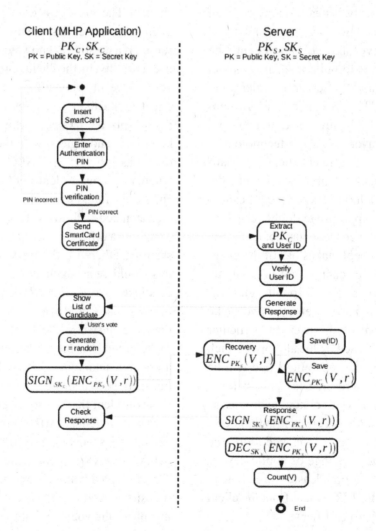

4.1 Usability

During the phase of client application development an usability study has been performed. It is important to underline that this system uses a structure and devices well-known to everybody. The application is accessed through a common TV and the remote control of STB, devices already used by millions of people.

To simplify as much as possible the operations which the user must perform, the use of buttons on the remote control was limited. The application can be used only by resorting at the arrow keys (*UP/DOWN* and *LEFT/RIGHT*) and by pressing *OK* button. Usually MHP applications exploit the four *coloured* buttons (red, green, yellow and blue), making more complicated the use of the interfaces. The interface consists of a sequence of screens thought to be easy to use and understand even for users subject to " digital divide". The application however fully comes in help of people by using a written guide (see Figure 3(a)) to give the user some basic hint for interacting with the interface in a correct way (audio-guide messages have also been implemented). The most difficult step for the user can be the typing of the PIN, but because it is simply numerical the operation is reduced to just press the code on the numeric keypad on the remote control, typically used to change TV channels, and then confirm with the OK button. It is important to highlight that at each step, in case of an error by the user, it is possible to go back. Both for the PIN and for any selection of the candidate, the pressure of the OK button displays a confirmation dialog (see Figure 3(b)). Without this check is not possible to proceed to the next step. It was also used a very specific criterion in the choice of using the arrow keys. Vertical arrows (UP and DOWN buttons) are used only for the selection of candidates/parties (see Figure 3(a)). These have the role to move the focus on the respective boxes of the candidates/ parties. While the horizontal arrows (LEFT and RIGHT button) are used only in the confirmation dialog to move the focus on YES (confirm) or NO (cancel) buttons (see Figure 3(b)).

4.2 Advantages and drawbacks

In this subsection advantages and drawbacks of the system are outlined and comparisons with classical voting systems and other electronic voting forms are carried out. Basically the proposed system allows the user to vote from home like the classical mail voting. Additionally the system encrypts the digital ballot and the communication towards the server with asymmetric key encryption. Besides the use of a smart card and a Personal Identification Number simplifies the authentication phase increasing at the same time the security level. A possible critic relies on the fact that such a system is not able to recognize whether a voter has actually cast his vote, because it's possible that the smart card and the PIN are used by someone else but the owner. It can be noted that the same critic can be arisen to a well known and accepted system like the mail voting. Another advantage of this system is the fact that the MHP application is broadcasted (i.e., with a *push* technology) to everyone making the Man In The Middle attack almost impossible. This kind of intrinsic security is given by the nature of the on-the-air broadcasting that can be modelled as a one-to-many scheme. Other possible drawbacks can come out from the structure of the system based on the client-server paradigm. The most attackable part of the system is the return channel that is exposed to MITM attacks. Similar attacks can be minimized by using HTTPS and performing a double security check from the client as requested by the protocol itself. Another clear advantage is the fact that the digital ballot can not be repudiated and the secrecy of the ballot itself ensured by the use of asymmetric cryptography properly implemented within the system. Besides, the use of the application does not affect the user in any way by demanding some particular cost. No extra hardware is needed to make the application run.

Figure 3. MHP application screenshots

(a)

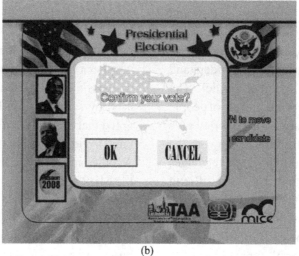

(b)

The only things needed is a commercial STB and at least a PSTN connection.

5 A REAL TEST BED (ELECTION NIGHT)

The entire architecture, in an ad-hoc setup, has been presented and tested, as a demonstration, on of November during the latest USA Presidential Elections. A convention named " Election Night", organized by the TAA (Tuscan American Association, http://www.toscanausa. org/Election_EN.asp) and sponsored by Tuscany Region (http://www.regione.toscana.it), was held in Florence (Italy) to wait for the actual result of the elections.

The architecture previously presented has been modified in order to simplify the voting phase during the Election Night. These changes have been necessary since a large number of people (about one thousand persons) were expected to cast their vote in few polling booths. The polling booths were equipped with a STB receiving the digital signal directly from a PC running a DVB-T/MHP object carousel and acting as a broadcaster. This PC used an appropriate hardware interface to modulate the digital signal to RF (Radio-Frequency) and sent it, via coaxial cable, to all STBs. These configuration has been adopted since no real broadcaster were available that night. Besides, since the STBs in use were fitted with the necessary connectors and interfaces, another PC were connected via Ethernet to each STBs to act like the server side machine as described above.

People who wanted to try the system, had to ask a hostess a smartcard with an associated dummy identity used during the tests. The voter, then, had to enter the polling booth and insert the card into the STB slot. The authentication phase, in this scenario, has been skipped since the smart card available were few and in order to speed up all the operations. In particular, the voter was not asked to unlock the card by entering the PIN code. The only security operation performed by the application was to check the presence of the card inside the slot to authorize the voter to go on. The following phases of voting took place as described in the previous chapters. During the night some exit polls has been simulated by projecting partial votes to a wall screen. People who took part in the convention expressed their appreciation for the initiative. The large number of voters clearly demonstrates that such a system matches the minimal usability requirements and that is easily comprehensible. A photograph of some tests can be seen at http://www.toscanausa.org/gallery/images/dnvye__C0B1305.jpg

6 CONCLUSION

The system presented in this paper is mainly aimed to reduce the " digital divide" in e-voting by exploiting DTT technology. People having mobility problems or leaving in weedy areas can vote by means of a STB and a PSTN connection even from their home. The security is ensured using HTTPS connection and an appropriate encryption of sensible data; in this case the user's vote. The encryption is operated by means of two pairs of asymmetrical keys owned respectively by the server and by the user's smartcard. The security protocol is similar to the ones designed for web based e-voting applications like SERVE (Jefferson et al., 2007a) and the estonian e-voting system (Mägi, 2007). The architecture is composed by a client application running on a STB and broadcasted by a trusted TV channel that is responsible to preserve its integrity. This application is able to communicate, via PSTN or digital connection, with a server that authenticates the user and eventually authorizes him to vote. The server stores his cyphered ballot, decoupling it from the user identity, until the scrutiny phase. The scrutiny takes place using a secret key used to decypher the encrypted ballots. This system is easily extending to other platform describe in the section 1 and not only. For the characteristics of the MHP standard, it is possible to reproduce this architecture in other system like: DVB-S (Satellite), DVB-C (Cable) or DVB-H (Handheld).

7 ACKNOWLEDGMENT

The authors would like to thank Tuscany Region for supporting the project and RTV38, Italian TV broadcaster, for the technical effort during testing phases and for contributing to the " Election Night" event.

REFERENCES

Chaum, D. (2004). Secret-ballot receipts: True voter-verifiable elections. *Security & Privacy*, *2*(1), 38–47. doi:10.1109/MSECP.2004.1264852

Chaum, D., Carback, R., Clark, J., Essex, A., Popoveniuc, S., Rivest, R., Ryan, P., Shen, E., & Sherman, A. (2008, May/June). Scantegrity II: End-to-End Verifiability for Optical Scan Election Systems Using Invisible Ink Confirmation Codes. *Security & Privacy*.

Chaum, D., Essex, A., Carback, R., Clark, J., Popoveniuc, S., Sherman, A., & Vora, P. (2008). Scantegrity: End-to-End Voter-Verifiable Optical-Scan Voting. *Security & Privacy*, *6*(3), 40–46. doi:10.1109/MSP.2008.70

Essex., et al. (2007). The Punchscan Voting System: Vo-Comp Competition Submission. *In Proceedings of the 1st Univ. Voting Systems Competition (VoComp)*. Retrieved from http://punchscan.org/vocomp/PunchscanVocompSubmission.pdf

Federal Election Commision. (2001). *Voting system Standards, Performance Standards, Introduction*. Retrieved from http://www.fec.gov/agenda/agendas2001/mtgdoc01-62/v1/v1s1.htm

Federal Election Commision. (2001a). *Voting System Standard*. Retrieved from http://www.fec.gov/agenda/agendas2001/mtgdoc01-62/overview.htm

Fisher, E. A., & Coleman, K. J. (2005). *The Direct Recording Electronic Voting Machine (DRE) Controversy: FAQs and Misperceptions*. Washington, DC: The Library of Congress.

Garera, S., & Rubin, A. D. (2007). An Independent Audit Framework for Software Dependent Voting Systems. *In Proceedings of the 14th ACM Conf. Computer and Comm. Security (CCS 07)* (pp. 256-265). New York: ACM Press.

Jefferson, D., Rubin, A. D., Simons, B., & Wagner, D. (2007). *A Security Analysis of the Secure Electronic Registration and Voting Experiment (SERVE), 2004*. Retrieved from http://www.servesecurityreport.org/. 21.01.2007

Jefferson, D., Rubin, A. D., Simons, B., & Wagner, D. (2007a). *A Security Analysis of the Secure Electronic Registration and Voting Experiment (SERVE)*. Retrieved June 13, 2007 from http://www.servesecurityreport.org/

Kohno, T., Stubblefield, A., Rubin, A. D., & Wallach, D. S. (2007). *Analysis of an Electronic Voting System, 2004*. Retrieved from http://avirubin.com/vote.pdf. 21.01.2007

Mägi, T. (2007). *Practical Security Analysis of E-voting Systems*. Master thesis, Tallinn University of Technology, Tallinn, Estonia.

This work was previously published in International Journal of E-Adoption, Volume 2, Issue 1, edited by Sushil K. Sharma, pp. 1-12, copyright 2010 by IGI Publishing (an imprint of IGI Global).

Chapter 7
Towards E–Society Policy Interoperability for Social Web Networks

Renato Iannella
NICTA, Australia

ABSTRACT

The move toward Policy-Oriented Web is destined to provide support for policy expression and management in the core web layers. One of the most promising areas that can drive this new technology adoption is e-Society communities. With so much user-generated content being shared by these social networks, there is the real danger that the implicit sharing rules that communities have developed over time will be lost in translation in the new digital communities. This will lead to a corresponding loss in confidence in e-Society sites. The Policy-Oriented Web attempts to turn the implicit into the explicit with a common framework for policy language interoperability and awareness. This paper reports on the policy driving factors from the Social Networks experiences using real-world use cases and scenarios. In particular, the key functions of policy-awareness—for privacy, rights, and identity—will be the driving force that enables the e-Society to appreciate new interoperable policy regimes.

1. INTRODUCTION

The e-Society has been a long term dream that the ICT community, amongst others, have moved towards with new technologies over the past decade. The engagement of citizens in e-Societies has enabled greater participation and opportunities for communities to offer "information commons" (Qui, 2008) for digital interactions. Today, we clearly have this dream realised with Social Networks. Social Networks - via the innovative use of Web 2.0 features - have also taken the ICT community by surprise with such rapid uptake and widespread content sharing.

DOI: 10.4018/978-1-4666-0041-6.ch007

Social Networks attempt to mimic and support normal society interactions and experiences. In many cases, these seem to be working well, such as keeping friends and family in contact and sharing status information. However, the wide-spread sharing of personal and corporate information within Social Networks (e.g., photos, documents) have an impact on policy support, such as privacy and rights management decisions. These issues have now become more relevant as Social Networks have empowered the end user to share even more private content with increasing global reach. Additionally, the providers that offer these services have an immense database of personal information at their disposal.

Generally, Social Networks "provide complex and indeterminate mechanisms to specific privacy and other policies for protecting access to personal information, and allow information to be shared that typically would not follow social and professional norms" (Iannella, 2009). There have been numerous attempts to solve this problem in the past but none have been really successful, nor applicable to the Social Networks community. A new approach is required to manage seamless policy interaction for the e-Society masses. The "Policy-Oriented Web" is an emerging idea to bring greater policy management technologies to the core web infrastructure. This will enable polices to interoperate across Social Network service providers.

In this paper we present e-Society use cases from Social Networks to highlight the driver for the adoption of new interoperable policy technologies. We then present an information model for the Policy-Oriented Web and show some example representations. Finally, we look at related works and conclude with how e-Society - via Social Networks - can lead to greater interoperability opportunities for policies across the wider Web.

2. E-SOCIETY USE CASE: SOCIAL NETWORKS

Social Networks, like FaceBook, Flickr, LinkedIn, Xing, YouTube, and MySpace, have been phenomenally successful. They have achieved this by providing simple yet user empowering features that digitally support the online social experience. In particular, the relative ease of sharing content with close colleagues and friends has driven Social Networks participation. However, this experience can have serious repercussions if the implicit arrangements under which content is shared are not known explicitly, or worse, are not respected.

Two recent examples have highlighted these negative experiences. The first was the use of photographs from Flickr in a commercial advertising program (Cohen, 2007). In this case, the image of a person was used by Virgin Mobile in billboard advertising. They had taken the image from Flickr as the photo owner (the person's friend) had selected a Creative Commons license that allowed commercial usage. This highlighted two issues; understanding the implications of commercial usage, and publishing images of your friends on public websites. The photo owner had assumed that commercial usage may have enabled him to participate in the financial rewards (it didn't). His friend who appeared in the photos also had no idea her image was being used, until it was too late (she was not impressed). The lack of understanding the requirement for "model release" permission in the license policy also contributed to this situation.

The second example involved photos from FaceBook being used by the mainstream media to report on the death of a defence force trooper (ABC Media Watch, 2007). The media had used his personal photos from his FaceBook profile - including photos of his family - to print in the national newspapers. At no time did they seek permission to reproduce these images. In some of the media responses to this issue, the assumption was stated that since the photos were on the Internet anyway, they were deemed "public domain" and you could basically do whatever you like with the images with little recourse.

Both of these cases involve sharing of photos on Social Networks and highlight challenges to owners and end users on the right level of respect for use of such content. To investigate this issue further, we looked at the processes for sharing photos on Facebook.

Like many Web 2.0 Social Networks, Facebook requires the account owner to certify - implicitly - that they have the right to distribute uploaded photos and that it does not violate the Facebook terms and conditions (see Figure 1). The latter is an eight page document of dense 'legal-ese' wording that not only is unlikely to be read by account owners, but rarely would be understood by the layperson.

Facebook allows you to add photos in named Albums to your account. You can then decide on who can see these photo albums with some simple image privacy controls. Figure 2 shows the options available including; Everyone, My Networks and Friends, Friends of Friends, and Only Friends.

However, when you choose the Customize options, additional detailed privacy controls are available (see Figure 3). Now you can be very specific, such as indicating which individual friends can see the photo ("Some Friends") and who cannot ("Except These People"). You can also specify specific Networks of friends as well.

Figure 1. FaceBook photo upload certification

Figure 2. FaceBook photo options

Figure 3. FaceBook photo privacy options

At this stage, when an end user - be they public, in your network, or a friend - sees your photo, they have the usual file manipulation controls in their web browser to "Save Image As" to the local disk (see Figure 4). Obviously the photo is now out of the reach of Facebook's privacy control mechanisms and can now be forwarded to anyone via email and other means, or printed in national newspapers, or plastered on billboards. So the privacy controls that we had carefully crafted in Facebook are now no longer available outside the domain of this Social Network.

Clearly the reason for this overriding of the Facebook privacy policy is the fact the a standard Web Browser has no knowledge of the policy and any embedded image in a web page can "normally" be saved to local disk. If we could design an enhancement to Facebook - if not all Social Networks - then we would consider a simple mechanism that informs the end user that the photo has some restrictions attached.

We don't envisage an "enforcement" mechanism, as this would not be consistent with the ethos of Social Networks, but an "accountability" mechanism would be sufficient and appropriate. This would allow, for example, images to be cached

Figure 4. Web browser "same image as..." menu

by the browser (for efficiency) but not explicitly saved outside the browser environment.

Figure 5 shows a hypothetical dialog that could appear instead of the "Save Image As" dialog (as shown in Figure 4). The key point is that this dialog - albeit simple - informs the end user of the privacy rules pertaining to the image and allows them to honour this (i.e. to cancel the request) or to continue with the file download, but being warned that this may be recorded for accountability purposes.

The image in Figure 4 is a picture of my cat Billie, and she is not too concerned about her image being published on FaceBook. The issue becomes really compounded, as we have already seen, when sharing pictures of your family, friends and colleagues. Facebook includes a feature whereby you can annotate photos and indicate the names of the people in the photo. These can be existing Facebook members or non-members. The image would then show their names (with a mouse-over their face) and, for members, would link to their profile.

Figure 6 shows an example of selecting my colleague's faces in a photo and assigning them to their Facebook identity. (Note that the images and names have been deliberately blurred in Figure 6 to protect their privacy). As with the photo of Billie, this photo can also be downloaded and shared bypassing the Facebook privacy policy. It also poses greater threat as my two colleagues in the photo also do not wish their image to be used for any other purpose than a corporate image of the project team.

However, we do now have the new possibility of checking the individual's policy needs since we have identified all the people in the photo. We could automatically notify each of them and ask if they would allow their friend (i.e., me) to publish the photo of them in his photo album and under the privacy policy I have designated. For example, I could allow the photo for complete public access, or limited to a network, or my friends. They could then respond based on this. This "policy negotiation" could also be automated to allow quicker responses, based on an individuals own privacy policy.

To summarise, Social Networks, like Facebook and others, have a tremendous opportunity now to look towards simple, yet powerful, policy support to match the community expectations when sharing content. The emerging Policy-Oriented Web can exploit these use cases as the driver to develop new web infrastructure. Future Web 2.0 services can be built upon this new web infrastructure to provide fair and accountable content sharing services.

Figure 5. New save dialog

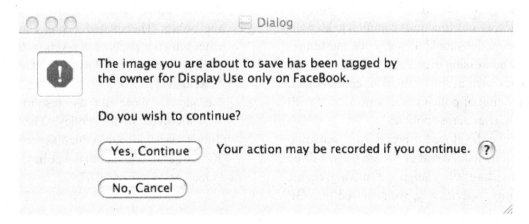

Figure 6. FaceBook: Photo friends tagging

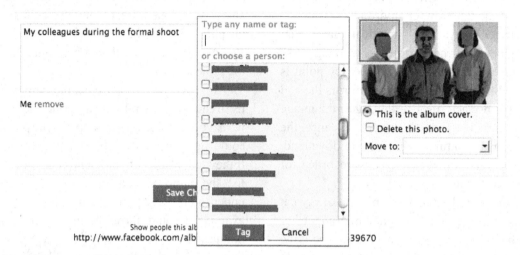

3. THE POLICY-ORIENTED WEB

The Policy-Oriented Web, also sometimes referred to as the Policy-Aware Web, is an emerging field that aims to address the need to manage multiple and conflicting policies in the future distributed service-oriented world. This will increase connectivity across disparate web systems and services as they can achieve a new level of automated interoperability, guided by declarative policies that can adapt to different contexts and environments. In an earlier position paper (Iannella et al., 2006) we outlined the major key strategic challenges posed by the Policy-Oriented Web. This included the need for a unified model that can adequately represent policies. Such a unified model - based on various policy requirements - will capture the core concepts and structures common to all policies. The model should also provide the framework for addressing even deeper policy-specific challenges such as the evaluation, enforcement, and reasoning of policies, and how to deal with inconsistencies across policies.

We have developed a preliminary semantic information model based on the analysis of three types of existing policy languages; privacy, rights, and identity. Specifically, we analysed the P3P

(Wenning & Schunter, 2006), ODRL (Iannella, 2002) and XACML (OASIS, 2005) languages and reviewed their information features, structures, and relationships to determine the commonalities across these policy languages. These three were chosen as they represent the most used languages for privacy (P3P), rights (ODRL) and access control (XACML). Each lacked the complete structure to be a general policy language on their own. For example, P3P lacks mechanisms to link to multiple parties, ODRL lacks negation, and XACML lacks inheritance.

The resultant Policy information model (shown in Figure 7) contains three primary classes that express the policy semantics:

- Action - these are the activities involved in the policy. The related Focus class indicates which aspects of the Action drive the policy, such as "Allow" or "Deny" or "Exclusive".
- Resource - these are the resources/content involved in the policy. The related Target class indicates which aspects of the Resource are relevant to the policy, such as "One" or "Any" or "All".

Figure 7. Policy information model

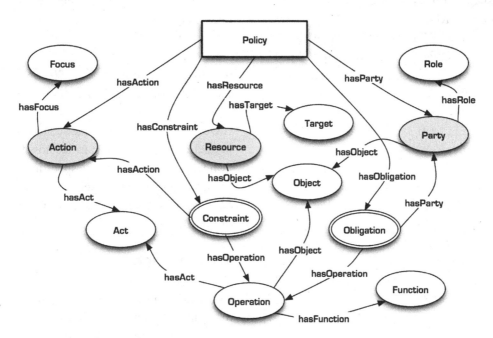

- Party - these are the people and organisations involved in the policy. The related Role class indicates which role the Party plays in relation to the policy, such as "Licensee" or "Consumer".

These three classes were found to be the core components from the policy languages analysed. Supporting these three classes are the following classes:

- Act - identifies specific acts that can be performed.
- Object - identifies specific entities.
- Function - identifies comparative operators.

A Policy can also include two other classes that modify the behaviour of Actions and Parties:

- Constraint - conditions that will limit an Action of the policy. This can cover a range of options from the fundamental (such as numeric, date ranges, geospatial)

to the more complex (such as a particular purpose or domain use).

- Obligation - requirements that must be met by a Party in order to satisfy the policy. This can also cover a wide range from the fundamental (such as payment) to the more complex (such as being tracked for usage).

Both the Constraint and Obligation classes are supported by the Operation class. The Operation class links instances of Act, Object, and Function classes to uniquely express the required operation. The Operation will enable reasoning services over policies as it will contain the fundamental data for policy expressions.

We have represented the Policy-Oriented Web Information Model (Figure 7) in RDF and RDF Schema (modeled using the Protégé tool). It was quite challenging in converting a typical information model (such as Figure 7) and mapping it into an RDF model. It some cases it was not clear how to best represent the information artifact, such as Focus and Deny, into the triple-based model of RDF.

The example RDF Schema snippet below shows the "hasObject" property with "Object" range and domain of "Operation", "Party", and "Resource" classes.

```
<rdf:Property rdf:about="urn:policy:1
0:hasObject">
  <rdfs:range rdf:resource="urn:polic
y:10:Object"/>
  <rdfs:domain rdf:resource="urn:poli
cy:10:Operation"/>
  <rdfs:domain rdf:resource="urn:poli
cy:10:Party"/>
  <rdfs:domain rdf:resource="urn:poli
cy:10:Resource"/>
</rdf:Property>
```

We have chosen just RDF and RDF Schema to keep the first iteration of the Policy-Oriented Web as "simple" as possible without over complicating the expression structures. This will be important to meet the technical needs of the Web 2.0 and Social Networks communities. We plan to also use RDFa as another encoding direct into HTML pages.

Others have proposed semantic expression of specific policy languages in the richer OWL language for rights (Hu, 2007; Garcia & Gil, 2006) and privacy (Kolari et al., 2005) policies. We envisage the future where use of such advanced semantic web languages will also be supported in the Web 2.0 platform of technologies. In the first iteration of the Policy-Oriented Web, we believe that basing it on the RDF language is the best compromise. The Policy-Oriented Web information model could also be expressed in OWL for more advanced reasoning and ontological features needed by high-end communities. However, this may lead to an unnecessarily complex language and lessen the appeal to the wider communities. Nonetheless, there should be support to extend the language for those requiring these features

and this will, at least, guarantee some level of interoperability.

4. POLICY-ORIENTED WEB FOR SOCIAL NETWORKS

If we now revisit some of the scenarios presented in Section 2, we can start to see how to apply the Policy-Oriented Web to the specific use cases for Social Networks. In particular, the two use cases of view control over photos, and publishing photos of your friends and colleagues.

4.1 View Rights

In this use case, we need to support the ability to define the scope of users who can view the photos in a photo album. Using Facebook, as an example, we need to support:

- all the public,
- all or some of your friends,
- all or some of your networks, and
- disallow one or more friends.

These would be expressed as Constraints in the Policy-Oriented Web model as part of a policy instance. The example below shows the RDF/XML snippet that would express that only people in your "Australia" network can view the photos.

```
<p:Constraint rdf:ID="view-aust-net-
work">
  <p:hasAction
rdf:resource="policy:render"/>
  <p:hasOperation
rdf:resource="group-australia-net-
work"/>
</p:Constraint>

<p:Operation rdf:ID="group-australia-
network">
  <p:hasAct
```

```
rdf:resource="policy:group"/>
  <p:hasFunction
rdf:resource="policy:equal"/>
   <p:hasObject rdf:resource="network-
australia"/>
</p:Operation>

<p:Object rdf:ID="network-australia"
  p:hasIdentity="urn:facebook:network
:australia"/>
```

These expressions capture the unique identifier for the Facebook Australia Network, and allows viewing (policy:render) for this network (policy:group) using the unique identifiers from the policy model semantics.

4.2 Friend's Privacy

In this use case, we need to allow your friends and colleagues that appear in your photos the ability to state whether they approve their image being published, including the scope of users who can view the photos. Using Facebook, as an example, we need to support the scenario of a friend tagging them on a photo and allow them to opt-out if they do not agree.

This use case is more complex in that it requires negotiation between the owner of the photo and the friends in the photo. We will not discuss the intricacies of policy negotiation (Arnab & Hutchison, 2007) in this paper, but highlight this as a requirement for the future Policy-Oriented Web.

Typically, we would see that users would have a default privacy policy as part of their account profile. This policy would express their preferences on how their image can be used in social network photo albums. Their privacy policy would then be compared to the "view rights policy" that one of their friends is proposing. If there is conflict then this would stop the publication (the default action) and the user may be asked to "consider" the policy and confirm/deny it manually.

For example, the below RDF/XML snippet shows a privacy-policy in which the user has denied viewing (render) for any resources containing their image for any Facebook Network.

```
<p:Policy rdf:ID="myPrivacy">
  <p:hasResource
rdf:resource="images-of-me"/>
   <p:hasAction rdf:resource="view-
deny"/>
   <p:hasOperation
rdf:resource="group-network"/>
</p:Policy>

<p:Operation rdf:ID="group-network">
  <p:hasAct
rdf:resource="policy:group"/>
   <p:hasFunction
rdf:resource="policy:equal"/>
   <p:hasObject
rdf:resource="network"/>
</p:Operation>

<p:Object rdf:ID="network"
  p:hasIdentity="urn:facebook:networ
k:all"/>

<p:Action rdf:ID="viewDeny"
p:hasFocus="deny" >
   <p:hasAct
rdf:resource="policy:render"/>
</p:Action>
```

The same model can be used to deny "public" and "friend" access (with appropriate identifiers from FaceBook). Conversely, if the user was happy to allow access for any network, friend, or public, then the "hasFocus" can simply be changed to "allow".

4.3 Toward Interoperability

Returning to the two real-world use cases described in Section 2, both of these should have been avoided with an appropriate policy expression and accountability across Social Networks and platforms. Today, however, even if the correct rights/privacy/access criteria were selected under the controlled Social Network environment, the lack of policy support at the operating system level (including the web browser) hinders policy conformance. This is one of the greatest challenges for the Policy-Oriented Web; to become pervasive across all platforms and services to enable any application to depend on open and interoperable policy-support services.

Looking back at the Flickr case, a rights policy could express that "Your Friends" in your photo have not given permission for their image to be reproduced (outside this specific Social Network). Figure 8 shows the permissions from Flickr for photos, which includes these constraints. In the FaceBook case, a similar policy could express that the family photos are not reproducible outside of Facebook.

Notice that the fundamental differences between Flickr (Figure 8) and FaceBook (Figure 3)

Figure 8. Flickr photo permissions

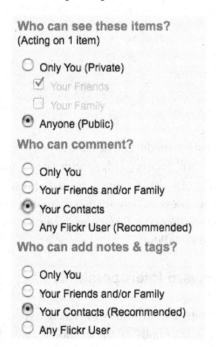

include some permissions (such as excluding named people and "networks" versus "groups") but are also similar in other respects. This means that at one level interoperability across these two Social Networks is possible if they share (and reuse) some of the core policy constructs. However, if one used "policy:group" and the other defined their own "flickr:family" then there will be some issues to overcome. More significant will be the lack of support for some features (eg exclusion of people) that only one Social Network supports.

The Flickr options (see Figure 8) also includes more permissions than just view (render). Specifically, they also allow for "commenting" and "tagging". However, when you look deeper at the Facebook implementation of "view" it does also allow commenting on photos. This implies that if you translate "view" from Flickr to Facebook then you must not allow "commenting" and "tagging", unless they are also specified. This leads to issues of conflict detection across these policies.

For example, this Act:

```
<p:Act p:hasIdentity="urn:facebook:v
iew"/>
```

is similar to:

```
<p:Act p:hasIdentity="urn:flickr:vi
ew"/>
<p:Act p:hasIdentity="urn:flickr:com
ment"/>
<p:Act p:hasIdentity="urn:flickr:t
ag"/>
```

However, the reverse is not true.

These two sets of Acts could be in direct conflict if not used correctly. As they currently stand, the process in determining this conflict may involve prior knowledge, most likely via humans mapping the two core parts of the different policy language ontologies, and building the conflict detection into the software application logic.

The longer term aim is to support services for ontology mappings to help automate this process. Ontology mapping is extremely difficult to generalise but significant research efforts are showing early promises (Euzenat & Shvaiko, 2007). We see this as a key feature of the Policy-Oriented Web and a future research challenge.

The challenges that lay ahead are for the Social Network communities to develop the common vocabularies (ontologies) for the policy expressions. This will enable a policy in Facebook to be supported in Flickr, for example. A greater challenge is the support in different platforms, like web browsers, to be aware that policies are attached to content. This is the long term goal of the Policy-Oriented Web.

5. THE POLICY-ORIENTED WEB CHALLENGES

The Policy-Oriented Web has significant challenges to meet future deployment realities. These ensuing research activities can be clustered into four areas:

. Policy Expression
. Policy Transparency
. Policy Conflict
. Policy Accountability

Policy Expression will focus on representing the interactions and dependencies between the critical policy languages for collaboration and sharing, such as Privacy, Rights, and Identity management. A policy language is a mechanism to declare a set of rules or statements that capture and express the requirements of individuals and organisations from a corporate, legal, best practices, and/or social perspective. Currently, these existing individual policy languages are missing an overall framework and architecture allowing the combination of different policy languages to interoperate and provide an accountable, enforce-

able, flexible and trusted experience for the web community.

The end goal is to develop a framework in which policy languages can coexist and share semantics and to support a wide range of policy functions. This poses fundamental challenges with each language having its own specific goals and context, but having a common impact on web objects when taken together. In particular, how they are harmonised to support open Policy Transparency of distributed policy information, conformance, and behaviour. An unintended consequence of transparency is that it sometimes "intensifies privacy concerns rather than engender trust" (Pollach, 2007) and these needs serious rethinking, redesign, and new approaches.

Policy Conflict is a major challenges of this activity to resolve policy contradictions. For example, it may happen that a user's privacy policy states that a service may not track the user's browsing history, while the service's rights policy says that the user may view the content provided the user's browsing history can be tracked. The first problem is identifying that a conflict exists. The second problem is what to do when the conflict is identified. The appropriate resolution may involve input from the user, and therefore the research must take into account issues surrounding human interaction with these policies.

Policy Accountability is another major challenge to detect policy breaches so that some modicum of accountability can be instilled in the web. This is a departure from the current approach of attempting to provide policy enforcement. Most attempts to provide enforcement on the web (for example, traditional digital rights management for multimedia content) have ended in failure, and are not well accepted by the web community. The accountability mechanism may support recording policy breaches that the user is completely aware of and the consequences of their actions and is a more "relaxed cooperative policy enforcement regime to not discourage users" (Bonatti et al., 2006).

We now review the policy implications for Social Networks using the four Policy-Oriented Web Challenges, in reference to the interoperability between Facebook (see Figure 3) and Flickr (see Figure 8) as a real-world use case.

5.1 Policy Expression

What is clear from Figures 3 and 8 is that the policy decision points are focussed on constraining who the end user party is or what group they are a member of. This is a different approach from past requirements (from the transaction-based DRM world) that was more interested in temporal, spatial and count-based constraints.

For Social Networks, the content owner can specify these types of limitations for who can access their content:

- Only the content owner (i.e. no one else)
- Specific (named) friends and colleagues (both allowed and not allowed)
- Family members
- All direct friends or colleagues
- Your second level friends or colleagues (ie friends of friends)
- All Groups (that the content owner is a member of) or some Groups
- Everyone (ie public)

Policy languages, such as ODRL Version 2.0 (Guth & Iannella, 2009a) will need to be expressive enough to handle these types of conditions. We have begun to look at the extensions needed by ODRL to meet this need (Governatori & Iannella, 2009). One immediate outcome has identified the need for a generic "anyone" party and membership semantics that need to be part of the ODRL Core Metadata 0 (Guth & Iannella, 2009b). This "anyone" party construct can then act as a constraint for smaller subsets of people and groups so that Duties, for example, can be specified.

The expression implication for Policy languages is a need for a "person" entity as well as a role indicator (such as friend, family, contact etc) and a group or membership mechanism.

5.2 Policy Transparency

In Social Networks it is important that there is awareness by all users of policies related to their actions (or inactions) and any consequences. In the examples shown in Figures 3 and 8, the owner of the content is selecting the policy options, but the end recipients (their friends and colleagues etc) are not typically made fully aware of these constraints since they will simply not see the content. For example, if the Flickr photo owner only allows "Commenting" to "Your Friends and Family", then their full list of "Contacts" will simply not know they have been disallowed. In the same case, what is the difference between adding a Comment or a Note to a photo that requires a separation of the two in Flickr, and why conflate "notes and tags" together? What if you wanted your family to add tags and your friends to add comments?

More interestingly, if a Facebook user allows "Friends of Friends" to see some content, then the friend-of-a-friend will not know why they have been granted access - just which they have. This could be very confusing if you then take away that right. The end recipient should be made aware that they have access to this content because they are a friend of a friend.

There are many challenges in this area that deal with how to best inform the end recipient why they have access rights to some content, and why they do not to other content. Policy management systems need to not only inform the user, but know of all the relevant polices related to that user. This implies some federation mechanisms across policy management systems. What is also important is making the end recipient aware of any consequences from not abiding by these policies.

5.3 Policy Conflict

Policy conflict becomes relevant when interoperability between Social Networks is considered. Today, there is very little of this occurring at the policy level. That is, you cannot take all your Flickr photos - together with their policy descriptions - and import them into Facebook - and preserve the policy conditions.

The interoperability issue can only be addressed by first having a common or consistent policy semantics that are supported by various Social Network providers. There needs to be common policy language that can be the lingua-franca of Social Network portability. Even with this in place, the concepts used in each Social Network will need to be harmonised to allow for the mapping between them. Conflicts will occur so there needs to be a way to resolve these, and most may not be machine-resolvable.

For example, in Figure 3 we see that Facebook has the concept of "Friends of Friends" and Flickr does not. So how can we translate a policy that allows content to be seen by Friends of Friends to a service that does not have this concept? Even harder, and more important, is to recognise that there is even a potential conflict point between the two service providers.

Policy conflict will be a long and tedious task to solve. Semantic Web technologies and other more formal logical approaches may be the answer, but much experimentation will be required.

5.4 Policy Accountability

Given that policy interoperability will be a difficult task solely for machines to manage, there is clearly a better model that needs to be involved less "enforcement" and more "cooperation" with users. Social Networks policy management should mirror the real world in which laws are made, people break laws, but they are aware of the consequences of their actions.

It would therefore be more feasible in the long term to allow Policies that are difficult to resolve (e.g., because of unknown semantics or conflicts) to be addressed by the end user. This means that the service can inform the user of the concern/conflict and allow them to make a decision as to what to do next. The process would also make it clear that their actions (either way) would be recorded for future accountability purposes. So the model is to trust the user first and if there is continual abuse of that trust, there is a mechanism to followup and resolve the issue.

Take the above example of "friends of friends" not being supported in Flickr (from a FaceBook policy). In this case the service would say that it does not support/understand this concept but will tell the end user that they can access the content - if they are a friend of Billie's friends. If they continue, then the service can record that fact for any future followup. The alternative would be simply to decline access and that would then have greater detrimental impact on the overall social experience.

6. RELATED WORK

Requirements for any new area of work are always important. A number of research goals in the area of semantic policies include (Bonatti et al., 2006):

- lightweight knowledge representation to reduce the effort for policy-oriented frameworks for specific communities,
- incorporation of controlled natural language syntax for expressing policy rules, and a
- relaxed cooperative policy enforcement regime to not discourage users.

Others (Kolari et al., 2006) indicate that the primary requirement is viewing policies from the privacy and business perspective so as to enable compatibility across the enterprise. Previous international workshops on Semantic Policies presented many papers on emerging requirements for the policy-oriented web, including trust and negotiation mechanisms. However, very few deal with e-Society and Social Networks as the driver and consider the policy requirements from that context.

There are some efforts now appearing on an initial functional architecture for the policy-oriented web. These include the three basic capabilities of (Weitzner et al., 2007):

- policy transaction logs to enable the assessment of past policy decisions, either in real-time or for post-processing,
- policy language framework that enables a shared policy vocabulary to evolve over time from overlapping communities on the web, and
- policy reasoning tools to enable polices to be evaluated and decisions made to assist the user.

There is also relevant work on privacy and identity management in the PRIME Project (Casassa-Mont et al., 2007) and POEM Project (Kaiser, 2007) that has developed detailed enterprise architectures that could be generalised to support policy management tasks within a Social Networks context.

Some frameworks (Clemente et al., 2005) are grounded on XML technology and define architectures consisting of policy management tools, policy databases, policy decision points, and policy enforcement points. Others follow this idea and extend the policy architecture based on a role-based access control model (Bhatti et al., 2005) or view-based access control (Koch & Parisi-Presicce, 2006) and a trading services model (Lamparter et al., 2006). Frameworks also classify policies into high-level and low-level (Pretschner et al., 2006) to reflect and support different enforcement capabilities.

There is a significant body of work that reviews and compares different Privacy languages (such as EPAL, P3P, XACML) and supporting frameworks (Kolari et al., 2005; Tonti et al., 2003; Anderson, 2005; Ardagna et al., 2005; Jensen et al., 2005). Their general conclusion is that a common approach in the future will simplify policy analysis and reduce inconsistencies and promote policy reuse across communities and enhance such policy protection on the web. We have found that our Policy information model (see Figure 8) moves towards this goal, and provides more relevant policy-semantics (over existing languages) to express such policies. For example, Parties and roles, and dual-focus Actions provide clearer semantic and functions more relevant to Social Network requirements.

The application of semantic web technologies to structured policy languages (e.g., XACML) has shown how its expressive power can easily accommodate such transformation and extensions but highlight several aspects for future research (Damiani et al., 2004) and specific needs for a policy language for defining security requirements (Kagal et al., 2003).

Investigation of privacy support in Social Networks has found that third-party access to user information (e.g., via open APIs such as OpenSocial) as potentially compromising (Felt & Evans, 2008) to users as the conformance to the user's policy is solely at the discretion of the third-party. Others found that the user model used for Privacy is not consistent with what is implemented by the Social Network providers (Chew et al., 2008) nor the way a user's privacy decisions are based on the relationship with the provider as well as other individuals (Grandison & Maximilien, 2008).

We have also been working on extending the ODRL rights expression language (Guth & Iannella, 2009a) to accommodate more general policy features. We expect that this will be the basic model that could be widely deployed given its success in the mobile community.

7. CONCLUSION

We have seen that Social Networks have become an "overnight" phenomenon - backed up by Web 2.0 technologies - and provide rich user experiences. We have also shown that some of these experiences are not socially (or legally) acceptable. This is a golden opportunity for the Policy-Oriented Web to play a more significant role in the e-Society. The core area would be to better express the semantics of policies covering the access to user-generated content, and users' personal preferences.

We have also defined the basis for a flexible information model that can underpin the Policy-Oriented Web and promote it as a new platform that will enable pervasive policy management across Web 2.0. We have shown some examples of applying the Policy-Oriented Web language to some use cases from real issues dealing with Social Networks. The current model is not complete and we expect that there will be a number of enhancements that can be applied to this preliminary semantic model with additional use cases, but the key idea is that we can begin to articulate the core concepts, classes, and relationships for a policy language framework. Future research areas will include policy conflict detection and accountability.

These are just the first steps in bringing policy-supportive technologies to the e-Society communities. These communities thrive on "simple" technologies that address their needs. The Policy-Oriented Web - as a semantic policy platform - will need to be integrated into the Web 2.0 style of technologies. This means more work is needed on the user interfaces for policy interactions and the integration with existing Web 2.0 platforms and deployment technologies. The end result should see the Policy-Oriented Web supporting more of the e-Society needs and evolving into a more user-focused technology platform.

ACKNOWLEDGMENT

NICTA is funded by the Australian Government as represented by the Department of Broadband, Communications and the Digital Economy and the Australian Research Council through the ICT Centre of Excellence program and the Queensland Government.

REFERENCES

Anderson, A. (2005). *A comparison of two Privacy Policy Languages: EPAL and XACML* (Sun Microsystems Labs Tech. Rep.). Retrieved from http://research.sun.com/techrep/2005/smli_tr-2005-147/

Ardagna, C., Damiani, E., De Capitani di Vimercati, S., Fugazza, C., & Samarati, P. (2005). *Offline Expansion of XACML Policies Based on P3P Metadata (. LNCS, 3579,* 363–374.

Arnab, A., & Hutchison, A. (2007, October 11-13). DRM Use License Negotiation using ODRL v2.0. In *Proceedings 5th International Workshop for Technology, Economy, and Legal Aspects of Virtual Goods and the 3rd International ODRL Workshop*, Koblenz, Germany.

Bhatti, R., Ghafoor, A., Bertino, E., & Joshi, J. B. D. (2005). X-GTRBAC: an XML-based policy specification framework and architecture for enterprise-wide access control. [TISSEC]. *ACM Transactions on Information and System Security, 8*(2), 187–227. doi:10.1145/1065545.1065547

Bonatti, P. A., Duma, C., Fuchs, N., Nejdl, W., Olmedilla, D., Peer, J., & Shahmehri, N. (2006). Semantic Web Policies - A Discussion of Requirements and Research Issues. In *Proceedings of the European Semantic Web Conference (ESWC 2006)* (LNCS 4011, pp. 712-724). New York: Springer.

Casassa-Mont, M., Crosta, S., Kriegelstein, T., & Sommer, D. (2007). *PRIME Architecture V2*. Retrieved March 29, 2007 from https://www. primeproject.eu/prime_products/reports/arch/ pub_del_D14.2.c_ec_WP14.2_v1_Final.pdf>

Chew, M., Balfanz, D., & Laurie, B. (2008, May 18-21). Mining Privacy in Social Networks. Web 2.0 Security and Privacy. In *Proceedings of the 2008 IEEE Symposium on Security and Privacy*, Oakland, California.

Clemente, F. J. G., Perez, G. M., & Skarmeta, A. F. G. (2005). An XML-Seamless Policy Based Management Framework. *LCNS, 3685*, 418–423.

Cohen, N. (2007, October 1). Use My Photo? Not Without Permission. *New York Times*. Retrieved from http://www.nytimes.com/2007/10/01/ technology/01link.html?ex=1348977600&en=1 82a46901b23f450&ei=5124&partner=permalin k&exprod=permalink

Damiani, E., De Capitani di Vimercati, S., Fugazza, C., & Samarati, P. (2004). *Extending Policy Languages to the Semantic Web* (LNCS 3140, pp. 330-343).

Euzenat, J., & Shvaiko, P. (2007). *Ontology Matching*. Berlin: Springer-Verlag.

Felt, A., & Evans, D. (2008, May 18-21). Privacy Protection for Social Networking Platforms. In *Proceedings of the Web 2.0 Security and Privacy at the 2008 IEEE Symposium on Security and Privacy*, Oakland, California.

García, R., & Gil, R. (2006, November). An OWL Copyright Ontology for Semantic Digital Rights Management. In Proceedings of the *IFIP WG 2.12 & WG 12.4 International Workshop on Web Semantics*, Montpellier, France.

Governatori, G., & Iannella, R. (2009, August 31-September 4). Modelling and Reasoning Languages for Social Networks Policies. In *Proceedings of the Thirteenth IEEE International EDOC Conference*, Auckland, New Zealand.

Grandison, T., & Maximilien, E. M. (2008, May 18-21). Towards Privacy Propagation in the Social Web. In *Proceedings of the Web 2.0 Security and Privacy at the 2008 IEEE Symposium on Security and Privacy*, Oakland, California.

Guth, S., & Iannella, R. (2009, September 23). *ODRL Version 2.0 Core Model* (Draft Specification). Retrieved from http://odrl.net/2.0/DS-ODRL-Model.html

Guth, S., & Iannella, R. (2009, September 25). *ODRL Version 2.0 Common Vocabulary* (Working Draft). Retrieved from http://odrl.net/2.0/ WD-ODRL-Vocab.html

Hu, Y. J. (2007). Semantic-Driven Enforcement of Rights Delegation Policies via the Combination of Rules and Ontologies. In *Proceedings of the Workshop on Privacy Enforcement and Accountability with Semantics, International Semantic Web Conference*, Busan, Korea.

Iannella, R. (2002, September 19). *Open Digital Rights Language* (Version 1.1 Specification). Retrieved from http://odrl.net/1.1/ODRL-11.pdf> and <http://www.w3.org/TR/odrl/

Iannella, R. (2009, January 15-16). Industry Challenges for Social and Professional Networks. In *Proceedings of the W3C Workshop on the Future of Social Networking*, Barcelona, Spain. Retrieved from http://www.w3.org/2008/09/msnws/papers/ nicta-position-paper.pdf

Iannella, R., Henricksen, K., & Robinson, R. (2006, October 17-18). A Policy Oriented Architecture for the Web: New Infrastructure and New Opportunities. In *Proceedings of the W3C Workshop on Languages for Privacy Policy Negotiation and Semantics-Driven Enforcement*, Ispra, Italy.

Jensen, C., Tullio, J., Potts, C., & Mynatt, E. D. (2005). *STRAP: A Structured Analysis Framework for Privacy* (Tech. Rep. No. GIT-GVU-05-02). Atlanta, GA: Georgia Institute of Technology.

Kagal, L., Finin, T., & Joshi, A. (2003, October 20-23). A Policy Based Approach to Security for the Semantic Web. In *Proceedings of 2nd International Semantic Web Conference (ISWC2003)*, Sanibel Island, Florida.

Kaiser, M. (2007, November). Toward the Realization of Policy-Oriented Enterprise Management. *IEEE Computer*, 57-63.

Koch, M., & Parisi-Presicce, F. (2006). UML specification of access control policies and their formal verification. *Software and Systems Modeling, 5*(4), 429–447. doi:10.1007/s10270-006-0030-z

Kolari, P., Ding, L., Shashidhara, G., Joshi, A., Finin, T., & Kagal, L. (2005, June 6-8). Enhancing Web privacy protection through declarative policies. In *Proceedings of the Sixth IEEE International Workshop on Policies for Distributed Systems and Networks* (pp. 57- 66).

Kolari, P., Finin, T., Yesha, Y., Lyons, K., Hawkins, J., & Perelgut, S. (2006). Policy Management of Enterprise Systems: A Requirements Study. In *Proceedings of the Seventh IEEE International Workshop on Policies for Distributed Systems and Networks*.

Lamparter, S., Ankolekar, A., Studer, R., Oberle, D., & Weinhardt, C. (2006, August 14-16). A policy framework for trading configurable goods and services in open electronic markets. In *Proceedings of the 8th International Conference on Electronic Commerce, Fredericton*, New Brunswick, Canada.

Media Watch, A. B. C. (2007). Filleting Facebook. *Australian Broadcasting Corporation (ABC)*. Retrieved October 29, 2007 from http://www.abc.net.au/mediawatch/transcripts/s2074079.htm

OASIS. (2005, February 1). *eXtensible Access Control Markup Language (XACML)* (Version 2.0, OASIS Standard). Retrieved from http://docs.oasis-open.org/xacml/2.0/XACML-2.0-OS-NORMATIVE.zip

Pollach, I. (2007, September). What's Wrong With Online Privacy Policies? *Communications of the ACM*.

Pretschner, A., Hilty, M., & Basin, D. (2006). Distributed usage control. *Communications of the ACM, 49*.

Qui, X. (2008). Citizen Engagement: Driving Force of E-Society Development. IFIP International Federation for Information Processing. In Wang, W. (Ed.), *Integration and Innovation Orient to E-Society* (*Vol. 252*, pp. 540–548). New York: Springer.

Tonti, G., Bradshaw, J., Jeffers, R., Montanari, R., Suri, N., & Uszok, A. (2003). Semantic Web Languages for Policy Representation and Reasoning: A Comparison of Kaos, Rei, and Ponder. In *Proceedings of the 2nd International Semantic Web Conference (ISWC2003)* (LCNS 2870, pp. 419-437). New York: Springer.

Weitzner, D. J., Abelson, H., Berners-Lee, T., Feigenbaum, J., Hendler, J., & Sus, G. J. (2007, June 13). *Information Accountability* (Tech. Rep. No. MIT-CSAIL-TR-2007-034). MIT Computer Science and Artificial Intelligence Laboratory.

Wenning, R., & Schunter, M. (2006, November 13). *The Platform for Privacy Preferences 1.1 (P3P1.1) Specification* (W3C Working Group Note). Retrieved from http://www.w3.org/TR/P3P11/

This work was previously published in International Journal of E-Adoption, Volume 2, Issue 1, edited by Sushil K. Sharma, pp. 13-29, copyright 2010 by IGI Publishing (an imprint of IGI Global).

Chapter 8

Electronic Voting Using Identity Domain Separation and Hardware Security Modules

Thomas Rössler

Secure Information Technology Center Austria (A-SIT), Austria

ABSTRACT

E-voting increasingly gains interest in e-Democracy and e-Government movements. Not only the technical security issues of electronic voting systems are of paramount importance, but also the necessity of following an all-embracing approach is challenging and needs to be addressed. This paper discusses e-voting as being a supreme discipline of e-Government. It introduces an innovative e-voting concept using the Internet as the voting channel. The concept introduced is based on Austrian e-Government elements and the Austrian identity management concept in particular. This paper presents a novel approach of building an e-voting system relying on two core principles: strong end-to-end encryption and stringent identity domain separation.

INTRODUCTION

Voting is the most important tool in democratic decision making. Therefore, elections and referenda should be accessible to as many people as possible. It is especially difficult for citizens living abroad to participate in elections.

DOI: 10.4018/978-1-4666-0041-6.ch008

The word e-voting is a general term that refers to any type of voting in electronic form. This work introduces a remote Internet e-voting concept that suits the needs of international election fundamentals—as formulated by the Venice Commission (Venice Commission, 2002) and the Council of Europe (Council of Europe, 2004a, 2004b)—and the needs of Austrian elections (Working-Group "E-Voting", 2004) in particular[1].

Today, the e-Government infrastructure is highly developed in many member states of the European Union. Austria in particular has actively pursued its e-Government strategy since the beginning and thus is today one of leading countries in Europe with respect to e-Government.

E-voting, seen as a special application of e-Government technologies, can be considered as being the supreme discipline of all e-Government applications due to its conflicting priorities of unique identification and perfect anonymity.

The proposed e-voting concept draws upon two principles in order to protect the election secrecy. On the one hand, the proposed e-voting system makes use of strong end-to-end encryption between the voter casting her vote and the electronic device responsible for counting. Thus, the cast vote is immediately encrypted by the voter after she has filled in her decision and is only decrypted for the single moment of counting. On the other hand, the proposed e-voting concept introduces a stringent domain separation model that has to ensure unique identification of voters during registration, but also guarantee perfect anonymity of cast votes. A special case in the introduced e-voting concept is that although votes are cast anonymously it is still possible to determine whether a given voter has cast her vote already or not. This mechanism is available during the election event only. This is important and a big advantage of the proposed scheme as it enables a voter to cast her vote conventionally at a polling station although she has decided to vote electronically. This characteristic of the proposed e-voting concept faces problems in connection with the Internet and the voter's local infrastructure as raised by the SERVE-report (Jefferson, Rubin, Simons, & Wagner, 2004) for instance.

From a technical perspective, the proposed e-voting concept makes use of Austrian e-Government components such as the Citizen Card (Hollosi, Karlinger, Rössler, & Centner, 2008; Leitold, Hollosi, & Posch, 2002; see also Rössler, Hayat, Posch, & Leitold, 2005). Although the core principles of this e-voting concept are versatile, the resulting e-voting concept is tailored to a certain degree for Austrian elections. Thus, the proposed e-voting concept has been named "EVITA" (Electronic Voting over the Internet - Tailored for Austria). The EVITA voting model aims to follow the process model of conventional postal elections which has two phases. In phase one, voters have to register and in phase two the voting process is carried out. Also from a technical perspective EVITA follows tight the model of postal elections. The EVITA scheme requires to encrypt the voter's decision without any identifying information and to attach additional voter related information to the encrypted vote. This corresponds to scenario of postal election scenarios where the vote is put into an inner envelope which itself is wrapped by an outer envelope that contains additional identifying information about the voter.

This paper introduces the core elements of the proposed EVITA-voting concept. The rest of this paper is organised as follows. The next section explains the core principles of the EVITA concept and introduces the dual approach of using strong end-to-end encryption and stringent identity domain separation. Section 3 and 4 further elaborate these core aspects—the creation of the identifiers following the Austrian electronic identity management in particular—in several sub-sections in detail. Section 5 briefly sketches the counting phase; in section 6 two additional elements of the EVITA-concept are accentuated: the structure of ballots and the principle of indirect voter authentication through cast votes. Finally conclusions are drawn.

CORE ELEMENTS OF THE EVITA SCHEMA

First of all, an e-voting schema (EVS) must guarantee that a voter's decision remains an inviolable secret. To do so, most of them use cryptographic mechanisms and principles. Existing e-voting schemes can be grouped as follows:

- EVS based on Homomorphic Encryption, e.g., (Cohen & Fischer, 1985; Cohen & Yung, 1986; Cramer, Gennaro, & Shoenmakers, 1997)
- EVS based on Mixing Nets, e.g., (Chaum, 1981; Juang & Lei, 1996; Hirt & Sako, 2000)
- EVS based on Blind Signatures, e.g., (Chaum, 1981; Fujioka, Okamoto, & Ohta, 1992; Okamoto, 1997)

To guarantee that a voter's decision remains an inviolable secret, two distinct general approaches seem to be promising. One approach is to have a voting scheme that prevents the vote from being spied on by applying cryptographic methods. Another approach for protecting the secrecy of the ballots is by removing any form of identifying information from the cast vote thus breaking any link between the voter and her cast vote. Both approaches have drawbacks and advantages. Furthermore, regarding the requirements given by the targeted use-cases neither approach by itself would be satisfactory.

In the first approach, the use of encryption algorithms seems to be adequate. Various strong encryption algorithms exist, so the question that remains is how and where to hold the decryption keys needed to decrypt votes. There are several schemes which do not need to decrypt votes in order to count them (e.g., schemes based on homomorphic encryption), but those approaches have limitations regarding write-in votes or they are too complex.

However, the use of strong encryption algorithms in order to protect the secrecy of ballots is no guarantee that these algorithms will be able to resist attack in the future. Due to the ever-increasing power of new computer systems it could become quite easy to crack a given encrypted vote by a brute force attack (e.g., by trying all encryption keys possible).

Therefore, using strong encryption mechanisms in combination with a comprehensive identity management concept in order to keep cast votes anonymous throughout the election and beyond are the key elements of the EVITA e-voting schema. Due to a sophisticated identification and authentication model that is based on the Austrian identity management concept[2], it can be ensured that the identity of a voter cannot be determined based on her cast vote, especially after the election. This eliminates the progressive weakness inherent to encryption algorithms.

ENCRYPTION USING A HARDWARE SECURITY MODULE

From the moment the voter makes her decision there is no more need to reveal it except for the reason of counting. There is no need to uncover the voter's decision, her vote respectively, at any other time. The aim is to achieve an end-to-end encryption of the cast vote between the voter and the counting device. At this point two questions arise. How to provide the voter with the encryption key and how to ensure that only the counting device is able to decrypt the vote. An obvious answer to the first question is to use an asymmetric encryption algorithm and a public key infrastructure. The latter question is more difficult to address as both technical and organisational measurements have to be put in place.

One technical solution for protecting the confidentiality of the private decryption key is to build the counting device on the basis of a hardware security module. Due to this, the private key used for decrypting of cast votes is solely stored in the hardware security module in a very secure way. However, additional organisational and technical measures are required in order to address the process of key generation and distribution. The private key—or any copy of it—must not exist outside the hardware security module without any technical or non-technical security measure.

In order to export, backup and (re-)import the private key of the hardware security module—which is necessary in real election scenarios—an adequate and sophisticated key management must be put in place. It would be a desirable to require the hardware security module to provide a key export and import mechanism following a defined shared key schema (e.g., see Desmedt, 1992, 1994; Desmedt & Frankel, 1989). If a shared key schema is provided, a dedicated organisational framework has to be defined that states how to distribute the key shares and to whom. The organisational framework as well as the legal framework of an election must state clearly how many shares are required at a minimum to import or reset the decryption key of the hardware security module. Furthermore, it must describe which organisations—or more generally which entities of the election process—are eligible to hold a key share. From an organisational and legal perspective, a shared key schema would be perfect for replicating the legal responsibilities of the participating political parties regarding the election.

The EVITA approach is to decrypt the vote only at the very single moment of counting; a cast vote remains encrypted at any time before and after counting. This contrasts with other e-voting approaches where votes are decrypted before counting. However, the counting device holds the decryption key for decrypting the votes within the counting process. It must meet the requirements of a hardware security module in order ensure that the key cannot be exported or stolen. Furthermore, the counting device must ensure that votes are decrypted only for the purpose of counting. There must not be any chance to learn decrypted votes by accessing the counting device by any means. It is not sufficient to use a hardware security module only for the purpose of securely holding the keys. Additional critical components of the counting device—critical with respect to revealing encrypted votes unintentionally—are the

counters used to compute the result. The counting device must not offer any possibility of finding out intermediate results or to observe the current status of the counting process. However, logs for recording information might be put in place throughout the counting process by the counting device in order to collect additional information that confirm the correctness of the count, e.g. for an election audit.

DOMAIN SEPARATION AND IDENTIFICATION MODEL

On the one hand, the process requires unique identification of the voter in the course of the registration procedure in order to record who has cast her vote. On the other hand, the cast vote must not be linkable to the voter. Although these requirements seem to be contradictory, the EVITA voting schema meets both requirements by introducing a sophisticated identification concept and domain separation schema (domain separation with respect to identity domains).

The concept of domain separation is based on the need-to-know principle since neither of the involved authorities—usually we have two authorities: a Registration Authority dealing with registration issues and an Election Authority dealing with the election itself—need to know the voter's unique identity (identifier). Usually it is sufficient to identify the voter within a dedicated context. This principle is also the underlying idea of the whole identity management of Austrian e-Government and the Citizen Card concept.

The Austrian identity management concept introduces a unique identifier for each citizen, called Source Personal Identification Number (sPIN), as well as identifiers for sectors of applications, called Sector Specific Personal Identification Numbers (ssPIN), in order to uniquely identify a citizen within a given sector of applications. It is important to note that a person's sPIN is only stored in her Citizen Card. There exists neither a register of sPINs nor is any authority or application allowed to handle or store them. Applications and authorities are only allowed to work with sector-specific identifiers which are derived from a person's sPIN by applying cryptographic one-way functions (the next section describes this derivation process in detail).

Since it was the aim to develop an e-voting schema that is fully compliant with Austrian e-Government elements, the EVITA voting schema adopts and extends the concept of sector-specific identifiers.

The EVITA voting schema follows a two phase approach, which differs between registration phase and election phase. Therefore, the identification schema needs to be discussed and developed in two levels. On the first level, the identification schema must handle registration issues. On the second level, the identification schema must offer the possibility to determine whether or not a voter has cast her vote already.

To clarify the requirements for the identification schema, here is a list of scenarios and phases where identification is necessary:

1. **During the registration phase:** The voter requests to vote electronically using her Citizen Card.
2. **During the election phase:** In the event the voter is unable to vote electronically—due to technical problems within the voter's technical environment etc.—the voter should have the possibility to visit a polling station in order to vote conventionally (this is a design requirement for the EVITA concept). At the polling station, the election officials must (electronically) identify the voter in order to determine whether she has already cast her vote via e-voting or not.
3. **During the election phase:** In the course of casting a vote electronically, the voting system should determine whether the voter has already cast a vote or not, in order to prevent double votes.

Although the second and the third scenarios appear to contradict the election secrecy at first glance, the proposed domain separation model is able to solve the problem. Thus EVITA proposes an identification schema that is built on the established identity management concept of Austrian e-Government and makes use of two different identifiers which are loosely bound to each other using cryptographic technologies.

From an organisational point of view, there are two different domains. The registration system has to identify the voter in existing registers and databases, such as the register of voters, the Central Resident Register, etc. The representation of a voter's identity must match existing records of registers and authorities; therefore, the first form of identity is taken directly from the conventional identity management system of the Austrian e-Government, i.e. a conventional sector-specific personal identification number (ssPIN). Since these registers are used for conventional elections as well, they usually contain additional information about the voter, such as her given name, name, date of birth, etc.

The information attached to the encrypted vote must contain some identification information in order to determine whether a voter has already cast her vote and thus prevent double votes. The latter question is important when conducting a conventional election in parallel and allowing e-voters to cast their votes by conventional means as well (in the event of technical problems, etc.).

So, two different domains and two different representations of a voter's identity appear necessary:

1. The first domain is denoted as Registration Domain and it deals with identifiers taken from the conventional Austrian e-Government (such as ssPIN).
2. The second domain is denoted as Election Domain and it deals with identifiers distinct from those of the Registration Domain.

A bidirectional link must not be allowed to exist between the identity representations of both domains. Nevertheless, it must be possible to prove whether or not a given voter has already cast a vote by checking the voter's identity representation in the Registration Domain.

Only in the event that an e-voter is not able to cast her vote electronically for some reason and thus shows up at a conventional polling station to cast her vote it is legitimate to search for the existence of the voter's vote. It must be noted that this is a strict uni-directional query from a given (conventional) identity to the appropriate cast vote. In terms of identity representations, it means that a corresponding identity representation in the Election Domain should be derivable from a given identity representation in the Registration Domain but not vice versa.

The requirement is to define two identity domains and two respective identity representations in which a corresponding identity representation in the Election Domain can be derived from a given identity representation in the Registration Domain. This requirement leads to having a link between identity representations from the Registration Domain and the corresponding personal identifiers of the Election Domain. Creating this link using simple derivation mechanisms—following the mechanism used for deriving a ssPIN from a given sPIN—is not satisfactory since the identity representations of the Registration Domain are conventional e-governmental identifiers and are based more or less on conventional identification information (such as name, date of birth, etc.). Without additional measures it would be too easy to find out a citizen's identity representation in the Registration Domain, and with this information find the corresponding identity representation in the Election Domain.

The EVITA voting schema suggests creating the link between the personal identifiers in the Registration Domain and the corresponding identifiers in the Election Domain as depicted in Figure 1. This sketch outlines both domains and the different forms of identifiers.

The Registration Domain deals with conventional electronic identifiers; i.e. sPIN and a sector-specific identifier which is specific to the election event (ssPIN(v)). In the course of crossing domains, the EVITA schema requires that a special personal identification number be derived that is only to be used within the Election Domain—referred to as a vPIN—from a given ssPIN(v). By applying a mathematical one-way function (HASH function), the link between the ssPIN(v) and the derived vPIN is uni-directional, pointing from the Registration Domain to the Election Domain. Furthermore, in order to have no permanent direct link between both identifiers, the derivation procedure applies secret keys.

Since the link between both domains is only necessary during the election event (according to the requirements defined before: after election there is usually no need to search for a voter's cast vote after polling stations have been closed), the secret keys that are used to create a vPIN from a given ssPIN(v) are needed during the term of the election event only and have to be destroyed immediately after the election event. This can be ensured on a technical level by using hardware security modules for generating and holding the keys. If the hardware security modules do not provide functionality for exporting the keys, there would not exist any copy of these secret keys outside the hardware security module, thus there would be no way to create a vPIN from a given ssPIN(v) without using the hardware security module. The link between ssPIN(v) and vPIN can be permanently broken by securely erasing the secret keys or by destroying the corresponding hardware security modules.

In order to prevent any kind of abuse, it is important to log whenever the system is used to transform a ssPIN(v) to a vPIN. The use of hardware security modules means that there is only one single point to control, so it is easy to apply

Figure 1. Cryptographic link between registration domain and election domain

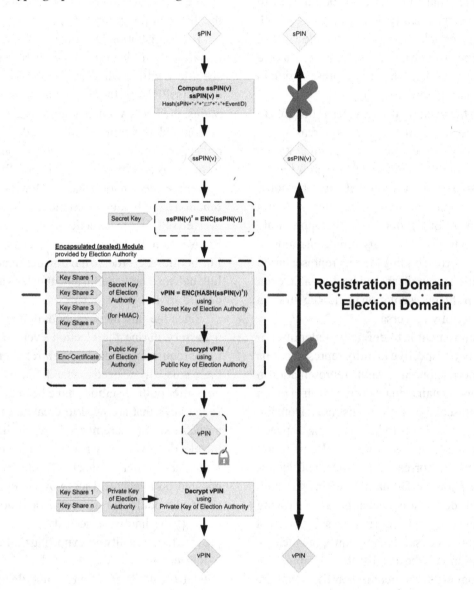

both technical and organisational mechanisms to prevent abuse.

Registration Domain: Creation and Use of ssPIN(v)

The voter registers for electronic voting using a process provided in the Registration Domain. Since the application for electronic voting requires discrete identity data as well, such as the voter's name, date of birth etc., a conventional sector specific identifier is used.

The registration service usually identifies the voter using her Citizen Card. This means that the registration process has access to the sPIN, and can also find out the application-specific sectoral identifier ssPIN(v). The ssPIN(v) is the conventional sectoral identifier specific to an election. The registration application contacts registers—such as the Central Resident Register or the electronic register of voters—using the ssPIN(v). As the ssPIN(v) conforms to the conventional identification schema of Austrian e-Government, every register is able to resolve the identifier and provide the requested information.

All actions taken in the registration phase correspond to conventional governmental processes. Therefore, the personal identifier used within the Registration Domain is a conventional sector-specific personal identifier. The sectoral identifier is derived from the voter's unique sPIN following the schema defined in the Austrian identification schema (Hollosi, & Hörbe, 2006). The following expression (see figure 2) shows the whole derivation process in detail.

Election Domain: Creation and Use of vPIN

In contrast to the Registration Domain, the Election Domain does not require any discrete identity information about the voter. It is not even necessary to identify the voter in person within the Election Domain since the processes of the Election Domain do not deal with identification but rather with authorisation. The election process is not interested in the unique identity of the voter. The only thing the voter has to prove is that she is eligible to vote.

There needs to be a way to track which voter has already cast a vote. This is necessary when running a conventional election process in parallel and considering the conventional election process as a fallback scenario for the electronic election. This implies that the officials at the polling station must be able to prove whether or not the voter has already cast a vote. It must be kept in mind that the voter at the polling station might only be carrying a conventional identity card, e.g. a passport, which leads to the requirement of having a link from a voter's conventional identity information through a sectoral identifier (ssPIN(v)) to her corresponding identifier of the Election Domain (vPIN).

The creation of a ssPIN(v) from a set of discrete identity information which is sufficient enough to identify the person uniquely is only possible with the help of the so called Source PIN Register Authority. Thus it is possible to determine a voter's ssPIN(v) based on the information given on her conventional identity card. As a consequence, the algorithm for creating the vPIN has to take the ssPIN(v) as input. Moreover, this creation algorithm must always yield the same vPIN for a given ssPIN(v). Since the link between ssPIN(v) and vPIN is only needed temporarily, there must be a way to remove the link relation permanently, for example, immediately after the election event. The algorithm given in the following equation (see figure 3) achieves both requirements:

The algorithm for creating vPINs is a logical continuation of the ssPIN(v) algorithm. Here again

Figure 2. The creation of a ssPIN(v)

$$ssPIN(v) = HASH(sPIN \oplus \text{"}ed\text{"})$$

sPIN	the voter's sPIN
'ed'	short-name of the sector, e.g. election and democracy (ed)
HASH	cryptographic one way function
$\oplus$	concatenation of two strings

Figure 3. The creation of a vPIN

$$vPIN = HMAC\big(ENC\big(ssPIN(v)\big)_{SK_{RA}}\big)_{SK_{EA}}$$

SK_{EA}	secret key of the Election Authority
SK_{RA}	secret key of the Registration Authority
HMAC	keyed hash function; e.g. realized through ENC(HASH(x))
ENC	symmetric encryption algorithm

the algorithm makes use of a one-way function (HASH function) in order to ensure uni-directionality. Contrary to the creation of the ssPIN(v), the algorithm for creating vPINs requires a secret security measure for both the Registration Domain and the Election Domain. This measure may be implemented in several ways, for instance by adding secret phrases or by applying cryptographic algorithms such as encryption algorithms or keyed HASH functions.

The proposed algorithm for creating a vPIN takes the previously created ssPIN(v) as input. First, the algorithm adds the secret of the Registration Domain to the ssPIN(v) by applying a symmetric encryption algorithm (e.g., 3DES, AES). Here the encryption algorithm makes use of a secret key which is under the sole control of the Registration Authority (i.e. the authority controlling the Registration Domain/Process). The resulting encrypted ssPIN(v) is further derived by applying a keyed HASH function as a one-way function. This keyed HASH function (HMAC) not only creates the HASH value for the given input but also combines it with a secret by applying a secret key provided by the Election Authority (i.e. the authority controlling the Election Domain/ Process). Instead of a HMAC, a sequence consisting of HASH function and encryption could be used as well.

As a result, the link between a vPIN and the underlying ssPIN(v) cannot be created without knowing both secret keys. Thus both secret keys are important elements of the vPIN-creation algorithm, which leads to a temporary link be-

tween the personal identifiers of both domains. In other words, both authorities have to cooperate to uncover a voter's identifier. Therefore, Registration Authority and Election Authority have to be separated by organisational means, which is common in elections.

Just involving secret keys in the derivation process as a technical measure is not sufficient. Additional organisational measures are required. The management of the secret keys is of crucial importance since possession of both secret keys enables the owner to create vPINs. Therefore, each secret key has to be provided and handled within the respective domain by the according authority and has to be handled appropriately. The use of a hardware security module is not only strongly recommended, but rather should be treated as a requirement for creating and holding the keys securely.

Figure 1 shows the proposed approach for handling both secret keys. This proposal suggests using a shared key schema for the handling of the Election Authority's secret key. The key shares should be held by the members and representatives of the election commission. In order to permanently break the link between the identifiers of both domains, it is sufficient to destroy at least one of both secret keys.

Figure 1 also highlights a second but very important issue in the vPIN creation process. Since a vPIN is created by using a specific ssPIN(v) as input, the creation process should be located within the Registration Domain. The process has to ensure that the vPIN that is created cannot be accessed by any entity in the Registration Domain. Therefore, the schema requires encryption of the vPIN for the Election Authority (Election Domain) immediately after it has been created.

Any technical implementation of the vPIN-creation process must follow the requirements stated above. In addition to all technical measures there is a strong need for organisational measures. Thus it is recommended that the Election Authority provide the technical implementation for dealing with its secret keys for the vPIN creation process by means of a sealed module (e.g. sealed hardware and electronically signed software) that contains a hardware security module holding all keys of the Election Authority (see "Encapsulated (sealed) Module" in figure 1).

SKETCH OF THE CAST VOTE AND COUNTING PHASE

For a complete understanding it is important to sketch the cast vote and counting process briefly. In order to cast a vote, the voter has simply to contact a server of the Election Authority which takes the voter's encrypted vote. As mentioned before, a cast vote consists of two parts: the inner part holding the encrypted vote which solely contains the voter's decision; the outer part holding at least the voter's vPIN in order to detect double votes and to mark which voter has cast a vote. During counting—which might take place any time later—the counting module removes the outer part of votes and just takes the encrypted inner part as input for counting. All encrypted parts become mixed up and fed into the counting device (i.e., a hardware security module) which decrypts votes and prepares the final result. The hardware security module of the counting device solely holds the private key to decrypt votes.

The EVITA approach is to decrypt the vote only at the very single moment of counting; a cast vote remains encrypted at any time before and after counting. This contrasts with other e-voting approaches where votes are decrypted before counting. However, when re-counts are considered, keeping votes encrypted is more advantageous. The counting device holds the decryption key for decrypting the votes within the counting process. It must meet the requirements of a hardware security module in order ensure that the key cannot be exported or stolen. Furthermore, the counting device must ensure that votes are decrypted only for the purpose of counting. There must not be any chance to learn decrypted votes by accessing the counting device by any means. It is not sufficient to use a hardware security module only for the purpose of securely holding the keys. Additional critical components of the counting device—critical with respect to revealing encrypted votes unintentionally—are the counters used to compute the result. The counting device must not offer any possibility of finding out intermediate results or to observe the current status of the counting process. However, logs for recording information might be put in place throughout the counting process by the counting device in order to collect additional information that confirm the correctness of the count, e.g. for an election audit. This information also must not be disclosed to anybody during counting as it can be used to reveal cast votes.

This sketch of the counting phase is very simplified. Important details, such as an additional signature on votes (before casting) to prevent manipulation of cast votes or the mechanism of indirect voter authentication, have been omitted.

ADDITIONAL ELEMENTS OF THE EVITA CONCEPT

This section finally emphasizes two additional elements of the EVITA-concept: the structure of ballots and the principle of indirect voter authentication through cast votes.

Ballot, Ballot Envelope, Ballot Card and Vote

The core data structure of the EVITA voting concept is the ballot, which consists of several elements. The ballot is a container which stores all required data elements for a voter during the election event. Thus, the content of a ballot is added to during different phases and grows incrementally. Figure 4 depicts all phases and elements of a ballot at a glance.

With respect to the syntactical structure of the ballot, the EVITA voting system strongly recommends the use of an XML structure since XML is not only one of the major basis technologies used in Austrian e-Government but also because a standardised XML language for election purposes already exists, i.e. EML (Borras, 2007).

OASIS has a technical committee that is responsible for developing EML being a standardised language for *"the structured interchange of data among hardware, software, and service providers who engage in any aspect of providing election or voter services to public or private organizations"* (Borras, 2007, p. 6).

It is highly recommended to incorporate international standards and definitions whenever possible (e.g., see the Council of Europe's recommendation (Council of Europe, 2004a), number 67 and 68). It is especially important to use standardised interfaces—and EML is considered a standardised interface—because it makes it easier for external election observers to verify the data flow between the modules of an e-voting system. Furthermore, using a standardised interface offers the opportunity to draw on existing products and systems if available.

Indirect Voter Authentication

The EVITA voting schema does not require the voter to sign her ballot before casting to prevent any manipulation of the ballot after being cast. Instead, this voting schema introduces an additional Asserting Authority which blindly signs the ballot. Thanks to the proposed registration and asserting processes of the EVITA voting schema, even the voter herself can be indirectly repetitively authenticated by her cast ballot.

Indirect voter authentication is based on the combination of the registration and asserting

Figure 4. Left: initial ballot. Middle: ballot after the encrypted vote has been added. Right: complete ballot containing the encrypted vote.

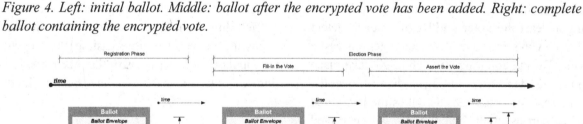

process. During the registration process, the voter is identified and authenticated by providing her Citizen Card. To be more precisely, identification and authentication requires the citizen to provide a SAML-assertion called Identity-Link which is stored on her Citizen Card and to create an electronic signature by using her Citizen Card. The Identity-Link is an XML-based data structure which combines the citizen's sPIN with her public keys that are used to verify her electronic signatures. The Identity-Link itself is signed by the issuing Source PIN Register Authority to confirm its authenticity. Therefore, using the Identity-Link it is possible to create the relation between a citizen's electronic signature and her claimed identity.

Based on this, the registration service creates the voter's voting credentials which are immediately encrypted by applying the voter's public key that is provided in the voter's Identity-Link. Thus it is ensured that the voting credentials that are returned—containing her blank ballot card and ballot envelope—are only able to be decrypted by the voter's Citizen Card. This implies that the person who is able to decrypt the voting credentials is the same person who registered and to whom the voting credentials have been issued.

The same argumentation is applicable to the asserting process. During the asserting process, the voter is identified and authenticated once again by providing her Identity-Link and an electronic signature. In addition, the voter provides her encrypted blinded ballot and asks the Asserting Authority to blindly sign it. As a result, the asserting service blindly signs the ballot and returns the resulting signature value encrypted with the voter's public key. Thus, the voter's blindly signed encrypted ballot is encrypted again for the voter who has been identified by the provided Identity-Link. Finally, after the voter has decrypted the signature value, she has to unblind it according to the blind signature schema applied. The decrypted and unblinded signature value resulting from the asserting process is further denoted as "assertion".

In order to ensure that the voter who requests for her vote to be asserted is the same person who is registered for e-voting and to whom the presented ballot has been issued, the Registration Authority provides the encryption key used to encrypt the voter's voting credentials during registration process to the Asserting Authority. Since both the Registration Authority and the Asserting Authority are located in the Registration Domain, both are allowed to handle the voter's ssPIN(v). Moreover, since the Registration Authority creates a list of e-voters based on the ssPIN(v), the Registration Authority should put the voter's encryption key on this list as well. Thus, with the help of this list, the Asserting Authority is able to decide whether or not the voter requesting for asserting is an eligible e-voter. The Asserting Authority is then able to encrypt the resulting assertion with the voter's public key that she has presented during the preceding registration process. This ensures that no other person other than the one who has been registered for e-voting during the registration process is able to decrypt and use the returned assertion.

Finally, before the voter casts her ballot, she has to decrypt the assertion received from the asserting service and add it to her ballot. Thus, the Election Authority might draw the following conclusions based on a cast ballot:

1. The cast ballot has been decrypted by the person who has registered for e-voting and to whom the underlying blank ballot has been issued during the registration process. This can be concluded because the blank ballot received during the registration process has been encrypted for the registered voter only.

2. The cast ballot has been asserted through the same voter who registered for e-voting and to whom the underlying blank ballot has been issued during the registration process. This can be concluded because the assertion returned to the voter is encrypted for this voter only by drawing on the voter's public

key stored by the Registration Authority during the registration process. Thus, the voter who has requested for e-voting and to whom the encrypted voting credentials have been issued during registration has compiled the cast ballot, and the cast ballot contains the decrypted assertion.

3. If the signature contained in the assertion of the encrypted cast ballot can be verified successfully, the cast ballot has been asserted by the identified voter.

Due to the conclusions 1), 2) and 3) and assuming that the voter has not lost her Citizen Card—and knows the secret codes needed to use it—or has not lent it to anyone else, the cast ballot can be assumed to be the ballot from the voter who has been registered for e-voting and to whom the blank ballot card has been issued. This means that the vPIN provided in the cast ballot

represents the voter who cast the ballot. Figure 5 depicts the principle of indirect voter authentication as used within the proposed e-voting schema.

CONCLUSION

The proposed e-voting solution relies on two core principles: strong end-to-end encryption and stringent domain separation. Both principles are closely coupled to Austrian e-Government solutions. The latter principle especially is an extension of the Austrian identity management concept. Due to the domain separation concept introduced, the e-voting concept is able to handle unique identification of voters while protecting the anonymity of cast votes with the simultaneous possibility of gaining knowledge about whether a given voter had cast a vote already (during the election event). Thus, the proposed e-voting scenario

Figure 5. Simplified illustration of indirect voter authentication

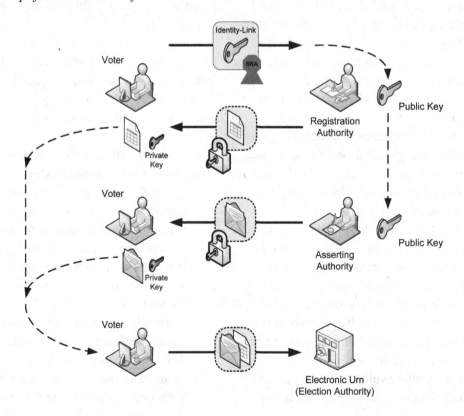

allows voters to cast their vote conventionally at a polling station on Election Day even though the voter might have registered for e-voting.

Allowing e-voters to cast their vote at the polling station as well—under extenuating circumstances—is an important element of the EVITA's embracing security concept which makes the EVITA concept different from other e-voting schemes. The use of the Internet inherently brings with it some risks that cannot be addressed by technical measures (i.e. network security elements, redundancy, etc.) alone, however they can be tackled by having a comprehensive technical, organisational, and legal security concept. So, allowing e-voters to cast their vote at the polling station is an organisational measure facing a possible break-down of the e-voting channel (e.g., due to DoS, etc).

REFERENCES

Borras, J. (2007). *Election Markup Language (EML) Version 5.0. Organization for the Advancement of Structured Information Standards (OASIS)*. Retrieved December 18, 2009 from http://docs.oasis-open.org/election/eml/v5.0/os/EML-Process-Data-Requirements-v5.0.pdf

Chaum, D. (1981). Untraceable electronic mail, return adresses, and digital pseudonyms. *Communications of the ACM, 24*(2), 84–86. doi:10.1145/358549.358563

Cohen, J., & Fischer, M. (1985). A robust and verifiable cryptographically secure election scheme. In *Proceedings of the 26th IEEE Symposium on the Foundations of Computer Science (FOCS)* (pp. 372-382). Washington, DC: IEEE.

Cohen, J., & Yung, M. (1986). Distributing the power of government to enhance the privacy of voters. In *Proceedings of 5th ACM Symposium on Principles of Distributed Computing (PODC)*, 52–62. ACM.

Council of Europe. (1950). *Convention for the Protection of Human Rights and Fundamental Freedoms*. Paris: Council of Europe.

Council of Europe. (2004a). *Recommendation Rec(2004)11 of the Committee of Ministers to member states on legal, operational and technical standards for e-voting*. Paris: Council of Europe.

Council of Europe. (2004b). *Explanatory Memorandum to the Draft Recommendation Rec(2004) of the Committee of Ministers to member states on legal, operational and technical standards for e-voting*. Paris: Multidisciplinary Ad Hoc Group of Specialists IP1-S-EE, Council of Europe.

Cramer, R., Gennaro, R., & Shoenmakers, B. (1997). A secure and optimally efficient multi-authority election scheme. In *Advances in Cryptology - Eurocrypt 97* (LNCS, pp. 103-118). Berlin: Springer Verlag.

Desmedt, Y. (1992). Threshold cryptosystems. In J. Seberry & Y. Zheng (Eds.), *Proceedings of Advances in Cryptology - Auscrypt '92* (LNCS 718, pp. 3-14). Berlin: Springer-Verlag.

Desmedt, Y. (1994). Threshold cryptography. In *European Trans. on Telecommunications* (pp. 449-457).

Desmedt, Y., & Frankel, Y. (1989) Threshold cryptosystems. In G. Brassard (Ed.), *Proceedings of Advances in Cryptology - Crypto '89* (LNCS 435, pp. 307-315). Berlin: Springer Verlag.

Fujioka, A., Okamoto, T., & Ohta, K. (1992). A practical secret voting scheme for large scale elections. In *Advances in Cryptology - Auscrypt 92* (pp. 244-251).

German, B. S. I. (2007). *Basissatz von Sicherheitsanforderungen an Onlinewahlprodukte (Version 0.18)*. Bonn, Germany: Bundesamt für Sicherheit in der Informationstechnik.

Gesellschaft für Informatik e. V. (2005). *GI-Anforderungen an Internetbasierte Vereinswahlen.* Germany.

Hirt, M., & Sako, K. (2000). Efficient receipt-free voting based on homomorphic encryption. In *Proceedings of the Eurocrypt 2000.*

Hollosi, A., & Hörbe, R. (2006). Bildung von Stammzahl und bereichsspezifischem Personenkennzeichen (SZ-bPK-Algo -1.1.1). *Platform Digital Austria, AG Bürgerkarte.* Retrieved May 12, 2007 from http://www.ref.gv.at

Hollosi, A., Karlinger, G., Rössler, T., & Centner, M. (2008). *The Austrian Citizen Card (Specification), Specification of the Austrian Citizen Card version 1.2.* Retrieved November 20, 2009 from http://www.buergerkarte.at/konzept/security-layer/spezifikation/aktuell/

Jefferson, D., Rubin, A. D., Simons, B., & Wagner, D. (2004). *A security analysis of the secure electronic registration and voting experiment.* SERVE.

Juang, W.-S., & Lei, C.-L. (1996). A collision free secret ballot protocol for computerized general elections. *Computers & Security, 15*(4), 339–348. doi:10.1016/0167-4048(96)00011-9

Leitold, H., Hollosi, A., & Posch, R. (2002). Security architecture of the Austrian citizen card concept. In *Proccedings of ACSAC'2002, Las Vegas, 9-13 December 2002* (pp. 391-400). Washington, DC: IEEE Computer Society.

Okamoto, T. (1997). Receipt free electronic voting schemes for large scale elections. In *Proceedings of Workshop on Security Protocols 97* (LNCS, pp. 25-35). Berlin: Springer Verlag.

Rössler, T. (2007). *Electronic Voting over the Internet – an E-Government Speciality.* Doctoral dissertation, Graz University of Technology, Austria.

Rössler, T., Hayat, A., Posch, R., & Leitold, H. (2005). Giving an interoperable solution for incorporating foreign eids in austrian e-government. In *Proceedings of IDABC Conference, 2005,* 147–156.

Venice Commission. (2002). *Code of Good Practice in Electoral Matters. European Commission for Democracy through Law.* Council of Europe.

Working-Group "E-Voting." (2004). *Abschlussbericht zur Vorlage an Dr. Ernst Strasser, Bundesminister für Inneres.* Austrian Federal Ministry for the Interior.

ENDNOTES

[1] In preceding work (Rössler, 2007) we worked out an exhaustive and all-embracing set of security requirements by following a standardised methodology (i.e., Common Criteria methodology). The security requirements have been created based on (legal) election fundamentals (Venice Commission, 2002; Council of Europe, 2004a, 2004b; Working-Group "E-Voting", 2004; Council of Europe, 1950) and existing security considerations (German BSI, 2007; Gesellschaft für Informatik e. V., 2005). These achievements serve the basis for the e-voting concept presented here.

[2] For further details about the Austrian electronic identity management system see (Leitold, Hollosi, & Posch, 2002) and (Hollosi & Hörbe, 2006).

This work was previously published in International Journal of E-Adoption, Volume 2, Issue 1, edited by Sushil K. Sharma, pp. 30-44, copyright 2010 by IGI Publishing (an imprint of IGI Global).

Chapter 9
Requirements and Properties of Qualified Electronic Delivery Systems in eGovernment:
An Austrian Experience

Arne Tauber
E-Government Innovation Center (EGIZ), Austria

ABSTRACT

Electronic mailing systems are the dominant communication systems in private and business matters. Public administrations deliver documents to citizens and businesses—subpoenas, legal verdicts, notifications, administrative penalties, and so forth. However, official activities are more strongly bound to legal regulations than in civil law. Delivery of crucial and personal documents raises the demand for qualified identification and non-repudiation services as featured by registered and certified mail in the paper world. Legal requirements for electronic delivery carried out by public administrations (eDelivery) cannot be fulfilled by standard mailing systems. Although the requirements for eDelivery systems may differ due to national legal regulations, this paper discusses common requirements and properties on an abstract level. Moreover, the author shows how these requirements have been addressed by introducing the Austrian eDelivery system for eGovernment applications.

INTRODUCTION

Electronic mail (eMail) has become the most popular communication method in our daily life – we are used to write and receive eMails when communicating with friends, families, relatives or even in business matters when submitting contracts or bids. This has been confirmed by a survey (Statistik Austria, 2008) reporting that about 90% of active internet users in Austria are using the internet for communication purposes.

DOI: 10.4018/978-1-4666-0041-6.ch009

Electronic communication is of great importance not only in the private and business sector. The delivery of documents such as notifications, administrative penalties, permits and laws, is a fundamental and resource-intensive task for governments and public administrations. For instance, the Austrian Treasury and Ministry of Justice deliver more than 44 million documents each year. The transition to electronic delivery systems (further denoted as eDelivery systems) is a key requirement towards service-oriented architectures in eGovernment. Electronic delivery has still to be considered as a value-added service and will not replace paper-based delivery at least for the next decades. Reduced costs associated with delays and saving paper, 7 x 24 availability and improved accessibility are the promises. Document delivery is one of the last steps in public proceedings and raises the demand for an electronic counterpart in order to avoid media-breaks for processes carried out fully electronically.

Due to the high penetration rate, eMail seems to be the first choice when looking for communication channels serving different kind of transactions – from citizens to administrations (C2A), administrations to citizens (A2C), businesses to administrations (B2A), administrations to businesses (A2B) as well as administrations to administrations (A2A). However, eMail does not have the same evidential quality as registered or certified mail does in the paper world. There is a lack of essential security requirements like integrity, confidentiality, non-repudiation and a qualified sender or recipient identification. In the same way as confidentiality can be ensured through the use of mail extensions like S/MIME or PGP, the research community has focused on several security and cryptographic value-added services ensuring the evidential eMail document exchange between senders and recipients. These extensions are known under the term Certified Electronic Mail (Oppliger, 2004).

In contrast to the private sector, official activities are more strongly bound to legal regulations than in civil law and applied tools and technologies have to be almost legally regulated. Especially the justice sector requires a recipient to prove her identity in a qualified way when receiving crucial documents. A typical example is a subpoena, a written command to a person to testify before a court. A signed proof of receipt guarantees that a recipient has picked up the delivery at a certain point in time and thus is valid evidence in public proceedings.

Several EU member states have already recognized the need for legal regulations concerning administrative deliveries. A number of domestic laws and regulations have been enacted in the last years providing the basis for qualified eDelivery systems. Austria has introduced its eDelivery system early in 2004. Looking at the national level of other EU member states, there are similar initiatives such as the Posta Elettronica Certificata (PEC) (Gennai, Martusciello, & Buzzi, 2005) in Italy, the Secure Mailbox System in Slovenia, the DigiDoc Portal in Estonia or the upcoming DE-Mail (DE-Mail, 2009) system in Germany (2010). From a local point of view, several Austrian ministries have launched a closed mailing system, e.g. the Austrian eDelivery system for legal relations (ERV) (Ornetsmueller, 2009) provided by the Ministry of Justice or the eDelivery system for communications with tax authorities (FinanzOnline - DataBox) provided by the Austrian Treasury.

Although the mentioned eDelivery systems are based on different national legal regulations and thus are implemented in different ways, this paper discusses common requirements on an abstract level. This is essential when going the path towards interoperability, especially in a pan-European context. With the approaching deadline of the EU Services Directive (Council of Europe, 2006) by the end of 2009, cross-border document exchange gets on the agenda of all EU Member States. This directive will require public administrations to send documents to service applicants in a qualified and evidential way, potentially to a system located in another Member State. There-fore, in the remainder of this paper we define a classification scheme or taxonomy of eDelivery systems by identifying common requirements as a basis for a harmonized framework towards interoperability. In Section 2 we introduce and discuss the term qualified eDelivery system. We further discuss common architectural aspects of eDelivery systems from an abstract point of view. In Section 3 common requirements and properties of eDelivery systems are discussed. Although these requirements and properties are specific to eGovernment, some can be found in the private sector as well. We continue in Sec-tion 4 with discussing the Austrian electronic delivery system for eGovernment applications to show how requirements, challenges and security technologies have been implemented nationwide on the large scale.

ARCHITECTURAL ASPECTS OF EDELIVERY SYSTEMS

In this section we introduce and discuss the term Qualified Electronic Delivery System and main architectural aspects of eDelivery systems. In the last years, research has mainly focused on Certified Electronic Mail (CEM), i.e., a number of value-added services enhancing the eMail protocol with security and cryptographic features so as to provide an evidential and fair document exchange between communication partners. CEM puts emphasis on the eMail communication protocol. However, in order to get a more general and abstract definition of communication systems providing evidential security features, we introduce the term Qualified Electronic Delivery System. According to this definition, a CEM based system is an eDelivery system, but the reverse case must not necessarily be true. Currently we can find two CEM systems in the European eDelivery landscape: the Italian PEC and the upcoming German DE-Mail system, which is currently in test stage, ready for going

into production in 2010. Other national systems are purely web-service based, e.g. the Estonian DigiDoc portal or the Slovenian Secure Mailbox. However, we can find hybrid systems as well. The Austrian Electronic Delivery System for eGovern-ment applications uses web-service communica-tion protocols in order to transport MIME based containers, supported by all eMail clients when delivered to the final recipient. As CEM systems are a subgroup of eDelivery systems, CEM proper-ties can be used to describe eDelivery systems as well. Most existing eDelivery systems have the following CEM properties: Non-Repudiation of Submission (NRS), Non-Repudiation of Delivery (NRD), weak stateful in-line trusted third parties (TTP), resilient or unreliable communication chan-nels and asynchronous timeliness. Ferrer-Gomilla, Onieva, Payeras, and Lopez (2009) provide a revisited list of all properties related to CEM.

From an abstract point of view, qualified eDelivery systems can be seen as a closed com-munication system providing different services for its participants. Technical, organizational and legal policies are usually defined by legal regulations on a local, regional or national level.

In each eDelivery system we can find at least three types of entities: delivery service providers (DSP), recipients and senders. Usually, all DSPs act as in-line TTP. In some systems we can find so-called lookup services, a kind of dictionary or white pages in order to locate recipients. In the Austrian case, the lookup service acts as on-line TTP issuing digital postmarks and is therefore an essential part of the communication flow of the entire system.

Similar to standard mail providers, DSPs run communication services allowing the submission and delivery of qualified deliveries. Compared to eMail systems, they provide some sort of mail handling services (MHS) with a mail transfer agent (MTA) for senders and a mail delivery agent (MDA) for recipients. It is practically impossible to provide a qualified delivery system on the large scale without TTPs. TTPs ensure strong (or weak) fairness between all communication partners and must follow legal regulations. They are usually approved by governmental controlling institutions. In each system, recipients have to register with at least one service provider and can receive deliveries depending on their identification and authentication quality. This means that recipients should only be able to get personal deliveries if, and only if, they are registered based on an official ID. Standard deliveries could even be picked up using a pretended identity like in standard mailing systems. Following the EU Signature Directive (Council of Europe, 1999), many EU member states have already rolled out electronic IDs (eID) based on qualified signature certificates. Such eIDs have the same legal impact as traditional official IDs in the context of public services. Qualified eDelivery systems for eGovernment applications are supposed to enable eIDs in order to be carried out fully electronically. This applies to registration processes as well as the qualified identification of recipients when picking up deliveries.

Depending on system domain policies, senders must not necessarily register with a service provider. However, authenticity of senders must be ensured in some way. SSL/TLS client authentication is e.g. a technology backing the requirement for an adequate authentication on the transport layer. On the message or application layer, electronic signatures could ensure a qualified authenticity of senders. If DSPs offer a value-added service, which enables the sending of deliveries, recipients could act as senders and vice versa.

In existing eDelivery systems we can find two main types of architectures. So-called coupled eDelivery systems require both senders and recipients to register with a DSP. This is illustrated in Figure 1. Authentication of entities is ensured by their associated DSPs and electronic deliveries are exchanged through inter-provider communication. A sender transfers the delivery to her provider, which is responsible to locate the recipient's provider and to route the delivery to its final destination. This kind of architecture reminds of the classic eMail communication architecture. Known representatives are the Italian PEC and the German DE-Mail system, both having underlying CEM architectures. Special cases are coupled eDelivery systems with just a single DSP, e.g. the Slovenian Secure Mailbox. All senders and recipients are registered with the same DSP and thus routing is trivial. Independent from the underlying communication architecture (eMail or web-services), coupled eDelivery systems usually use the eMail address format as the standard way of addressing recipients. Therefore, a lookup service is not necessarily required and routing is as easy as in standard mailing systems.

Figure 2 shows the main architecture of so-called decoupled eDelivery systems. The hallmark of these systems is that only recipients are required to register with a DSP. Senders must locate the recipient's DSP and transfer the delivery to this provider. Therefore, a direct inter-provider communication is not required. However, it may not be explicitly forbidden. Consider the case a recipient wants to send a delivery through her DSP. In this case the DSP puts itself in the role of a sender. If the recipient's address data does not give an indication to her DSP, a prior recipient lookup will have to be carried out. This may also be the case, if such an operation is required by law, e.g. in the Austrian case, where the lookup service acts as on-line TTP and issues digital postmarks required for delivery transmission.

There are a number of approaches ensuring a reliable addressing of recipients. Unique identifiers are a common way to address entities in communication systems. As already stated, coupled eDelivery systems use identifiers based on the well-known eMail address format, e.g. givenname.familyname@systemprovider.it. In this way, citizens can provide their eDelivery address when applying for public services. Another approach is the use of unique national IDs. Austria and Estonia address recipients in this way. For this purpose, Austria introduced a so called delivery specific personal identification number

Figure 1. Main architecture of coupled eDelivery systems

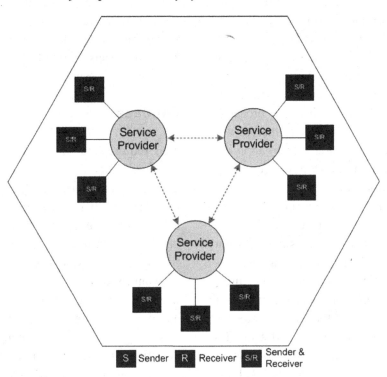

Figure 2. Main architecture of decoupled eDelivery systems

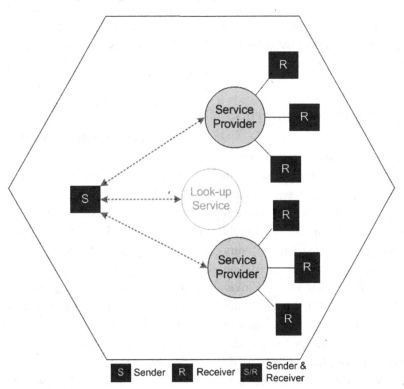

(PIN) – a derivation of a citizen's assigned unique identification number held in the base registers – the Central Residents Register (CRR) and the Supplementary Register for persons who do not have a registered address in Austria. For data protection reasons, public authorities are not allowed to use the CRR number in public proceedings. The delivery specific PIN is therefore a derivation using strong cryptography by applying a Triple-DES encryption with a following one-way SHA-1 hash function. Austrian citizens are not necessarily obliged to provide any information to the administration in order to be addressable. Although eMail addresses are a common format and easy to remember for citizens, unique national IDs are of help when public proceedings are initiated by the administration, e.g. in case of traffic offense penalties. If the eMail address is not known to the administration or if a lookup service may not be available, recipient addressing may become challenging. However, national IDs enable an easy and automatic addressing scheme, even if an administration was never in direct contact with the recipient.

The considerations made so far are on an abstract level and may quite differ by means of implementation issues for different member states.

REQUIREMENTS AND PROPERTIES

In this section we discuss common requirements and properties of qualified eDelivery systems in eGovernment. The classification of requirements is based on the investigation of several national delivery systems. These systems were already named in this paper and are the Austrian eDelivery system for eGovernment applications, the Italian PEC, the German DE-Mail system and the Slovenian Secure Mailbox. The first three named are "de jure" systems, meaning they are systems in the context of eGovernment and operating under particular national laws. The latter one is a "de facto" system, operating on a contractual basis

between the system provider and its customers. Beyond CEM based security requirements, we therefore discuss further requirements, properties and aspects related to legal regulations and eGovernment issues.

Fairness

This requirement defines the fair exchange of expected items. This core CEM property is an essential requirement ensuring that no participating entity is in an advantageous situation following the completion of a document exchange. The research community defines several CEM fairness properties, whereas only strong and weak fairness are relevant for qualified eDelivery systems. Strong fairness is fulfilled if, and only if, both the sender and the recipient get the expected items or none of them gets the expected items. Weak fairness is fulfilled if, and only if, both the sender and the recipient get the expected items or only one gets the expected items, but the other party has evidence of not having received the expected items. All "de jure" systems ensure strong fairness by law. Even in most private sector delivery systems strong fairness is an essential requirement. This results from the fact that all qualified eDelivery systems have at least one (in-line) TTP ensuring this requirement.

Non-Repudiation Services

A fair and evidential document exchange requires a qualified eDelivery system to implement several non-repudiation services. Most eDelivery systems provide services for Non-Repudiation of Submission (NRS) and Non-Repudiation of Delivery (NRD). The former gives evidence to public authorities of having sent the delivery at a certain point in time. The latter gives evidence to public authorities that a recipient has picked up the delivery at a certain point in time. This is determinant, e.g. for the commencement of the period for appeal. Qualified eDelivery systems should also provide non-repudiation services offering protection against false denial of involvement as described in RFC 2828 (Shirey, 2000). There exist a number of non-repudiation services for this kind of message related actions. Non-Repudiation of Origin (NRO) and Non-Repudiation of Receipt (NRR) are two examples. The latter provides an electronic delivery confirmation with a proof of receipt containing a timestamp and an electronic signature of the receiving unit (either the recipient herself or her delivery service provider). Implementation guidelines concerning non-repudiation protocols are specified by the standards ISO/IEC (1989, 1996, 1998).

Qualified Identification and Authentication

Qualified identification is a fundamental requirement for public administrations when delivering documents tagged as personal. In the postal world, recipients have to prove their identity by showing their passport, identity card, driver's license or another official ID. The recipient gets the delivery only in exchange of a qualified identification and a personal signature. This is part of a fair exchange. The qualified identification is usually required for certified mail services in the course of administrative or judicial procedures only. Private registered mail services usually don't authenticate the recipient signing the receipt.

Qualified eDelivery systems in eGovernment must therefore guarantee that recipients are identified and authenticated in a qualified and reliable way. This has to apply at least for the registration procedure. All investigated eDelivery systems support a qualified registration procedure with the national electronic identity (eID). These eIDs are all based on qualified certificates defined in Annex I of the EU Signature Directive 1999/93/EC (Council of Europe, 1999). Qualified signatures based on these eIDs are thus legally equivalent to handwritten signatures. The directive further ensures mutual recognition of eIDs throughout the EU and facilitates interoperability efforts. A German citizen may potentially authenticate herself at the Italian PEC using her German eID card. In the course of a delivery pick-up, authentication levels may range from low qualities (simple SMTP based username/password authentication) to high two-factor authentication qualities (eID). This usually depends on the type of non-repudiation service (e.g. NRR usually requires a high quality), legal regulations and domain policies. Until now, we talked only about identification and authentication of recipients. A fair system must ensure the same for senders. In coupled eDelivery systems we can find almost the same authentication mechanisms for senders and recipients. In decoupled systems sender authentication (NRO) may be ensured by applying electronic signatures on the transport, message or application layer.

Trust

There is a consensus in the research community that a fair and efficient communication system requires TTPs (Oppliger, 2007). All investigated and most existing eDelivery solutions have in-line TTPs, whereas a few have additional on-line TTPs, e.g., Austria. CEM research advises the use of off-line TTPs (so-called optimistic protocols) or on-line TTPs in order to avoid communication bottlenecks caused by in-line TTPs, where a TTP acting as intermediary is involved in each communication step. However, the implementation of existing systems with in-line TTPs shows the opposite. This results from the fact that in-line TTPs increase control of communication and information flows to a maximum. A TTP involvement in each step further leads to a better understanding of the system by users and increases trust in the system. Citizens shall innately trust the eDelivery system they are using. Therefore, entities acting as TTP in a "de jure" system must be approved by governmental controlling institutions.

Standard communication systems such as eMail have their limitations and cannot provide non-repudiation services. Even in most certified mailing systems there is a lack of qualified authentication and identification. In the remainder of this section we discuss further requirements and properties that may be part of qualified eDelivery systems depending on national legal regulations. Several security-related requirements and properties can already be handled by certified or even standard mailing systems with some extensions.

Security and Privacy

Analogous to the privacy of correspondence in the paper world, eDelivery systems may require that the content of deliveries cannot be altered and can be solely disclosed to the recipient. All investigated "de jure" systems support an optional end-to-end encryption (E2EE), thus ensuring confidentiality between the sender and the recipient so that no third party can access the message content. If no E2EE is applied, at least a secured communication channel is required for message transmission. This applies to all steps including message submission from sender to her DSP, inter-provider transmission and message delivery from the recipient's DSP to the recipient herself.

Data privacy protection must primarily be assured for personal data and unique national identifiers. In "de jure" systems the handling of sensitive data is regulated by national laws. This concerns the exposure of personal data through lookup services or white pages as well as the exposure of personal data to third parties in the course of message transmission. Qualified eDelivery systems must not be vulnerable to data theft attacks. In the eMail world, spammers exploit search engines or use Trojan horses for collecting eMail addresses in order to send illicit advertising mail (SPAM) or to thieve digital identities. This must be prevented in the context of qualified eDelivery systems through legal, technical and organizational provisions.

Representation

An eDelivery system should support communications between citizens and administrations (C2A, A2C) as well as communications between businesses and administrations (B2A, A2B). Businesses, associations and other corporate bodies usually have one or more authorized representatives, e.g., the registered manager of a company or other authorized employees. Special cases are professional representatives such as attorneys at law, notaries, tax consultants, etc. Depending on national regulations, they often have power of representation for their clients without the need of a written mandate. It must be ensured in a technical or organizational way that accounts belonging to corporate bodies can only be created by authorized representatives. The same applies for the pick-up of deliveries. All investigated eDelivery systems have enabled support for corporate bodies being able to receive electronic deliveries. However, Austria is the only country featuring an automated representation mechanism. This is called empowerment through electronic mandates (Rössler, 2009).

Delivery Qualities

In the paper world, postal operators offer special value-added services like registered or certified mail. The latter provides a proof of delivery and a proof of receipt including the recipient's signature. We call such value-added services *Delivery Qualities*. A delivery quality determines the complete supply chain of a letter, e.g. the number of evidences, authentication levels, and confidentiality as well as signature qualities. The same applies for qualified eDelivery systems. Legal regulations may require different quality levels concerning administrative deliveries. These levels could range from standard deliveries with no further requirements to qualified deliveries offering non-repudiation services. Delivery qualities may further define dedicated recipient groups, e.g., that a delivery can only be picked up by the recipient herself and not even by an authorized representative.

Standards

Service architectures, protocols and interfaces must be standardized to ensure interoperability and extensibility. This facilitates the deployment of an eDelivery system on the large scale by allowing new entities (senders, DSPs, etc.) to be easily integrated in the system. Standards are a driving force. They encourage the private and the public sector to take up development efforts so as to provide more and better services for recipients. This will inevitably lead to a higher degree of utilization by recipients and sender. Open standards further ensure transparency and freedom of choice. This can be of help when thinking towards interoperability, especially in the context of cross-border and on the large scale. The ETSI Registered E-mail Standard (REM) (ETSI, 2008) defines a common format for evidences for use in CEM systems. It works against the growth of a heterogeneous CEM landscape by ensuring system interoperability with standardized XML, CMS or PDF evidences. So far, the ETSI standard has been taken up by the UPU, which works on an extended version named Postal Registered eMail (PReM) (Universal Postal Union, 2008).

Absence

We can find the CEM timeliness property in eDelivery systems as well. Synchronous timeliness (Ferrer-Gomilla et al., 2009) is given, if the protocol can be terminated in a finite and known amount of time. However, citizens may not be able to pick up deliveries, e.g., when being on vacation or being hospitalized. This may eventually lead to legal consequences. Qualified eDelivery systems should therefore allow the absence of recipients concerning commencements of the period for appeal.

Accessibility

Secure and reliable communication in standard communication systems is typically based on end-to-end encryption (E2EE). Due to the diversity of software products and cryptographic tools, complexity is rapidly increasing with the number of participants. This circumstance hinders the dissemination of secure systems as can be seen in the case of standard mailing systems. Several protocols for certified eMail communications have been proposed so far, e.g., (Schneier & Riordan, 1997; Al-Hammadi & Shahsavari, 1999) including TTPs (Oppliger & Stadlin, 2004; Puigserver, Gomila, & Rotger, 2005). Qualified eDelivery systems should be designed in a way that recipients shall not get in touch with cryptographic functions such as signature creation, signature verification, evidence creation and E2EE. These operations should be carried out by service providers acting as TTP. Even if entity communication between senders and service providers or an inter-provider communication has to fulfill a number of requirements in terms of software and protocol security, the recipient should not be burdened with such complex processes. An eDelivery infrastructure should rather ease the access to the system allowing the use of commodity products such as eMail clients or web browsers. This could be achieved by enhancing standard mailing system in order to meet the requirements discussed in this section. For instance, Posta Elettronica Certificata (PEC) in Italy followed this approach.

Lookup Service

If allowed by legal regulations, a look-up service could facilitate the search for a particular recipient. Such a service could be useful in heterogeneous or federated delivery systems featuring a broad range of DSPs. In eDelivery systems with multiple DSPs and where the final DSP is not deducible from the recipient's address data, a sort of lookup service is essential. In some systems, entry of recipients in a lookup service or register is voluntary (DE-Mail system), whereas in other systems it is compulsory (Austria). A CEM eMail address usually implies that a recipient is registered with a DSP and is addressable by electronic means. A unique national ID does not. Each citizen, whether registered with a DSP or not, has such a unique ID. This is the case in Austria, and without a lookup service, a sender may not determine whether a recipient is addressable by electronic means and with which DSP a recipient is registered with. In a single DSP solution like Slovenia, recipients can still be addressed by their tax numbers without the presence of a lookup service. Nevertheless, it is essential that data privacy protection must have high priority in the context of lookup service.

THE AUSTRIAN DELIVERY SYSTEM FOR EGOVERNMENT APPLICATIONS

In this section we discuss how the considerations made so far have been implemented on a national level by introducing the Austrian eDelivery system for eGovernment applications. Policies and general requirements are laid down by the Austrian eGovernment Act – enacted on 1st March 2004 – which provides the legal basis to facilitate electronic communications with public bodies. In the remainder of this section we discuss architectures, main process building blocks, open standards and security technologies backing the Austrian eDelivery system.

Figure 3 shows the architecture and the basic eDelivery process flow of the Austrian eDelivery system for eGovernment applications. From an abstract point of view, the main entities are as follows:

Delivery Service providers: as long as legal, technical and organizational provisions are fulfilled, any public body or business can operate as DSP. A DSP can only be approved by the Federal Chancellery and must offer a number of basic services such as the delivery of administrative deliveries and the non-repudiation services NRD and NRR.

Recipients: all Austrian citizens and businesses can register with any service providers. Once the citizen or business is registered, all public administrations are able to address the recipient by electronic means. Electronic delivery is free of charge for recipients.

Senders: all Austrian public bodies are allowed to deliver documents to registered recipients.

Lookup service: the main lookup service can be seen as a register holding the data of all recipients. Service providers are therefore required to communicate the data of all registered recipients to the lookup service.

As illustrated in Figure 3, the main eDelivery process flow can be described as follows:

(1) Registration with service providers can only be carried out with the Austrian citizen card, the official electronic identification (eID) for online public services. Moreover, the citizen card offers the option to create qualified electronic signatures. As stated by the EU Signature Directive, qualified signatures have the same legal impact as handwritten signatures. The security architecture of the Austrian citizen card is described in detail in (Leitold, Hollosi, & Posch, 2002). Registration with service providers is explicitly voluntary as electronic delivery can be seen as an add-on service to traditional means of carrying-out delivery of printed documents. Registration of corporate bodies is based on so called electronic mandates. As citizen cards are only issued to physical persons, the Austrian eGovernment movement has developed an XML-scheme (Rössler, 2009) for electronic mandates, the technical vehicle for acting on someone else's behalf. Electronic mandates are digitally signed XML structures and can be stored on a citizen's eID. For instance, a

Figure 3. Architecture and process flow of the Austrian eDelivery system

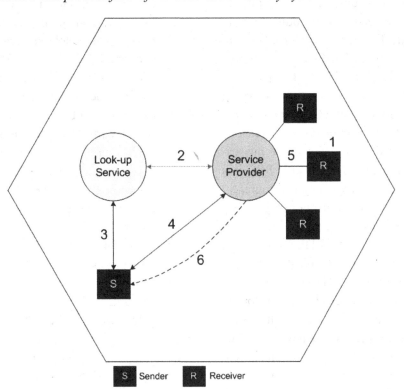

registered manager of a company can apply for an electronic postal mandate and accordingly act on behalf of the company when registering with a service provider. Postal mandates are available for representation of both corporate bodies and physical persons.

(2) Service providers must communicate the recipient's registration data to the central lookup service in order to be found by public authorities. Among personal data like delivery specific PIN, given name, family name, date of birth, eMail address, a service provider has to communicate an optionally supplied X.509 encryption certificate for end-to-end encryption, the recipient's preferred document formats - e.g., PDF or MS-Office - and declared absence times. End-to-end encryption between senders and recipients is only applied if the recipient explicitly desires this additional security layer

by providing an X.509 encryption certificate in order to receive encrypted eMails.

(3) In order to search for particular recipients, public authorities are forced to register with the central look-up service. The registration process is based on SSL/TLS X.509 client certificates having an appropriate attribute indicated by the Austrian eGovernment OID (Hollosi, Leitold, & Rössler, 2007) to assure that only public authorities can register with the lookup service. Using object identifiers (OID) to define appropriate attributes is a common practice in public key infrastructure (PKI). The supplied certificate must be used for searching recipients at the lookup service as well as for transmission of deliveries to service providers. Public authorities are allowed to search for recipients using particular parameters such as given name, family name, date of birth and the eMail

address. Public authorities are not always aware of the citizen's eMail address, e.g. in the case of traffic offence penalties. They are therefore recommended to use the encrypted unique delivery specific PIN for searching recipients that can be obtained by querying a frontend service of the Central Residents Register (CRR). For data protection reasons public authorities are never in the possession of the plain delivery specific PIN, it is rather protected using strong cryptography (RSA 1024bit) and can only be decrypted by the lookup service. Requests to the lookup service are sent using a HTTPs GET request based on SSL client authentication. Search parameters are passed as HTTP GET encoded parameters. Returned search results are based on an XML structure containing all service providers a recipient is registered with. For data protection reasons the lookup service must provide a limited result set only - the web service location of the service provider, preferred document formats and an optional encryption certificate, if the recipient has supplied one. In case of absence or a recipient has never registered with a service provider, a not found answer will be returned by the lookup service.

(4) If a recipient could be found, public authorities transmit the delivery to the web-service location of the service provider returned by the lookup service. SSL client certificates with a public authority OID assure authenticity of senders on the transport layer. Public authorities are advised to electronically sign documents before delivery to assure authenticity on the application layer (Non-Repudiation of Origin). With 2011 all administrative processes bound to the General Administrative Process Law (General Administrative Process Law, 1991) are obliged to digitally sign official copies. The transmission of electronic deliveries is based on the Soap with Attachments (SwA)

protocol supplying a MIME container. The SOAP part contains particular data to identify the recipient's delivery account such as the encrypted delivery specific PIN as well as additional metadata concerning unique reference numbers or delivery qualities. Attached binary documents are supplied within the MIME part of the SwA message. If a recipient has supplied a certificate for end-to-end encryption, an S/MIME container is supplied respectively. The use of (S) MIME containers ensures interoperability with standard eMail clients. Service providers can either provide the MIME container in a well structured form through a web-interface or forward the container to the recipient's standard eMail account.

(5) After having stored the delivery into the recipient's account, service providers must notify the recipient by electronic means, e.g., eMail or SMS that a delivery is ready to be picked up. If the delivery will not be picked up within 48 hours, a second notification is sent out. The recipient can pick up the delivery logging in at the web interface of the service provider with her citizen card and signing a delivery confirmation with her qualified signature certificate. The delivery confirmation is an XML document and must be signed following the XMLDSIG (Eastlake & Reagle, 2002) standard. Recipients can optionally login using a standard mail client. In this case the delivery confirmation must be signed by the service provider. The Austrian eDelivery system distinguishes between two delivery qualities - qualified deliveries (RSa) and standard deliveries.

(6) RSa requires a service provider to return the signed confirmation back to the sending public authority either by eMail or a SOAP based web service. If a recipient does not pick up the delivery in time, an appropriate non-delivery confirmation is returned as well.

So far, not all Austrian citizens are registered for electronic delivery and printed documents are still dominating the world of delivery. In order to encourage public authorities to integrate their services into the eDelivery system, the Austrian eGovernment movement has developed the concept of dual delivery. This concept follows the fire-and-forget pattern allowing all kinds of deliveries to be carried out over one single interface. If a recipient cannot be found querying the lookup service, the document will be printed out and delivered using conventional channels, e.g. by post.

The low frequency of electronic deliveries a year raises the demand for synergies with the private sector to make systems deployed on the large scale economic. Certified mail is a fundamental vehicle in the private sector when delivery of crucial documents asks for a qualified proof of receipt. Legal provisions allow businesses to make use of the Austrian eDelivery system with limitations. By using national and international standards a specification meeting the requirements for shared use of both governmental and business processes has been published this year. A service following this specification has recently been put into practice by an approved service provider and other providers are encouraged to follow suit.

With the introduction of the EU Service Directive (Council of Europe, 2006), cross-border eGovernment gets on the agenda of all EU member states. The ongoing EU Large Scale Pilot "STORK" (Ivkovic, Leitold, & Rössler, 2009) aims to achieve interoperability by bridging public services based on different legislations. Austria has the lead of Pilot 4, the so called eDelivery pilot focused on coupling eDelivery systems of different Member states.

CONCLUSION

Registered mail is a fundamental vehicle in the paper world. With respect to electronic communications, standard mailing systems do not meet the requirements for an adequate qualified delivery. Several EU member states have already put into place qualified eDelivery services based on domestic legal regulations. Even if at first sight these systems seem to quite differ from each other, common requirements and properties such as qualified identification and non-repudiation services can be identified. We further discussed architectural characteristics of eDelivery systems on an abstract level by identifying the main entities and common addressing schemes in such systems. A classification and a deeper understanding of eDelivery systems is an essential requirement towards an interoperable framework on a pan-European level.

As an example the Austrian eDelivery system facilitating electronic communications with public bodies is discussed. This use case demonstrates how requirements and properties discussed so far have been implemented on basis of Austrian legal regulations. Open standards and security technologies backing the Austrian eDelivery system are discussed as well.

REFERENCES

Al-Hammadi, B., & Shahsavari, M. (1999). Certified exchange of electronic mail (CEEM). In *Proceedings of the Southeastcon*, *99*, 40–43.

Council of Europe. (1999). *Directive 1999/93/EC on a Community framework for electronic signatures*.

Council of Europe. (2006). Directive 2006/123/EC of the European Parliament and of the Council of 12 december 2006 on services in the internal market.

DE-Mail. (2009). *Richtlinie für Bürgerportale (Version 0.98)*. Bonn, Germany: Bundesamt für Sicherheit in der Informationstechnik.

Eastlake D., & Reagle, J. (2002). *XML Signature Syntax and Processing (W3C Recommendation)*.

ETSI. (2008). Electronic Signatures and Infrastructures. *ETSI TS, 102,* 640.

Ferrer-Gomilla, J., Onieva, J., Payeras, M., & Lopez, M. (2009). *Certified electronic mail: Properties revisited. Computers & Security.* Atlanta, GA: Elsevier.

General Administrative Process Law. (1991). *AVG – Allgemeines Verwaltungsverfahrensgesetz. Bundesgesetzblatt 1991/51 idF Bundesgesetzblatt 2004/10.* Austria.

Gennai, F., Martusciello, L., & Buzzi, M. (2005). A certified email system for the public administration in Italy. In P. Isaías & M. Nunes (Eds.), *IADIS International Conference WWW/Internet 2005* (Vol. 2, pp. 143-147).

Hollosi, A., Leitold, H., & Rössler, T. (2007). *Object Identifier der öffentlichen Verwaltung.* Austria.

ISO/IEC. (1989). ISO/IEC 7498-2:1989. *Information processing systems – Open systems interconnection – Basic Reference Model – Part 2: Security Architecture.*

ISO/IEC. (1996). ISO/IEC 10181:1996. *Information technology – Open systems interconnection – Security framework in open systems.*

ISO/IEC. (1998). ISO/IEC 2788:1998. *Information technology – Security techniques – Non-repudiation.*

Ivkovic, M., Leitold, H., & Rössler, T. (2009). Interoperable elektronische Identität in Europa. In *7. Information Security Konferenz (Krems)* (pp. 175-190).

Leitold, H., Hollosi, A., & Posch, R. (2002, December 9-13). Security architecture of the Austrian citizen card concept. In *Proccedings of ACSAC'2002* (pp. 391-400).

Oppliger, R. (2004). Certified Mail: The Next Challenge for Secure Messaging. *Communications of the ACM, 47,* 75–79. doi:10.1145/1012037.1012039

Oppliger, R. (2007). Providing Certified Mail Services on the Internet. *Security & Privacy, 5,* 16–22. doi:10.1109/MSP.2007.15

Oppliger, R., & Stadlin, P. (2004). A certified mail system (CMS) for the Internet. *Computer Communications, 27,* 1229–1235. doi:10.1016/j.comcom.2004.04.006

Ornetsmueller, G. (2007). *WEB-ERV ERV Service (Version 1.1).* Austria.

Puigserver, M. M., Gomila, J. L. F., & Rotger, L. H. (2005). Certified e-mail protocol with verifiable third party. In *Proceedings of the 2005 IEEE International Conference on e-Technology, e-Commerce and e-Service* (pp. 548-551).

Rössler, T. (2009). Empowerment through Electronic Mandates – Best Practice Austria. *Software Services for e-Business and e-Society. IFIP Advances in Information and Communication Technology, 305,* 148–160.

Schneier, B., & Riordan, J. (1997). A certified e-mail protocol. In *Proceedings of ACSAC '97: the Annual Computer Security Applications Conference* (pp. 232-238). Washington, DC: IEEE Computer Society Press.

Shirey, R. (2000). Internet Security Glossary.

Statistik Austria. (2008). *ICT Usage in Households.* Austria: Bundesanstalt Statistik Österreich.

Universal Postal Union. (2008). *Postal Registered eMail (PReM), Functional Specification (Version 0.52).*

This work was previously published in International Journal of E-Adoption, Volume 2, Issue 1, edited by Sushil K. Sharma, pp. 45-58, copyright 2010 by IGI Publishing (an imprint of IGI Global).

Chapter 10
Employees' Perceptions of Biometric Technology Adoption in E-Government:
An Exploratory Study in the Kingdom of Saudi Arabia

Thamer Alhussain
Griffith University, Australia

Steve Drew
Griffith University, Australia

ABSTRACT

This paper discusses an exploratory study of government employees' perceptions of the introduction of biometric authentication at the workplace in the Kingdom of Saudi Arabia. The authors suggest that studying the factors affecting employees' acceptance of new technology will help ease the adoption of biometric technology in other e-government applications. A combination of survey and interviews was used to collect the required data. Interviews were conducted with managers and questionnaires were given to employees from two different government organisations in Saudi Arabia to investigate the employees' perceptions of using biometrics. The results of this study indicate a significant digital and cultural gap between the technological awareness of employees and the preferred authentication solutions promoted by management. A lack of trust in technology, its potential for misuse and management motives reflect the managers' need to consider their responsibilities for narrowing these gaps. It was apparent that overcoming employees' resistance is an essential issue facing biometric implementation. Based on the research the authors recommend that an awareness and orientation process about biometrics should take place before the technology is introduced into the organisation.

DOI: 10.4018/978-1-4666-0041-6.ch010

1 INTRODUCTION

New technologies constantly evolve new dimensions to daily life. They can be used to provide interactions between users and their governments through electronic services. Governments are looking for more efficient and effective uses of technology in order to electronically deliver their services (Alharbi, 2006; Scott, 2005). Electronic government (e-government) has therefore become an important world-wide application area.

With e-government applications, users are required to provide governments with personal information which necessitates an efficient, secure technology to provide reliable methods, particularly for users' identification as well as secure information systems. Thus, the implementation of e-government is facing important issues such as information security, user authentication and privacy in which biometric authentication is a potential solution to deal with such concerns (Dearstyne, 2001). It can provide reliable identification of individuals as well as the ability for controlling and protecting the integrity of sensitive data stored in information systems (McLindin, 2005). As a result, several governments have implemented biometric authentication systems in order to efficiently and securely provide their services.

However, the adoption of biometrics in e-government has become a major component of political planning for several governments. In particular, user acceptance can be an essential factor for the successful implementation of biometrics (Ashbourn, 2004; Giesing, 2003; Scott, 2005). Moreover, users can have a direct impact on the operational performance of biometric systems, so their concerns need careful consideration, even if their concerns are fairly rough and ill defined (Ashbourn, 2004).

This paper discusses a study conducted in the Kingdom of Saudi Arabia of government employees' perceptions of the introduction of biometric authentication at the workplace in 2008. The aim is gain an understanding of factors affecting the employees' acceptance of biometrics and to advise on how to successfully adopt biometrics in e-government applications. The paper is structured as follows. The relevant literature is reviewed followed by the description of the empirical study that involved a descriptive survey and interviews of the managers and employees in two organisations.

2 BACKGROUND

To introduce the context in which this study was undertaken it is necessary to consider the concepts of e-government and biometric authentication and how they relate to the technological sophistication of the major users. Saudi Arabia presents a unique set of cultural and technology uptake circumstances that have implications for management of a digital divide. We discuss the background to this enquiry in the following sections.

2.1 E-Government

Electronic government involves the citizens of that country in certain government activities in order to help solve problems. E-government provides unparalleled opportunities to streamline and improve internal governmental processes, enhance the interactions between users and government, and enable efficiencies in service delivery (Scott, 2005). It refers to the use of information technology by government agencies in order to enhance the interaction and service delivery to citizens, businesses, and other government agencies (Alharbi, 2006; AlShihi, 2006). Thus, there are four categories of e-government applications which are: Government-to-Citizen (G2C); Government-to-Business (G2B); Government-to-Government (G2G); and Government-to-Employee (G2E) (AlShihi, 2006).

2.2 Saudi Arabia and its Adoption of Technology

The Kingdom of Saudi Arabia is located in the Southern-Eastern part of the Asian continent. It occupies 2,240,000 sq km (about 865,000 sq mi) (The Saudi Network, n.d.). The total population reached 26,417,599 in mid-2005, compared with 24.06 million in mid-2004, reflecting an annual growth rate of 2.9 percent; however, 5,576,076 million of the population is non-Saudis (Central Department of Statistics & Information, 2009).

Regarding Information Technology in the Kingdom of Saudi Arabia, national e-government program has been launched, early 2005, under the name Yesser, an Arabic word meaning "simplify" or "make easy". It plays the role of the enabler / facilitator of the implementation of e-government in the public sector. Its objectives include raising the public sector's efficiency and effectiveness; providing better and faster government services, and ensuring availability of the required information in a timely and accurate fashion. Yesser vision is that by the end of 2010, everyone in the Kingdom will be able to enjoy world class government services offered in a seamless, user friendly and secure way by utilizing a variety of electronic means (E-government Program (Yesser), 2009).

With biometric technology, the Kingdom of Saudi Arabia has started the use of biometrics in e-government applications only a couple of years ago and it is trying to widely implement this technology. However, the implementation of biometrics was not successful in a number of Saudi government agencies which caused them to stop using this technology, and the concerns of users were an important factor in this.

In our study, we noticed that the Saudi case represents some specificity such as the technology deficiency and difficulty of its repatriation as the most technologies are imported from overseas. It is also noticed that a lot of users do not have much confidence in the computerized systems which proves the necessity to take into account users' perceptions and requirements for successful implementation of such e-government application.

2.3 Digital and Cultural Gap

Digital divide refers to the gap between the group of people that are very familiar and have good access to high technology and those who do not (Blau, 2002). It can be a result of several reasons such as a lack of financial resources, great education, and computer literacy. However, the digital divide makes the successful of e-government applications challenging (Al-Shehry, Rogerson, Fairweather, & Prior, 2006).

In the case of Saudi Arabia, a digital divide can be caused by the lack of knowledge and experience with technology, for instance, people in rural areas and inner city neighborhoods may have less internet access than others, while those who have never used computers may simply be reluctant to use the new technology (Alharbi, 2006). Moreover, Al-Shehry and others (Al-Shehry, Rogerson, Fairweather, & Prior, 2006) indicated that there is a significant risk of a digital divide in Saudi society and even among employees in public sector since there are a large number of people and employees that are still not computer-literate. Evidence of digital and cultural gap between the technological awareness of government employees and increasing need to deal with new technology can be realized in the result section.

2.4 Biometric Authentication Technology

Biometric technology provides a range of automated methods which can used to measure and analyze a person's physiological and behavioral characteristics (Wayman, Jain, Maltoni, & Maio, 2005). Physiological biometrics includes fingerprint recognition, iris recognition, facial recognition, and hand recognition. Behavioral biometrics contains voice patterns and signatures, which are usually taken for identification and verification purposes. Basic authentication is usually based on something somebody knows, like a pin or a password, or something somebody has, like a key, passport or driver's license. The limitations of these authentication measures in some application areas have led to the development and adoption of biometric technology which is now used to identify individual behaviors and characteristics (Wayman, Jain, Maltoni, & Maio, 2005).

Biometric technology usually involves a scanning device and related software which can be used to gather information that has been recorded in digital form (Bolle, Connell, Pankanti, Ratha, & Senior, 2004). Having digitally collected the information, a database is used to store this information for comparison with the previous records. When converting the biometric input, namely the already collected data in digital form, this software can now be used to identify the specific inputs into a value that can be used to match any data previously collected. By using an algorithm, the data points are then processed into a value that can be compared with biometric data in the database (Bolle, Connell, Pankanti, Ratha, & Senior, 2004).

2.5 Examples of Biometric Technology in E-government Applications

By using biometric technology, e-government aims to give its citizens improved services with efficient and secure access to information by providing reliable identification of individuals as well as the ability for controlling and protecting the integrity of sensitive data stored in information systems. Most researchers such as Ashbourn (2004), Bonsor and Johnson (n.d.), Scott (2005), and Wayman et al. (2005) argue that a wider use of biometric technology can be applied to e-government projects. Currently biometric technology is used for applications like e-voting to ensure that voters do not vote twice. With biometric technology, governments are better able to prevent fraud during elections

and other transaction types. Moreover, biometric technology has most recently been used to ensure correct working times are recorded and that only authorized personnel have access to government property and resources.

Biometric technology can also be used by e-governments for business. For instance, banks frequently adopt a facial feature recognition system to ensure that there is a reduced potential for theft. For example, photos are taken on the bank slips which are stored on computer software. As a result, this has avoided the issue of fraudulent bank slips when withdrawing money at ATMs. These technological advances in authenticating dealings with business have helped the government to conduct its activities more effectively and more securely (Bonsor & Johnson, n.d.).

In business transactions there is frequently the need for full authentication of employees to ensure that, in case of any problem, management is in a position to identify the person responsible for that act. Commercial applications may also require full identification capability, digital certificates, human interface, and one or more authentication devices to ensure that the business can run safely and effectively. People are also in a position to do their business with increased trust. Digital trust through public key cryptography, strong authentication and certification allows greater transaction confidence as long as that organisation has a certified identity as an effective and trustworthy company (Ashbourn, 2004).

Biometric technology is also used in the identification of citizens by e-government applications. Every nation could ethically be able to identify its citizens and differentiate non-citizens by using variations of national identification cards, visas, and passports with biometric data encoded within. Prior to the use of biometric data with such documents they were too easily forged or altered to allow unauthorized access to resources and facilities. As a result many nations have avoided the use of mechanisms such as a national identity card in the past.

Effective e-government biometric applications to authenticate and identify citizens have effectively been used in reducing the issues of illegal immigration, access bottlenecks in busy facilities and high costs of employing security personnel. A good example is the United States whereby, since "September 11", it has widely adopted biometric technology. Two laws were made in the United States as a first mass deployment of biometrics. Seven million transportation employees in the United States incorporate biometrics in their ID cards. Moreover, in order to closely control visitors who enter and leave the country, all foreign visitors are required to present valid passports with biometric data; consequently, over 500 million U.S. visitors have to carry border-crossing documents which incorporate biometrics (Ashbourn, 2004).

Several European governments have also started to implement the use of biometrics. The U.K. government has established issuing asylum seekers with identification smart cards storing two fingerprints. General plans have also been made to extend the use of biometrics throughout the visa system in the U.K. as well as in France, Germany and Italy (Scott, 2005).

The Australian Customs established an automated passenger processing system, that is, the e-passport SmartGate at Sydney and Melbourne airports, and it aims to introduce self-processing by employing facial recognition systems to confirm identities and streamline the travelers" facilitation procedures (The Annual Report of the Australian Customs Service (ACS), 2005).

E-government facilities use the various types of biometric identification in order to control certain illegal behavior. For example, the Japanese government plans to use biometric technology in passports to tackle illegal immigration and to enable tighter controls on terrorists. This will be applied within a computer chip which can store biometric features like fingerprints and facial recognition (Scott, 2005).

Other e-government applications are using the biometrics for certain defense bases for secure areas. For instance, hand recognition has been used at the Scott Air Force Base to save more than $400,000 in manpower costs through their metro-link biometric access gate (Frees, n.d.).

2.6 The Use of Biometric Technology in the Kingdom of Saudi Arabia

The Kingdom of Saudi Arabia, as other countries, has implemented biometrics in several places as follows:

- The Directorate General of Passports has implemented fingerprint technology in several cities in the Kingdom for foreign people. This system will be implemented in all cities in the Kingdom in order to accurately identify more than 7 million foreign people, which will be done through issuing or renewing their residences cards.
- Fingerprint technology has also been applied on employees for attendance in several government agencies such as Ministry of Interior, Ministry of Foreign, the General Organisation for Technical Education and Vocational Training, the Royal Commission for Jubail and Yanbu, and Supreme Commission for Tourism.
- Furthermore, a number of agencies such as the Ministry of the Interior, the Ministry of Foreign Affairs, and the Saudi Monetary Fund have implemented biometrics on employees for special security cases like entering via some doors in their buildings.
- However, the Ministry of the Interior has started to apply fingerprint technology within the national ID card for citizens, as approved by the Council of Ministers on 23rd of May 2005.

2.7 Concerns about the Use of Biometric Technology

While biometrics can provide a high level of authentication through identifying people by their physiological and behavioural characteristics, there are also several negative aspects. Biometrics can sometimes be ineffective when using the various styles of identification. For instance, fingerprints can be saturated, faint, or hard to be processed with some of devices, particularly if the skin is wet or dry. Hand recognition can sometimes be ineffective when the hand is damaged, thereby no results will be obtained to match with the images already in the database. Few facilities have databases or hardware to employ iris recognition, which makes the upfront investment too high to initiate a worldwide iris ID system. Biometric technology has also been criticized for its potential harm to civil liberties. This is because people have been denied access to the various regions and countries simply because they do not have the correct identities for those places. Moreover, there is potential for people's privacy to be violated with this new technology (Bolle, Connell, Pankanti, Ratha, & Senior, 2004).

3 METHODOLOGY

The review of the current literature on biometric applications guided our research and the literature on methods available for an exploratory study. Given the exploratory nature of the study the two research questions were aimed at providing descriptive information on the perceptions of current and potential users of biometric application. The research was designed to answer the following questions.

1. What are the managers' perceptions regarding the use of biometric authentication in e-government applications?

2. What are the employees' perceptions regarding the use of biometric authentication in e-government applications?

Given the two distinctive groups of people – managers and employees - involved the research was carried out in two distinct stages.

Method of sampling was purposive. This method of sampling (Maxwell, 2005) is a strategy in which "particular settings, persons, or activities are selected deliberately in order to provide information that can't be gotten as well from other choices" (p. 88). A selection of knowledgeable interviewees was approached.

The literature on user acceptance of new technology was used to design the questionnaire. The interviews were to discuss the questions in more detail and to gain further understanding on the factors that influence the use of biometric application, such as authentication.

Two distinct stages were designed in this research, each using a different method and each with a particular focus. A mix of qualitative methods and user groups provides rigor through triangulation and quantitative techniques provide useful trend analysis. Thus the use of the multiple or mixed methodology with both qualitative and quantitative aspects compensates for the weakness of one method via the strengths of the other method (McMurray, Pace, & Scott, 2004). A combination of qualitative and quantitative methods in the research "may provide complementary data sets which together give a more complete picture than can be obtained using either method singly" (Tripp-Reimer, 1985, p. 197). Additionally, the use of multiple qualitative methods enhances the richness and validity of the research (McMurray, Pace, & Scott, 2004). In particular, interviews were conducted with managers and questionnaires were given to employees in order to investigate their perceptions regarding the use of biometrics.

3.1 Interviews

Interviews with knowledgeable individuals are recommended as an appropriate method to narrow down the scope of the research and investigate the range of issues (Sekaran, 2003). In this research, face-to-face interviews were conducted in the Kingdom of Saudi Arabia with eleven managers of the General Organisation for Technical Education and Vocational Training and the Royal Commission for Jubail and Yanbu. However, the participants were selected at different management levels. In order to obtain personally meaningful information from the participants, open-ended questions were used for the interviews (McMurray, Pace, & Scott, 2004).

3.2 Questionnaire

The questionnaire was used for data collection for this research as it is an efficient means to gain data from a large participant group, it is an appropriate method to answer the research questions, and it is an effective method to investigate people's attitudes and opinions regarding particular issues (Fraenkel & Wallen, 2000). In this research, a total 101 participants completed the questionnaire, and they are all employees in one of these two organisations: the General Organisation for Technical Education and Vocational Training and the Royal Commission for Jubail and Yanbu.

3.3 Data Collection and Analysis

As mentioned, the data of this research were collected through face-to-face interviews and questionnaires as well as the literature review. The justification for using different techniques for collecting the data is triangulation to provide verification. Triangulation refers to the use of several different methods or sources in the same study in order to confirm and verify the data gathered (McMurray, Pace, & Scott, 2004).

In the interview, all participants were asked if the interview could be recorded, and none of them objected. The expected maximum time for each interview was 60 minutes; however, the actual time for each recording was about 25 to 40 minutes. Notes were taken during each interview as a safeguard against recording failure. Afterwards, all interviewees' answers were categorized according to each question of the interview and they are presented in the results section.

In the questionnaire, permission from the surveyed organisations as well as all the managers of the participating employees is gained to distribute the questionnaire to the employees. However, all responses were stored in the SPSS (Statistical Package for the Social Science) software which was used for the analyses. Statistical analysis includes the frequency and the percentage of each category of the responses for each answer, the Chi square value and its level of significance.

4 RESULTS

It is noteworthy that the two investigated organisations implemented fingerprint scanners for proving employees' attendance. Previously, manual signature recording was the official process for proving employees' attendance in most agencies in the Kingdom of Saudi Arabia. In this process, the employee has to sign and record attendance twice a day, at the beginning of the work day and at the end as well. This process has several negatives, because the employees may sign for others and may not write the correct time of signing. Therefore, this was not an effective or efficient process for recording attendance, and was considered a good reason for implementing biometric technology.

However, in this section we will present just a number of our survey questions which are relevant to detecting problems in this context and seeking solutions to reducing the digital and cultural gap.

4.1 Interview Results of Managers

A question by question analysis is presented as follows:

4.1.1 What Cultural Gap Do You Perceive Between the Employees' Level of Technological Experience and the Level of Biometric Technology That is Being Deployed?

This question investigates the cultural gap between the employees' level of technological experience and the level of biometric technology that is being deployed in their organisation. Nine of the respondents to this study agreed that there is a cultural gap between the employees' technical cultural levels and the level of technology being used, but they attributed this gap to different reasons, as follows:

- Four respondents attributed the technical cultural gap of the staff to their levels of technological literacy.
- Two respondents attributed the technical cultural gap to the employees' age; that is, the older the employee, the wider the gap.
- One respondent attributed the cultural gap to a perception that use of this technology indicates a level of mistrust of employees by management causing them not to want to use the technology
- Two respondents did not attribute the cultural gap to a particular reason.
- Two other respondents did not agree that there is a cultural gap at all.

4.1.2 Do You Accept a Level of Responsibility for Narrowing This Cultural Gap?

This question investigates the managers' perceived responsibility for narrowing the cultural gap between their employees' level of technological experience and the level of biometric technology.

- Five of the interviewed managers felt that they are responsible for narrowing the cultural gap; they proposed procedures concentrating on enhancing employee awareness of technology and its utilities.
- Four respondents did not consider that it was their responsibility to narrow the cultural gap.

4.1.3 Have You Experienced Any Difficulties in Dealing With This Technology? If So, What Were They?

This question investigates the managers' points of view regarding the difficulties in dealing with biometric technology in their workplace. Regarding the difficulties being experienced, 11 responses were presented by the interviewees, distributed among the following categories:

- Employee resistance (11 respondents);
- Disabling and breaking the fingerprint device by some employees (4 respondents);
- System failures (5 respondents); and,
- System unable to take fingerprints from some users (7 respondents).

4.1.4 What are the Main Barriers (Inconveniences) of Applying Biometric Technology in Your Organisation?

This question investigates the managers' point of view regarding the main barriers of applying biometric technology in their organisations.

- All responses to this issue were related to digital and technological culture as well as resistance to change that was evidenced by the employees at the beginning of the deployment.

4.1.5 How Do You Think the Use of Biometric Technology Affects Self Perceived Social Level of Your Employees?

This question investigates the social impact of the use of biometric technology on the employees themselves and among their society. A wide range of responses were provided regarding the social impact of the fingerprint technology; these responses showed contradictions regarding the effects on hardworking employees.

- Six respondents said that there were positive effects as regulation became stricter.
- Five respondents highlighted the negative effects of using this technology.

However, they attributed the positive and negative effects to the following:

- Three respondents raised the issue of mistrust concerns that the employees may feel. They feel the perception that their managers do not trust them and that this may reflect badly on them in their society as other people may mistrust them as well.
- Four respondents commented that this type of regulative technology has reported positive effects on all types of employees, especially when comparing with other employees who do not use this technology. For example, one response said that I feel proud with my friends that I use this new technology while they do not.

To sum up, managers' responses to all questions indicated that there is a digital and cultural gap evidenced by the technological awareness of employees and the preferred authentication solutions promoted by management. This digital and cultural gap creates a resistance to change by the employees which reflects on the acceptance and adoption of new technologies such as these.

4.2 Questionnaire Results of Government Employees

As mentioned before the questionnaire was distributed to 101 government employees and a question by question analysis is presented in this section. Questions were presented as a five point Likert scale (1 to 5) where 1 is the lowest level of importance and five is the highest. There was an "opt out" option if the respondent did not know the importance or relevance of the question's concept. Likert responses have been generalised to provide a preliminary analysis view.

4.2.1 How Important Do You Think the Use of Biometric Technology is to the Organisation?

Responses to this question examine the users' points of view regarding the level of importance that the employees think the organisation places on the use of biometric technology. The responses were as the following:

- No one of the respondents think that it is not important.
- 23.8% feel that it is important.
- 13.9% feel that it is very important.
- A minority (45.5%) of the respondents have no idea of the importance of using fingerprint technology in their workplace.

4.2.2 How Important Do You Think it is That There Should Be an Awareness of This Technology Before its Implementation?

Responses to this question examine the users' points of view regarding the importance of awareness before implementation of the used biometric technology. The concept of awareness includes aspects of notification, information and education of employees. All respondents classified the level of importance as follows.

- Only 5% of the respondents feel that it is not necessary to promote employee awareness of the technology before the implementation.
- 15.8% think that it is important.
- A majority (52.56%) of the respondents perceived that it is very important to have awareness before using fingerprint technology.

4.2.3 Do You Think That the Use of This Technology in Your Workplace Means That Employers Mistrust Employees?

Responses to this question examine the users' points of view regarding the perception of employer mistrust created by introducing and using biometric technology. There is a significant difference among employees' responses as follows.

- 33.7% of the respondents state that it does not mean mistrust.
- 11.9% think that it means mistrust.
- 22.8% think that it certainly means mistrust.
- 33.7% of the respondents are unsure if it means mistrust or not.

5 DISCUSSION

The results indicate that nine of the interview respondents agreed that there is a digital/cultural gap created by the employees' low familiarity with technology and the organisation's adoption of biometrics. This has been supported by several studies; for instance, Ashbourn (2004) stated that education is an essential phase that users need. The organisation that is going to implement such biometric technology has to communicate with users in order to provide them with a good understanding and overview about biometrics, how this technology works, and the reasons for its implementation. Moreover, if this information

is presented in an attractive and truly informative manner, the organisation will achieve much in warming users towards the project and raising their confidence regarding the implementation of this technology.

In addition, this result reflects some of the literature findings regarding the challenges in the implementation of e-government in the Kingdom of Saudi Arabia. These might be summarized as the weakness due to the lack of social and cultural awareness of the concepts and applications of e-government, the extent of computer illiteracy, as well as the deficiency of the official education curricula in addressing the information age. However, the result of this study supports the finding which reveals that there is a need programs related to the application of e-government (Alshareef, 2003; Alsuwail, 2001).

Only five of the interviewed managers felt that they are responsible for narrowing the technological cultural gap. This result concurs with Ashbourn's (2004) finding that managers need some in-depth training in order to understand the various issues regarding the introduction and use of such technology. In particular there is a need to be able to fulfill their roles regarding the ongoing running of the application and user acceptance and understanding. Therefore, such training may lead managers to narrow the technical cultural gap.

It is important to note that employee resistance is an essential issue facing organisations, as mentioned by all respondents through their answers to several questions. Several employees have tried to prevent the use of this technology in many ways. Four interviewees clarified that some employees had tried to break down the device which meant that some managers had to install cameras in order to catch the person and prevent this from happening. Furthermore, some employees tried to distort their fingers by injuring them or rubbing them on wood in order to make the system unable to read their fingerprints in an attempt to prove this technology to be ineffective. In addition, this result relates with the literature finding where Alsuwail (2001) and Alshareef (2003) confirmed resistance by employees to change as one of the challenges of implementing e-government in the Kingdom of Saudi Arabia. This has been supported by Feng (2003) who stated that one of the main barriers to implementing e-government is the need for change in individual attitudes and organisational culture. Furthermore, user acceptance and perception problems relating to the implementation of the new technology have been clarified by Giesing (2003) as factors that would prevent an organisation from implementing or adopting biometric technology.

Furthermore, the interviews provided a wide range of responses regarding the social impact of the fingerprint technology. Six respondents said that there were positive effects through the regulation of attendance and working hours. On the other hand, five respondents highlighted the negative effects of using this technology, which relate to the literature finding by Coventry (2005) who highlighted the weakness of the social and cultural awareness of the concepts and applications of e-government. Coventry continued that the usability and acceptance of biometric services can be affected by the context of use as well as the social issues, such as the perceived benefits to the user and the perceived privacy risks. Application contexts with obvious, apparent benefits and low risks may lead to greater perceptions of usability and higher acceptance opinions of biometrics than contexts where there are little obvious benefits and high risks.

On the other hand, a minority (45.5%) of the employees had no idea of the importance of using fingerprint technology, which may relate to the shortage of any awareness program that the employees could undertake before using such technology. This supports the challenges of implementing e-government in the Kingdom of Saudi Arabia which indicate a scarcity of information programs related to the application of e-government, the deficiency of the official education curricula in addressing the information age, and the lack of computer literacy among citizens (Alharbi, 2006; Alshareef, 2003; Alsuwail, 2001).

A small majority (52.56%) of the respondents perceived that it is very important to have an awareness of the introduction and implications of the technology through information and education programs before using fingerprint technology. Change resistance might also be a key factor here. In fingerprint technology contexts in Saudi Arabia, many people raise the issue of radiation risks that they think are associated with using these systems, as well as the disease transfer by every employee touching the same point, which was also illustrated in other responses to the interviews. These concerns will simply be reduced as the levels of awareness increase, and as the usual habits continue after adaptation to this technology takes place. As stated, a weakness of the social and cultural awareness of the concepts and applications of e-government has been noted in the literature by Alshareef (2003) and Alsuwail (2001) as well as a scarcity of education programs related to the application of e-government. Moreover, Alharbi (2006) clarified that society lacks awareness about e-government advantages and benefits. However, a study by Giesing (2003) noted that the employees expressed the need for more information about biometric technology in general and for more detailed information on the specific biometrics that will be used, as they only had basic knowledge of biometrics. Giesing's study shows that employees would like to know more regarding biometric technology, such as background information, advantages and disadvantages, user guides on the use of the biometrics, technical specifications, the storage of biometric data, as well as the security and privacy issues. Furthermore, Ashbourn (2004) stated that the education phase of implementing technology is very important for users in order to provide them with a good understanding and to make them more confident in its use.

A significant 33.7% of the respondents to the survey section of this study do not know whether introduction of this technology indicates mistrust and 22.8% of them think the use of this technology certainly means employers mistrust employees. This may be attributed to various factors including a lack of awareness through consultation, notification, information, and general levels of computer literacy. The scarcity of programs related to the application of e-government may also explain these some of the results. As 33.7% of respondents do not feel that it signifies mistrust of employees and these may relate to the proportion of the user population with higher levels of the familiarity with technology, its adoption, convenience and usefulness which they may have experienced elsewhere.

6 CONCLUSION

A study was undertaken to investigate government employees' perceptions of factors relating to the introduction of biometric authentication at the workplace. This was undertaken to determine how best to gain employees' acceptance of biometric in order to successfully adopt biometrics in e-government applications. Results supported a number of findings reported in literature regarding user acceptance and adoption of biometrics and e-government technology. Analysis of results shows that an awareness and orientation process about biometrics should take place before the technology is introduced into the organisation. This is highlighted as all managers expressed employees' resistance to the technology's installation at the beginning of its implementation. The employees should be made aware about the use of the new technology, the purpose of its implementation and the benefits. Since about half of the managers had not considered their responsibilities for narrowing the digital and cultural gap regarding the fingerprint technology, it is recommended that managers should be made aware of their responsibilities in this issue. They should recognize that digital and cultural gap in technological awareness exists and that they have to act as leaders and

role models for their employees. Finally, as the managers have a big part of the responsibility to successfully implement biometric technology in their organisations, they need to gain a detailed understanding of this technology and preferably have a basic background about Information Technology as well.

7 FURTHER RESEARCH

While this research has investigated users' perceptions regarding the use of biometric in e-government applications, further research is recommended to focus in more detail on the users' concerns, such as familiarity, trust, and convenience. In addition, more research should be done to better understand the relationship between each concern of the users' perceptions. Moreover, since this research indicated the importance of an awareness program for users before the implementation of such biometrics, more specific studies about what users need to know and the best methods to inform them regarding this science are recommended.

REFERENCES

Al-shehry, A., Rogerson, S., Fairweather, N., Prior, M. (2006). *The Motivations for Change towards E-government Adoption: Saudi Arabia as a case Study, eGovernment Workshop*. West London: Brunel University.

Alharbi, S. (2006). *Perceptions of Faculty and Students toward the Obstacles of Implementing E-Government in Educational Institutions in Saudi Arabia (Tech. Rep.)*. Morgantown, West Virginia: West Virginia University.

Alshareef, T. (2003). *E-Government in the Kingdom of Saudi Arabia, Applicational Study on the governmental mainframes in Riyadh City*. Riyadh, Saudi Arabia: King Saud University.

AlShihi, H. (2006). *Critical Factors in the Adoption and Diffusion of E-government Initiatives in Oman*. PhD thesis, Victoria University, Australia.

Alsuwail, M. (2001). *Directions and local experiences, Foundations and Requirements of E-Government*. Paper presented at the E-Government Conference, Institute of Public Administration, the Kingdom of Saudi Arabia.

Ashbourn, J. (2004). *Practical biometric from aspiration to implementation*. London: Springer.

Blau, A. (2002). Access isn't enough: Merely connecting people and computers won't close the digital divide. *American Libraries*, *33*(6), 50–52.

Bolle, R., Connell, J., Pankanti, S., Ratha, N., & Senior, A. (2004). *Guide to Biometrics*. New York: Springer.

Bonsor, K., & Johnson, R. (n.d.). How Facial Recognition Systems Work. *How Stuff Works*. Retrieved October 1, 2007 from http://computer.howstuffworks.com/facialrecognition.htm

Central Department of Statistics & Information (CDSI). (2009). Retrieved from http://www.cdsi.gov.sa

Central Intelligence Agency (CIA). The Word Fact Book. (2009). Retrieved from https://www.cia.gov/library/publications/the-world-factbook/

Coventry, L. (2005). *Usable Biometrics, Security and usability* (pp. 181–204). London: University College London, Human Centered Systems Group.

Dearstyne, B. (2001). E-business, e-government and information proficiency. *Information Management Journal, 34*(4).

E-government Program (Yesser). (2009). *The Ministry of Communications and Information Technology*. Retrieved from http://www.yesser.gov.sa

Feng, L. (2003). Implementing E-government Strategy is Scotland: Current Situation and Emerging Issues. *Journal of Electronic Commerce in Organizations*, *1*(2), 44–65.

Fraenkel, J., & Wallen, N. (2000). *How to design & evaluate research in education*. New York: McGraw-Hill.

Frees, R. (n.d.). Biometric technology improves identification security. *U.S. Air Force*. Retrieved March 3, 2008 from http://www.af.mil/news/story.asp?id=123084564

Giesing, I. (2003). *User response to biometric* (pp. 95–135). Pretoria, South Africa: University of Pretoria.

Maxwell, J. A. (2005). *Qualitative Research Design: An Interactive Approach* (2nd ed.). Thousand Oaks, CA: Sage Publication.

McLindin, B. (2005). *Improving the Performance of Two Dimensional Facial Recognition Systems*. South Australia, Australia: University of South Australia.

McMurray, A., Pace, R., & Scott, D. (2004). *Research: a commonsense approach*. Melbourne, Australia: Thomson Social Science Press.

Scott, M. (2005). An assessment of biometric identities as a standard for e-government services. *Services and Standards*, *1*(3), 271–286. doi:10.1504/IJSS.2005.005800

Sekaran, U. (2003). *Research Methods for Business: A Skill Building Approach* (4th ed.). New York: John Wiley & Sons Inc.

The Annual Report of the Australian Customs Service (ACS). (2005). Retrieved from http://www.customs.gov.au/webdata/resources/files/ACSannualReport0405.pdf

The Saudi Network. (n.d.). Retrieved January 14, 2009 from http://www.the-saudi.net/

Tripp-Reimer, T. (1985). Combining qualitative and quantitative methodologies. In Leininger, M. M. (Ed.), *Qualitative research methods in nursing* (pp. 179–194). Orlando, FL: Grune & Stratton.

Wayman, J., Jain, D., Maltoni, H., & Maio, D. (2005). *Biometric Systems: Technology, Design and Performance Evaluation*. New York: Springer.

This work was previously published in International Journal of E-Adoption, Volume 2, Issue 1, edited by Sushil K. Sharma, pp. 59-71, copyright 2010 by IGI Publishing (an imprint of IGI Global).

Chapter 11

Diffusion of E–Learning Practice in an Educational Institution:
Organizational Learning Attributes and Capabilities

Keith Thomas
The Chinese University of Hong Kong, China

Paul Lam
The Chinese University of Hong Kong, China

Annisa Ho
The Chinese University of Hong Kong, China

ABSTRACT

Successful knowledge transfer or diffusion of e-learning practice goes beyond precursor incentives and anticipated rewards for the individual lecturer. It also involves wider enabling of learning attributes and cultural capabilities in an organization. This paper examines how some of these attributes and capabilities play out in an educational institution in the context of web-enabled technology. An organizational-learning model is used to examine diffusion of practices after initial design and development. This paper is based on a case study of eight course-level e-learning projects in a university based in Hong Kong. The study illustrates a number of issues and challenges for the wider uptake of the initial idea from the individual course to the programme and wider institution.

INTRODUCTION

What we know about knowledge transfer or diffusion across an organization is greatly exceeded by what we do not know (Huber, 2001). Mirroring this

DOI: 10.4018/978-1-4666-0041-6.ch011

observation, other research suggests motivational factors are negatively correlated with knowledge sharing (Taylor & Wright, 2004), and hence there is a need to look beyond incentives and rewards to learning attributes and capabilities in an organization (Szulanski, 1996; Taylor & Wright, 2004). This wider view similarly complements literature on the dynamics of interactions (Staber & Sydow, 2002; Hyland, Davison, & Sloan, 2003; Thomas & Bose, 2006), the need to create framework conditions to stimulate people within and outside organizations (Lundvall & Nielsen, 2007), and the value of social networks (Schoenmakers & Duysters, 2006). In face of this compelling evidence, no matter how well-intentioned, any effort without the necessary preconditions is likely to be doomed to failure, defined in this case by the absence of wider uptake of any initial individual technology-based teaching and learning initiative (Taylor & Wright, 2004).

A starting point to understanding organizational learning (OL) is to view it as more than an aggregation of individual learning. While individual learning is necessary, alone it is not sufficient (Argyris & Schon, 1978; Kim, 1993). Correspondingly, the necessary extra conditions can be described as creating and transferring knowledge (Nonaka, Toyama, & Konno, 2000) or as learning embedded in organizational memory or institutionalized in systems, structures and practices (Berends, Boersma, & Weggeman, 2003). This paper explores the process of transferring e-learning knowledge from the individual course and teacher to the wider community. The focus is on the process and character of knowledge sharing or diffusion associated with teacher and classroom-based interventions. In this context, teachers are no more well-intended practitioners intent on imparting knowledge than students are simply learners of a subject; rather, teachers, like students, are social beings and they respond to the social, political and organizational context around them (Laurillard, 1994). The introduction, survival and dispersal of new technology is, using a medical metaphor, somewhat akin to a new species invasion of an ecology, in this case the university. Typically, slow adoption of technology by teachers has been a long-standing issue; research has focused on schools as social organizations and on sets of factors associated with teachers, such as attitudes and expertise with

technology. Much of this research is in isolation; nor is there an apparent framework to unify the studies (Zhao & Frank, 2003).

This study seeks to shed light on some of the challenges and opportunities for both individual teachers and institutions in relation to e-learning diffusion. As Solomon and Chowdhury (2002) advised, 'evaluative inquiry' for OL and change is more than a means to an end, and it is more than skills that results in increased competence or improved classroom effectiveness. A significant effect of evaluative inquiry is the fostering of relationships among organization members and the diffusion of their learning through the organization. Thus, the process also serves as a transfer-of-knowledge process (Solomon & Chowdhury, 2002), such that inquiry provide avenues for growth, for both individual and organization.

Organizational Learning and Diffusion

OL, which is the collective process of acquisition and creation of competencies that modify how situations are managed and transform the situation themselves (Stevens & Dimitriadis, 2002), is of great interest as it links individual learning with organizational behavior and change. Organizations in turn are best understood in terms of four distinct and co-equal forms of knowledge: explicit, tacit, individual, and group knowledge (Cook & Brown, 1999), where knowledge and knowing (or 'knowing in action') are seen as mutually enabling. To explain this distinction, rather than the more static view of knowledge, 'knowing in action' refers to situated practice around varying forms of social interaction in what literature describes as communities of practice (Amin & Roberts, 2008). Thus, knowledge is a tool of knowing (Blackler, 1995) and it is a generative dance between knowledge and knowing that is a powerful source of innovation.

Two broad perspectives in OL are evident: individual and social, although due to the intrinsic complexity of OL, there are few attempts to combine individual and OL in an integrative approach (Stevens & Dimitriadis, 2002). The first, individual learning, is a functional viewpoint; organizations are not super-persons and they learn only in so much as the individuals in them learn (Mumford, 1991; Kim, 1993). Accordingly, organizational memory represents a shared understanding of routines, procedures, rules and documents. The perspective is functionalist as it assumes reality can be described objectively and there is little effort to change conditions in relation to power. The second, a social interpretative view, sees the organization as an evolutionary entity, constantly creating meaning and identity (Boreham & Morgan, 2004; Yorks, Neuman, Kowalski, & Kowalski, 2007). This latter view, increasingly the mainstream view, emphasizes the subjective nature of knowledge and of learning being situated or context-dependent (Ortenblad, 2002). Rather than a dichotomous stance, this study takes an integrated view that seeks to incorporate insights from both views into a practical application of collective learning and effective diffusion of a service offering e-learning. In furthering this objective, as Stevens and Dimitriadis (2002) noted, the transformation of any service itself may also require the transformation of some elements of the service concept.

The primary challenge for OL is *diffusion* of knowledge (Zemke, 1999), which in simple terms means linking or extending individual learning (Ghosh, 2004). The knowledge or practice (in a form of tacit knowledge) of one individual can influence others in the organization. However, the challenge appears to be in facilitating or allowing a feedback loop that connects the individual and the collective. It can be done through factors that facilitate knowledge transfer at the individual level through the different levels of an organization – in the case of an educational institution, to other individual teachers, the faculty group and finally to the wider organization. Notably, any transfer will reflect the structure and activities of the group

and what happens within individual psyches and how the resultant experiences are projected back into group life (Stacey, 1993). What this observation highlights is a little appreciated influence of psychological needs, including defences against anxiety, and the need to integrate individuals into the group over concern of wider social needs.

From the social perspective, the social system determines social structures and related activity, and OL is filtered and facilitated by group-based mechanisms that *legitimize* and *synthesize* (Nonaka & Takeuchi, 1995; von Krogh & Roos, 1995; Thomas & Bose, 2006). From this perspective, culture, structure, resources and other considerations can act as potential *barriers to learning* and diffusion (Tamuz, 2001; Walshe, 2003). Collectively, these issues are encapsulated in the concept of *absorptive capacity*, a concept that refers to the ability (potential or realized) within an individual (or group) to recognize the value of new or external information, to assimilate it and apply it to organizational ends (Cohen & Levinthal, 1990; Lane, Koka, & Pathak, 2002). While there has been little attention on how absorptive capacity is created and developed in an organization, studies highlight effective internal knowledge sharing and integration as being critical (Lane et al., 2002). Other studies treat absorptive capacity as a cognitive barrier (Minbaeva, Pedersen, Bjorkman, Fey, & Park, 2002), arising from, for example, differences in worldviews (of the environment and economy), perceptions of vulnerability, adaptive capacity and risk, and also competition among issues for public attention and a space on political agendas. Conversely, variable conceptualizations of barriers to adaptation, such as for climate-change assessments or best-practice management, can also contribute to low adaptive capacity (Preston & Stafford-Smith, 2009). For these reasons, if we are to facilitate adaptation and diffusion, it seems fundamental that we address social, cultural and even economic phenomena.

Individual and wider social processes involved in OL can be described as a cyclic or spiral relationship. A composite framework that abstracts the various components and their interrelationships are shown in Figure 1. The cycle portrays initially an inner circle of individual experiences in terms of new practice prompted by an *external stimulus* that must first be *recognized and interpreted* in terms of current mental models, routines and procedures. *Experimentation and search*, through dialogue and problem-solving workshops, help consolidate this practice for subsequent critique by a process of *internal selection, articulation and codification* that is followed by a process of *feedback and iteration*. The cycle either improves the initial individual service or connects these routines to the wider organization by way of a larger spiral (or cycle) of diffusion (Zollo & Winter, 2002, pp. 340, 345). The model provides a framework to explain the links across individual, group and organization levels, while describing OL as a process involving attributes such as interpretation, experimentation, codification and feedback. The approach also reveals the importance of institutionalization of the entire process. Diffusion, thus,

can be enhanced by relational practices – space for the creation of shared meaning, reconstituted power relationships and by cultural tools to mediate learning and makes it sustainable (Boreham & Morgan, 2004). These attributes are collectively an organization's absorptive capacity.

THE STUDY

The Information Technology Services Centre (ITSC) and the Centre for Learning Enhancement And Research (CLEAR) are collectively responsible for the planning and implementation of e-learning projects in The Chinese University of Hong Kong. Part of this role is an e-learning Expo (http://www.cuhk.edu.hk/elearning/expo), run annually, with the aim of providing opportunities for teaching staff to showcase course-based e-learning projects developed through the previous year. The study interviewed eight teachers, professors and instructional staff, who took part in the eLearning Expo in 2008. These teachers, who

Figure 1. Organizational learning cycle (adapted from Harvey & Brown, 1996)

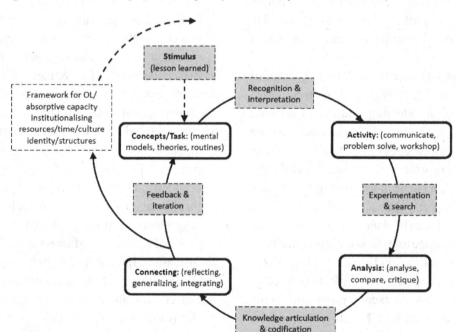

Table 1. Disciplines and the e-learning strategies used by teachers in the study

Teacher	Discipline	Type of strategies	Objectives
1	Language	Multimedia learning module	Self-learning of Putonghua (Chinese)
2	Medicine	Learning resources and quizzes	Consolidation of taught knowledge
3	Science	Video clips of presentations	Students learn from each other
4	Physical education	Video clips of demonstrations	Students have a chance to view the procedures clearly and repeatedly
5	Science	Online discussions with students	Consolidation of knowledge taught or not taught
6	Medicine	eCases	Application of knowledge on authentic problems
7	Engineering	Wiki	Students exchange information and opinions
8	Medicine	Animations	Better explanation of concepts

applied e-learning strategies in their own courses to varying degrees of success, represent a range of disciplines and a variety of strategies (see Table 1). These included web functions, multimedia-rich strategies, and web 2.0 activities, such as the wiki.

The learning objectives associated with these projects were quite varied. Nonetheless, a case-study approach to this research helped explore adaptive behavior in individuals and interpret the findings using the preceding OL concepts and related behavioral approaches.

The researchers met each of the teachers in a focus-group meeting (average 45 minutes each). The teachers were told the main object of the meeting in advance and were invited also to complete a brief survey as preparation for this meeting. This survey explored the sense of ownership and evaluation of the respective projects in terms of perceived benefits or payoffs teachers obtained or expected from their project, while more generally encouraging interview subjects to review and reflect on the design process and outcomes prior to the interviews. This method minimized the warm-up time needed at the beginning of each meeting and allowed maximum opportunity for well-considered responses, rather than on-the-spot ideas that were conjured in a hurry. The approach proved useful and the researchers found the feedback collected in the interviews to the point and in-depth.

All interviews were audio-recorded. Detailed summary notes were compiled immediately after these meetings based on notes, collective recollection and recordings. Completing this process, all summary notes were circulated among the researchers for review and amendment as necessary to ensure they were accurate and comprehensive. The researchers using qualitative thematic analysis, with comments grouped and regrouped into similar themes and sub-themes. Periodic meetings were also held by the researchers to look at the qualitative analyses and how they should be interpreted.

FINDINGS

The Inner (Individual) Learning Cycle

The information collected at the teacher interviews generally confirmed that the various strategies of course-level interventions and individual processes in the illustrated OL cycle happened iteratively and generally smoothly. In other words, the teachers were able to experiment in design and achieved to a greater or lesser degree their initial expected objectives. Through this process of development, teachers described moving from basic designs concerns (what to do and how) to concern over look (appearance) and then to a critical focus on functionality in terms of teaching and learning. Evidence of effectiveness in terms of learning outcomes came from both formal and informal evaluation sources. For example, some teachers compared students' performance in assignments across the years (teachers 2, 4 and 8), some solicited students' opinions on the e-learning strategies through focus-group meetings or surveys (teachers 2, 3, 4, 6 and 8), and some observed students in and outside class, or had informal conversations with them about the new strategies (teachers 1 and 5). It was also clear that many of the teachers evaluated the e-learning strategies using multiple methods.

Because of the e-learning activities, the teachers were satisfied that:

- The students spent more time on learning (teachers 2, 4 and 6);
- Students could better understand difficult concepts that were previously only poorly illustrated by static textbooks pictures and diagrams (teacher 8);
- Students had the opportunity to apply knowledge on realistic cases (teacher 2);
- Student learning was more active, asking questions and participating in discussion (teacher 5);
- Students were even more motivated in class (teacher 4);
- The coverage of content went beyond the syllabus (teachers 5 and 6);
- Students appreciated teacher's effort and course evaluation scores were generally better that previous years (teacher 2 and 4);
- Students learned new skills and showed some improved ability to solve problems (teacher 6); and
- There was evidence students enjoyed the online resources and found them useful (teacher 2).

Teachers attributed the success of their e-learning strategies to a number of factors. Factors related to themselves included: strong motivation, fuelled by enthusiasm for teaching excellence (teachers 2, 4, 5, 6, 7 and 8); not being overly worried about applying technology (teachers 2, 5 and 7); and the belief that technology would enhance teaching practice (teachers 5, 6, 7 and 8). A number of factors reflecting the social system were also important:

- Students were very ready and willing to change (teachers 4 and 7);
- Support provided either by the department or by the University, in the form of monetary grants, technical services and/or consultations in regard to e-learning pedagogical design. In general, the teachers remarked that the support (limited as it was) had great impact on their work and workload, and that ITSC support in particular was most helpful as it came at the critical times, usually at the beginning of their planning and development stage (teachers 2, 3, 5, and 8); and
- An internal departmental climate (teacher 6) characterized by good communications, a collegial long-term relationship with doctors, personal credibility and relevant information technology (IT), audio-visual (AV) and subject-based (biological) knowledge.

In sum, teachers achieved considerable success in developing and applying e-learning strategies to their courses – the individual component of OL. Success to this extent was not related to technology, as much as to social context.

The Wider (Organizational) Spiral

Teachers were then asked to consider whether they were aware of any extension on their strategies into the wider teaching and learning environment. Four situations were described: uptake of the strategies by the same teacher in other courses

Table 2. Diffusion of e-learning strategies used by teachers

Teacher	To other courses	To fellow colleagues	To other teachers	Outside University
1	No (self-learning resource)	No	Presented in Expo	No
2	No (content different)	Yes/No (talked to friends)	Presented in Expo	Writing a journal article
3	No	No	Presented in Expo	No
4	No (self-learning resources)	No (thought they were too busy)	Presented in Expo	Writing a journal article
5	No	No	Presented in Expo	No
6	Yes (departmental level resource – high utility)	Yes (many department staff involved)	Presented in Expo	No
7	Yes	Yes/No (talked to friends)	Presented in Expo	No
8	Yes, applied for funding for another set of animations	No	Presented in Expo	Writing a journal article

taught by him/herself; transfer of the strategy to other colleagues in the teacher's same department; transfer of the strategy to other teachers in the same university; and transfer of strategies to people outside the university. These situations broadly distinguish between low-end OL or transfer to a wider adoption and diffusion of lessons learned. The exchanges can occur in various forms, from formal meetings and conferences to informal gatherings. The responses, as summarized on Table 2, show a general lack of wider diffusion.

Teachers participating in this study overall reported transfer of e-learning strategies difficult, even to other courses taught by them. This problematic nature in knowledge transfer reflected the fact that many of the strategies were emergent, quite topic-specific and involving unanticipated time-consuming creation of online learning materials (e.g., cases of teachers 2, 6 and 8). Sometimes, staff perceptions got in the way. As teacher 5, for example, remarked that other student groups might not welcome the same strategy and consequently he did not use the same online discussion strategy in another course in which the students were actually majoring in the subject. The reason given is evidence of a cognitive barrier: a belief that 'only students who took the course as an elective or as a general-education course would welcome free-flow, open-ended

discussions' enabled by the e-learning intervention.

Adoption of e-learning strategies by teachers in the same departments was not evident. Most respondents remarked the general culture was not conducive to sharing their respective e-learning strategies – in effect, a lack of an expansive learning environment reflective of a cultural and social barrier. Some teachers (2 and 7) did explain their projects to fellow colleagues in informal situations, but these teachers doubted it led to any real uptake by their colleagues. As they remarked, teachers tend to have their own styles of teaching. As well, it seemed that many of the e-learning strategies were not directly transferable to other courses and teachers. For uptake by other teachers, either specific e-learning project development is needed or at the very least teachers need to be helped to overcome the hurdle of learning a new set of online teaching skills, while mastering the selected technology. Both conditions, in combination with a lack of strategic thinking reflected by an inability to look beyond and outside the immediate course, and power-based relationships in the departments, tended to mitigate adoption and extension of lessons learned at individual levels.

Noting Gronn's (2003) call for distributed leadership, there is a need to recognize the dynamic interplay between structure, culture and agency in knowledge transfer. In this sense, the only apparent structure supporting diffusion of e-learning strategies to other teachers in the university is an annual eLearning Expo. There is, however, little evidence that this activity, while well attended by other teachers, displaying a range of e-learning projects and providing a useful discussion forum, leads to any uptake in e-learning. However, as some teachers (2 and 6) remarked, it was easier to get the attention of like-minded teachers in another department than teachers in their own. Any diffusion of strategies by teachers to people beyond the University is typically achieved through journal articles or conference papers. There is evidence of effort being given to disseminate respective experience and insights, but as some teachers (2 and 5) remarked, the motivation to write a paper with a teaching and learning focus is also not counted as serious research in their field. Thus, the motivation to publish and so disseminate lessons learned is diminished.

Other attributes related to this seeming non-existence of wider diffusion include:

- Unlike technologies that entertain people and/or make life convenient for users, e-learning strategies can often increase teachers' workload, especially in the preliminary stages of project development.
- Diffusion was not the original objective: rather the main objective being to use the strategies in teaching their own course or courses.
- Lack of skills to promote e-learning: by teachers to effectively explain the strategies or have access to evidence to persuade others that the strategies work.
- Lack of a culture of teaching innovations: the majority of the teachers did not teach this way and so it was very rare, especially in team-teaching situations, that any teacher does something very different from the rest of the teaching team.

- Lacking of affirmation from the organization: use of e-learning strategies was not seen as a strong indicator of performance in teaching and learning. Hence, aside from receipt of a development grant, there was no tangible action taken to recognize the effort to develop e-learning interventions from any of the departments.

DISCUSSION

In discussing policy implications to support diffusion there is an important caveat: the sample and, consequently, the findings are not representative of the whole institution where the study was conducted. However, in sampling a small cross-section of the population, this study does flag the need for deeper investigation into how individual and OL can be integrated in terms of building organizational *absorptive capacity*. There is also apparent value in exploring how technology use has changed teachers and the wider institution. A parallel study objective would be to explore what has changed and perhaps more importantly, see what has been maintained and why?

In this study, the evidence, consistent with literature, is that no matter how well-intentioned, any wider uptake of individual technology-based teaching and learning initiatives is unlikely to be a success without necessary preconditions. The primary purpose of this study was to focus on the process and character of knowledge sharing or diffusion associated with teacher-led, classroom-based e-learning interventions. A secondary intention through evaluative inquiry was to foster relationships among teachers, a process that serves as a transfer-of-knowledge process. This secondary intention was largely achieved, but is not specifically addressed in this subsequent discussion. In terms of the primary objective of this study, there are clear framework conditions or attributes that are identified. Building on the reported findings, the broad framework condi-

Figure 2. An illustration of relationships and key attributes

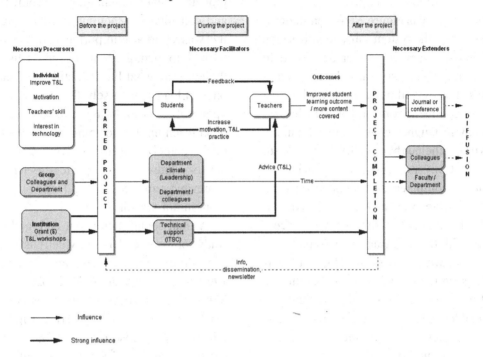

tions and associated relationships are illustrated in Figure 2. These conditions are shown in terms of necessary precursors, facilitators and extenders that apply to the respective phases of the project, before, during and after. The inner (individual) component of OL is shown in white, while the outer (collective) component of OL is shown in grey.

Individual (Teacher–Leader) Factors Influencing Diffusion

Using an ecological metaphor, uptake of new technologies as the result of an external signal can be described as typically entering through a permeable membrane, represented by a receptive teacher (Zhao & Frank, 2003). Other teachers may be uncertain of the value of technology or need for change; hence, similar to any invasion by an exotic species into an ecosystem, some ideas survive, many do not. The interaction of the receptive teacher and the technology is at the centre of the recognition, interpretation and experimentation stage, with initial perceptions based on a perceived

value of the technology, which in turn reflects the wider context and in particular the teacher's own history and pedagogical practices, as well as an assessment of the costs associated with using the selected technology. Characteristically, projects were lonely and time-consuming; both are crucial conditions for successful uptake and they reflect, in a large part, the wider ecosystem of the faculty. As the project advanced, through experimentation and codification stages, technology begins to be modified to suit the teacher's needs. What helped this process was the perceived user-friendliness of the Google platform and related features that allowed easy uptake by the teacher and afforded greater student utility; a typical example is the utility of podcasting as a teaching tool.

At a personal level, being self-motivated and intellectually committed helped sustain teachers and allowed them to stay engaged. Personal motivation aside, a key factor was the perceived intrinsic return on effort in terms of better teaching practice and students' learning, as well as the expected extrinsic benefit during performance appraisal. These conditions are implicit in the circular feedback loop shown in Figure 2 between students and teachers. That the system subsequently saved teaching time encouraged further development effort of learning objects such as videos, podcasts and e-cases. The overall personal reward is best captured by a comment from one teacher who said 'that after having taught the same course for many years, this project helped her regain her enthusiasm for teaching'. Conversely, issues such as having a five-year-old computer with outdated software presented unnecessary obstacles to project development. In the medical example, having access to a patient with the necessary symptoms was a practical issue, while access to ITSC staff was a systemic issue for all and typically resulted in constant time delays. Finally, and consistently at an individual level, teachers were appreciative of the follow-up represented by the interview process. This was seen as a welcome, if unintended, show of institutional interest in their ongoing efforts.

Social-Structural Connections for Diffusion

Some framework conditions that supported e-learning development at a social-system level included what is described as collegiality of co-development. Being part of a small team helped spur and sustain interest. Having the support of technical support staff was a key advantage, for design and functionality and consequent extension of project goals, as well as the simple opportunity to delegate tasks. Another key condition influencing diffusion related to students themselves. As teachers noted, there was a general ready uptake by students. These students were generally younger and more willing to use e-learning packages, especially if it did not create extra work and provided ready access to knowledge in bite-sized chunks as required. Another structural condition that supported uptake (although not diffusion) of e-learning technology was the support provided by the department or by the University – in terms of

monetary development grants, technical services and consultative teaching and learning support that was reported as important in fitting e-learning tools into pedagogical design. This support, though somewhat limited, still had great impact on workload. Conversely, the primary obstacle to uptake of e-learning was the apparent reluctant by other teaching staff to commit any effort because of the perceived time involved. Another social barrier related to senior professors tending to be somewhat removed from the innovative work of more junior teaching staff.

A final social factor that emerged from this study concerns leadership. Much has been written and said of both leadership and OL (Abernathy, 1999; Senge, 1999; Johnson, 2002; Gronn, 2003; Martineau, 2004). As noted earlier, any transformation of this service offering (incorporating e-learning) will also require a transformation of some elements of the service concept. More simply, leadership is not an add-on; it is a necessary precondition and it is central to OL (Cooksey, 2003). Leadership is also central to diffusion at the wider social (outer spiral) level and Senge's three critical roles for leaders in learning organizations: *designer, steward* and *teacher* (Senge, 1995; Senge, 1999) highlights a fundamental shift from depending on senior leaders to facilitate, mentor and empower, to staff needing to evolve into leaders in their own right. This shift goes beyond ownership of process and outcomes to accepting responsibility for process and outcomes. In terms of implementing and then diffusing e-learning practice across the University, teachers and project developers need to grasp the idea of distributed leadership.

CONCLUSION

This paper used an OL framework to examine diffusion of knowledge based on a practice-based approach to OL. What that model presented was the opportunity to see OL as two distinct, but interlinked learning processes – individual and collective. We report the progress of a number of e-learning innovators and discuss how to organize and encourage knowledge transfer for e-learning projects. The findings overall support the body of evidence in knowledge-management literature that motivation and reward factors are insufficient to influence knowledge sharing and sustained diffusion. The study also confirms what learning literature suggests: that individual learning is necessary, but alone is insufficient. Rather, the extra conditions for successful OL involve embedding lessons in organizational memory or in respective systems, structures and practices. This paper foregrounds what literature has described as framework conditions for successful transfer – social context, discussed in terms of 'individual teacher–leader attributes' and the 'social-structural connections' necessary to foster e-learning diffusion. The primary issue is seemingly not about locating and using suitable technology, but about creating the supportive social context, including distributed leadership, to leverage a knowledge spiral at both individual and organizational levels. Based on the findings, one of the reported issues at an individual and collective level (group and institutional) is time. When we dig deeper, there is another significant component that is linked to cultural bias, which makes the institution resistant to change. Both issues deserve further exploration.

REFERENCES

Abernathy, D. J. (1999). A chat with Chris Argyris. *Training & Development, 53*(5), 80–84.

Amin, A., & Roberts, J. (2008). Knowing in action: Beyond communities. *Research Policy, 37,* 353–369. doi:10.1016/j.respol.2007.11.003

Argyris, C., & Schon, D. (1978). *Organizational learning: A theory of action perspective*. Reading, MA: Addison Wesley.

Berends, H., Boersma, K., & Weggeman, M. (2003). The structuration of organizational learning. *Human Relations, 56*(9), 1035–1056. doi:10.1177/0018726703569001

Blackler, F. (1995). Knowledge, knowledge work and organizations: An overview and interpretation. *Organization Studies, 16*(6), 1021–1046. doi:10.1177/017084069501600605

Boreham, N., & Morgan, C. (2004). A sociocultural analysis of organisational learning. *Oxford Review of Education, 30*(3), 307–325. doi:10.1080/0305498042000260467

Cohen, W. M., & Levinthal, D. A. (1990). Absorptive capacity: A new perspective on learning and innovation. *Administrative Science Quarterly, 36*(1), 128–152. doi:10.2307/2393553

Cook, S. D., & Brown, J. S. (1999). Bridging epistemologies: The generative dance between organizational knowledge and organizational knowing. *Organization Science, 10*(4), 381–400. doi:10.1287/orsc.10.4.381

Cooksey, R. (2003). Learnership in complex organizational textures. *Leadership and Organization Development Journal, 24*(4), 204–214. doi:10.1108/01437730310478075

Ghosh, A. (2004). Learning in strategic alliances: A Vygotskian perspective. *The Learning Organization, 11*(4/5), 302–311. doi:10.1108/09696470410538206

Gronn, P. (2003). *The new work of educational leaders*. London: Sage Publications.

Harvey, D., & Brown, D. R. (1996). *An experimential approach to organizational development*. Upper Saddle River, NJ: Prentice Hall.

Huber, G. (2001). Transfer of knowledge in knowledge management systems: Unexplored issues and suggested studies. *European Journal of Information Systems, 10*(2), 72–79. doi:10.1057/palgrave.ejis.3000399

Hyland, P., Davison, G., & Sloan, T. (2003). Linking team competences to organizational capacity. *Team Performance Management, 9*(5/6), 97–106. doi:10.1108/13527590310493873

Johnson, J. R. (2002). Leading the learning organization: Portrait of four leaders. *Leadership and Organization Development Journal, 23*(5), 241–249. doi:10.1108/01437730210435956

Kim, D. H. (1993). The link between individual and organizational learning. *Sloan Management Review, 35*(1), 37–50.

Lane, P. J., Koka, B., & Pathak, S. (2002). A thematic analysis and critical assessment of absorptive capacity research. In *Proceedings of the Academy of Management, BPS: M1, Academy of Management*.

Laurillard, D. (1994). Multimedia and the changing experience of the learner. In M. Ryan (Ed.), *Proceedings of the Asia Pacific Information Technology in Training and Education Conference (APITITE94)* (Vol. 1, pp. 19-24). Brisbane, Australia: APITITE.

Lundvall, B.-A., & Nielsen, P. (2007). Knowledge management and innovation performance. *International Journal of Manpower, 28*(3/4), 207–223. doi:10.1108/01437720710755218

Martineau, J. (2004). Laying the groundwork: First steps in evaluating leadership development. *Leadership in Action, 23*(6), 3–8. doi:10.1002/lia.1044

Minbaeva, D., Pedersen, T., Bjorkman, I., Fey, C. F., & Park, H. J. (2002). MNC knowledge transfer, subsidiary absorptive capacity and HRM. In *Proceedings of the Academy of Management*.

Mumford, A. (1991). Individual and organizational learning. *Industrial and Commercial Training, 23*(6), 24–31. doi:10.1108/EUM0000000001581

Nonaka, I., & Takeuchi, H. (1995). *The Knowledge-creating company: How Japanese companies create the dynamics of innovation*. New York: Oxford University Press.

Nonaka, I., Toyama, R., & Konno, N. (2000). SECI, Ba and leadership: A unified model of dynamic knowledge creation long range planning. *Long Range Planning, 33*(1), 5–34. doi:10.1016/S0024-6301(99)00115-6

Ortenblad, A. (2002). Organizational learning: A radical perspective. *International Journal of Management Reviews, 4*(1), 87–100. doi:10.1111/1468-2370.00078

Preston, B. L., & Stafford-Smith, M. (2009). Framing vulnerability and adaptive capacity assessment: Discussion paper. *CSIRO Climate Adaptation Flagship Working paper Number 2*. Retrieved from http://www.csiro.au/org/ClimateAdaptationFlagship.html

Schoenmakers, W., & Duysters, G. (2006). Learning in strategic technology alliances. *Technology Analysis and Strategic Management, 18*(2), 245–264. doi:10.1080/09537320600624162

Senge, P. (1995). *The fifth discipline: The art and practice of a learning organization*. Sydney, Australia: Random House.

Senge, P. (1999). Learning leaders. *Executive Excellence, 16*(11), 12.

Solomon, M. J., & Chowdhury, A. M. R. (2002). Knowledge to action: Evaluation for learning in a multi-organizational global partnership. *Development in Practice, 12*(3/4), 346–354. doi:10.1080/09614520220149000

Staber, U., & Sydow, J. (2002). Organizational adaptive capacity. *Journal of Management Inquiry, 11*(4), 408–424. doi:10.1177/1056492602238848

Stacey, R. (1993). *Strategic management and organizational dynamics*. New York: Pitman Publishing.

Stevens, E., & Dimitriadis, S. (2002). New service development through the lens of organizational learning: evidence from longititudinal case studies. *Journal of Business Research, 57*, 1074–1084. doi:10.1016/S0148-2963(03)00003-1

Szulanski, G. (1996). Exploring internal stickiness: Impediments to the transfer of best practice within firms. *Strategic Management Journal, 17*, 27–43.

Tamuz, M. (2001). Learning disabilities for regulators: The perils of organizational learning in the air transportation industry. *Administration & Society, 33*(3), 276–302. doi:10.1177/00953990122019776

Taylor, W. A., & Wright, G. H. (2004). Organizational readiness for successful knowledge sharing: Challenges for public sector managers. *Information Resources Management Journal, 17*(2), 22–37.

Thomas, K., & Bose, S. (2006). The human face to knowledge management: Extending the knowledge spiral. *The International Journal of Knowledge. Culture and Change Management, 6*(9), 33–44.

von Krogh, G., & Roos, J. (1995). A perspective on knowledge competence and strategy. *Personnel Review, 24*(3), 56–76. doi:10.1108/00483489510089650

Walshe, K. (2003). Understanding and learning from organizational failure. *Quality & Safety in Health Care, 12*(2), 81–82. doi:10.1136/qhc.12.2.81

Yorks, L., Neuman, J. H., Kowalski, D. R., & Kowalski, R. (2007). Lessons learned from a 5-year project within the Department of Veterans Affairs: Applying theories of interpersonal aggression and organizational justice to the development and maintenance of collaborative social space. *The Journal of Applied Behavioral Science, 43*(3), 352–372. doi:10.1177/0021886307301431

Zemke, R. (1999). Why organizations are still not learning. *Training (New York, N.Y.), 36*(9), 40.

Zhao, Y., & Frank, K. A. (2003). Factors affecting technology uses in schools: An ecological perspective. *American Educational Research Journal, 40*(4), 807–840. doi:10.3102/00028312040004807

Zollo, M., & Winter, S. G. (2002). Deliberate learning and the evolution of dynamic capabilities. *Organization Science, 13*(3), 339–351. doi:10.1287/orsc.13.3.339.2780

This work was previously published in International Journal of E-Adoption, Volume 2, Issue 3, edited by Sushil K. Sharma, pp. 1-13, copyright 2010 by IGI Publishing (an imprint of IGI Global).

Chapter 12
Investigating the Attitude of Students Towards Online Learning

Zerrin Ayvaz Reis
Istanbul University, Turkey

ABSTRACT

The evolution of Internet has provided an opportunity for offering online learning. The old online learning models are getting replaced by new e-learning models. Many universities worldwide have started offering e-learning or online learning through a variety of online learning methods. In fact, the current e-learning models are revolutionizing the instructional content delivery, learning activities, and social communication. Although online learning environments are becoming popular, there is minimal research on learners' attitudes toward online learning environments. The purpose of this study is to explore learners' attitudes toward online learning. Over 300 participants participated. The findings of this study of students' perceptions and attitudes toward online learning not only will help assess pedagogical approach but also help university officials prepare Internet-based online education delivery.

INTRODUCTION

Online learning can be defined as all forms of teaching and learning through Information and Communication Technologies (Guir-Rosenblit, 2005). This includes any course content that is

DOI: 10.4018/978-1-4666-0041-6.ch012

delivered through the use of the Internet, audio and videotape, CD-ROM, satellite broadcast, MP3 players, podcasts, interactive television, PDAs, email, and blogs. Online learning is a relatively new phenomenon that is growing in a significant number of universities around that world, enhancing the learning and teaching processes. Enhancements include incorporating text, audio, video, and animation into course lectures; retrieving information from online journals, periodicals, and newspapers; including simulations and multi-media presentations in the classroom; enhancing communication and collaboration between professors and students; and uploading course content and tests to university websites. It should be apparent that the benefits of online learning to both students and professor have endless possibilities as we are only in the beginning stages of online learning adoption. Technology based online learning helps educators and students overcome time and place barriers. Bork and Gunnarsdottir (2001) described that technologies have benefited teaching and learning environments. Technology-based online learning can benefit students and institutions in terms of course availability, affordability, and convenience (Deal, 2002). Using information technology in online learning can change the commuter student's experience by offering opportunities to interact with an instructor and other students and be engaged in the environments that are not bound by time and place (Kruger, 2000).

Online learning has slowly become a part of Universities across the globe. A variety of information systems (IS) have since allowed online learning to become much more interactive for the online student utilizing such things as sharing video, audio, discussion board, and live interactions via the internet with students and professors. These types of changes make the online learning atmosphere far closer to on-campus learning (Ferratt & Hall, 2009).

Adults have experienced the largest benefit of online learning, making it possible for them to return to school and further their education while continuing to work (Li, 2007). Zhao et al. (2009), showed in a survey they collected of 300 students that approximately 75% of them where 25 years old or older. Over 50% of U.S. students have gone back to college or started college after starting professional career (Hiltz & Turoff, 2005). Online learning has been extremely popular to this demographic because of it flexibility, lack of commuting time, availability 24 hours a day, and typically flexible, to a point, deadlines (Zhao et al., 2009).

Online learning has also seen its fair share of growing pains. Over the years the main complaints to this style of learning has been problems submitting homework and papers, correspondence with professors primarily through email, learning curve involved for the technology required, and lack of face to face interaction with other students (Perreault et al., 2002). Unfortunately most universities are tackling these types of issues on their own, typically creating a duplication of efforts in solving the same problem as well as universities not pooling their resources and money to enable the best possible solution for everyone (Barker & Holley, 1996). Many IS software platforms have been created to help facilitate online learning as well as providing a widespread solution to general problems encountered by professors and students including Adobe Acrobat Pro, Blackboard, WebCT, and Moodle (Li, 2007). However there is still more room to improve and with the use of more IS systems and software online learning can become an even better environment to learn in, even over on campus learning.

Nowadays, technology in online education has extended its capability to reach students and university learning goals. Interactive and non-interactive learning have increased their role in online education. Berge (1999) mentions that interaction is an important component to learner satisfaction and it helps maintain student persistence in courses. Moore (1989) classified communication in interaction learning between 1) participants and materials, 2) participants and instructors, and 3) among participants. These classifications allow flexibility in the design of interactive learning programs (Northrup, 2002).

University professors and instructors who have taken on the challenge of teaching classes via online learning have undergone many different changes including how to alter their teaching methods to be the most successful for on campus and online learning students. Additionally online students have much different expectations of professors, expecting them to be readily available to answer questions at all times via email – causing high amounts of mental pressure on the instructor (Li, 2007). Along the same lines, universities are also held to a different standard by online students requiring more technical help, more course software to facilitate their courses, and many other new resources an on-campus only institution would not require (Hiltz & Turoff, 2005).

Kruger (2000) suggests using new technology applications in the classroom only if they are more effective and can improve student learning. Students' technology skills should also be assessed before implementing new technology in the classroom. Online learning instructors need to be able to motivate students despite the lack of eye contact in this environment (Sherry, 1996; Cornell & Martin, 1997; Barker & Baker, 1995). Because of the lack of eye contact and face-to-face interaction, some educators are concerned that online learning is not as effective as traditional learning (Kruger, 2000).

Another aspect including in this study is attitude. Attitude, as defined by Collins Cobuild English Dictionary (1998), means "something that people think and feel about it." Thurstone and Chave (1946) define an attitude as "the degree of positive or negative affect associated with some psychological object." The psychological object in Thurstone's definition is any phrase, person, symbol, idea, or institute toward which people's opinions can differ positively or negatively (Edwards, 1957). Attitudes are considered to have three components: 1) affect, what the individual feels toward the attitude object; 2) behavior, the individual's intention to act toward the attitude object in a particular way; 3) cognition, the individual's beliefs, knowledge structures and thoughts about the attitude object (Smalley, Graff, & Saunders, 2001; Gall, Gall, & Borg, 2002).

Attitudes and opinions of students toward each criterion of technology-based online learning can be used to help institutes and organizations develop online learning to meet students' needs. Valenta, Therriault, Dieter and Mrtek (2001) mentioned that instruction for web-based courses can be better designed by first understanding student opinions. Also Webster and Hackley (1997) stated that "students' opinions regarding technology and online learning may have significant effects on the success of the method. Researchers have generally argued that the successful implementation of any new technology depends on factors related to user attitudes and opinions". Therefore, to be able to improve the quality of online learning in to meet students' expectations, the attitude of students toward technologies used in online learning and the factors affecting their choice to take such courses should be taken into account. This study intends to investigate the factors that influence students' choice to take online learning courses and the attitude of students toward the technologies used in online learning.

REVIEW OF THE LITERATURE

In the beginning online learning typically consisted of CD-ROM discs and packets of information through the mail. The student would complete modules on their own mailing back their work or commuting to campus on select dates for tests (Barker & Holley 1996). Over the years online learning continually evolved mostly due to information systems creating pathways for more interactive learning as well as IS software and websites to make all the components of the course more feasible. Internet based IT systems have allow face to face meetings, "live" learning classroom environments, and website submission portals to easily get and submit assignments and grades (Hiltz & Turoff, 2005).

Perreault et al. (2002) stated that most of the problems associated with online learning consisted of trouble submitting assignments, difficulty learning the technology required to take the course, lack of face-to-face interaction with professors and students, and lack of ability to obtain help outside of class time. Information systems software has been created over the years to make receiving assignments, submitting assignments, taking tests, and allowing students to collaborate with each other (Li, 2007). Course management systems like Blackboard gives the student a "virtual" classroom allowing instructors to post comments, lecture notes, and links to additional study material, students to turn in assignments, and even administer exams. The course management system automates much of course grading or at a minimum calculates up to date student grades and provides them quick feedback to how they are doing in the class (Li, 2007).

Many universities have now realized the need for student and instructor training and the need for the institution to better support both the instructor and student. From students to professor's administrative assistants everyone must have critical IT skills when participating in or facilitating online learning, requiring universities to continue to heavily invest in training (Santhanam et al., 2008). Perreault et al. (2002) discusses the need for institutions to provide technical support and training to both faculty and students for all of the online systems course management systems, give instructors access to distance-learning curriculum developers to better shape their teaching, allow multiple means for communication between students and between students and professors, and finally provide numerous resources including CD-Roms to help students learn. Many of the course management systems allows students to utilize interactive "help" sections to better learn the management systems so that the student can be successful in the class. If the student and professor are properly trained to use the different software and required tools (computers), by the end of the course Aziz et al. (2010) found that over 75% of the students agreed that IT was a helpful tool al-

lowing them to be more engaged in learning and that 72% of the students felt computers made the course material easier to understand.

Furthermore Meissonier et al. (2006) went on to state that not only do online learning instructors require additional training and resources but also require a technical team responsible for helping to design and post the professor's curriculum on-line. An incentive system for professors and instructors also must be put in place for those willing to tackle the challenge of distance teaching, recognizing that more work, training, and preparation is required for these types of classes (Meissonier et al., 2006).

As information systems become more advanced the lack of face-to-face communication is quickly fading. Ferratt and Hall (2009) describe the need for online learning to be based on what they call "learning via virtually being there." The author's vision combines both the current technologies discussed previously with new limitless future technologies. With these IS technologies in addition to future technologies, online learning can create an environment very similar to on-campus learning but provide the additional benefits of flexibility, unlimited access to course materials and lectures, and ability for students to easily interact with professors and other students (Hiltz & Turoff, 2005). An IS enabled online learning environment like "learning via virtually being there", described by Ferratt and Hall (2009), will heavily weaken the geographic monopolies enjoyed by many universities (Hiltz & Turoff, 2005).

Another area that IS systems have addressed is the ability for online students to obtain help outside of class time (Li, 2007). A course management site like Blackboard allows students to post questions in a discussion board for other students to read and answer or for the professor to reply an answer to the student. The main avenue of correspondence between professors and students continues to be email which can cause professors to feel the need of constantly checking email and message boards to meet the student's needs (Li, 2007).

Anakwe et al. (1999) states that management attitudes and practices are deeply rooted in the individual's cultural beliefs and in respect to online learning, differences in cultural beliefs would also exert the need for different learning styles. The simplest hurdle that needs to be addressed is some students taking online learning courses have a different native language than English. If the course management tool was able to convert the text and course materials into their native language a better understand might be provided. Furthermore "online learning as a technology evokes different meanings and reactions amount individuals with different cultural orientations" (Anakwe et al., 1999, p. 238).

There are many hurdles that online learning needs to cross and it is very questionable if it will ever be a "finished" design due to its heavy dependence and ties with the ever growing field of technology. Institutions need to provide better training courses for students and teachers as well as the proper resources for professors to be successful. Currently professors are carrying much of the load when it comes to online teaching inducing higher levels of stress (Meissonier et al., 2006). Additional new software programs and other information systems need to be created to enhance the learning via "virtually being there" atmosphere that Ferratt and Hall (2009) showed was the best learning environment for students.

Most research efforts were focused on establishing the effectiveness and credibility of such online learning courses (Moore & Thompson, 1997). Many institutes are concerned about the quality of their online learning programs. Most universities and post-secondary institutes all over the world are trying to offer online learning programs that have the same quality as those in traditional classroom settings (Dolezalek, 2003). Instructors who use online education must offer learning experiences to off-site students that will be equal in terms of quality and quantity as that offered to traditional students (Swan & Jackman, 2000). Many higher education institutes offer their courses in online learning for economic reasons (Merisotis & Phipps, 1999). The concern in computer-mediated learning environments is unlike two-way interactive video conferences, where students and the instructor can communicate with each other by talking or seeing each other as in a conventional classroom; computer-mediated learning requires special abilities of students and more technical support if students are to have online interaction fully (Merisotis & Phipps, 1999). Distance education is firmly established not only as an alternative for the delivery of higher education but as a need (Maushak & Ellis, 2003). However, online learning approaches are not always a solution to alternative ways was for the delivery of higher education (Williams, Paprock, & Covington, 1999).

Much research has been done in this area to assure the quality and effectiveness of online learning. "Online instruction classes should meet the same quality standards as traditional lecture classes and these standards can be evaluated the same way" (Ryan, 2000, p. 78). Moreover, success of students can also be evaluated by comparing lecture and online class assessments and final outcomes (Ryan, 2000). Students' performances, such as the outcomes between online learning and traditional learning, have been examined in many studies. Most of them found that there are no significant differences in learning outcome of online learning students (see Ryan, 2000; Carswell, Thomas, Petre, Price, & Richards, 2000; Schulman & Sims, 1999; Szulc, 1999).

The relationship between student grades and performance in online education and traditional courses has been considered in many studies, with reassuring results. A number of researchers have reported the consistent result that there is no significant difference in student learning associated with the course setting environment (Szulc, 1999). Thomas L. Russell, a professor at North Carolina State University, has collected and reviewed more than 300 dissertations, articles, studies, and research papers that have been published from 1928 to 1998 and cited and published them in 1999 in the book *The No Significant Difference Phenomenon*. That research investigated the online learning outcomes and grades of students using several types of learning media, such as postal, satellite, Internet, video tapes, and CDs. Those studies found no significant differences in learning outcomes and grades of students (Russell, 1999). Even though, that research was conducted with different methodologies, most of them yielded similar results.

Schulman and Sims (1999) conducted their research by comparing pretest and posttest scores of 40 undergraduate students in online courses and 59 undergraduate students in traditional courses. The results show that pretest scores of students in the online courses were significantly higher than those of students in traditional class. However, the posttest scores of students in the online course and in the traditional course did not have significant differences. In their sample, Schulman and Sims assumed that students who choose to enroll in the online courses may have been better prepared for the course than the students who chose the traditional way. Hoffmann (2002) also mentioned that students in online learning felt that they had to work harder and they could learn as much as in a traditional classroom.

Szulc (1999) investigated 44 enrollment records in nine courses from six departments at Christopher Newport University that offered online learning. The study used students' final grades to determine if the online course had prepared students as well as the traditional course. Szulc found that there was no significant difference in the final grades between students in online learning settings and students in traditional settings. Szulc concluded that the online course in this study had prepared students as well as the traditional course.

Another example from a study by Carswell, Thomas, Petre, Price, and Richards (2000) used learning style, background questionnaires and learning outcomes to compare between online courses and traditional courses. Based of the finding of the study, the learning outcomes of both groups shown no discrimination in grades.

Hofmann (2002) recommended that Internet-based online learning is more effective than traditional classroom learning because students in Internet-based learning had no other options but to become active learners. Online students may be better prepared for the course than students in traditional settings (Shulman & Sims, 1999). Hoffmann also found that students in Internet-based online learning have more courage to ask questions than in a traditional classroom setting. In traditional classroom, the setting actually does not require input from students unless the instructor chooses. Several students did not contribute in class discussions unless they were called on by the instructor to do so (Hoffmann, 2002). Bennett (2001) mentioned that the collaboration between the instructor and students is one of the main strengths of internet-based online learning. Chat room, discussion boards, and email force students to communicate with their instructors and their colleagues.

Another research conducted by Richard Ryan (2000) compared the quality between an online course and a traditional course. Ryan found that the final grades for participants in the online setting and participants in the traditional lecture setting were not significantly different for either course offering. Moreover, students in online courses considered themselves as more professional than students in the lecture classes. Students in online courses felt that they had more opportunities to work independently at their own pace and they felt more comfortable communicating with others anonymously. They thought that these were two main advantages of working online (Ryan, 2000).

Sullivan (2002) had concern about the gender differences issue in this kind of learning environment. Sullivan analyzed the data in the following categories: context, flexibility, achieving academic goals, face-to-face interaction, shy and quiet students, self-discipline and self-pace, and family and children. He used two open-ended questions to evaluate students' experience in these issues in the online environment. The finding showed that positive comments about online environment were as high as negative comments. Most of the negative comments were directed to specific teaching strategies, specific course design issues, and technical related problems.

Most of studies conclude that online learning courses compare favorably with traditional classroom based learning. Students in these studies had high satisfaction and enjoyment. Students in online learning had similar grades and test scores as in traditional classroom. They even had the same attitude toward the course (Merisotis & Phipps, 1999). However, some research found that average scores of students in online courses or computer-based courses were higher than students in traditional courses (see Gubernick & Ebeling, 1997; Vasarhelyi & Graham, 1997; Copper, 2001; Carswell, Thomas, Petre, Price, & Richards, 2000).

METHODOLOGY

This study attempted to answer the research questions; what is the overall attitude, which consists of affective, behavioral and cognitive components, of students toward the technologies used in their learning?; what is the attitude of students toward the interaction in a technology-based learning environment?; what is the attitude of students toward the quality of the technologies used in online learning? The population for this study based on a random sample for participation. The targeted group, which was used in this study, was undergraduate students at Mid-West University, at USA. Participants were limited to only those majoring in Business Administration. Participants in this study included both men and women who were currently enrolled or have experiences in technology-mediated online learning course(s)

during the time of conducting this research. Students in online learning classes used the same lectures via video stream, the same textbooks and the same exams. However, students were required the take the final exam on-campus.

Borg and Gall (1989) stated that the Likert technique is usually the easiest method for developing an attitudinal measurement instrument. The survey method can be used to ask every participant the same questions and collect the result of each question with a large amount of inputs. In this study, several questionnaire items had been reviewed from the literature. The questionnaire items were developed from Thomerson and Smith (1996), German (1988), Loyd and Loyd (1985), Kekkonen-Moneta and Moneta (2002), Cramer, Havice, and Havice (2002), Delcourt and Kinzie (1993). Smalley, Graff, and Sauders (2001), Hassan and Shrigley (1984) and Kinzie, Delcourt, and Powers (1994). These items include closed questions that allowed limited responses (multiple choice questions), open questions that allow participants to fill out their information, and check boxes that allowed participants to check all boxes that apply to their cases.

The survey questionnaire had two sections. The first section was demographic information. In this section, participants were asked to provide information regarding the range of age, gender, highest completed degree, location of residency, employment status, and student status. The second section was used to measure students' attitudes. This section consisted of three parts. Each part consisted of a set of Likert scale items. Participants were asked to answer these questions. The first part asked students' level of agreement for each statement. Students were asked to rate their agreement on a scale of 1 to 5, 1 being "strongly disagree", 2 being "disagree", 3 being "neutral", 4 being "agree", and 5 being "strongly agree" (Kinzie, Delcourt, & Powers, 1994). This part was used to answer question one, two, three, and four. For the overall attitude towards technology-based learning, three components of attitude were measured: affective, cognitive and behavioral. The score for each item may be added together to obtain an overall measure of attitudes (Kinzie, Delcourt, & Powers, 1994). In the second part, participants were asked if they have ever used any type of technologies such as Internet, Satellite Broadcasting, and Television Broadcasting, in their learning. The check boxes were provided for participants to check if they have used the technologies. Then participants were asked to rate the usefulness of each technology on a scale of 1 to 5, 1 being "Not useful, 2 being "Somewhat useful", 3 being "Moderate useful", 4 being "Useful", and 5 being "Very useful". This part was additionally used to answer question four.

The web questionnaire was posted on InQsit website and was distributed to online learning students via email with the explanation of the purpose of this study. Students were asked to complete the questionnaire on the web site during June to July 2004. The InQsit questionnaire was set to bypass login information and allow anonymous response. Therefore, the names and identities of students were not asked in any parts of the survey.

The participants of this study were student volunteers; therefore no extra credits or rewards were given. Students who participate in this study were expected to complete all questionnaire items and click the submit button to submit the answers for the web questionnaire. For the paper questionnaires, participants were expected to complete all questionnaire items and return the paper to the questionnaire distributors.

Method of Analysis

What is the overall attitude, which consists of affective, behavioral and cognitive components, of students toward the technologies used in their learning?, 2) What is the attitude of students toward the interaction in a technology-based learning environment?, 3) What is the attitude of students toward the quality of the technologies used in

online learning?, The sample mean score of each category was calculated and then used to compare with the hypothesized mean score for that category to find if they have a significant difference. If there was no significant difference between the hypothesized mean score and the sample mean score, students were considered to have neutral attitudes toward the component. If significant difference was found, students were considered to have either positive or negative attitudes. The sample mean score was used to analyze whether the attitude in that category was positive or negative. If the sample mean score was significantly higher than the hypothesized mean score, students were considered to have positive attitude towards that component. If the sample mean score was significantly lower than the hypothesized mean score, students were considered to have negative attitudes toward that component.

Frequency distribution was used to show which cases fall into the various categories of a variable and how the cases are distributed across the categories of a variable (Arney, 1990). The Analysis of Variance (ANOVA) was used to compare the mean of more than two groups in the demographic survey, such as age, marital status and employment status. From these analysis, the statistical significant was used to identify if students who had positive or negative attitudes.

ANALYSIS AND FINDINGS

In this study, the web questionnaires were sent to 500 students via email. For the web questionnaire, 330 responses were received, which was 79.75 percent. The raw data that had been collected from the questionnaire was entered to SPSS program to be analyzed.

However, some entries had to be discarded due to disqualifying of participants. In this study, the sample group consisted of undergraduate and graduate students. Therefore, the entries with other program levels were discarded.

The total of entries that were included in analysis of this study was 307 entries. After the disqualified entries were discarded, the final 307 responses were entered into SPSS and were used to support the answers of the research questions. The frequency tables, t-tests, and other statistical results are performed.

The hypothesis on research question on what is the overall attitude, which consists of affective, behavioral and cognitive components, of students toward the technologies used in their learning was supported. Moreover, the sample mean score was also significantly higher than the hypothesized mean score. Students were considered to have positive attitudes toward affective component. The hypothesis on what is the attitude of students toward the interaction in a technology-based learning environment was also supported. In this also, the sample mean score was significantly higher than the hypothesized mean score. Students were considered to have positive attitudes toward interaction. Hypothesis on what is the attitude of students toward the quality of the technologies used in online learning was also supported. In this hypothesis too, the sample mean score was also significantly higher than the hypothesized mean score. Students were considered to have positive attitudes toward quality.

These results are consistent with research that shows that students exhibit greater motivation and attitude towards technology when course content interests them and when they perceive some personal relevance with the content (Smart and Cappel, 2006). Smart and Cappel (2006) in their study suggest *"that computer users' prior experience with technology affects their attitudes about technology in general and the greater amount of experience users have with technology the higher the levels of users' satisfaction in learning to use new technology"*. The result of this study confirms that students with more experience with technology and e-learning had more motivation and better attitude towards technology based learning. According to the report on Evaluation of Evidence-Based Practices in Online Learning: A Meta-Analysis and Review of Online Learning Studies from the U.S. Department of Education, Office of Planning, Evaluation, and Policy Development (www.ed.gov/about/offices/list/opepd/ppss/reports.html) on average, students of online learning performed better than those with face-to-face instruction. This also shows that students are developing positive attitude to technology based learning.

Discussion and Summary

The impact of new online learning technologies on higher education will grow considerably in the future and will impact all areas of education including teaching, learning, and research (Guri-Rosenblit, 2005). Undeniably online learning technologies promise innovative and stimulating opportunities to enhance the quality of education and shape the generation and distribution of knowledge to both on-campus and distance universities. Because online learning technologies are at the earlier stages of adoption, research is inconclusive about its actual effectiveness in the university setting.

Based on the findings of this study, online learning students had positive attitudes toward technology-based online education, which consistent with positive attitudes of students. Most studies show that more women are enrolled in online learning environment than men (Gibson, 1998; Cooper, 2001). In this study, a higher number of responses were also received from female students (51.8 percent). However, statistics of demographic survey showed some different students' characteristics. Most studies found that average age of online learning students is higher than students in traditional settings (Szulc, 1999; Gibson, 1998; Cooper, 2001; Gibson & Graff, 1992). In this study, 74.3 percent were in the age range of 19 to 24, which is comparable with average age in traditional classrooms. Cooper's study (2001) showed that most online learning students were full-time employees and it was difficult for them to get a degree by attending the class at fixed times in contrast with this study, which most students described themselves as unemployed (78.5 percent).

Thompson stated in Gibson (1998), typically, students that are attracted to online education are those who are at a geographic online from an institute. In this study, the most responses (49.8 percent) were received from students in Bangkok and metropolitan areas. Some studies reported that females also felt that online environment was more welcoming for shy and quiet students than males. Sullivan (2001) claimed that females missed the interaction of the traditional classroom setting more than males. Significant difference was not found in this issue between male and female students in this study. These differences of findings may be influenced by culture differences. For the reason of taking online learning, some studies indicated that flexibility of online learning was the main advantage (Sullivan, 2001). In Taiwan, the finding of Kung's study (2002) showed that 70 percent participants believe that subject matter was important.

On the other hand, the finding of this study found the result differently from students. Midwest students believed that work requirement was more important than the subject matter. However, the interest in subject matter also received a high mean score. In this globalization of technology, computers are faster, bandwidth is increasing, and new applications rapidly come out and it is hard to identify the breakthrough. The use of existing and emerging technologies in higher education will continue to enhance the learning experience of all technology-based online learning students. The advancement of technology offers commuter students stronger relationships between instructors and classmates. Instructors can provide students quick feedback about assignments and quick answers about students' questions through asynchronous communication methods rather than the written comments that usually take days or weeks after the assignment is submitted. Students can also communicate, discuss, and ask questions with their peers or instructors at real-time through synchronous communication methods (Kruger, 2000).

Implications and Recommendations

Even though the findings of this study show positive attitudes of students towards technology-based online education, the development of online education should be continued. Moreover, the findings show that many students still have not had experience with technology that they considered useful. Institutes and instructors should provide students more opportunity to explore those technologies in their learning. For example, students considered Internet as a useful resource, but some students still have not used Internet in their learning. E-mail is one of the powerful communications and students considered it useful. However, teachers and students' technical skills should be considered before employing new applications. Because technical skills of students and instructors may not be sufficient for the optimal online education in some applications, institutions should provide training sessions to both students and instructors so that students will be able to use technology in their learning more effective and instructors can develop their courses and material in the format the best suit students' technical ability. Both instructors and students should be encouraged to use other technologies that the institutes provide. As this study shows positive attitudes of students in online learning, other organizations can also use the findings of this study to develop their training sessions.

Assumptions and Limitations

The main assumptions in this study were; participants clearly read and understand the content of each question; participants have experience in online learning. Each participant responded to either the web or paper questionnaire no more than one time. The participants in this study are limited to students of university at Midwest USA. The participants in this study are limited to students majoring in Business Administration. The participants in this study are limited to undergraduate and graduate students. Therefore, the findings may vary from other research conducted with students at other levels. Since this study was based on a random sample of students, the results and findings from this study may vary from selected target groups. The results of this study are limited by the sample size of participants.

REFERENCES

Anakwe, U. (1999). Online learning and Cultural Diversity: Potential Users' Perspective. *The International Journal of Organizational Analysis, 7*(3), 224. doi:10.1108/eb028901

Arney, W. R. (1990). *Understanding statistics in the social sciences*. New York: W.H. Freeman.

Aziz, T., Khan, M., & Singh, R. (2010). Effects of Information Technology Usage on Student Learning: An Empirical Study in the United States. *International Journal of Management, 27*(2), 205–217.

Barker, B., & Baker, M. (1995). Strategies to ensure interaction in telecommunicated online learning. In *Proceedings of the 11th Annual Conference on Teaching and Learning,* Madison, WI (pp. 17-32).

Barker, R., & Holley, C. (1996). Interactive Online learning: Perspective and Thoughts. *Business Communication Quarterly, 59*(4), 88–97. doi:10.1177/108056999605900409

Bennett, R. E. (2001). How the Internet will help large-scale assessment reinvent itself. *Education Policy Analysis Archives, 9*(5).

Berge, Z. (1999). Interaction in post-secondary web-based learning. *Educational Technology, 39*(1), 5–11.

Borg, W. R., & Gall, M. D. (1989). *Educational Research: An Introduction* (5th ed.). White Plains, NY: Longman.

Bork, A., & Gunnarsdottir, S. (2001). *Tutorial online Learning: Rebuilding our education system*. New York: Klumar Academic/Plenum Publishers.

Carswell, L. T., Petre, M., Price, B., & Richard, M. (2000). Online education via Internet: the student experience. *British Journal of Educational Technology, 31*(1), 29–47. doi:10.1111/1467-8535.00133

(1998). *Collins Cobuild English Dictionary*. London: Harper Collins Publishers Ltd.

Cooper, L. W. (2001). A comparison of online and traditional computer applications classes. *T.H.E. Journal, 28*(8), 52–56.

Cornell, R., & Martin, B. L. (1997). The role of motivation in web-based instruction. In Khan, B. H. (Ed.), *Web-Based Instruction* (2nd ed., pp. 93–100). Englewood Cliffs, NJ: Educational Technology Publications Inc.

Cramer, S., Havice, W., & Havice, P. (2002) Attitudes toward computer-mediated online training. *The Journal of Technology Studies.*

Deal, W. F. III. (2002). Online Learning: Teaching technology online. *Technology Teacher, 61*(8), 21–27.

Delcourt, M., & Kinzie, M. (1993). Computer technologies in teacher education: The measurement of attitudes and self-efficacy. *Journal of Research and Development in Education, 27*, 35–41.

Dolezalek, H. (2003). Online degree. *Training (New York, N.Y.), 40*(5), 26–32.

Edwards, A. L. (1957). *Techniques of Attitude Scale Construction*. Englewood Cliffs, NJ: Prentice Hall Inc.

Ferratt, T., & Hall, S. (2009). Extending the Vision of Online learning to Learning via Virtually Being, There and Beyond. *Communications of AIS, 2009*(25), 425-435.

Gall, M. D., Gall, J. P., & Borg, W. R. (2002). *Educational Research: An Introduction* (7th ed.). Boston: Allyn and Bacon.

German, K. E. (1988). Attitudes toward computer instruction. *Journal of Computers in Mathematics and Science Teaching, 7*(1-2), 22–28.

Gibson, C. (Ed.). (1998). *Online Learners in Higher Education*. Madison, WI: Atwood Publishing.

Gibson, C., & Graff, A. (1992). Impact of adults' preferred learning styles and perception of barriers on completions of external baccalaureate degree programs. *Journal of Online Education, 7*(1), 39–51.

Gubernick, L., & Ebeling, A. (1997). I got my degree through E-mail. *Forbes, 159*, 84–92.

Guri-Rosenblit, S. (2005). Distance education' and 'online learning': Not the same thing. *Higher Education, 49*, 467–493. doi:10.1007/s10734-004-0040-0

Hassan, A. M. A., & Shrigley, R. (1984). Designing a likert scale to measure chemistry attitudes. *School Science and Mathematics, 84*(8), 659–669. doi:10.1111/j.1949-8594.1984.tb09581.x

Hiltz, S., & Turoff, M. (2005). EDUCATION GOES DIGITAL: The Evolution of Online learning and the Revolution in Higher Education. *Communications of the ACM, 48*(10), 59–64. doi:10.1145/1089107.1089139

Hoffman, D. W. (2002). Internet-Based online learning in higher education. *Tech Directions, 62*(1), 28–33.

Kekkonen-Moneta, S., & Moneta, G. B. (2002). E-learning in Hong Kong: comparing learning outcomes in online multimedia and lecture versions of an introductory computing course. *British Journal of Educational Technology, 33*(4), 423–433. doi:10.1111/1467-8535.00279

Kinzie, M., Delcourt, M., & Powers, S. (1994). Computer Technologies: Attitudes and self-efficacy across undergraduate disciplines. *Research in Higher Education, 35*(6), 745–767. doi:10.1007/BF02497085

Kruger, K. (2000). Using Information Technology to Create Communities of Learners. *New Directions for Higher Education, 109*, 59–70. doi:10.1002/he.10907

Kung, S. (2002). Factors that affect students' decision to take online learning courses: A survey study of technical college students in Taiwan. *Educational Media International, 39*(3-4), 299–305.

Li, X. (2007). Intelligent Agent–Supported Online Education. *Decision Sciences Journal of Innovative Education, 5*, 311–331. doi:10.1111/j.1540-4609.2007.00143.x

Loyd, B., & Loyd, D. (1985). The reliability and validity of an instrument for the assessment of computer attitudes. *Educational and Psychological Measurement, 45*, 903–908. doi:10.1177/0013164485454021

Maushak, N. J., & Ellis, K. A. (2003). Attitudes of graduate students toward mixed-medium online education. *The Quarterly Review of online. Education, 4*(2), 129–141.

Meissonier, R., Houzé, E., Benbya, H., & Belbaly, N. (2006). Performance Factors of A "Full Online Learning": The Case of Undergraduate Students in Academic Exchange. *Communications of AIS, 2006*(18), 2-33.

Merisotis, J. P., & Phipps, R. A. (1999). What's the Difference? Outcomes of online vs. traditional classroom-based learning. *Change, 31*(3), 12–18. doi:10.1080/00091389909602685

Moore, M. (1989). Three types of interaction. *The American Journal of Online Education, 3*(2), 1–6.

Moore, M. G., & Thompson, M. M. (1997). *The effects of online learning.* University Park, PA: American Center for the Study of Distance Education, Pennsylvania State University.

Northrup, P. T. (2002). Online learners' preferences for interaction. *The Quarterly Review of online. Education, 3*(2), 219–226.

Perreault, H., Waldman, L., & Alexander, M. (2002). Overcoming Barriers to Successful Delivery of Online learning Courses. *Journal of Education for Business, 77*(6), 313. doi:10.1080/08832320209599681

Russell, T. L. (1999). *No significant difference phenomenon.* Raleigh, NC: North Carolina State University.

Ryan, R. (2000). Student assessment comparison of lecture and online construction equipment and methods classes. *T.H.E. Journal, 27*(6), 78–84.

Santhanam, R., Sasidharan, S., & Webster, J. (2008). Using Self-Regulatory Learning to Enhance E Learning-Based Information Technology Training. *Information Systems Research, 19*(1), 26–47. doi:10.1287/isre.1070.0141

Sherry, L. (1996). Issues in online Learning. *International Journal of Educational Telecommunications, 1*(4), 337–365.

Shulman, A. H., & Sims, R. L. (1999). Learning in an online format versus an in-class format: An experiment study. *T.H.E. Journal, 26*(11), 54–57.

Smalley, N., Graff, M., & Saunders, D. (2001). A revised computer attitude scale for secondary students. *Educational and Child Psychology, 18*(3), 47–57.

Smart, K. L., & Cappel, J. J. (2006). Students' Perceptions of Online Learning. *Journal of Information Technology Education, 5*(1), 201–219.

Sullivan, P. (2001). Gender differences and the online classroom: male and female college students evaluate their experiences. *Community College Journal of Research and Practice, 25*, 805–818. doi:10.1080/106689201753235930

Sullivan, P. (2002). "It's easier to be yourself when you are invisible": Female college students discuss their online classroom experiences. *Innovative Higher Education, 27*(2), 129–144. doi:10.1023/A:1021109410893

Swan, A. K., & Jackman, D. H. (2000). Comparing the success of students enrolled in online education courses vs. face-to-face classrooms. *The Journal of Technology Studies, 29*(1), 58–63.

Szulc, P. (1999). Reassessing the assessment of online education courses. *T.H.E. Journal, 27*(2), 70–74.

Thomerson, J. D., & Smith, C. L. (1996). Student perceptions of the affective experiences encountered in online learning courses. *The American Journal of Online Education, 10*(3), 37–48.

Thurstone, L., & Chave, E. (1946). *The measurement of attitude.* Chicago: University of Chicago Press.

Valenta, A., Therrirault, D., Dieter, M., & Mrtek, R. (2001). Identify student attitudes and learning styles in online education. *Journal of Asynchronous Learning Networks, 5*(2).

Vasarhelyi, M., & Graham, L. (1997). Cybersmart: Education and the Internet. *Management Accounting,* 32-36.

Webster, J., & Hackley, P. (1997). Teaching effectiveness in technology-mediated online learning. *Academy of Management Journal*, *40*(6), 1282–1310. doi:10.2307/257034

Williams, M., Paprock, K., & Convington, B. (1999). *Online Learning: The essential Guide*. Thousand Oaks, CA: Sage.

Zhao, J., Alexander, M., Perreault, H., Waldman, L., & Truell, A. (2009). Faculty and Student Use of Technologies, User Productivity, and User Preference in Online learning. *Journal of Education for Business*, *84*(4), 206–212. doi:10.3200/JOEB.84.4.206-212

Chapter 13
Adoption of PBL to Online Environments:
Student's Perspectives

Fatih Gursul
Istanbul University, Turkey

Hafize Keser
Ankara University, Turkey

Sevinc Gulsecen
Istanbul University, Turkey

ABSTRACT

This study's aim is to find out student's perspectives on online and face-to-face problem-based learning approaches. The study was conducted at the Department of Computer Education and Instructional Technologies, Faculty of Education, Hacettepe University. Participants were 42 freshman students attending the department during fall of 2006-2007. These students were put into two groups—the online problem-based learning group and the face-to-face problem-based learning group. The research was conducted on Mathematics-I while implementing the topic of 'derivation'. The content analysis statistical technique is used, as well as a questionnaire consisting of open-ended questions, which perform as a data collection tool to find out the views of the students in context to the process.

INTRODUCTION

It is a cliché to say that people live in the Information Age. So, we can't say it. We will say that humanity has never been more in love with information than it is now. Information saturates our personal and our professional lives. It not only affects our experience, it pretty much is our experience. Music is information, language is information numbers are information, and pictures are information. Information, just as energy and matter, is even considered to be basic element of the universe itself (Stonier, 1996).

With promises of rich information resources readily available, successful use of the World Wide Web within an instructional setting is tied

DOI: 10.4018/978-1-4666-0041-6.ch013

directly to a pedagogical approach that promotes inquiry-based learning (Sammons, 2003; Piccinini & Scollo, 2006). Inquiry-based learning can have many definitions and can be compared directly to other forms of instruction such as problem-based learning (Harrison et al., 2002; Etnon, 2008).

Learning from problems is a situation of human existence. In our attempts to solve the many problems we come across every day, learning occurs. In looking for offices in an unfamiliar building, or addresses in an unfamiliar town, we finally find our way. In filling out income tax statements, learning occurs, just as in trying to find out why the car won't start. Although we may not be consciously aware, these problem situations are all learning experiences that are providing us with information and knowledge that we can apply to future problems (Barrows & Tamblyn, 1980).

Researchers have provided a number of definitions regarding problem-based learning. Bubonics (2001) defined problem-based learning as a curricula and learning approach which exposes the students to an ill-structured problem taken from real life and develops the students' problem solving strategies, knowledge, experiences and skills during the problem-solving process. Cunningham and Corderio (2000) emphasized that the key to problem-based learning is the use of a real-life problem in problem solving process. In addition Duch et al. (2001) stated that problem-based learning is an educational strategy helping the students to construct the questioning and communication skills which they need in their daily lives.

Today, problem-based learning is becoming more widespread all around the world. For instance, 80 percent of the medical faculties in the US use problem-based learning approach (Bubonics, 2002, p. 2). Considering the literature review on problem-based learning, it can be concluded that this approach, appearing as a traditional and campus-based one, is also an approach that works online when integrated with a proper and rational technology (McLinden et al., 2006). Computer and

Web in particular are having a strong impact on education. These tools must clearly be regarded as versatile aids rather than as a replacement for face to face teaching methods (Pragnell et al., 2006). Although there is a vast amount of research and literature available on face-to-face problem-based learning (Barrows, 1993; Bubonic, 2001; Duch, 1995; Cunningham & Corderio, 2000; Greening, 1998; Major, 1998; Major & Palmer, 2001; Savery & Duffy, 1996; Savin-Baden & Major, 2004), currently some studies have studied PBL when utilized in the online environment (Sendag & Odabasi, 2009; Chu et al., 2009; Tseng et al., 2007).

Problem-based learning seems to fit into the new technology-based model for higher education. It is adaptable for on-line delivery, benefits from the wealth of information available from the Internet, and requires the communication afforded by email and conferencing tools. Further, problem-based learning supports collaborative learning even at a distance (Orril, 2000). Further, online PBL is sometimes referred to as distributed PBL and is a version of PBL that is useful to learners who are separated from their tutors by distance. Learning is mediated through online technologies within a shared, 'virtual' distributed learning environment (Wheeler et al., 2005). While many of current models of online educational approaches focus on teacher-centered learning, Online PBL needs to be focused on team oriented knowledge-building discourse (Savin-Baden & Wilkie, 2006, p. 7).

In literature, many studies have been and are still being conducted on problem-based learning. The studies generally compare problem-based learning environment with traditional educational environments (Deveci, 2002; Katwibun, 2004; Ozel et al., 2005; Gunhan, 2006; Tandogan, 2006; Uslu, 2006; Gulsecen & Kubat, 2006; Tavukcu, 2006; Ciftci et al., 2007; Arici & Kidiman, 2007; Akinoglu & Tandogan, 2007; Gulsum & Sungur, 2007). A small number of the studies on problem-based learning deal with a comparison of online collaborative learning and traditional learning environments (Mayer, 2004; Valaitis et al., 2005; Ozdemir, 2005; Lopez-Ortiz, 2006; Kennedy, 2007). We have been able to find only one research, carried out by Luck and Norton (2004) on the comparison of online problem-based learning and face-to-face problem-based learning approaches. Also, this study was not based on mathematics but on the subject Educational Management at Department of Pre-School Education and Management. On the other hand, we have not been able to find any studies comparing the students' perspectives in online collaborative problem-based learning and face-to-face collaborative problem-based learning in the field of mathematics. The purpose of this study is to obtain findings which will be helpful for eliminating this gap and ambiguity.

METHOD

Research Model

For this study, the experimental method, one of the qualitative research models, was used. The experimental research explains the cause-effect relation; in other words, the effect of one variable on other variables is examined. Since this paper compared the effect of online and face-to-face problem-based learning on student views.

Participants

The study was conducted at Department of Computer Education and Instructional Technologies, Faculty of Education, Hacettepe University. The subjects were 42 freshman students attending to this department at the fall term of 2006-2007 academic year. These students were put into two groups as online problem-based learning and face-to-face problem-based learning. These groups were formed use of random sampling technique via the SPSS (Statistical Package for Social Sciences for Windows, 11.0) program. Through this pro-

gram, each group was divided into 5 sub-groups, in online problem-based learning and face-to-face learning groups, 4 subjects in 8 sub-groups and 5 subjects in the other two sub-groups. The research was conducted on Mathematics-I during the implementation of the subject 'derivative'.

Data Collection Tools

In this research two different data collection tools were used. First one is the Survey to determine the Students' opinions about the Processes, the second one is the teaching materials used by students and designed by the researcher in Blackboard Learning Management System.

The Survey to Determine the Students' Opinions about the Processes

A students' opinions determining survey composed of 7 open ended questions is enhanced to ascertain the students' perceptions and perspectives about face to face PBL and Online PBL environments. In the development process of survey the related literature is scanned and a survey composed of 8 questions is developed by the researcher. It is applied to two field specialists for convenience and availability of the survey. In accordance with the feedback, one question is picked out and a final survey composed of 7 questions is gained. The survey follows the questions below:

1) The problems experienced by students between each other during application processes of online and face-to-face problem-based learning,
2) The problems experienced by students with the teacher during application processes of online and face-to-face problem-based learning,
3) The problems experienced by students in access to resources during application processes of online and face-to-face problem-based learning,

4) The elements found enjoyable by students during the processes of online and face-to-face problem-based learning,

5) The elements acquired by students during application processes of online and face-to-face problem-based learning,

6) The elements of application processes of online and problem-based learning which have an effect on students' daily lives,

7) The way perspectives of students on mathematics during application processes of online and problem-based learning.

Teaching Material

In this study, we designed a teaching material introduced on the web in order to develop problem-based learning activities. For this, we used Blackboard Learning Management System, which allows one to design teaching materials on the web (e.g., Hacettepe, University of Cincinnati, University of Newcastle, University of Leicester, Ohio University, University of Cambridge use Blackboard Learning Management System for problem-based learning practices). The material designed on Blackboard and the pilot scheme of the problem-based learning environment was carried out on the teacher candidates taking the subject Computer at their first grades at Department of Primary School and Pre-School Education, Faculty of Education, Hacettepe University, (N=70). The purpose of this pilot scheme was to determine any possible problem and difficulty on Blackboard (Gursul & Altun, 2007). The Blackboard environment was revised and operationalized in accordance with the results obtained from the pilot scheme.

Prior to the study, the well-structured and ill-structured sample problems were analyzed regarding the subject derivative. Problem 1 used in the study was inspired by a research project titled "The 'Catwalk': Representing What You Know" and broadcasted on an educational television station in USA (This program can be watched on the link.learner.org/channel/workshops/pupmath/workshops/wk6trans.html). The problem 2, on the other hand, was adapted in Turkish from a problem under the title "Fundamental Concepts of Differential Calculus" on web page of Wofforg Academics (Original problem can be accessed on the link http://www.wofford.org/ecs/ScientificProgramming/DifferentialCalculus/material.htm).

Online problem-based research groups were exposed to mathematics instruction through the use of Blackboard Teaching Management System. The training of the groups was completed by the researcher within seven weeks' time. Software on web, e-mails, e-groups and e-books were used in a way that would enable this environment to provide the students with opportunities for developing their skills and methods in order to adapt to and change new situations. For student-student and student-teacher interaction, we used both simultaneous lesson-counseling through Microsoft Msn Messenger and the instruments as phone and e-mail. In order to minimize the problems experienced between the teacher and students, during the online simultaneous learning, we announced the students about which group would be provided with online teaching at which hours through online communication, and the rules to be complied with in online environment. Each group took a one-hour simultaneous lesson a week with the teacher at the hours announced previously. In addition, each group was provided with the opportunity of having simultaneous negotiation with the teacher (via mto191@hotmail.com, an address taken for the lesson) between 8.30 am and 5.00 pm on Monday, Wednesday, Thursday and Friday and between 1.00 pm and 2.30 pm on Tuesday.

As for the group provided with mathematics instruction through face-to-face problem-based learning, the practice lasted for seven weeks. The process was carried out by the researcher in classroom.

FINDINGS

The Problems Experienced by Students between Each Other During Application Processes of Online and Face-to-Face Problem-Based Learning

Figure 1 includes the problems experienced by students in online groups between each other during application process of problem-based learning.

As can be concluded from Figure 1, the problems experienced by students in online problem-based learning environment between each other have been categorized as access (21 answers), festive holiday (3 answers), obstacles to decision-making process (2 answers), technological disturbances/problems (1 answer) respectively.

Figure 2 shows the problems experienced by students in face-to-face groups between each other during the process of problem-based learning.

As can be seen from Figure 2, the problems experienced by students in face-to-face problem-based learning environment between each other have been categorized as access (17 answers), festive holiday (5 answers), final week (3 answers), degree of intra-group intimacy (2 answers), task sharing /responsibility (2 answers) respectively.

When one considers the problems experienced by students between each other in online and face-to-face problem-based environments, it is observed that similar problems have been expressed for both environments. Although the problem of access constitutes the basic problem for students in both environments, it has been observed that the students in online environments experience this problem at a higher level. The cause underlying this situation is not being able to access to Internet and to establish concurrent communication. Another problem, festive holiday, has been suffered in online environments at a lower level. The reason for this is that although the students are physically in different environments, online learning environments that remove the boundaries provide instruments which enable interaction.

Figure 1. The problems experienced by students between each other during application process of online problem-based learning

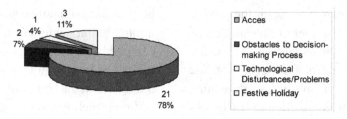

Figure 2. The problems experienced by students between each other during application process of face-to-face problem-based learning

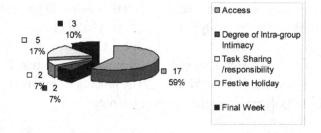

Figure 3. The problems experienced by students with the teacher during application process of online problem-based learning

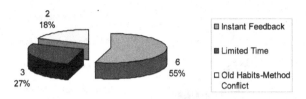

The Problems Experienced by Students with the Teacher during Application Processes of Online and Face-to-Face Problem-Based Learning

Figure 3 includes the problems experienced by students in online groups with the teacher during application process of problem-based learning.

As can be concluded from Figure 3, the problems experienced by students in online problem-based learning environment with the teacher have been categorized as instant feedback (6 answers), limited time (3 answers), old habits-method conflict (2 answers) respectively.

Figure 4 shows the problems experienced by students in face-to-face groups with the teacher during the process of problem-based learning.

As can be seen from Figure 4, the problems experienced by students in face-to-face problem-based learning environment with the teacher have been determined to be only instant feedback (3

Figure 4. The problems experienced by students with the teacher during application process of face-to-face problem-based learning

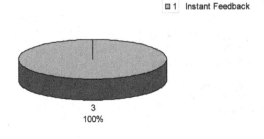

answers). This problem has been expressed by referring to student remarks.

While a very small number of answers (3 answers) in face-to-face problem-based learning environment has cited the condition in which the teacher cannot provide instant feedback as a problem, the students in online problem-based learning environment have also expressed the problems "limited time" and "lack or scarcity of experienced towards online learning" as well as the problem "instant feedback". Another element that brings limitation to learning in online environments is the fact that instant feedback is not provided. As stated above, the fact that a larger number of students have expressed this problem seems to support the limitation of this kind of environments.

The Problems Experienced by Students in Access to Resources during Application Processes of Online and Face-to-Face Problem-Based Learning

Figure 5 includes the problems experienced by students in online groups in access to resources during application process of problem-based learning.

As can be concluded from Figure 5, the problems experienced by students in online problem-based learning environment in access to resources have been categorized as old habits/method conflict (6 answers), sufficient/insufficient time for experts (4 answers), technical inadequacies (2 answers), reliability of resources (2 answers),

Figure 5. The problems experienced by students in access to resources during application process of online problem-based learning

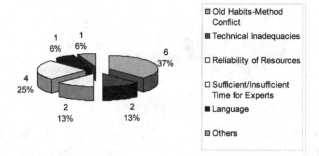

language (1 answer) and others (1 Student) respectively.

Figure 6 shows the problems experienced by students in face-to-face groups in access to resources during the process of problem-based learning.

As can be seen from Figure 6, the problems experienced by students in face-to-face problem-based learning environment in access to resources have been classified as sufficient/insufficient time for experts (11 answers), language (6 answers), old habits/method conflict (5 answers) and reliability of resources (2 answers) respectively.

There is a similarity between problems experienced by online and face-to-face problem-based learning environments in access to resources. Both environments have suffered problems such as lack of experience regarding problem-based learning, limited time for experts to whom they can consult and language. Especially students who encounter with an ill-structured problem in

problem-based learning for the first time have suffered the problems above since they do not know which resource to use and how, where and why to use it.

The Elements Found Enjoyable By Students during the Processes of Online and Face-to-Face Problem-Based Learning

Figure 7 includes the elements found enjoyable by students in online groups during application process of problem-based learning.

As can be concluded from Figure 7, the elements found enjoyable by students in online problem-based learning environment have been categorized as increased friendship relations (14 answers), positive effect of method opportunities (11 answers), independence in terms of space (8 answers), focus on a common purpose (5 answers), increased awareness towards researching (1 answer) and other (3 answers) respectively.

Figure 6. The problems experienced by students in access to resources during application process of face-to-face problem-based learning

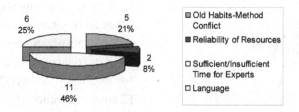

Figure 7. The elements found enjoyable by students during application process of online problem-based learning

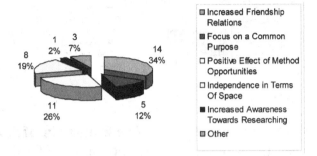

Figure 8 shows the elements found enjoyable by students in face-to-face groups during the process of problem-based learning.

As can be seen from Figure 8, the elements found enjoyable by students in face-to-face problem-based learning environment have been classified as increased friendship relations (11 answers), increased awareness towards researching (6 answers), focus on a common purpose (5 answers) and other (5 answers) respectively.

The leading one among elements found enjoyable by students in both environments is increased friendship relations. The second enjoyable element is increased awareness towards researching in face-to-face environment and positive effect of problem-based learning method in online environment. Considering these results, it can be argued that online problem-based learning approach affects the students in a positive manner and the instruments towards this approach (msn, Blackboard, e-mail, phone) are found enjoyable by students.

The Elements Acquired By Students during Application Processes of Online and Face-To-Face Problem-Based Learning

Figure 9 includes the elements acquired by students in online groups during application process of problem-based learning.

As can be concluded from Figure 9, the elements acquired by students in online problem-based learning environment have been categorized as positive effect of method opportunities (12 answers), group work (11 answers), increased awareness towards researching (9 answers) and others (5 answers) respectively.

Figure 10 shows the elements acquired by students in face-to-face groups during the process of problem-based learning.

As can be seen from Figure 10, the elements acquired by students in face-to-face problem-based learning environment have been classified as positive effect of method opportunities (12

Figure 8. The elements found enjoyable by students during application process of face-to-face problem-based learning

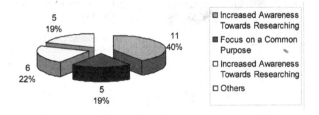

Figure 9. The elements acquired by students during application process of online problem-based learning

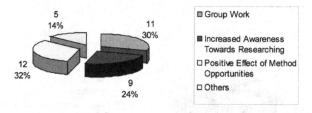

answers), group work (9 answers), increased awareness towards researching (9 answers), establishing correlations between mathematical subjects (3 answers) and others (8 answers) respectively.

There is a similarity between elements acquired by students in online and face-to-face problem-based learning environments following the application. The leading one among these elements is the adoption of problem-based learning method by students and group work. Group work has been found more positive in online problem-based learning environment when compared to face-to-face problem-based learning environment. From that point of view, we can argue that online problem-based learning approach is at least as much adopted as face-to-face problem-based learning approach.

The Elements of Application Processes of Online and Problem-Based Learning Which Have an Effect on Students' Daily Lives

Figure 11 includes the elements affecting the daily lives of students in online groups during application process of problem-based learning.

As can be concluded from Figure 11, the elements of application process of online problem-based learning which have an effect on students' daily lives have been categorized as sense of transfer (8 answers), increased using internet technologies (3 answers), group work (2 answers) and others (2 answers) respectively.

Figure 12 shows the elements affecting the daily lives of students in face-to-face groups during application process of problem-based learning.

As can be concluded from Figure 12, the elements affecting the daily lives of students in face-to-face problem-based learning environment

Figure 10. The elements acquired by students during application process of face-to-face problem-based learning

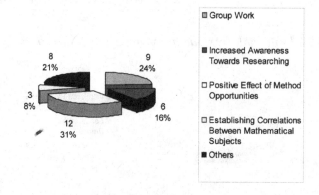

Figure 11. The elements of application process of online problem-based learning which have an effect on students' daily lives

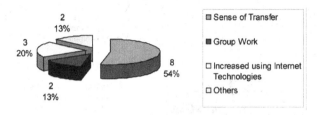

Figure 12. The elements of application process of face-to-face problem-based learning which have an effect on students' daily lives

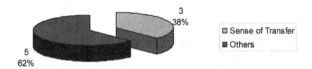

have been classified as sense of transfer (3 answers) and others (5 answers) respectively.

The students in online problem-based learning environment (54%) have expressed that they can transfer the skills they have acquired to their daily lives at a higher rate when compared to the students in face-to-face problem-based learning (38%). The use of Internet technologies (forum, msn, data bases, search engines, etc.) has been expressed as another significant element that can be used by the students in online problem-based learning environment.

The Way Perspectives of Students on Mathematics during Application Processes of Online and Problem-Based Learning

Figure 13 shows the way perspectives of students on mathematics in online groups change during the application process of problem-based learning.

As can be concluded from Figure 13, the effects on the way students in online problem-based learning environment consider mathematics have been classified as overcoming mathematics pho-

Figure 13. The effects of application process of online problem-based learning on students' perspectives on mathematics

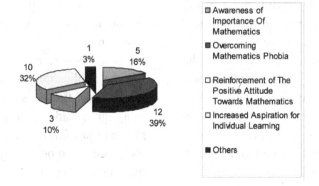

Figure 14. The effects of application process of face-to-face problem-based learning on students' perspectives on mathematics

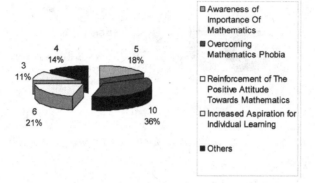

bia (12 answers), increased aspiration for individual learning (10 answers), awareness of importance of mathematics (5 answers), reinforcement of the positive attitude towards mathematics (3 answers) and others (1 answer) respectively.

Figure 14 shows the way perspectives of students on mathematics in face-to-face groups change during the application process of problem-based learning.

As can be concluded from Figure 14, the effects on the way students in online problem-based learning environment consider mathematics have been classified as overcoming mathematics phobia (10 answers), reinforcement of the positive attitude towards mathematics (6 answers), awareness of importance of mathematics (5 answers), increased aspiration for individual learning (3 answers) and others (1 answer) respectively.

There is a similarity between perspectives of students in online and face-to-face problem-based learning environments following the application. Overcoming mathematics phobia has been expressed as the most notable effect in both environments. Another similar element is the conclusion that the students in both environments have recognized the significance of mathematics. This can be based on the fact that well-structured problems are chosen from real life in problem-based learning. In addition, considering that increased aspiration for individual learning is higher for

students in online problem-based learning (32%) than for students in face-to-face problem-based learning (3%), one can conclude that individual learning is more adopted by students in online problem-based learning environment than the students in face-to-face problem-based learning environment.

DISCUSSION AND SUGGESTIONS

Hammel et al. (1999) stated that students perceived that a PBL approach adopted consistently across the curriculum contributed to the development of information management, critical reasoning, communication, and team-building skills; however, identified challenges were time and role management, information access, instructor versus PBL expectations and practices, and coping with the ambiguity of knowledge and reasoning. Our studies seem to support these findings in both online and face to face problem-based learning environments.

Based on the researcher's experiences during the application process, it can be said that it will make the decision-making process easier to assign a leader or to guide for each group in the simultaneous discussion groups. In addition, the process can be managed more effectively by making the students' participation in group discussions on online more planned and organized. In order to reduce the problem of teacher-learner interaction, an assistant teacher may be provided in a way that will help the teacher. While carrying out such practices, one should pay attention not to include days such as festive holidays with the aim of not disrupting learner motivation and preventing process delays. The application will be more efficient and effective if the students at online practice have computers and access to the internet at home or dormitory where they stay.

The appropriate instruments and methods should be selected so as to make teacher-learner and learner-learner interaction more effective. Another study on this issue could form groups by taking students' cognitive skills and gender factor into account. In this study, the results obtained from the online and face-to-face problem-based learning environments could be compared in terms of these variables.

This study has been conducted on ten groups, half of which in online problem-based learning environment (21 students) and half of which in face-to-face problem-based learning environment (21 students). This has been regarded as the limitation of the study. The number of groups and students could be higher in other similar studies in order to obtain more reliable generalization.

REFERENCES

Akinoglu, O., & Ozkardes Tandogan, R. (2007). The effects of problem-based active learning in science education on students' academic achievement, attitude and concept learning. *Eurasia J. Math. Sci. & Tech. Ed.*, *3*(1), 71–81.

Arıcı, N., & Kıdıman, E. (2007). Mesleki ve teknik orta öğretimde probleme dayali öğrenme yönteminin akademik başariya ve öğrenmenin kaliciliğina etkisi. *e-Journal of New World Sciences Academy*. Retrieved September 13, 2007, from http://www.newwsa.com/makale_ozet.asp?makale_id=118

Barrows, H., & Mayers, A. (1993). *Problem based learning in secondary schools*. Unpublished monography, Springfield, IL.

Barrows, H. S., & Tamblyn, R. M. (1980). *Problem-based learning: an approach to medical education*. New York: Springer Publishing Company. ISBN 0826128416, 9780826128416

Bubonic, E. J. (2001). *Improving student learning and attitude throuhg problem–based learning*. Unpublished master's thesis, Ashland University, Ashland, OH.

Chu, H. C., Chen, T. Y., Lin, C. J., Liao, M. J., & Chen, Y. M. (2009). Development of an adaptive learning case recommendation approach for problem-based e-learning on mathematics teaching for students with mild disabilities. *Expert Systems with Applications*, *36*(3), 5456–5468. doi:10.1016/j.eswa.2008.06.140

Çiftçi, S., Meydan, A., & Ektem, I. S. (2007). Sosyal bilgiler öğretiminde probleme dayali öğrenmeyi kullanmanin öğrencilerin başarisina ve tutumlarina etkisi. *Selçuk Üniversitesi Sosyal Bilimler Enstitüsü Dergisi. Sayı*, *17*, 179–190.

Cunningham, W. G., & Corderio, P. A. (2000). *Educational administration: A problem-based aproach*. Boston: Allyn & Bacon.

Derry, J. S. (2005). eSteps as a case of theory-based web course design. In A. M. O 'Donnell, C. E. Hmelo-Silver, & G. Erkens (Eds.), *Collaborative learning, reasoning, and technology* (pp. 171-197). New York: Routledge.

Deveci, H. (2002). *Sosyal bilgiler dersinde probleme dayali öğrenmenin öğrencilerin derse ilişkin tutumlarina, akademik başarilarina ve hatirlama düzeylerine etkisi*. Unpublished, doctoral dissertation, Eskişehir University, Eğitim Bilimleri Enstitüsü.

Duch, B. J. (1995). *What is problem-based learning?* Retrieved October 1, 2007, from http://www.udel.edu/pbl/cte/jan95-what.html

Duch, B. J., Groh, S. E., & Allen, D. E. (2001). *The power of problem-based learning.* Sterling, VA: Stylus Publishing.

Etnon, R. (2008). The use of the world wide web in learning and teaching in higher education: reality and rhetoric. *Innovations in Education and Teaching International, 45*(1), 15–23. doi:10.1080/14703290701757401

Exley, K., & Dennick, R. (2004). *Small group teaching: tutorials, seminars and beyond* (pp. 76–94). New York: Routledge Group.

Greening, T. (1998). Scaffolding for success in problem-based learning. *Medical Education Online, 3*(4). Retrieved October 2, 2007, from http://www.med-ed-online.org/f0000012.htm

Gülseçen, S., & Kubat, A. (2006). Teaching ICT to Teacher Candidates Using PBL: A Qualitative and Quantitative Evaluation. *Journal of Educational Technology & Society, 9*(2), 96–106.

Gülsüm, A., & Sungur, S. (2007). Effectiveness of Problem-Based Learning on Academic Performance in Genetics. *Biochemistry and Molecular Biology Education, 35*(6), 448–451. doi:10.1002/bmb.97

Gunhan, B. C. (2006). *İlköğretim II. kademede matematik dersinde probleme dayali öğrenmenin uygulanabilirliği üzerine bir araştirma.* Unpublished doctoral dissertation, Dokuz Eylül University, Eğitim Bilimleri Enstitüsü.

Gürsul, F., & Altun, A. (2007). okul öncesi ögretmen adaylarinin karma yöntemle yapilan bilgisayar dersine ilişkin görüsleri. *Uluslar Arası Ögretmen Yetiştirme Politikaları ve Sorunları Sempozyumu* (pp. 12-14). Mayıs, Bakü: Azerbaycan

Hammel, J., Royeen, C. H., Bagatell, N., Chandler, B., Jensen, G., Loveland, R., & Stone, G. (1999). Student perspectives on problem-based learning in an occupational therapy curriculum: a multiyear qualitative evaluation. *The American Journal of Occupational Therapy., 53*, 199–206.

Harrison, C., Comber, C., Fisher, T., Haw, K., Lewin, C., Lunzer, E., et al. (2002). *ImpacT2: The Impact of Information and Communication Technologies on Pupil Learning and Attainment* (ICT in Schools Research and Evaluation Series, No. 7). London: DfES/BECTa. Retrieved from http://partners.becta.org.uk/index.php?section=rh&rid=13606

Katwibun, D. (2004). *Middle school students' mathematical dispositions in a problem-based classroom.* Unpublished doctoral dissertation, Oregon State University, OR.

Kennedy, S. J. (2007). Learning and transfer compared in two teaching methods: online problem-based learning and the traditional lecture method. Unpublished doctoral dissertation, Capella University, MN.

Lopez-Ortiz, B. I. (n.d.). *Online collaborative problem-based learning: Design, facilitation, student work strategies and supporting technologies.* EdD dissertation, Teachers College, Columbia University, NY.

Luck, P., & Norton, B. (2004). Problem-based management learning-better online? *The European Journal of Open and Distance Learning (EURODL).* Retrieved October 5, 2007, from http://www.eurodl.org/materials/contrib/2004/Luck_Norton.htm

Malopinsky, L., Kirkley, J., Stein, R., & Duffy, T. (2000, October 25-28). An instructional design model for online problem based learning (pbl) environments: The learning to teach with technology studio. In *Proceedings of the selected research and development papers at the 23rd National Convention of the Association for Educational Communications and Technology*, Denver, CO (Vol. 1-2).

Mayer, C. L. (2004). *An analysis of the dimensions of a Web-delivered problem-based learning environment*. Unpublished doctoral dissertation, University of Missouri, Columbia, MO.

McLinden, M., McCall, S., Hinton, D., & Weston, A. (2006). Participation in online problem-based learning: insights from postgraduate teachers studying through open and distance education. *Distance Education, 27*(3), 331–353. doi:10.1080/01587910600940422

Orrill, C. H. (2000, April 24-28). Designing a PBL Experience for online delivery in a six-week course. In *Proceedings of the Annual Meeting of the American Educational Research Association*, New Orleans, LA.

Özdemir, S. (2005). *WEB ortamında bireysel ve işbirliğine dayalı problem temelli öğrenmenin eleştirel düşünme becerisi, akademik başarı ve internet kullanımına yönelik tutuma etkileri*. Doctoral dissertation, Gazi University, Eğitim Bilimleri Enstitüsü, Ankara, Turkey.

Özel, M., Timur, E., Özyalın, Ş., & Danışman, M. A. (2005). Modüler tabanli eğitim programinda matematik ve jeofizik bütünleşmesi. *Dokuz Eylül Üniversitesi, Mühendislik Fakültesi. Fen ve Mühendislik Dergisi, 7*(2), 101–112.

Piccinini, N., & Scollo, G. (2006). Cooperative Project-based Learning in a Web-based Software Engineering Course. *Journal of Educational Technology & Society, 9*(4), 54–62.

Pragnell, M. V., Roselli, T., & Rossano, V. (2006). Can a Hypermedia Cooperative e-learning Environment Stimulate Constructive Collaboration? *Journal of Educational Technology & Society, 9*(2), 119–132.

Sammons, M. (2003). Exploring the New Conception of Teaching and Learning in Distance Education. In Moore, M. G., & Anderson, W. G. (Eds.), *Handbook of Distance Education* (pp. 387–400). Mahwah, NJ: Lawrence Erlbaum Associates.

Savin-Baden, M., & Wilkie, K. (2006). *Problem-Based Learning Online*. Berkshire, UK: Open University Press.

Sendag, S., & Odabasi, F. (2009). *Effects of an online problem based learning course on content knowledge acquisition and critical thinking skills*. Computer and Education.

Stonier, T. (1996). Information as a basic property of the universe. *Biosystem, 38*(2), 135–140. doi:10.1016/0303-2647(96)88368-7

Tandoğan, R. Ö. (2006). *Fen eğitiminde probleme dayali aktif öğrenmenin öğrencilerin başarilarina ve kavram öğrenmelerine etkisi*. Unpublished master's thesis, Marmara Üniversitesi, Eğitim Bilimleri Enstitüsü.

Tavukçu, K. (2006). *Fen bilgisi dersinde probleme dayali öğrenmenin öğrenme ürünlerine etkisi*. Unpublished master's thesis, Zonguldak Karaelmas University, Sosyal Bilimler Enstitüsü.

Tseng, K. H., Chiang, F. K., & Hsu, W. H. (2007). Interactive processes and learning attitudes in a web-based problem-based learning (PBL) platform. *Computers in Human Behavior, 24*(3), 940–955. doi:10.1016/j.chb.2007.02.023

Uslu, G. (2006). *Ortaögretim matematik dersinde probleme dayali öğrenmenin öğrencilerin derse ilişkin tutumlarina, akademik başarilarina ve kalicilik düzeylerine etkisi*. Unpublished master's thesis, Balıkesir University, Fen Bilimleri Enstitüsü.

Valaitis, R. K., Sword, W. A., Jones, B., & Hodges, A. (2005). Problem-based learning online: perceptions of health science students. *Health Sciences Education, 10*(3), 231-252. New York: Springer.

Wheeler, S., Kelly, P., & Gale, K. (2005). Influence of online PBL on teachers. *Research in Learning Technology, 13*(2), 125–137.

ENDNOTE

This study has been extracted as a summary from the doctorate thesis titled "The Effect of The Online and Face-to-face Problem-based Learning Approaches on Student Achievement Level and Their Attitudes towards Mathematics" and conducted under Prof. Dr. Hafize Keser at Department of Computer Education and Instructional Technologies, Ankara University.

This work was previously published in International Journal of E-Adoption, Volume 2, Issue 2, edited by Sushil K. Sharma, pp. 19-34, copyright 2010 by IGI Publishing (an imprint of IGI Global).

Chapter 14
Wiki Interaction Tracks in Geometry Learning

Wajeeh Daher
An-Najah National University, Palestine and Al-Qasemi Academic College of Education, Israel

ABSTRACT

The constant comparative method (Lincoln & Guba, 1985) was used to analyze preservice teachers' discussions and interactions in wiki discussion sections regarding geometric lessons that were written by other preservice teachers in the year before. The data was compared for the following interaction aspects of knowledge building: dialogical actions, participants' roles, and discussion tracks. Research shows that building their content and pedagogic content knowledge, the preservice teachers together with the lecturer used mainly proposing, asking, requesting, arguing, presenting, and moving the discussion forward as dialogical actions. Proposing and asking were used for various goals such as proposing various ideas and actions, and asking about different issues concerned with geometric content and pedagogic content knowledge. The lecturer asked questions more than the preservice teachers, while the preservice teachers proposed more than the lecturer. The knowledge building was collaborative in nature, and one important aspect which enabled the collaboration is the topology of the wiki discussion section. This topology enables presenting the content of the messages; not just the titles, where the contents are presented as having the same level and thus the same importance.

INTRODUCTION

Wikis are used and constructed by students for various targets. Taylor (2006) describes the advantages that wikis offer: (1) it is available 24 hours a day (2) it is easy to navigate, easy to be searched and easy to make contributions to (3) Changes, new information and successful improvisations can be quickly documented, and (4) new, revised or alternative worksheets can be attached for subsequent use by anyone. Grant (2006) says that "Wikis have been heralded as one of a number of new and powerful forms of software capable of

DOI: 10.4018/978-1-4666-0041-6.ch014

supporting a range of collaborative ventures and learning activities." Forte and Brukman (2007) say that wikis can be used by students not just as a kit for writing to learn, but a kit for public knowledge building in schools. Head and Eisenberg (2009) found that higher education students use Wikipedia as a unique and indispensible research source for conducting their researches. They add that this collaborative, community-based online source gave students a big picture and language contexts for their research projects. Head and Eisenberg (ibid) report that in 8 out of 11 of the student discussion sessions there was a strong consensus among students that their research process began with Wikipedia.

The wiki technology then serves various educational functions for teachers and students. So, preservice teachers would benefit from being introduced to this technology.

LITERATURE REVIEW

Wikis in Education

Tonkin (2005) identifies four categories of the wiki use in the education field:

1. Single-user: This use allows individual students to write and edit their own thoughts. So, it's useful for revision and monitoring changes in understanding over a period of time.
2. Lab book: This use enables students to peer review notes kept online by adding commentary, annotations or other additions to existing lecture notes, seminar discussions, lesson plans, etc.
3. Collaborative writing: This use can be used by a team for joint project or research such as a group initiative, essay or presentation.
4. Knowledge base: Through collaborative entries, students can create course content

that supplements and extends delivered material.

Challenges to Wiki's Use in Education

Reynard (2009) points at three challenges to wiki use in instruction. The first challenge is to create meaningful assignment to motivate students' learning. Reynard suggests that this can be done through: building a dynamic and not static assignment, the assignment should demand every student fully participating, and the assignment should use students' participation to move their learning forward. The second challenge involves grading the students' work in the wiki environment. Reynard (2009) says that students should be graded for all their work's stages in the wiki environment, where the grading should take into consideration the following stages: working with and building on existing information, inputting new information, and synthesis of information into useful ideas for the project or work at hand. The third challenge to wiki use in instruction is the kind of collective knowledge requested in the assignments. Assignments should involve complex problems which don't have obvious or preset solutions, and students should have adequate time for carrying out these assignments collectively.

Leuf and Cunningham (2001) suggest that wikis can support the delivery of class curriculum and projects, as well as the discussion during the process of creating and sharing knowledge. Raman, Rayn, and Olfman (2005) examined the use of wikis in facilitating the creation of a knowledge management system. They chose the wiki technology for its following characteristics: (1) Wiki technology is easy to install (and free), (2) Wiki technology provides capability for easy access and editing, (3) Wiki technology allows a class to develop a knowledge base readily, and (4) Wiki technology can aid knowledge creation and sharing in both corporate and academic settings." Raman, Rayn, and Olfman (ibid) found that the students lacked initiative and the enthusiasm to discover for themselves how best to maximize the value potential of wiki technology. Furthermore, they concluded that effective implementation and use of a wiki to support knowledge management for effective teaching and learning is contingent upon familiarity of both students and instructors with the technology, level of planning involved prior to system implementation and use in class, class size, and the ability to motivate students to learn from one another based on the principles of discovery learning

Effectiveness of Wikis as Learning Environments

Coutinho and Bottentuit Junior (2007) describe a collaborative learning experience of post graduate students who attended a program on research methods in education, where the experience involved the use of wikis in advanced collaboration. They point that the feedback received from students shows that wikis can be effective in learning environments; however, the evidence obtained, regarding the potential of wikis to promote learning in the ZPD zone, was clearly inconclusive: students enjoyed working in groups but they did not believe group works to have better quality; neither that they learned more working in teams than working individually.

Wikis as Collaborative Educational Environments

Kessler (2009) studied student-initiated attention to form in wiki-based collaborative writing among pre-service Non-Native Speaker (NNS) English teachers. He found that the overall tendency among these NNS English teachers, when editing each other's wiki-posts, was to focus on meaning rather than form. When the teachers revised the form, they did so with some additional attention to the content, so this revision of form wasn't just an isolated incidence of error-correction. The teach-

ers deferred to meaning, design and style rather than grammatical errors. When asked to explain their behavior, the teachers responded that they didn't attend to grammatical errors because they had no problem understanding the meaning of the sentences.

Grant (2006) described a wiki project in which three ICT 9th grade classes took part. The teachers assigned students to random groups of between six and nine students, each with their own separate wiki. The students were required to work in their groups on a history-based research project regarding innovations in technology since 1950. They were asked to present their project in the wiki. Grant (ibid) says that the students worked on their own wiki pages, and very few edited material on others' pages. The interviewed students agreed that it was better to write one's own page rather than edit someone else's. From the other side, the students considered commenting on each other's design of the wiki pages as acceptable and legitimate practice, and did so. The author concluded that knowledge-building network did not arise in this experiment, and explained that this happened because the students imported practices of individualized written texts and assignments from their school community.

Wilkinson and Huberman (2007) pointed at the following measures that serve to compute the collaboration in editing an article in wikis: (1) the number of edits on an article, (2) the number of contributors, (3) visibility or relevance of the article, and (4) age of the article. Meishar-Tal and Tal-Elhasid (2008) say that in educational wikis, the number of contributors shouldn't be taken into account when measuring collaboration, and instead the relative diversity of contributors should be taken into account. They define relative diversity as the ratio between the number of actual contributors and the number of potential contributors. For example, potential contributors could be the number of group members who work on a wiki article. Meishar-Tal and Tal-Elhasid added to the previous measures another measure which they called 'intensity'. They defined 'intensity' as the number of edits that the contributors did; this should be taken into account proportionally to the relative diversity of the collaboration.

Wikis as Environments for Educational Dialogue or Interactions

Cohen (2009) described the process of creating a mathematical dialogue by means of a collaborative editing of a wiki document about the mathematical term 'function'. She reported that the majority of practitioners who were involved in her research did not participate in editing the term, saying that they experienced difficulty with an on-line dialogue as opposed to face-to-face discussion. At the same time, the participation of the practitioners who participated in editing the term contributed to an improvement in the information about the term "function".

Aharony (2008) found the following types of interactions in the discussion section of a wiki that was constructed by 19 undergraduate second-year students who participated in an information-management academic program: Courtesy, instructor's comments (supportive comments, style and bibliography, substantive comments), students' constructive comments (structure and bibliography comments, clarification, expanding the assignment, deep comments), and students' response to their classmates (communication with the instructor, emotional reaction, technical and structural comments, appreciation, direct response to other students' comments, substantive deep comments).

Research Rationale and Goal

Robinson (2006) says that the use of wikis in education has increased dramatically over the last few years, and wiki entries and conference sessions abound. He adds that there is still a lot of confusion about what wikis are and how to use them. Though much of this confusion has cleared in the past three

years, there are still many issues regarding wikis use in education that should be researched. One such issue is the discussion potentialities of the wiki environment. One essential component of an electronic learning environment is the forum which facilitates communication among the participants of the learning environment. In the case of the wiki environment we have the discussion section which enables communication among the participants. What potentialities does this section have? Which dialogical actions and tracks of actions does it facilitate? The questions are especially important in the case of learning geometry. Various researchers point at the importance of learning geometry for school learners and the difficulties that those learners confront learning it. Providing preservice teachers with a building tool of geometry lessons (as the wiki) should be a key component of their teaching preparation, for it would help them to a great extent in their future teaching of geometry. This preparing won't be efficient if it doesn't include a discussion tool that enables them to discuss geometry lessons. This research wants to examine the potentialities of the wiki environment to enable various types discussing actions and tracks of actions regarding geometry lessons. Doing so will make us know if wiki provides an appropriate environment for teachers and learners to discuss geometry lessons, teaching and learning.

Research Questions

1. What dialogical actions do preservice teachers carry out when discussing wiki-based geometry lessons?
2. What discussion tracks of actions are preservice teachers engaged with when discussing wiki-based geometry lessons?
3. What learning and teaching roles do preservice teachers and their lecturer play when discussing wiki-based geometry lessons?

Methodology

Research Setting and Sample

The study was carried out in a college wiki. This wiki is used by the college preservice teachers for various learning goals: describing and discussing their projects, writing and discussing their assignments, writing lessons, etc. In this research I will examine the discussion pages in the geometry wiki. These pages are involved with discussing geometry lessons that preservice teachers from former years built. The preservice teachers who built the lessons and those who discussed them are second year preservice teachers in the mathematics department. This study examines the discussions held in the first semester of the academic year 2008-2009 by 26 preservice teachers, regarding the lessons built in the first semester of the academic year 2007-2008 by 24 preservice teachers.

Working in a wiki environment, second year preservice teachers of the mathematics specialization who participate in the advanced geometry course go through three stages with their wiki environment learning: (1) examining and discussing geometry lessons that were built by preservice teachers from the previous academic year (2) editing the lessons according to the discussion in the first stage, and discussing this editing (3) writing new geometry lessons. This study reports the first stage of working with the geometry wiki

Data Collecting Tools

The data was collected from the discussion sections of 24 wiki pages which included a geometry lesson each. These discussion sections had one to four discussion themes each. Table 1 describes the number of wiki discussion sections that had one theme, two themes, etc.

Table 1. distribution of the number of themes

Number of themes	Number of wiki sections
1	4
2	8
3	7
4	4
Total number of wiki sections	23

Data Analyzing Tools

The texts in each discussion section (57 texts in total) were analyzed using the constant comparative method, as described by Lincoln and Guba (1985). This method compares the data until categories and themes emerge. The data was compared for the following interaction aspects: dialogical actions, participants' roles, and discussion tracks. Dialogical actions are the actions that the participants in the discussion do during their discussion, for example criticizing, notifying, etc. The participants' roles are the roles that the participants in the discussion play towards each other, for example watching, directing, etc., and the discussion tracks are the sequences of actions/interactions during a discussion; for example ask – inquire – argue - explain.

FINDINGS

The Teacher's Dialogical Actions and Role in the Wiki Geometric Discussions

Acceptance Dialogical Actions

The teacher accepts:

After various dialogical actions, the teacher sometimes accepted a student's definition, suggestion, argument, etc.

The teacher accepts with withdrawal:

Sometimes the teacher accepted the main claim of the student and at the same time criticized part of it. For example, the teacher accepted a student's claim that a square is a rectangle, but criticized mentioning the length of edges in the definition.

The teacher accepts and promotes the discussion further:

The teacher usually didn't just accept the students' statements but promoted them further, for example, when a student claimed that two intersecting lines reminded her of an angle, the teacher required her to compare the two situations and discuss their similarities and differences.

The teacher supports:

The teacher supported students when suggesting a right suggestion or raising an important issue, for example when suggesting correctly using a specific term in place of another one, or when suggesting to give different examples on a term and not just one.

The teacher argues:

The teacher argued regarding: (1) the correctness of a student's claim (2) the efficiency of a student's suggestion.

The teacher confronts and promotes the discussion further:

The teacher confronted some students' claims, giving them new information and asking them to think about the issue again. Sometimes the teacher confronted the students' claims by showing them the contradictions in those claims.

Notifying Dialogical Actions

The teacher informs:

Sometimes the teacher wrote just to inform the students that he was following their discussions. The teacher also wrote to inform the students (1) about a formatting problem, for example not writing the angle symbol using the wiki language (2) that there was no link between a page and the previous page (3) that a definition did not follow a specific criterion.

The teacher acknowledged the students' contribution:

Usually this was done when a student claimed a correct claim, suggested a good suggestion, attracted the attention to an important point, etc.

The teacher encourages:

In this case, the teacher encouraged the students to participate in the discussion, for example by asking them about their opinion, their preference or their history regarding the learning of geometry.

The teacher attracts the students' attention:

The teacher attracted the students' attention to other dimensions of the issue discussed, for example that the discussed issue is not only about the aesthetic of a definition, but also about its being ambiguous or clear.

The teacher moves the discussion forward:

Doing so, the teacher requested students to elaborate more on their comments, suggestions or opinions.

Requiring Dialogical Actions

The teacher asks:

When asking, the teacher asked about the following: (1) how to define a geometric term, (2) what alternative definitions there are for a specific geometric term, (3) whether a definition fulfills some definition criterion, (4) whether a definition is sufficient (5) the difference between a given definition and a proposed one (6) the efficiency of a suggested definition.

The teacher requests:

When requesting, the teacher requested the students to: (1) go to geometry books or to the internet to look for the definition of a geometric term, or how a specific topic is introduced, or how a theorem is proved (2) find alternative definitions for a specific geometric term.

Suggesting Dialogical Actions

The teacher proposes:

The teacher proposed to (1) add drawings to a lesson (2) write mathematical formulae algebraically and verbally at the end of presenting a new topic.

The teacher gives an opinion:

The teacher gave his opinion regarding contend and pedagogic content knowledge, for example, what it means to define, what it means to write geometric proof, etc.

The teacher defines:

The teacher gave an exact definition when the students discussed this definition but couldn't arrive at its exact statement.

The teacher describes:

For example the teacher described how to write mathematical formulae in the wiki language

The Teacher's Roles

The teacher played different roles, writing in the wiki discussion section. These roles varied, starting from watching what was going on in the discussion section and ending with presenting the participants with information. Between those two ends, the teacher had different roles; for example, directing, motivating, encouraging. I will describe these roles below:

The teacher watches:

Sometimes the teacher watched what was going on without interfering. This usually happened when the students could manage their geometry learning alone.

The teacher directs:

The teacher directed the students by informing them, asking them questions, proposing to them alternative actions, requesting them to do specific actions, or moving the discussion forward.

The teacher motivates:

The teacher motivated students to pursue their study regarding geometry concepts by accepting their claims, supporting them, and implying directions of examinations.

The teacher encourages:

The teacher encouraged students to pursue their study by acknowledging their contribution, and by talking to them by names or as members in the same learning group as him.

The teacher presents:

Sometimes the teacher presented information to a participant or participants. This usually happened after some discussion to which students contributed but couldn't arrive at the exact concept, idea or statement.

The Student's Dialogical Actions and Role in the Wiki Geometric Discussions

Acceptance Dialogical Actions

The student accepts:

The student accepted the teacher's and other students' suggestions or ideas, for example that a lesson should include a suggested definition or drawing.

The student accepts and promotes the dialogue further:

Sometimes, students, not only accepted a suggestion or an opinion, but promoted it further, adding to it or explaining why it is correct.

The student argues:

The students argued regarding: (1) the correctness of a proof (2) the correctness of a definition (3) the appropriateness of a lesson's element to the goal of the lesson (4) the need to prove the formulae that we give to pupils.

The student criticizes:

The students criticized: (1) the absence of a definition for a specific term (2) the inexistence that a definition criterion is not satisfied (3) the statement of a definition (4) the absence of a drawing in a lesson (5) the absence of sufficient examples in a lesson (6) the absence of sufficient exercises in a lesson (7) formatting aspects of the text, like the font size or the background color.

Notifying Dialogical Actions

The student informs:

The students informed others regarding finding some problems with the text that they read, for example, one student wrote that she didn't find a needed definition for the rectangle in the lesson.

Requiring Dialogical Actions

The student asks:

When students asked they asked about issues similar to those that were mentioned by the teacher. In addition students asked about (1) design issues like the formatting of a wiki page or the appropriateness of a picture to a geometric subject (2) the meaning of a specific sentence or a word in a sentence (3) the reason for a specific feature of the lesson, for example the absence of exercises in a lesson.

Suggesting Dialogical Actions

The student proposes:

The students proposed to: (1) change some formatting aspect, like the font size or color; introduce a geometric topic in an alternative way, (2) change the definition of a specific term (3) how to teach a specific topic (4) how to correct a proof of a specific theorem (4) how to write a specific equation (5) include a specific drawing (6) include a specific element in the definition of a geometric term (7) write answers for the exercises (8) how to teach a specific topic.

The student gives an opinion:

For example regarding how a topic should be presented to students.

The student explains:

When the student explained, she explained a suggestion that she suggested, a claim that she claimed, etc.

The student defines:

Usually, the students defined geometrical terms, like shapes.

The student describes:

Usually students described the properties of geometric shapes.

The student corrects:

Usually, students corrected their writings according to the feedback they got from the teacher or other students.

The student presents:

The students presented what they were required to do, for example, they presented a definition or the correction of a definition, or examples on a new topic, etc.

The Students' Roles

The students' main roles were: watching, presenting, arguing and directing.

Dialogic Tracks

Now I describe the tracks of dialogic actions which the students and teacher were involved with. Figure 1 describes one such dialogical track.

Figure 1 is an example of a 'solo' track. This is a track which involves just one participant. It can be characterized further as: a student dialogue, a dialogue which has one message, a dialogue which has three types of contents (criticizing, explaining and proposing), a non-saturated dialogue; i.e., a dialogue that could have been continued: the student could have been required to give a complete proof according to her explanation.

Figure 2. describes a second dialogical track.

Figure 2 is an example of two-participant track, a track which involves two types of participants; one student and the teacher, a track which has four types of contents: suggesting, informing, correcting and asking. It's also an example of a track of a 'saturated' dialogue. This is a dialogue which couldn't be pursued further. It's also a five-message track.

Figure 3 describes a third dialogical track in another wiki geometry lesson.

Figure 3 describes two-participant track, a track which is teacher-involved, a four-message track, a track of 6 types of content: informing, defining, describing, asking, presenting and requiring. It's also a non-saturated track, because the student could have pursued the dialogue but he didn't do so.

Figure 1. A dialogical track in the discussions section of one wiki lesson

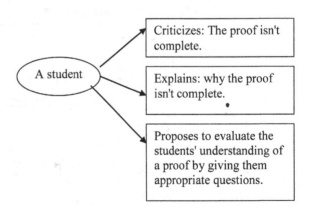

Figure 2. A second dialogical tracks in the discussions section of a wiki lesson

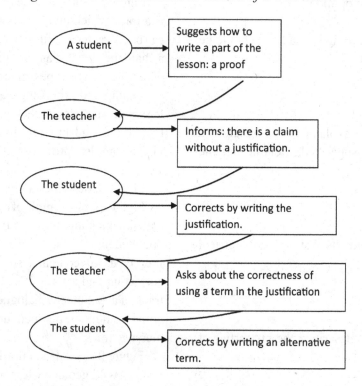

Figure 3. A dialogical track in the discussions section of another wiki lesson

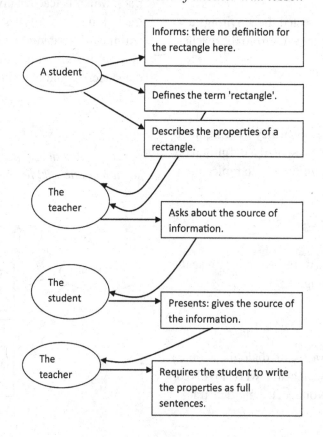

Figure 4. A different dialogical track in the discussions section of another wiki lesson

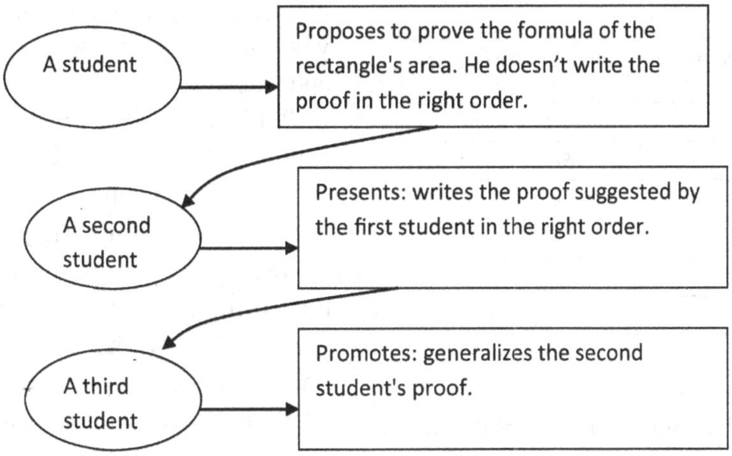

Figure 4 describes students-only track of dialogic actions.

Figure 4 is an example of a multi-student track. This is a track in which the teacher didn't interfere. Other characteristics of the track are: a three-student track, a three-message track, a track that involves three types of content: proposing, writing and generalizing. This track could be considered saturated.

So, dialogical tracks in the wiki discussion sections can be characterized according to the following six aspects: (1) Number of participants (2) Type of participants (3) Number of dialogue contents (4) Types of dialogue contents (5) Number of messages (6) Saturation of the dialogue. In addition to these characteristics, wiki dialogical tracks can be characterized according to (7) the order of its dialogical actions.

The following tables describe the distribution of the dialogical tracks according to those categories.

Table 2 describes the distribution of dialogical tracks according to the number of participants participating in them. .

We see from table 2 that in most of the wiki tracks 2-4 participants were involved.

Table 3 describes the distribution of dialogical tracks according to the type of participants participating in them.

We see from Table 3 that the teacher was involved with more than half of the dialogical tracks.

Table 4 describes the distribution of dialogical tracks according to the number of dialogue contents.

Table 2. Number of participants in the dialogical tracks (N=57)

Number of participants	Percent of wiki tracks
1	12.28%
2	22.81%
3	42.11%
4	19.3%
5	3.5%

Table 3. Type of participants in the dialogical tracks (N=57)

Number of participants	Percent of wiki tracks
Students only	47.37%
Students and the teacher	52.63%

Table 4. Number of dialogue content types in the dialogical tracks (N=57)

Number of dialogue content types in one wiki track	Percent of wiki tracks
1	8.77%
2	12.28%
3	22.81%
4	33.33%
5	12.28%
6	10.53%

Table 4 shows than more than half of the dialogical tracks were involved with three to four dialogue contents.

Table 5 describes the distribution of dialogical tracks according to the type of dialogue contents.

Table 5. Types of dialogue contents in the dialogical tracks (N=57)

Dialogue content in one wiki track	Percent of wiki tracks
Acceptance: • Acceptance • Acceptance with withdrawal • Criticizing • supporting • Accepting with promoting • Confronting with promoting • Arguing	• 8.77% • 12.28% • 12.28% • 8.77% • 8.77% • 10.53% • 43.86%
Notifying: • informing • acknowledging the students' contribution • encouraging • attracting the students' attention • moving the discussion forward	• 10.53% • 10.53% • 10.53% • 10.53% • 35.09%
Requiring: • Asking • Requesting	• 36.84% • 24.56%
Suggesting: • proposing • giving an opinion • explaining • defining • describing • correcting • presenting	• 61.40% • 8.77% • 17.54% • 29.82% • 10.53% • 10.53% • 75.44%

We see from Table 5 that 'suggesting' is the main category of dialogical actions used by the wiki participants to discuss geometry, its learning and teaching.

Table 6 describes the distribution of dialogical tracks according to the number of messages.

We see from Table 6 that most of the dialogical tracks had 3-4 messages.

Table 7 describes the distribution of dialogical tracks according to the Saturation of the dialogue.

Table 7 shows that most of the wiki dialogical tracks were saturated or almost saturated regarding the treatment of the issue they involved. Issues that were not saturated were not treated at all, issues that were semi saturated were treated but one of the issues that they involved was not treated. Issues that were almost saturated involved issues that were almost fully treated but one participant at least didn't carry out a requested action, for example he was required to explain why he used a specific term but didn't give any explanation. Issues that were saturated had issues which were all completely treated

Table 6. Number of messages in the dialogical tracks (N=57)

Number of messages in one wiki track	Percent of wiki tracks
1	5
2	7
3	21
4	24

Table 7. Saturation dialogical tracks (N=57)

Saturation type	Percent of wiki tracks
Not saturated	8.77%
Semi saturated	19.3%
Almost saturated	38.6%
Saturated	33.33%

Order of Dialogical Actions in a Track

Some tracks started with proposing which is a 'suggesting' dialogical action:

- Proposing – arguing – asking – defining – arguing - defining.
- Proposing – arguing – asking – presenting – arguing – presenting – asking – presenting.
- Proposing – arguing – supporting – asking – presenting – asking.
- Proposing – arguing – asking - arguing.
- Proposing – asking – arguing – notifying – presenting – asking.

Other 'suggesting' dialogical actions which started wiki tracks were: giving opinion and presenting, as in the following tracks:

- Giving an opinion - arguing - proposing - presenting.
- Presenting - accepting with withdrawal – asking – asking - presenting.

Other tracks started with an 'acceptance' dialogical action:

- Rejecting – proposing – arguing – asking – arguing – presenting.
- Confronting – presenting – asking – presenting – proposing – arguing – asking – arguing – accepting and promoting – asking – arguing – presenting.

Some tracks began with a requiring dialogical action:

- Asking – arguing – arguing – presenting – asking – arguing – presenting.

As could be seen, when tracks began with proposing, arguing or asking followed and then a suggesting action. When we have a saturated track, it ends with presenting. It is also noticeable that an accepting action follows a suggesting action.

Interactions

There were various types of interactions between the participants in the wiki discussion section. Initiated teacher's or student's dialogue triggered different types of dialogic actions and interaction. Below I describe the different types of triggered actions and interactions.

Table 8 describes the actions/interactions triggered by a student's initial actions.

DISCUSSION

Dialogical Actions

Augar, Raitman, and Zhou (2004) say that wikis can be used to facilitate computer supported collaborative learning, CSCL. This is what happened in the reported preservice teachers' learning that occurred in a wiki environment: second year preservice teachers collaborated to discuss and deepen their knowledge in geometric content and pedagogic content knowledge. Collaborating, they did various dialogical actions. These dialogical actions are of four main types: Accepting, notifying, requiring and suggesting. These four types are of complementary nature: accepting is used to exchange ideas and move the discussion forward. Notifying is used for administrative goals; especially to direct the participants and promote learning. It was used not only by the teacher but by the students too. Requiring is used to make the participants do things, and suggesting is used to give some goods for the participants. It could be suggested that these four components are essential for effective and successful learning in any learning setting, especially the electronic setting.

Table 8. Triggered actions/interactions by initiated actions

Initial action	Triggered actions/interactions
Proposing	Accepting the proposal, acknowledging the importance of the proposal, supporting the proposal, rejecting the proposal, requiring the clarifying of the proposal, discussing the proposal, developing the proposal.
Asking	Trying to answer, giving implication of the right answer, proposing a way to the right answer, giving information, and arguing.
Requesting	Clarifying, trying to do, doing.
arguing	Arguing, accepting, supporting, rejecting.
explaining	Arguing, supporting, rejecting, requesting further explanation.
Giving an opinion	Arguing, supporting, rejecting, requesting further explanation, giving opinion.
defining	Accepting, rejecting, and arguing with or against the definition's statement.
describing	Accepting, rejecting, and arguing with or against the description's statement.
correcting	Accepting, rejecting, and arguing with or against the correction.
Informing	Accepting, rejecting, arguing with or against what is informed, and doing according to what is informed.
Implying	Clarifying, explaining, and doing as implied.
encouraging	Doing,
Criticizing	Accepting, rejecting, arguing with or against the criticism, and doing according to the criticism.

Dialogical Interactions

Augar, Raitman, and Zhou (2004) point that wikis enable the exchange of ideas and the facilitation of group interaction. This research looks at three aspects of this exchange: the type of participants in the exchange, the triggered actions/interactions from a dialogical action, and the tracks that represent this exchange.

Regarding the triggered actions/ interactions, we saw that a dialogical action may result in various actions/ interactions. The dialogical actions that triggered more actions/ interactions were proposing and asking. Proposing and asking were wide range actions; they were used to propose various ideas and actions, and ask about different issues that were concerned with geometric content and pedagogic content knowledge. The teacher asked more than students, while students proposed more than the teacher. This can be explained by the directing role of the teacher who asked to direct the students to verify or develop geometric concepts, while he didn't propose directly ideas or actions because he probably wanted the students to ar-

rive at these actions and ideas by themselves, as a consequence of his directing. Thus the study of geometry and geometry writing and teaching, in the wiki dialogical environment, was characterized by a teacher who directed and students who exchanged ideas and suggested taking specific actions. The discussion of the two other issues regarding the participants' types and the dialogical tracks will follow.

Participants' Roles

The Teacher's Role

The teacher's role can be summarized as: watching, directing, encouraging, motivating, and presenting. As reported in the finding, the teacher played the presenting role scarcely; when the students didn't arrive by themselves at the exact definition of a geometric term or the proof of a geometric theorem. This happened after discussing the definition or the proof with the students. Thus the main role played by the teacher was directing. Bjørgen (1991), as reported by Ljoså

(1998), describes four different conceptions of what it means to be a teacher: (1) the sculptor who takes full responsibility for the presentation of all relevant material and controls the schedule, the curriculum and the work of the students (2) The entertainer who feels responsible for arousing the interest of the student and make it easy for them to grasp the central issues of her subject (3) the coach who believes that results depend on the work done by each student, and sees himself as catalyst for this work. (4) The manager who looks at the classroom as a working place, and considers her task to be managing the joint efforts effectively towards the best possible result. The role of the teacher, in the wiki geometry learning that this article reports, is more a coach than any other role, but he also was a manager and an intertainer.

The Student's Role

The students' main roles were: watching, presenting, arguing and directing. The students did more presenting than the teacher because this is what they were expected to do when suggesting changes to improve the wiki geometric texts. Arguing was one of the main dialogical actions of students because this is how they defended or justified their suggestion. Overall, the students' role was to develop last year students' knowledge and, doing so, to produce their own knowledge. Discussing last year students' knowledge and suggesting ways to develop it turned the knowledge from acquired into constructed. The students not only constructed their own knowledge but directed other students to build their own knowledge. The students weren't independent in deciding what to learn, but they were independent in deciding which text to discuss and which aspect of the text to treat. They were also independent in their choice of other students to direct or accompany in the process of building geometric knowledge. It can be said that the students were active partners in the building of geometric knowledge (Sperlich & Spraul, 2007).

Characteristics of the Dialogical Tracks in the Wiki Discussion Section

Looking at characteristics that characterize the dialogical tracks in the wiki discussions section, the following seven aspects were found:

1. Number of participants.
2. Type of participants.
3. Types of dialogue contents.
4. Number of dialogue contents.
5. Number of messages.
6. Saturation of the dialogue.
7. Order of dialogic actions.

Let's discuss each of these aspects.

Number of Participants

The number of participants in a wiki track varied from one to five, but in most of these tracks 2-4 participants were involved, so the wiki enabled mostly two types of dialogical interaction: one-to-one interaction and a group interaction, where three participants or more participated in the group interaction. We shouldn't neglect extremes situations, where just one participant participated in the dialogical track or five participants participated. The first situation could have happened in one of three cases: (1) The participation was not noticed by any participant apart from this who wrote it (2) the participation didn't need further pursuing, for example it criticized something and corrected it (3) the participation needed pursuing but no participant pursued it. The third case could have happened for its relative unimportance to the other participants, or the other participants didn't know how to treat the issue that the participation described. The issues that attracted more participants involved issues related to pedagogic content knowledge. This could have happened because beliefs regarding pedagogic content knowledge may vary across teachers, but content knowledge

Figure 5. Topology of the electronic forum

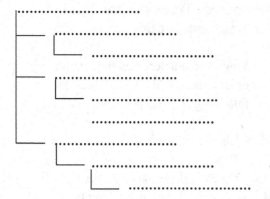

should be the same if we consider the right content knowledge that teachers should own.

If we compare the 'number of participants' aspect in the wiki discussion section and the electronic forum (on mathematical content knowledge or pedagogic content knowledge), we find that the discussion in an electronic forum is generally one-to-one, while the discussion in a wiki environment could be a group discussion too. This finding can be explained by the different topologies of the two environments. The topology of the electronic

forum looks as in Figure 5 while the topology of the wiki discussion section looks as in Figure 6.

The participant who enters the electronic forum meets just the titles of the messages, while the participant who enters the wiki discussion section meets all the messages texts. This characteristic of the wiki discussion section would probably encourage this participant to read the messages and respond.

Type of Participants

Almost fifty percent of the wiki tracks were students-only. This suggests that discussions in the wiki environment could be totally held by students, and thus wiki discussions support students in building their knowledge independently. This claim is supported by Mason (1998) who says that discussion among students on specific topic has the potential to motivate inquiry and to create a learning context in which collaborative knowledge occurs.

Figure 6. Topology of the discussion section in the wiki

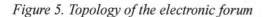

Types and Number of Dialogue Contents

Students and teacher used various dialogue contents to discuss and develop geometry content and pedagogical content knowledge. They inquired about these types of knowledge and requested improvement and development of the given texts. These inquiring and requesting caused the students and the teacher to suggest various dialogical actions and thus exchange and build geometric knowledge. The high percentage of suggesting actions wasn't triggered only by the requiring actions but by the other actions: accepting and notifying. What the high percentage of suggesting actions implies is that this type of actions is essential for students' knowledge building. The students learned by doing, by making mistakes and correcting (Mysliwiec, 2008).

More than half of the dialogical tracks had three to four dialogue contents. This implies the importance of the combination of dialogue contents to the construction of knowledge, here geometric content and pedagogic knowledge.

Saturation of the Dialogue Track

Two issues attract our attention here: third of the wiki tracks were saturated and more than third of them were semi saturated. These two facts point that more than two thirds of the wiki tracks had issues which were fully treated. The second fact, though, points that the participants didn't follow or utilize the discussion to treat all the relating issues that were raised. This could have happened because a participant felt or knew he/she presented a right answer, so why to bother and come back to find out if there was any new dialogical action related to his/her own?

Mason's (1998) found that the sharing of what participants knew through discussion helped to activate important thought processes. This happened in this research too; the students shared their knowledge regarding content and pedagogic geometric knowledge to develop it and raise it to a new level (in the saturated tracks). This research's findings agree with the findings of Mason (1998) and Pontecorvo (1990, as reported by Black, 2005) that students' discussion has the potential to motivate inquiry and create learning contexts in which collaborative knowledge occurs. The findings also agree with Bauman (1997) who says that interactions between faculty and students motivate students to engage in tasks pedagogically and emotionally.

Order of Dialogic Actions

Some elements of the order of dialogic actions depend on the assignment required from the students; some elements depend on the dialogical action itself, while other elements depend on the students' preferences. The assignment required the students to discuss the geometric lessons in order to develop them. So, the students started the dialogical track by proposing how to do that or by rejecting or confronting some elements of the existing lesson. Some students started the track by asking about elements in the existing lesson. They probably did that as a preparation for proposing some development to the lesson or for presenting such development.

Some dialogical actions triggered specific actions, for example, proposing triggered mostly arguing, while asking triggered mostly presenting. These relations hold in a specific context, for example in a context of an assignment in a specific topic like developing geometric lessons.

Different students used different order of dialogical actions, for example some students preferred to start their participation by proposing to act in a specific way, others preferred first to reject or confront the existing material and then to propose, while some students preferred to ask first about the existing lesson and then to propose how to develop it. These preferences probably depended on two factors: the characteristics of the student and his/her confidence regarding the geometric knowledge in question. If the student is confident he/she would probably propose how to develop the lesson, otherwise he/she would verify first regarding his/her doubts, and then propose. Characteristics determine if the student rejects a component of the lesson plan or proposes how to develop it without stating a rejection. This relation between the participants' characteristics and participants' behavior in the electronic forums is mentioned by ChanLin (2008) who points that learning and actions in online discussions is related to individual differences of students.

CONCLUSION

Teaching and learning geometry effectively can be accompanied by difficulties (Orrill, 2006). This research shows a successful way to learn about geometry and teaching geometry; the wiki discussions way. Preservice teachers who were required to develop pre-written geometry lessons used wiki discussions to build their own geometric content and pedagogic content knowledge. This was done in part by the preservice teachers alone and in part with the directing of the lecturer. Building their content and pedagogic content knowledge, the preservice teachers and lecturer used mainly the following dialogical actions: proposing, asking, requesting, arguing, presenting, and moving the discussion forward. Proposing and asking were used for various goals: to propose various ideas and actions, and ask about different issues concerned with geometric content and pedagogic content knowledge. The lecturer asked questions more than the preservice teachers, while the preservice teachers proposed more than the lecturer. The knowledge building was collaborative in nature, and one important aspect which enabled the collaboration is the topology of the wiki discussion section. This topology enables presenting the content of the messages; not just the titles, where the contents are presented as having the same level and thus the same importance.

REFERENCES

Augar, N., Raitman, R., & Zhou, W. (2004, December 5-8). Teaching and learning online with wikis. In R. Atkinson, C. McBeath, D. Jonas-Dwyer, & R. Phillips (Eds.), *Beyond the comfort zone: Proceedings of the 21st ASCILITE Conference*, Perth, Australia (pp. 95-104). Retrieved from http://www.ascilite.org.au/conferences/perth04/procs/augar.html

Bauman, M. (1997). *Online learning communities*. Retrieved December 2, 2002, from http://www-personal.umd.umich.edu/~marcyb/tcc-l.html

Bjørgen, I. A. (1991). *Ansvar for egen læring*. Trondheim, Norway: Tapir.

Black, A. (2005). The use of asynchronous discussion: Creating a text of talk. *Contemporary Issues in Technology & Teacher Education*, 5(1). Retrieved from http://www.citejournal.org/vol5/iss1/languagearts/article1.cfm.

ChanLin. L. J. (2008). Individual Differences in Computer-Mediated Communication Individual Differences in Computer-Mediated Communication. *Journal of Educational Media & Library Sciences, 45*(4), 505-524. Retrieved from http://joemls.dils.tku.edu.tw/45/45-4/505-524.pdf

Cohen, D. (2009). The Impact of Wiki-Based Collaborative Environment on Mathematical Dialogue. In *Proceedings of the Learning in the Technological Era, Chais Conference on Instructional Technologies Research* (pp. 64-69).

Coutinho, C., & Bottentuit, J., Jr. (2007). Collaborative Learning Using Wiki: A Pilot Study With Master Students In Educational Technology In Portugal. In C. Montgomerie & J. Seale (Eds.), *Proceedings of World Conference on Educational Multimédia, Hypermedia e Telecommunications (ED-MEDIA)*, Vancouver, CA (pp. 1786 -1791). Retrieved from https://repositorium.sdum.uminho.pt/bitstream/1822/6720/1/Edmedia2007.pdf

Forte, A., & Bruckman, A. (2007). *Constructing text: Wiki as a toolkit for (collaborative?) learning*. Retrieved February 19, 2009, from http://www.wikisym.org/ws2007/_publish/Forte_WikiSym2007_ConstructingText.pdf

Grant, L. (2006). *Using Wikis in Schools: a Case Study*. Retrieved April 5, 2009, from http://www.futurelab.org.uk/resources/documents/discussion_papers/Wikis_in_Schools.pdf

Head, A., & Eisenberg, M. (2009). *Finding Context: What Today's College Students Say about Conducting Research in the Digital Age*. Retrieved from http://www.projectinfolit.org/pdfs/PIL_ProgressReport_2_2009.pdf

Kessler, G. (2009). Student initiated attention to form in autonomous wiki based collaborative writing. *Language Learning & Technology, 13*(1), 79–94. http://llt.msu.edu/vol13num1/kessler.pdf.

Leuf, B., & Cunningham, W. (2001). *The wiki way: Quick collaboration of the web*. Boston: Addison-Wesley.

Lincoln, Y. S., & Guba, E. G. (1985). *Naturalistic Inquiry*. Thousand Oaks, CA: Sage.

Ljoså, E. (1998). *The Role of University Teachers in a Digital Era*. Retrieved from http://www.lnks.no/eurodl/shoen/eden98/Ljosa.html

Mason, L. (1998). Sharing cognition to construct scientific knowledge in school context: The role of oral and written discourse. *Instructional Science, 26*, 359–389. doi:10.1023/A:1003103213786

Meishar-Tal, H., & Tal-Elhasid, E. (2008). measuring collaboration in educational wikis: a methodological discussion. In *Proceedings of the 6th Meytal conference*, Haifa, Israel.

Mysliwiec, T. (2008). Telling, Doing, Making Mistakes, and Learning. *The Teaching Professor*. Retrieved from http://www.facultyfocus.com/articles/effective-teaching-strategies/telling-doing-making-mistakes-and-learning

Orrill, C. (2006). What Learner-Centered Professional Development Looks Like: The Pilot Studies of the InterMath Professional Development Project. *The Mathematics Educator, 16*(1), 4–13.

Pontecorvo, C. (1990). Social context, semiotic mediation, and forms of discourse in constructing knowledge at school. In H. Mandl, E. DeCorte, S. N. Bennett, & H. F. Friedrich (Eds.), *Learning and instruction, European research in an international context Vol. 2:1. Social and cognitive aspects of learning and instruction* (pp. 1-26). Oxford, UK: Pergamon Press.

Raman, M., Ryan, T., & Olfman, L. (2005). Designing knowledge management systems for teaching and learning with wiki technology. *Journal of Information Systems Education, 16*(3), 311–321.

Reynard, R. (2009). 3 Challenges to Wiki Use in Instruction. *Campus Technology*. Retrieved from http://campustechnology.com/Articles/2009/02/11/3-Challenges-to-Wiki-Use-in-Instruction.aspx?p=1

Robinson, M. (2006). Wikis in education: social construction as learning. *Community College Enterprise*. Retrieved from http://findarticles.com/p/articles/mi_qa4057/is_200610/ai_n17191876

Sperlich, A., & Spraul, K. (2007). Students As Active Partners: Higher Education Management in Germany. *Innovation Journal, 12*(3). Retrieved from http://www.innovation.cc/peer-reviewed/sperlich11final1draft.pdf

Taylor, G. (2006). *The Wiki as a collaborative tool for staff and students in Secondary Schools*. Retrieved from http://www.decs.sa.gov.au/learningtechnologies/files/links/Web_2_tools2006_Taylor.pdf

Tonkin, E. (2005). Making the Case for a Wiki. *ARIANDE*, 42. Retrieved from http://www.ariadne.ac.uk/issue42/tonkin

Wilkinson, D. M., & Huberman, B. A. (2007). *Assessing the value of cooperation in wikipedia.* Retrieved from http://arxiv.org/PS_cache/cs/ pdf/0702/0702140v1.pdf

Chapter 15
An Evaluation of WebCT Course Content Management System at the University of Botswana

Adeyinka Tella
University of Ilorin, Nigeria

S. M. Mutula
University of Botswana, Botswana

Athulang Mutshewa
University of Botswana, Botswana

Angelina Totolo
University of Botswana, Botswana

ABSTRACT

This study evaluated a WebCT course content management (CCMS) system at the University of Botswana. Survey methodology was used and questionnaires were distributed to 503 students selected from six faculties, and an in-depth interview were conducted involving (20) twenty lecturers who teach via the WebCT platform. Findings reveal that, generally, WebCT CCMS is doing well at the University of Botswana and that the system has been a success. The results also confirm the quality of course materials uploaded on the system, that is, service quality and the quality of the teaching and learning via the system. Furthermore, by learning through WebCT, students are able to self regulate their learning and, given the opportunity, they are ready to use and continue learning using the WebCT platform. Results also indicate that generally students are satisfied with the performance of WebCT and that there are many benefits associated with the system in context to teaching and learning at the university. Problems associated with WebCT CCMS that are experienced by staff and students of the University include access, network /server failure, lack of link between ITS and WebCT, lack of teaching expertise using WebCT, and failure to remove completed courses from the system.

DOI: 10.4018/978-1-4666-0041-6.ch015

INTRODUCTION

The use and adoption of WebCT is gaining popularity in higher education the world over (Alhhayat et al., 2004). WebCT course content management system is a class of Information System that manages teaching and learning. It is a system developed to support and enhance the organizational processes of content creation, storage and retrieval, transfer, delivery and application. WebCT is an integrated, user–machine system for providing information or content to support teaching and learning operations, management, analysis and decision-making. Based on these actions, it is thus clear that WebCT is similar to early Information system ideas as defined by Delone and Maclean (1992, 2003), and Davis and Olson (1985). To these authors, an "information system collects, transmits, processes, and stores data on an organization's resources, programmes, and accomplishments. The system makes possible the conversion of these data into management information for use by decision makers within the organization; and thereby produces information that supports the management functions of an organization. However, it is generally accepted that the evaluation of information systems is complex. Evaluation from multiple, interrelated success dimensions on both a stakeholder and technical perspective is more likely to capture changes in performance than one single item or even a set of financial measures (Segars & Grover, 1998). WebCT evaluation is recognized as one of the problematic issues that can be interpreted in many different ways.

Ferguson, Hilder, and Kelly (2005) have pointed out that one hardly needs to labour the point that information systems evaluation is a critical activity. Given the overwhelming scope and emergence of course content management system in the e-learning environment, it is important for information system professionals to develop the means to evaluate this new service and delivery system. As observed by Ferguson et al., (2005), there has been considerable research into the evaluation of information systems. The considerable financial investment by organizations in information systems underlines the importance of evaluation for IS researchers and practitioners (Saarinen, 1996, p. 103). Evaluation occurs twice in the traditional structural systems analysis and design approach: first, in the feasibility phase in which an attempt is made to establish the likely impact and cost, and, second, in the form of a post-implementation evaluation, which is an attempt to measure the impact the system has actually had (Smithson & Hirschheim, 1998, p. 160, Serafeimidis, 2002, p. 172). This second approach focuses on issues of whether the project was delivered on time, whether the budget was enough and whether it met the specifications (Smithson & Hirschheim, 1998, p. 162). The second approach to evaluation of information systems indicated above is chosen for this study. This is because it is an attempt to measure the benefits of WebCT course content management system after implementation to determine its success in terms of its actual benefits on the primary consumers who are the students.

It should be noted that the evaluation of the WebCT system can be done from various perspectives. For instance, the system can be evaluated from the point of view of the administrative and academic staff; the technical staff and the content of the system. However, an evaluation of the success of the system from the students' perspective was chosen in this study because they are the primary users of the system.

Several problems associated with WebCT have been identified in the literature. For instance, the inability to meet the usability requirements of the students or staff members, confusing navigation systems and multiple screen designs within the same course (Storey et al., 2000). According to the UB WebCT Report 2007, WebCT off campus access is still unpredictable and unstable. For instance, there were several reports of access problem, students' assignments submissions not being sorted out by IDs and surname, lost or forgotten passwords, the failure of either the server or the network, students' long distance from courses, classmates and instructors, logging problem, and long download time for many files with large sizes. Students at the University of Botswana seem to be experiencing most of these problems associated with WebCT system, and this is why this study focuses mainly on the students.

Studies on course management systems or e-learning in general have largely focused on online course content creation; proportion of students using online content, online content development, securing content, the quality of content online, the management of students' marks and course materials (Educause Centre of Applied Research, 2003; Eyitayo, 2005; Leem & Lim, 2007; Lowe & Kaplan, 2007; Morgan, 2003). Despite the increasing use of course content management systems for teaching and learning, little attention has been given to examining issues of its evaluation, which are central to e-learning implementation (Drury, 1998; Gatian, 1994). A limited number of studies have evaluated course content management systems in e-learning environments. The evaluation of course content management systems deserves special attention because it is a contemporary information system whose evaluation has not been sufficiently reported in the literature (Zacharias et al., 2002). Seddon (1997) observes that limited studies have attempted to use a high profile IS model such as the Delone and Mclean IS Success Model as a lens to evaluate the success of e-learning-course content management systems. Most of the information system success models that have been used to determine information system success are borrowed from Delone and Mclean success model; but the number of studies addressing evaluation or success of e-learning systems are relatively small (Quinn et al., 2005; Squires & Preece, 1999).

Research on assessing the evaluation of information systems has been ongoing for nearly three decades (Hussein et al., 2007). However, the scope and approach of these IS evaluation studies has varied greatly, with little consensus on measures of IS success, thus complicating the comparison of results across studies and confounding the establishment of a cumulative research tradition (Gable, Sedera, & Chan, 2003). The key issues that arise which are part of what this study addressed include limited studies that have used Delone and Mclean IS success model to evaluate e-learning course content management success. Generally, the focus has been on other information system success and not course content management system success. Moreover, previous studies have focused more on the output of information system and not on the output of course content management system. Heeks (2000) approximates that 20-25% of ICT-related projects in developed countries are never implemented or are abandoned immediately following implementation while a further 33% fail to achieve their major goals or they simply do not produce the desirable outcomes. Much of the research on course content management systems is done in Europe, North America and Asia but very few studies of this nature have been undertaken in Africa. Related studies in developing countries would provide a comparative picture with those in developed countries and help address some gaps in the literature in this area. This study wishes to address these issues by adapting Delone and Mclean's Model and using it to evaluate the success of WebCT course content management system at the University of Botswana.

The contribution of this study to the field of information management research cannot be under-estimated. Firstly, evaluating WebCT course content management system is considered as an innovation to information research. This is because limited studies are available on the subject matter. The University of Botswana implemented WebCT in 2002 and has invested significant resources in e-learning in terms of ICT infrastructure and staffing. The University needs to know the level of e-learning success to justify continued investment in this programme. Moreover, WebCT has been reported to pose a number of challenges not only at UB but beyond. Parts of these challenges were earlier identified in the background to the study. In-depth investigation of these challenges is necessary for adequate and proper interventions. The evaluation of e-learning at UB would help towards achieving the university's vision of becoming a centre of excellence in the world. Wang et al. (2007) point out that in order for e-learning systems to be used effectively in an organization; there is need to measure or evaluate their success and/or effectiveness.

An evaluation of WebCT course content management system is important for reviewing resource provision, process improvement and re-engineering, quality of learning at the university, return on investment and capacity building to mention but a few. Little research has been carried out to address the evaluation of WebCT course content management system within organizations particularly in education context (e.g., Kerrey & Isakson, 2000; Zhang & Nunamaker, 2003) using Delone and Mclean Model. And those that exist have been undertaken largely in the context of developed world particularly among the corporate organizations. As pointed out above, most researches on course content management systems are concentrated in Europe, North America and Asia. Studies of this nature have hardly been undertaken in Africa. The developing country context of related studies would provide a comparative picture with developed countries and help address some gaps in literature in this area.

OBJECTIVES OF THE STUDY

The main objective of the study is to evaluate WebCT Course Content Management system at the University of Botswana using Delone and Mclean IS Success model. The specific objectives are to:

1. Evaluate the WebCT system quality, course content quality and support service quality provided for WebCT.

2. Determine the quality of teaching and learning and how students self-regulate their learning through WebCT.
3. Find out the students Intention to use/use and students' satisfaction with WebCT.
4. Investigate the benefits of WebCT to students.
5. Find out the challenges faced by students when using WebCT.

Based on the identified objectives, the study answered the following research questions:

1. How successful is WebCT at the University of Botswana?
2. What is the quality of WebCT system, course content and support services provided from the perspective of the students?
3. What is the quality of teaching and learning, and how do students self-regulate their learning through WebCT?
4. What is students' intention to use/use and the level of students' satisfaction with WebCT?
5. What are the benefits of WebCT to students and what challenges are faced by the students when using WebCT at the University of Botswana?

METHODOLOGY

A combination of positivist approach (associated with quantitative studies) and interpretive approach (associated with qualitative studies) was used in this study. Quantitative paradigm was applied as dominant approach using survey design. The justification for using quantitative which is in line with positivism was based on Kaplan and Duchon (1988), Kaplan and Maxwell (2005), and Allen's (1995) position. These authors point out that the dominant approach to information technologies studies has been based on a positivistic research in which researchers examine the effects of one or more variables on another. Through positivism, the researcher creates, tests, and explains the empirical reality that is being investigated. This explanation also called scientific theory is made up of constructs that belong exclusively to the observing researcher as opposed to observed human subjects" (Lee, 1991, p. 351). Qualitative paradigm was used as a less dominant approach to compliment the quantitative data. This was done by sampling small sample of faculty/lecturer using WebCT at the University of Botswana. The debate surrounding the use of both quantitative and qualitative research methodologies in a single research design has been spluttering, in the social sciences and sciences where the idea was raised by (Campbell & Fiske, 1959; Allen, 1995). The use of the two methods was supported by the argument that in spite of the mutually exclusive nature of the two methods, aspects from different paradigms can be combined in one research design (Wildermuth, 1993). This study used the Information System Success Model (ISSM) as a lens to evaluate the success of WebCT course content management systems at the University of Botswana. Quantitative paradigm was applied using *students at the University of Botswana* as the unit of analysis.

This present study adapts and extends the updated Delone and Mclean IS success model. The study focused on the evaluation of WebCT course content management systems at the University of Botswana and falls within the context of information systems research. This study was done in the light of the need to search for the appropriate model to evaluate the success of course content management systems. The literature review has so far revealed variables and constructs used in evaluation of information systems. These variables are most common to the constructs of IS success in Delone and Mclean success model (see Figure 1).

Though many studies have attempted to extend the Delone and Mclean Original IS Success Model, (Seddon, 1997), some have done so to overcome the shortcomings of Delone and Mclean use construct while, others have done so to suit the context in which their studies have been conducted. The current study attempted to adapt and extend the updated Delone and Mclean IS success model to evaluate the WebCT course content management systems at the University of Botswana. This is supported by Wu and Wang (2006) argument that, although Delone and Mclean proposed an updated conceptual IS success model, it clearly needed further validation before it could serve as a basis for the selection of appropriate IS measures. In addition, researchers have to choose several appropriate success measures based on the objectives and the phenomena under investigation, as well as consider possible relationships among the success dimensions when constructing the research model. Going by this

Figure 1. The updated Delone and Mclean model (2003, p. 24)

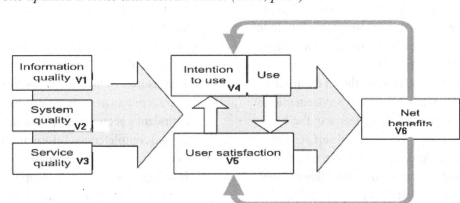

Adapted from DeLone & McLean, 2003

argument, some appropriate CCMS success measures (e.g. teaching and learning quality and learners' self-regulation) will be added to the updated Delone and Mclean model to capture the phenomenon under study, namely, evaluation of CCMS in an education setting/context. Teaching and learning quality is added to the constructs based on the fact that researches have proved over the years that technology enhances and improves teaching and learning (ECAR, 2005; Morgan, 2003; US Department of Education, 2007), etc. Moreover, this study was conducted in an educational setting focusing on teaching and learning. Therefore the needs to include variables that reflect this setting are germane.

The perception of quality in teaching and learning by users with regard to course content management system is assumed to increase the use of the system and eventually to the success of the system. It is on this assumption that this research was premised. It intended to find out if the quality of teaching and learning in an e-learning environment could determine the success of WebCT course content management system at the University of Botswana. On the other hand, students' self-regulated learning is added, based on the observation that students utilise applications to construct more complicated meanings. However, not all learners are able to manage their learning process and master the content at hand, especially in e-learning course content management system environments (Neiderhuser & Stoddart, 2001). Thus CCMS can provide the support to guide learners in the use of the appropriate tools to help them acquire, for example, the strategic knowledge to collect and organize data and then demonstrate what they have learned (Niederhuser & Stoddart, 2001). The extent to which CCMS system makes learners to self-regulate their learning the better is its success. Therefore, students' self-regulated learning is considered critical to the measure of success in academic context. It is on this premise that student self-regulated learning is considered as one of the CCMS success constructs in this study.

As applied to this study, the independent variables are CCM system quality, Course content quality, CCM support service quality, and teaching and learning quality, student self-regulated learning, and intention to use/use, user satisfaction, and net benefits. The dependent variable on the other hand is course content management system success (see Figure 2).

In the application of IS Success Model to this study, the success constructs identified by Delone and Mclean (2003) and the additional ones by the researcher will be defined in the manner described below:

System Quality (V1, modified variable): This is taken directly from Delone and Mclean (2003) and refers to an overall quality of hardware and software of WebCT CCMS and to the elements of the system that affect the end user in the way they interact and use the system. The quality of course content management system in this study was determined by the degree of the availability of the system on request; reliability: how CCMS is error free, response time: the time taken to respond to the user's request (e.g., download time) are examples of qualities that are valued by users of course content management system.

Course Content Quality (V2 modified variable): The course content quality in this study is defined as the judgment by (the students) of the degree to which course content management systems are provided with valuable content, with regard to the defined needs of the students. The quality of course content is measured by its timeliness, relevance of course content to students' needs, usefulness to students, accuracy, importance, availability, and completeness. Information quality in IS research refers to output that information system provides. Since the output of information system is information in IS research, in this study; content quality was used because

Figure 2. Adaptation and modification of model Delone and Mclean (2003)

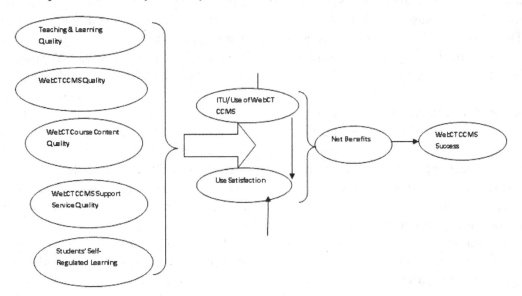

the output of course content management system is the content it produce. Therefore content is used instead of information.

Service Quality (V3, modified variable): Service quality is considered as the overall support delivered by the CCMS service provider or support rendered to the students in the CCMS environment or platform. It applies regardless of whether this support is delivered by the IS department, CCMS support team, a new organizational unit, or outsourced to an Internet service provider (ISP).

Learning and Teaching Quality (V8, added variable): This is concerned with an improved quality of teaching and learning as perceived by the students. This is because the core business of course content management system is learning and teaching. Therefore, in this study the teaching and learning quality will mean the improvement in the way courses are delivered, through CCMS platform and the quality of tutors' interaction with the students on the platform. This was measured by the perception of users (students) in terms of learning and teaching improvement on a five points scale.

Learners' Self-Regulated Learning (V7, added variable):Schunk and Zimmerman (1994) defined self-regulated learning as "the process whereby students activate and sustain cognitions and affects that are systematically oriented toward an attainment of their goals". Cognitive self-regulation can be taught to students (Hwang & Liu, 1994). CCMSs should inspire, motivate, and guide students to develop self-regulated learning cognitive skills. This means that students are guided in order to play an active role in learning, become self-organized, self-directed, independent, and actively participate in the learning process to construct their knowledge (Vovides et al., 2006). According to the constructivist learning theory, students utilise open applications to construct more complicated meanings. However, not all learners are able to manage their learning process and master the content at hand, especially in e-learning environments. This is where CCMS can provide the support to guide learners in the use of the appropriate tools to help them acquire, for example, the strategic knowledge to collect and organize data and then demonstrate what they have learned (Niederhuser & Stoddart, 2001). This construct is defined in this study as the way learners actively participate and take decisions regarding their learning.

The opportunity learners have to self-regulate their learning under CCMS can go a long way in determining the success of the system. Students' self-regulated learning is considered as one of the CCMS success factors in this study because it is critical for measuring success of a system in educational context. Therefore, with this variable, what was measured is the way learners self-regulated their learning under the course content management system. This was measured using a modified learners' self-regulated scale developed by Schunk and Zimerman (1994). This scale was developed to measure the students' self regulated learning. It was hoped students would be able to play an active role in learning, become organised, self-directed, self-independent, and actively participate in the learning process to construct their own knowledge via course content management system would determine the success of the system.

Intention to Use/Use of Course Content Management System (V4, modified variable): This construct is concerned with issues such as the amount of hours spent on using the course content management system by students. The use of course content management system was examined using both objective and subjective measurements. Objective measurements concentrated on the behavioral aspect of the system. Common objective measurements include the amount of time used, frequency, intensity with respect to total services rendered or individual service encounters, and specific system functions used or not used. Also, the course content management system was assessed subjectively; i.e., treated as a surrogate for perceived CCMS benefits. To this end, attitudinal measurements related to technology acceptance such as perceived system usefulness, ease of use, ease of learning,

convenience of access, and user support were also considered. The intention to use is known to be a strong predictor of information system use in IS research (Davies et al., 1989; Venkatesh et al., 2003) which is one of the most influential models in the information system domain explaining IS adoption and use. Therefore, a high intention to use is more likely to lead to high CCMS use, and then in turn increase net benefits and eventually success of CCMS. This variable was assessed using indicators such as motivation for use, nature of use (voluntary and mandatory), frequency of use, access and availability.

Users Satisfaction (V5): This construct is concerned with perceptions of satisfaction by the students in terms of individual outcomes on a pleasant-unpleasant continuum (Naylor et al., 1980). User satisfaction in this study refers to the degree to which an individual user is satisfied with his or her overall use of the course content management system under consideration. Collective findings from prior IS research has suggested that user satisfaction is a strong and critical manifestation of a system's success (Delone & Mclean, 1992, 2003). User satisfaction has been extensively studied in IS research. As a result, several measurement inventories have been developed and validated. These inventories provide an adequate starting point for measuring user satisfaction in the targeted University of Botswana. In this study, this variable was measured using the modified user satisfaction scale where users (students) indicate how satisfied they were using CCMS at the University of Botswana upon a five point scale. Indicators that were used to measure satisfaction include relevance, dependability, accuracy, usefulness, adequacy and effectiveness.

Net Benefits (V6): This is an idealized comprehensive measure of the sum of all past and expected future benefits of CCMS, without including past and expected future costs, attributes to the use of course management system (Wu & Wang, 2006). It is the valuation of the benefits of course content management systems to the students.

Any use of resources, including the time taken in building course content management system at UB, learning to use, and using the course content management system. To measure Net Benefits, one had to adopt some stakeholders' (students) points of view about what is valuable and what is not about course content management system as suggested by (Seddon, 1997). Net benefits in this study were measured by the perception of users on how valuable the course content management system to them was. This was measured using a modified net benefit sub-scale used by Wang et al. (2003).

Net benefits included the increased performance of individual student's learning or individual academic staff's teaching activities. For a University of Botswana student, important net benefits resulting from the use of a course content management system included improvements in the learning outcome and performance, decision-making, the quality of the (students) produced by the University though the system. It has been suggested that learning outcomes, performance and decision making should be measured using quantitative terms (Wang et al., 2003). Through the virtual service connections, students can learn and enhance their knowledge. By actively participating in virtual service connection, a student can become more visible to their peers. Net benefits are also concerned with improved performance at the University of Botswana, improved outcome/outputs, quality of graduates, cost reduction as well as increased work volume.

WebCT Course Content Management System Success (V9, dependent variable): In this study, course content management system's success refers to the degree to which the person evaluating the system believes that the stakeholder (students) in whose interest the evaluation is being made is better off. In other words, the success CCMS is the extent to which the system supports the fulfillment of the objectives that underpin its implementation at the University of Botswana in terms of its conformity to the resources (costs

and time) assigned to it and the improvement of teaching and learning. Therefore, the success of the course content management system in this study was determined by the success construct in the research model developed for this study. This includes CCMS quality, content quality, support service quality, teaching and learning quality, student self-regulated learning, user satisfaction and net benefits of CCMS. The addition of responses to all the eight CCMS success constructs in this study amount to the measure of CCMS success score.

The target population of this study consist of undergraduate students and lecturers at the University of Botswana using course content management systems. The following is the profile of the study population (UB WebCT Report, 2007; UB Fact and Figures, 2006/07).

- There are 16, 238 number of students;
- Students are distributed in 7 faculties and 42 departments;
- 8,000 students were using CCMS across all faculties;
- About 258 faculty/lecturers were delivery their course via CCMS

A simple random probability sampling was used to select sample from the students' population. Generally, the sample size was determined from the total number of students 8,000 who are users of CCMS at the University of Botswana (UB WeCT Report, 2007. The students' population distribution of WebCT CCMS per faculty was not available. Sample selection was based on Israel (2003) model. The model posits that given a total population of N, if ±5% is taken for precision levels where confidence level is 95% and P=.5, the sample (n) should = X (Israel, 2003) (see Table 1).

By applying the Israel Model to this study, the total population of students enrolled for WebCT courses N= 8,000, if ±5% (e) is taken for precision levels where the confidence level is 95% and P=.5, the sample (n) = 381. The sampling frame for this

Table 1. Israel sample selection table

Size of Population	Sample (n) for precision (e) of:			
	±3%	±5%	±7%	±10%
5,000	909	370	196	98
6,000	938	375	197	98
7,000	959	378	198	99
8,000	976	381	199	99
9,000	989	383	200	99
10,000	1,000	385	200	99
15,000	1,034	390	201	99

study was a register containing WebCT courses and number of student users per faculty at UB and the UB WebCT 2007 Report which contained information on students who are using the course content management system at the University. It was from this report that the sample for this study was taken following Israel's (2003) model.

SAMPLE SELECTION PROCEDURE

Faculties were censured. Within each faculty, a core course was chosen at each year of study (core courses are compulsory foundation courses which all students must offer and pass before graduation). This means that 4 core courses were chosen from each faculty. The total number of students taking each of the core courses was identified and added to give a total for each faculty. From this total, ±10% was taken for precision. This represent sample for each faculty

DATA COLLECTION PROCEDURE

Data was collected from the students through the survey questionnaire. The aim of the questionnaire was to ascertain how students perceive the success of CCMS. The questionnaire was self-administered by the researchers in respective faculty during a core course. Instruction and direction on how to respond to the items in the questionnaire were read by the researcher. Out of the 600 questionnaire administered to the students, 503 were returned giving 84% response rate and of the 22 lecturers in charge of the courses delivered on WebCT where questionnaire was administered to students, only 20 accepted to be interviewed giving 91% response rate. The two response rates of 84% and 91% achieved are considered good in survey research (Babbie, 2004, p. 261) and the high response rate was largely attributed to the clear instructions and informed consent of the respondents that was sought before collecting data (See Appendix I).

DATA COLLECTION INSTRUMENTS

Questionnaire was used to gather data from the respondent (students) in this study. The items in the questionnaire were adapted from various previous IS success measures. The design of the questionnaire was informed by literature review, previous survey questionnaires used in similar studies, the statement of problems, research problems.

The following domain constructs were included in the questionnaire:

Criterion measure (Success of CCMS), System quality, Content quality, Service quality: learning and Teaching quality, Self- Regulated Learning, Intention to use/ System use, User satisfaction, Net benefits and Challenges of using WebCT CCMS. Items in the questionnaire were rated on a 4 point likert scale with end points of '4' Strongly Agree, and 1 Strongly Disagree; the two midpoints was '3' Agree and '2' Disagree.

The survey questionnaire consisted of 4 pages containing 40 items. The questionnaire comprised two Parts. Part 1 required the demographic information of the participants. These include age, gender, educational level, job level, department, and length and years of service. Part 2 contained the items sub-dived into ten sections each containing items on each of the construct in this study.

- **Section A** covered (items 1-4). The items covered the aspect of CCMS success at the University of Botswana.
- **Section B** covered (items 5-9). The items in this section covered aspect of CCMS quality.
- **Section C** covered (items 10-13). The items in this section covered Course Content Quality.
- **Section D** covered (items 14-16). The items in this section covered Support Service Quality.
- **Section E** covered (items 17-19). The items in this section covered Teaching and Learning Quality.
- **Section F** covered (items 20-23). The items in this section covered Student Self-Regulated learning.
- **Section G** covered (items 24-28). The items in this section covered Intention to Use/ Use of CCMS.
- **Section H** covered (items 29-34). The items in this section covered Use satisfaction.
- **Section I** covered (item 35-39). The items in this section covered Perceived Net benefits of CCMS.
- **Section J**. (40). There is only one item in this section and it covers challenges of using CCMS.

All items from section A-I are closed ended items while the only item in section J is open ended (See detail in Appendix 1). A four point's likert scale was used for all the closed ended items ranging from Strongly Agree-SA; Agree-A; Disagree-D and Strongly Disagree- SD. NS – Not Sure/Indifferent was excluded from the response choice to overcome the neutral and don't know responses (Hussien et al., 2007); and moreover to avoid distortion of results. The questionnaire was hand distributed to the participants. The questionnaire was pre-tested on sub-part of the envisage population to ascertain the validity and reliability of its items. It was assumed that since most questions were based on previous empirical studies, they had already been validated.

INTERVIEWS QUESTIONS

In addition to questionnaire described above, interview was used to gather detailed and in-depth information from academic staff on how the WebCT CCM system has affected quality of learning and teaching, its benefits and challenges to the teaching and learning at the University of Botswana. (See Appendix 2 for the Interview questions). Interview questions were also pilot tested to ascertain the validity and reliability and how the data can adequately compliment the quantitative data. Respondents' permission was sought for tape recording their responses. The permission was granted by some of the respondents while others resented. Some of the respondents who did not allowed their responses to be recorded assisted the researcher to summarise their responses to all the interview questions. Furthermore, the researchers wrote the responses of some respondents as they were being interviewed. This was later transcribed.

Instrument Reliability

Reliability in this study was evaluated by assessing the internal consistency of the items representing each factor using Cronbach Alpha. The 40 item questionnaire had a reliability of 0.91, exceeding the minimum standard of 0.80 suggested for basic research (Wang & Tang, 2003). The reliability of each factor was as follows: Criterion Measure, $r = 0.68$; System Quality, $r = 0.68$; Content Quality, $r = 0.61$; Service Quality, $r = 0.30$; Teaching and Learning Quality, $r = 0.60$; Self-Regulated Learning, $r = 0.74$; Intention to Use/Usage, $r = 0.53$; User Satisfaction $r = 0.61$; Net Benefits, $r = 0.75$ and Challenges of Using WebCT System $r = 0.11$. These indicate that nearly all the sections of the items in this study are reliable for use in this study except the Service quality and Challenges

Table 2. Distribution of respondents' by faculty (N = 503)

Name of faculty	Frequency	Percentage %
Faculty of Business	99	19.7
Faculty of Education	89	17.7
Faculty of Engineering Technology	97	19.3
Faculty of Humanities	52	10.3
Faculty of Science	106	21.1
Faculty of Social Sciences	60	11.9
Total	**503**	**100.0**

Table 3. Distribution of respondents across department (N = 503)

Department	Frequency	Percentage %
Accounting and Finance	76	15.1
Architecture and Planning	13	2.6
Chemistry	44	8.7
Civil Engineering	51	10.1
Educational Foundations	22	4.4
Electrical Electronics	15	3.0
Environmental Science	62	12.3
Language and Social Science Education	5	1.0
Library and Information Studies	37	7.4
Management	23	4.6
Mechanical Engineering	16	3.2
Physical and Health	58	11.5
Political and Administrative Studies	46	9.1
Population Studies	6	1.2
Primary Education	4	.8
Statistics	8	1.6
TRS	15	3.0
Urban and Regional Planning	2	.4
Total	**503**	**100.0**

sections that have lower reliability co-efficient. However, these were used in this study but the two sections need to be revalidated in case of future use. The lower value of reliability of co-efficient of the service quality and Challenges of WebCT CCMS sections could be due to the small number of participants used during the validation of the questionnaire. Table 2 contains information about item purification on the questionnaire.

Results

The demographic characteristics of the students in this study are presented as follows. The students were asked to indicate their faculty. The results are shown in Table 2.

The distribution of the students according to faculty shows that 21.1% of them were from the faculty of science, 19.7% were from the faculty of Business, 19.3% were from the Faculty of Engineering and Technology, 17.7% are from Faculty of Education, 11.9% were from the Faculty of Social Sciences and 10.3% were from the Faculty of Humanities. This data indicate that more students from the Faculty of Science participated in the study than other faculties.

Respondents were asked to indicate their department. The results are shown in Table 3.

The distribution of the students across departments shows that the students were distributed in 18 out of 42 departments in the University of Botswana. The findings show that 15.1% of the students were from the department of Accounting and Finance. The department of Environmental Science follows with 12.3% while 11.5% were from the department of Physical and Health Education. The data reveal that 10.1% of the respondents were from the department of Mechanical Engineering, 9.1% from the department of Political and Administrative Studies, while 8.7% and 4.4% were from the department of Chemistry and Educational Foundations respectively. None of the students who were WebCT users from each of the remaining participating departments exceeded to 4%.

Table 4. Respondents distribution by year of study (N = 503)

Year of Study	Frequency	Percent
Year 2	173	34.4
Year 3	124	24.7
Year 4	179	35.6
PGDE/PGD	27	5.4
Total	**503**	**100.0**

Key- PGDE/PGD = Post Graduate Diploma in Education/ Post Graduate Diploma

Respondents were asked to indicate their year of study. The results are shown in Table 4.

The students' distribution according to their year of study shows that 35.6% of them were from year 4 while 34.4% were from year 2. The data further reveal that 24.7% were from year 3 and 5.4% were post graduate diploma in education PGDE/PGD students. These findings show that there were more students who are WebCT users in year four than other years or levels of study.

Respondents were asked to indicate their gender. The results were shown in Table 5.

The distribution of students using WebCT according to gender shows that there was a slight difference in the distribution along gender lines. The results in Table 8 show that 53.7% were female while 46.3% were male.

This part presents the results of the survey conducted to evaluate the WebCT CCMS. The purpose was to determine the CCM system quality, content quality, support service quality, learning and teaching quality, self-regulated learning, intention to use/use, user satisfaction and net benefits of WebCT course content management system.

Table 5. Respondents distribution by gender

Student Gender	Frequency	Percent
Male	233	46.3
Female	270	53.7
Total	**503**	**100.0**

Success of WebCT at the University of Botswana

The objective was to find out the success of WebCT CCMS at the University of Botswana. The results are shown in Table 6.

The results in Table 6 show that 81.3% of the respondents strongly agreed that the impact of WebCT course content management CCMS on learning at UB has been positive while 18.9% disagreed and strongly disagreed. Furthermore, 78.1% strongly agreed that the impact of WebCT CCMS on them as students has been positive, while 82.1% indicated that they strongly agreed and agreed from their own perspective as students that the performance of WebCT system at the University of Botswana is beneficial; while 71.2% strongly agreed that they perceived the system to have been a success at the university. Looking at the responses to the items on the overall measure of WebCT success at the University, it is clear that the number of those who strongly agreed and agreed was far more than those who disagreed and strongly disagreed. These results indicate generally that WebCT course content management system is doing well at the University of Botswana and hence the system has been a success. Having answered the main research question for this study, the results in Tables 10 to Table 19 provide answers to the specific research questions for the study.

The Quality of WebCT System, Course Content and Support Services

The objective was to find out how the students perceived the quality of WebCT Course Content on WebCT and support services provided. The results are shown in Table 7, Table 8, and Table 9.

The results in Table 7 reveal that 60.2% of the respondents strongly agreed that the systems 'availability is high while 39.2% strongly disagreed. The data also show that 81.5% indicated

Table 6. Evaluation of WebCT course content management system success N = 503

S/N	Criterion Measure (Success of CCMS)	SA	A	D	SD
1.	Overall the impact of WebCT course content management system on learning at UB has been positive	103 (20.5)	306 (60.8)	74 (14.7)	20 (4.0)
2.	Overall the impact of WebCT course content management system on me has been positive	95 (18.9)	299 (59.4)	81 (16.1)	28 (5.6)
3.	The performance of WebCT course management system at UB to me as student is beneficial	135 (26.8)	278 (55.3)	69 (13.7)	21 (4.2)
4.	From my own perspective as UB student, use of WebCT CCMS is a success.	94 (18.7)	264 (52.5)	108 (21.5)	37 (7.4)

Note: Strongly agree and agree were collapsed to strongly agree

Disagree and strongly disagree were collapsed to strongly disagree

Table 7. Quality of WebCT course content management system N = 503

S/N	WebCT Course Content Management System Quality	SA	A	D	SA
1.	WebCT Course content management system availability is very high	68 (13.5)	238 (47.3)	166 (33.0)	31 (6.2)
2.	WebCT Course content management system is easy to use	100 (19.9)	310 (61.6)	75 (14.9)	18 (3.6)
3.	WebCT Course management system is user-friendly	115 (22.9)	292 (58.0)	79 (15.7)	17 (3.4)
4.	WebCT Course content management system provides interactive Features between users and system	73 (14.5)	305 (60.6)	109 (21.7)	16 (3.2)
5.	WebCT Course content management system provides high-speed access to Information.	90 (17.9)	230 (45.7)	145 (28.8)	38 (7.6)

Note: Strongly agree and agree were collapsed to strongly agree

Disagree and strongly disagree were collapsed to strongly disagree

Table 8. Content quality of courses on WebCT CCMS (N = 503)

S/N	Content Quality	SA	A	D	SD
1.	I think course content is always presented in a useful format	85 (16.9)	288 (57.3)	112 (22.3)	18 (3.6)
2.	Course content management system provides up-to-date information	65 (12.9)	282 (56.1)	129 (25.6)	27 (5.4)
3.	Course content management system provides course Content/information that seems to be exactly what I need.	56 (11.1)	260 (51.7)	163 (32.4)	24 (4.8)
4.	Course content management system provides content/information relevant to my discipline.	72 (14.3)	317 (63.0)	98 (19.5)	16 (3.2)

Note: Strongly agree and agree were collapsed to strongly agree

Disagree and strongly disagree were collapsed to strongly disagree

Table 9. Quality of support service (N = 503)

S/N	Service Quality	SA	A	D	SD
1.	The WebCT CCMS system provides a proper level of on-line assistance and explanation.	51 (10.1)	274 (54.5)	146 (29.0)	32 (6.4)
2.	The IT department/e-learning support staff are always available for consultation.	50 (10)	150 (29.8)	193 (38.4)	110 (21.8)
3.	The IT department/e-learning support staff provide satisfactory support to users using the WebCT course management system at UB.	57 (11.3)	200 (39.8)	157 (31.2)	89 (17.7)

Note: Strongly agree and agree were collapsed to strongly agree
Disagree and strongly disagree were collapsed to strongly disagree

Table 10. Teaching and learning quality and WebCT CCMS (N = 503)

S/N	Teaching and Learning Quality	SA	A	D	SD
1.	Learning through WebCT course management system is stress free.	60 (11.9)	230 (45.7)	169 (33.6)	44 (8.7)
2.	Learning through a course content management system is easier.	64 (12.7)	253 (50.3)	150 (29.8)	36 (7.2)
3.	Course content management system aides active learning	78 (15.5)	273 (54.3)	112 (22.3)	40 (8.0)

Note: Strongly agree and agree were collapsed to strongly agree
Disagree and strongly disagree were collapsed to strongly disagree

that the system is easy to use while 18.5% strongly disagreed. Responses to WebCT course management system is user-friendly show that those who strongly agreed (80.9%) were more than those who strongly disagreed. Moreover, the results show that the system provides interactive features between users and the system with 71.1% who strongly agreed, while 24.9% strongly disagreed. Similarly, the data reveal that respondents strongly agreed that the system provides high speed access with 63.6% indicating that they strongly agreed while 36.4% strongly disagreed to the statement. It is clear from these results that respondents who strongly agreed to the measure of quality of WebCT system were more than those who disagreed and strongly disagreed. This indicates generally that the quality of WebCT to the respondents is very high.

The results in Table 8 show that 74.2% strongly agreed that course content on WebCT is always presented in a useful format while 25.9% strongly disagreed. The results also show that 69% strongly

agreed that the system provides up-to-date information to them while 31% strongly disagreed. Furthermore, the results reveal that 62.8% strongly agreed that the system provides course content that seems to be exactly what they need while 38% were indifferent to this. Moreover, 77.3% indicated that they strongly agreed that the system provides content/information that is relevant to their discipline/course of study, while 22.7% strongly disagreed. Looking at the percentage of responses to the measure on content quality, it is clear that the percentage of strongly agreed outnumber the percentage of strongly disagreed. This implies that the content of courses on WebCT course content management system at the University of Botswana is of a high quality. This answers the third research question for this study.

The results in Table 9 reveal that 64.6% indicated that they strongly agreed that WebCT system provides a proper level of on-line assistance and explanation while 35.4% strongly disagreed. The data also show that 39.8% strongly agreed that the

IT department / e-learning support staff are always available for consultation, while 60.1% strongly disagreed. On whether or not the IT department/ e-learning support staff provide satisfactory support to users using the WebCT system at the University, 51.1% strongly agreed while 49.9% strongly disagreed. From these results, it is clear that there is only a slight difference in the percentage of strongly agreed compared to the percentage of strongly disagreed. Overall, though, the result shown the students strongly agreed. Although, the result confirms that the support service is of high quality.

The Quality of Teaching and Learning, and Students Self-Regulated Learning through WebCT

The objective was to find out the quality of teaching and learning via WebCT and how students self-regulate their learning at the University of Botswana. The results are shown in Table 10 and Table 11.

The results show that 57.6% strongly agreed that learning through the WebCT course content management system is stress free while 42.4% strongly agreed. The results further show that 63% strongly agreed that learning though the WebCT system is easier while 37% strongly disagreed. Moreover, 69% strongly agreed that the WebCT system fosters active learning while on the other

hand, 30.2% strongly disagreed. Looking at the responses to the items, it is clear that strongly agree responses to the teaching and learning quality of WebCT is greater than those of strongly disagree. This implies that the quality of teaching and learning through WebCT CCMS at the University of Botswana is high and of a good quality. This hereby answers the fifth research question on this study.

The results in Table 11 show that 65% strongly agreed that the WebCT system allows them to ask questions in order to make sure they understand the material and courses they have been studying and offered. On the other 34.2% strongly disagreed to the statement. The findings also reveal that 75.4% strongly agreed that the WebCT system helps them to answer assignment and quiz questions while 24.6% strongly disagreed. Furthermore, 54.6% strongly agreed that the WebCT helps them make decisions on things that they need to learn before offering courses on the platform, while, 45.4% strongly disagreed. In addition, the results reveal that 60.5% strongly agreed that the WebCT system enable them to monitor their learning progress while 39.5% strongly disagreed. Comparing the percentage of strongly agreed with strongly disagree on this issue of self-regulated learning; it is clear that the WebCT has enabled the learners to self-regulate their learning activities.

Table 11. Students self-regulated learning and WebCT CCMS (N = 503)

S/N	Self-regulated learning	SA	A	D	SD
1.	WebCT CCMS allows me to ask myself questions to make sure I understand the material and courses I have been studying and offered.	80 (15.9)	251 (49.9)	147 (29.2)	25 (4.9)
2.	WebCT CCMS helps me to practice exercises/answer assignment and quiz questions.	97 (19.3)	282 (56.1)	100 (19.9)	24 (4.8)
3.	WebCT CCMS helps me decide on the things I will need to do to learn before offering a course.	64 (12.7)	211 (41.9)	179 (35.6)	49 (9.7)
4.	WebCT CCMS enables me to control my learning progress	57 (11.4)	247 (49.1)	154 (30.6)	45 (8.9)

Note: Strongly agree and agree were collapsed to strongly agree
Disagree and strongly disagree were collapsed to strongly disagree

Students' Intention to Use/Use and Students' Satisfaction with WebCT

The purpose was to find out the students intention to use/use and students satisfaction with the WebCT CCMS at the University of Botswana. The results are shown in Table 12 and Table 13.

The results in Table 12 show that 56.7% strongly agreed that their frequency of using WebCT course content management system is high while 43.3% indicated that they strongly disagreed. The response to the item 'If WebCT course content management system was not man-datory, I would still use it' reveals that 64.6% strongly agreed that if the system was not manda-tory they would still use it; while 33.3% indi-cated that they strongly disagreed. Results on the item 'I spend many hours per week with the We-bCT course content management system' show that 41.8% strongly agreed that they spend long hours per week on the WebCT CCMS while 48.2% strongly disagreed to the statement. Responses to the item 'I do not spend long hours per week on WebCT course content management system' show that 73.6% strongly agreed to the statement; while 32.4% strongly disagreed. Responses to the last

Table 12. Intention to use/usage of WebCT CCMS (N = 503)

S/N	Intention to use/Content Management Usage	SA	A	D	SD
1.	The frequency of my using WebCT course content management system is high	87 (17.3)	198 (39.4)	162 (32.2)	56 (11.1)
2.	If WebCT course content management system was not mandatory, I would still use it.	78 (15.5)	247 (49.1)	126 (25.0)	52 (10.3)
3.	I spend many hours per week with WebCT course content management system.	55 (11.0)	155 (30.8)	219 (43.5)	74 (14.7)
4.	I do not spend long hours per week with WebCT CCMS.	138 (27.5)	232 (46.1)	89 (17.7)	44 (8.7)
5.	Assuming I have access to WebCT CCMS, I intend to use it	130 (25.9)	297 (59.0)	57 (11.3)	19 (3.8)

Note: Strongly agree and agree were collapsed to strongly agree
Disagree and strongly disagree were collapsed to strongly disagree

Table 13. Users' satisfaction and WebCT CCMS (N = 503)

S/N	User Satisfaction with CCMS	SA	A	D	SD
1.	The course content management system is efficient	88 (17.5)	285 (56.7)	102 (20.3)	28 (5.6)
2.	I find the CCM system dependable	73 (14.5)	239 (47.5)	155 (30.8)	36 (7.2)
3.	I am satisfied with the accuracy of the system	91 (18.1)	234 (46.5)	139 (27.6)	39 (7.8)
4.	The output of the system(content) is presented in a useful format	78 (15.5)	300 (59.6)	100 (19.9)	25 (5.0)
5.	The system is adequate to meet the information processing needs of my area of responsibility	78 (15.5)	266 (52.9)	129 (25.6)	30 (6.0)
6.	Over-all, I am satisfied with the system	105 (20.9)	237 (47.1)	116 (23.1)	45 (8.9)

Note: Strongly agree and agree were collapsed to strongly agree
Disagree and strongly disagree were collapsed to strongly disagree

item 'Assuming I have access to WebCT CCMS, I intend to use it' show that an overwhelming majority (84.9%) of the respondents strongly agreed that if they have access to WebCT CCMS, they would use it while 15.1% strongly disagreed. These results show that the percentage of students who strongly agreed compared to strongly disagree. On the third item in the table is very close. In spite of this, the result still confirms the fact that respondents made good use of WebCT CCMS and still have the intention of using it.

The results on users' satisfaction with the WebCT system reveal that 71.2% strongly agreed that the WebCT system is efficient while 28.8% strongly disagreed. On the response to the second item, 'I find the CCM system dependable, the findings reveal that 62% strongly agreed that they find the system dependable while 38% strongly disagreed. Responses to the item 'I am satisfied with the accuracy of the system' show that 64.6% strongly agreed that they are satisfied with the accuracy of the WebCT system while 35.4% strongly disagreed. Data on the fourth item 'The output of the system (content) is presented in a useful format' reveal that 75.1% strongly agreed and agreed that the output of WebCT system is presented in a useful format while 24.9% strongly disagreed. Also, 68.4% strongly agreed while 31.6% strongly disagreed that the WebCT system is adequate to meet the information processing needs of their area of responsibility. Overall, 68% strongly agreed that they are satisfied with the WebCT CCMS while 32% strongly disagreed. However, this percentage is not as high as 78-80% reported in the UAE Laptop project Web based learning; but since, the 68% is far above the average (50%), it can be concluded that CCMS is a success at the University of Botswana. It is clear from these results that users are satisfied with the output of WebCT followed by its efficiency, its adequacy in meeting information processing needs of the users and moreover its dependability. These results show clearly that users are generally satisfied with the WebCT course content management system at the University of Botswana thereby answering the 7th research question on the study.

The Benefits of WebCT to Students and Challenges Faced When Using Webct at the University of Botswana

The purpose was to find out the benefits of WebCT CCMS to the users at the University of Botswana. The results are shown in Table 14 and Table 15.

Results on whether the WebCT CCMS helps in improving the students' learning performance shown that 77.7% strongly agreed while 22.3% strongly disagreed. The results reveal further that

Table 14. Net benefits and WebCT CCMS (N = 503)

S/N	Net Benefits	SA	A	D	SD
1.	The course content management system helps me improve my learning performance	116 (23.0)	275 (54.7)	87 (17.3)	25 (5.0)
2.	The CCMS helps me think through problems.	72 (14.3)	235 (46.7)	174 (34.6)	22 (4.4)
3.	The CCMS enables the University to respond more quickly to change regarding teaching and learning.	114 (22.7)	195 (38.8)	152 (30.2)	42 (8.3)
4.	The CCMS helps the University to produce better products.	103 (20.5)	221 (43.9)	130 (25.8)	54 (10.7)
5.	The course content management system helps the University save cost relating to teaching and learning.	119 (23.7)	219 (43.5)	111 (22.1)	54 (10.7)

Note: Strongly agree and agree were collapsed to strongly agree
Disagree and strongly disagree were collapsed to strongly disagree

Table 15. Challenges of using WebCT CCMS (No = 503)

S/N	Challenges of using WebCT CCMM	No	Frequency	Mean	SD
1.	Access problem	503	400	1.54	.50
2.	Network/Server failure	503	366	1.29	.46
3.	Long download time for large adobe and PPT files	503	355	1.32	.47
4.	Long on problem	503	244	1.56	.50
5.	Loss or forgotten password	503	209	1.63	.48

Note: Strongly agree and agree were collapsed to strongly agree
Disagree and strongly disagree were collapsed to strongly disagree

61% strongly agreed that WebCT helps them to think through problems while 39% strongly disagreed. Furthermore, results show that 61.5% strongly agreed that WebCT CCMS enables the university to respond more quickly to change regarding teaching and learning. However, 38.5% strongly disagreed, while, 64.4% strongly agreed that WebCT has helped the university to produce better products in terms of the quality of graduates. The results further show that 67.2% strongly agreed that WebCT CCMS helps the university to save costs relating to teaching and learning. On the other hand, 32.3% strongly disagreed with the statement. It can be inferred from these findings that besides the benefits of the WebCT CCMS there are other benefits such as improvement in learning and teaching, helping students thinking through problems, facilitating quick response to change regarding teaching and learning, enhancing better products and save costs relating to teaching and learning.

The results in the table show that access as the most common problem faced by users of WebCT course content management system at the University of Botswana has a frequency Mean of 1.54 and SD of 0.50. This is followed by network/server failure which was indicated by 366 respondents with a Mean of 1.29 and SD 0.46. The next problem is long download time for large adobe and PPT files indicated by 355 respondents with Mean 1.32 and SD 0.47. Other results follow in this order: long on problem indicated by 244 respondents

with a Mean of 1.56 and SD of 0.50 and loss or forgotten password indicated by 209 respondents with the Mean 1.63 and SD 0.48. These results clearly show that all challenges are significant and need to be dealt with. Other challenges identified by the respondents regarding their use of WebCT at the University of Botswana are: assignment submission problem, completed courses not removed from the system, course information not uploaded on time, difficulty in opening important documents, inadequate information on courses, unavailability of Information on the area of study, invalid links and lack of access outside campus, irrelevant course content on WebCT, unwillingness of IT staff to help everyday, late opening of computer labs, virus interruption, and few hours operation of computer labs in some faculties e.g., Faculty of Engineering Technology (FET), course materials not regularly updated, shortage of computers relative to students' population, and lastly, course content do contain outdated information and courses not registered by students do appear under their profile.

From the interviewed respondents, it was evident that many problems are being encountered in the process of using WebCT at the University of Botswana for teaching and learning. One common problem which was mentioned by nearly all the interviewed respondents is the issue of limited access by both the lecturers and the students. This ranged from the number of computers available not being commensurate with the number of students.

One respondent stated thus: "I teach large classes, 70 students sometimes; therefore computers are not enough in the laboratory for all students". The majority pointed out that sometimes when they want to use the laboratory they found that it is booked by another person. This means they have to wait for the other lecturer to finish. It is also observed that most of the computer laboratories on campus cannot contain more than 60 students at a time and there are courses with 80 students or more. Some respondents pointed out that access to computers is not always possible, especially after working hours.

The issue about the lack of a link between ITS and WebCT was also pointed out. A respondent had this to say regarding this matter: "ITS and WebCT are independent of each other making the job becoming unpleasant. WebCT do not have all the names of students registered, and there is also the fact that most of the time registered students on ITS are different from those registered on WebCT".

Findings also reveal that as a result of using this system for teaching and learning gives an opportunity to download class notes, assignments and other course materials. Students therefore are reluctant to attend classes. On this issue, one respondent states that "students tend not to come to class the moment they get the handout for the day. I normally tell my students to take advantage of having the handout before the class, but they should not stop coming for classes because the handouts do not carry everything that the lecturer teaches". Similarly, another respondent said "a major problem is the significant drop in students' attendance for lectures which unfortunately is affecting and will continue to affect their performance in the courses".

Another problem identified is the unavailability of the network. It was pointed out that sometimes the system can be very slow even during class time and some other times. A respondent explained that the Internet is slow, and one cannot switch into one's lesson before time because another lesson is in session. The Internet may not even come up at all. Still on this network problem, another respondent had this to say, "With logging-in and with general network performance (last year it was actually not possible to log-in from outside), this defeats the issue of students learning anytime, anywhere associated with CCMS". Other respondents point to the fact that they find it difficult to design courses by themselves to the point where it would be more interesting to the students.

Furthermore, the results reveal another important problem regarding the fact that the content uploaded for previous years always appears in the course content. Also, some respondents pointed out that most of the problems are technical, like students forgetting their password or access code, and sometimes the slow response of the technical team. One respondent stated that "there is also a problem of staff not really participating; it is not related to my course but it is a problem. Using WebCT is not only to put some material there for students to see but also to use the system for assessment, communication etc. That requires time and effort, it will not happen without some incentives". This respondent tried to emphasize that the majority of staff, particularly lecturers, do not show interest and willingness to use the system for teaching and learning.

It was revealed that preparing materials like course notes and handouts for students wastes a lot of time. This section has revealed the fact that there are problems with the use of WebCT for teaching and learning at the University of Botswana and most of these have been elaborated.

CONCLUSION

Based on the evaluation of WebCT CCMS and on the review of relevant studies undertaken internationally and locally, it can be concluded that WebCT CCMS has achieved tremendous success at the University of Botswana. The quality of WebCT system, content of course materials uploaded on the system, support service quality, quality of the teaching and learning via the system are all very high. Furthermore, by learning through the system students are able to self regulate their learning, and given an opportunity, the students are ready to continue learning on the platform. Results also indicate that generally students are satisfied with the performance of the WebCT CCMS and that there are lots of benefits associated with the system as far as teaching and learning at the university is concerned.

Recommendations

Based on the findings of this study, the following recommendations were made. The university needs to further enhance the support services provided for the users of WebCT course content management system. Teaching and learning is the core business of an e-learning system and this was shown to of good quality thereby determined the WebCT success evaluation. However, there is need for improvement in the quality of teaching and learning through WebCT at the university. The content of the materials (course note, PPT, assignments, other activities) on WebCT should be improved upon.

Improving the quality of the WebCT system calls for increasing access to the system. The access points to WebCT system at present are very minimal. In the light of this, the university should consider it a matter of urgency to increase access points to the WebCT at the university. This will enable more access to the system.

In order to improve the quality of the content of the system, there is need for the people in charge of the system at the university (e.g., WebCT Administrator or UB e-learning support team) to consider making sure that information relevant to courses they are teaching is uploaded on the system. In other words, there is a need for course content quality control. This is necessary to ensure all the content on the system is up to standard. In addition, completed courses should

be removed from the system to avoid conflicting with current active courses.

There is need for improved support service provided to WebCT users at the University of Botswana. The WebCT support staff should always consider making themselves available for assistance bearing in mind that the system is all about technology and it can develop technical faults at any time. The University of Botswana should consider increasing the number of WebCT support staff on campus. By doing so, readymade assistance will always be available to users whenever they encounter problems in the process of using WebCT CCMS at the university.

Lecturers are called upon to consider always engaging learners in activities that do promote independent, self-directed learning so that they can be active and life-long learners. As said by (Shovein, 2006) a quality online course is characterized by engaging activities that motivate learners. This should be the target for all lecturers. Such activities should be capable of developing appropriate cognitive, affective, and psychomotor skills. The activities should encourage critical thinking, creativity and problem solving. Activities and materials presented on WebCT should be presented sequentially in order of difficulty. Learners should consider interacting more with one another in order to benefit from the experience and professional expertise of one another.

Students need to increase the number of hours they spend using WebCT on campus. If this is done, it will force the university authority is to acknowledge that the success of the system is inevitable when students use it for their learning. The issue of access is still relevant here. Many students use the system only if they know they will be successful. In the light of this, the university should consider building more computer laboratories on campus so that students' can use the WebCT CCMS.

There is a link between quality and budget earmark for undertaken courses on WebCT. It should be noted, therefore, that tutoring and the development of specific content increases quality but requires a lot of funds. The university should see to this by making more funds available for upgrading the system so that it can accommodate more content.

Implication for Practice

This study has several implications for the success of e-learning and its effectiveness. The empirical results emphasized the importance of assuming a multi-dimensional approach. Therefore, it is important for educational institutions implementing e-learning to put emphasis on various system levels. As indicated by Delone and Mclean (2003) the quality of information, system quality, service quality, system use, user satisfaction, and net benefit determine the effectiveness of the system. Designing strategies to improve only one variable is an incomplete if the effects of the others are not considered. The results of this study will encourage WebCT managers/administrators to include the measures of content quality, system quality, service quality, teaching and learning quality, self-regulated learning, intention to use/use, user satisfaction and net benefits into their evaluation techniques of whatever e-learning system they use notwithstanding the overall evaluation, the WebCT evaluation questionnaire developed for this study can be used to compare the success of an e-learning system with specific factors (i.e., content quality, system quality, support service quality, teaching and learning quality, self-regulated learning, user satisfaction and net benefits). If any tertiary institution implementing e-learning finds itself lacking in any of these dimensions, then it can do a more detailed analysis and take the necessary corrective actions.

Aside from an overall evaluation, the WebCT evaluation questionnaire developed in this study can be used to compare success for e-learning system with specific factors (i.e., content quality, system quality, support service quality, teaching and learning quality, self-regulated learning,

user satisfaction and net benefits). If any tertiary education institution implementing e-learning finds itself lacking in any of these dimensions or factors, then it may do a more detailed analysis and take necessary corrective actions. The WebCT CCMS evaluation questionnaire was designed to be applicable across a broad spectrum of e-learning systems, and to provide a common framework for comparative analysis. This framework (Figure 3) can be adapted, modified or supplemented to suit specific practical needs of a particular e-learning environment. It is observed and noted that aside from quality of teaching and learning with self-regulated learning which reflects the core business of e-learning, there are still other relevant variables that can be added. These two variables are expected to help future researcher come up with other variables that reflect this core business of e-learning.

In ensuring success of e-learning system in tertiary education institutions, e-learning policy makers should borrowed ideas from the results on this study. This should contribute to the success of their e-learning system.

REFERENCES

Al-Ayyat, S., Bali, M., Ellozy, A., Kosheiry, M., Mansour, M., & Pappas, W. (2004). Two years into WebCT: Perceptions of AUC Students. In *Proceedings of the 2nd International E-learning Conference*. Retrieved August 14, 2008, from http://acs.aucegypt.edu/Presentations/studsurvey.pdf

Allen, D. (1995). Information systems strategy formation in higher education institutions. *Information Research, 1*(1). Retrieved February 28, 2008, from http://informationr.net/ir/ir/1-1/paper3.html

Babbie, E. (1990). *Survey Research Methods*. Belmont, CA: Wadsworth Publishing Company.

Campbell, D. R., & Fiske, D. W. (1959). Convergent and discriminant validation by multitrait-multimethod matrix. *Psychological Bulletin, 56*(2), 81–105. doi:10.1037/h0046016

Davis, F. D. (1989). Perceived Usefulness, Perceived Ease of Use, and User Acceptance of Information Technology. *Management Information Systems Quarterly, 13*(3), 319–340. doi:10.2307/249008

Davis, F. D., Bagozzi, R. P., & Warshaw, P. R. (1989). User Acceptance of Computer Technology: A Comparison of Two Theoretical Models. *Management Science, 35*(8), 982–1003. doi:10.1287/mnsc.35.8.982

Davis, G., & Olson, M. (1985). *Management information systems: conceptual foundations, structure and development*. New York: McGraw-Hill.

Delone, W. H., & Mclean, E. R. (1992). Information system success: The quest for the dependent variable. *Information Systems Research, 3*(1), 61–95. doi:10.1287/isre.3.1.60

Delone, W. H., & Mclean, E. R. (2003). The Delone and Mclean information system success: A ten years update. *Journal of Management Information Systems, 19*(4), 30–36.

Drury, D. H. (1998). A hierarchical structural model of information systems success. *Infor*, (3). Retrieved January 15, 2008, from http://findarticles.com/p/articles/mi_qa3661/is_199802

Educause Center for Applied Research ECAR. (2003). Supporting e-learning in higher education. *Educause Report*. Retrieved April 5, 2007, from http://www.educause.edu.ecarl

Eyitayo, O. T. (2005). Experimenting e-learning with a large class. *International Journal of Education and Development using Information and Communication Technology, 1*(3), 160-171.

Ferguson, S., Hider, P., & Kelly, T. (2005). *Information systems evaluation and the search for success: lessons for LIS research*. Retrieved July 22, 2008, from http://www.alia.org.au/publishing/alj/54.3/full.text/ferguson.hilder.kelly.html

Gable, G. G., Sedera, D., & Chan, T. (2003, December 14-17). Enterprise systems success: A measurement model. In *Proceedings of the twenty-fourth international conference on information systems*, Seattle, WA (pp. 576-591).

Gatian, A. W. (1994). Is user satisfaction a valid measure of system effectiveness? *Information & Management, 26*(3), 119–131. doi:10.1016/0378-7206(94)90036-1

Heeks, R. (2000). *Reinventing government in information Age*. London: Routledge Press.

Hussein, R., Abdu-Karim, N. S., Mohamed, N., & Ahlan, A. R. (2007). The influence of organizational factors on information system success in e-government agencies in Malaysia. *Electronic Journal of Information Systems in Developing Countries, 29*(1), 1–17.

Hwang, B., & Liu, Y. (1994). A study of proportional reasoning and self-regulation instruction on students' conceptual change in conceptions of solution.

Israel, G. D. (2003). *Determining sample size*. Retrieved February 10, 2007, from http://edis.ifas.edu

Kaplan, B., & Duchon, D. (1988). Combining Qualitative and Quantitative Methods information system research: a case study. *Management Information Systems Quarterly, 12*(4), 571–586. doi:10.2307/249133

Kaplan, B., & Maxwell, J. A. (2005). *Evaluating the organizational impact of healthcare information system* (2nd ed.). New York: Springer.

Kerrey, B., & Isakson, J. (2000). The power of the Internet for learning: Moving from promise to practice. *Report of the Web-based education commission to the president and the congress of the United States*. Retrieved July 22, 2008, from http://www.ed.gov/offices/AC/EBEC/FinalReport/WBECReport.pdf

Lee, A. S. (1991). Integrating Positivist and Interpretive Approaches to Organizational Research. *Organization Science*, (2): 342–365. doi:10.1287/orsc.2.4.342

Leem, J., & Lim, B. (2007). The current status of e-learning and strategies to enhance educational competitiveness in Korean Higher education. *International Review of Research in Open and Distance Learning*, 8(1), 1–18.

Lowe, N. J., & Kaplan, R. (2007, September 5-7). Reflections on the changing use of Web-CT in a business communication course. In *Proceedings of the 9th Annual Conference on World Wide Web Applications*, Johannesburg, South Africa. Retrieved from http://www.zaw3.co.za

Morgan, G. (2003). Faculty use of course management systems. *Educause Research Study*, 2, 45–46.

Naylor, J. C., Prichard, R. D., & Ilgen, D. R. (1980). *A theory of behaviour in organizations*. London: Academic Press.

Niederhauser, D., & Stoddart, T. (2001). Teacher's instructional perspectives and use of educational software. *Teaching and Teacher Education*, 17, 15–31. doi:10.1016/S0742-051X(00)00036-6

Quinn, C. N., Alem, L., & Eklund, J. (2005). *A pragmatic evaluation methodology for an assessment of learning effectiveness in instructional system*. Retrieved March 15, 2008, from http://www.testingcentre.com/jeklund/Interact.htm

Saarinen, T. (1996). An expanded instrument for evaluating information systems success. *Information & Management*, 31(2), 103–118. doi:10.1016/S0378-7206(96)01075-0

Saarinen, T. (1996). An expanded instrument for evaluating information systems success. *Information & Management*, 31(2), 103–118. doi:10.1016/S0378-7206(96)01075-0

Schunk, D., & Zimmerman, B. (1994). *Self-regulation of learning and performance. Issues and educational applications*. Hillsdale, NJ: Eribaum.

Seddon, P. B. (1997). A Respecification and Extension of the DeLone and McLean Model of IS Success. *Information Systems Research*, 8(3), 240–253. doi:10.1287/isre.8.3.240

Segars, H. A., & Grover, V. (1998). Strategic planning success: an investigation of the construct and its measurement. *Management Information Systems Quarterly*, 22(2), 139–163. doi:10.2307/249393

Serafeimidis, V. (2002). A Review of Research Issues in Evaluation of Information Systems. In van Grembergen, W. (Ed.), *Information Systems Evaluation Management*. Hershey, PA: IRM Press.

Smithson, S., & Hirschheim, R. (1998). Analysing Information Systems Evaluation: Another Look at an Old Problem. *European Journal of Information Systems*, 7(3), 158–174. doi:10.1057/palgrave.ejis.3000304

Squires, D., & Preece, J. (1999). Predicting quality in educational software: Evaluating for learning, usability and the synergy between them. *Interacting with Computers*, 5(11), 467–483. doi:10.1016/S0953-5438(98)00063-0

Storey, V. C., Straub, D. W., Stewart, K. A., & Welke, R. J. (2000). A conceptual investigation of the e-commerce industry. *Communications of the ACM*, 43(7), 117–123. doi:10.1145/341852.341871

University of Botswana. (2007). *WebCT Report*. Botswana: University of Botswana: Center for Academic Development.

University of Botswana. (2007). Facts and Figures. In *University Fact Book*. Botswana: University of Botswana.

US Department of Education. (2007). *Connecting students to advance courses online: Innovations in Education (WestEd)*. Washington, DC: US Department of Education Office of Innovation and Improvement.

Venkatesh, V., Morris, M. G., Davis, F. D., & Davis, G. B. (2003). User acceptance of information technology: toward a unified view. *Management Information Systems Quarterly*, *27*, 425–478.

Vovides, Y., Sanchez-Alonso, S., & Nickmans, V. M. (2007). The use of e-learning course management system to support learning strategies and to improve self-regulated learning. *Educational Research Review*, *2*(1), 64–74. doi:10.1016/j.edurev.2007.02.004

Wang, S., & Tang, T. I. (2003). Assessing customer perceptions of Web sites service quality in digital marketing environments. *Journal of End User Computing*, *15*(3), 14–31.

Wang, Y. S., Wang, H. Y., & Shee, D. Y. (2007). Measuring e-learning systems success in an organizational context: Scale development and validation. *Computers in Human Behavior*, *23*(4), 792–1808. doi:10.1016/j.chb.2005.10.006

Wildermuth, B. M. (1993). Post-positivist research: two examples of methodological pluralism. *The Library Quarterly*, *63*, 450–467. doi:10.1086/602621

Wu, J.-H., & Wang, Y.-M. (2006). Measuring KMS success: A respecification of the DeLone and McLean's model. *Information & Management*, *43*, 728–739. doi:10.1016/j.im.2006.05.002

Zacharias, P., Vassilopoulos, K., & Poulymenakou, A. (2002). *Designing online learning courses: Implications for usability*. Retrieved March 15, 2008, from http://wwwjapit.org/zacharias_eta102.pdf

Zhang, D., & Nunamaker, J. F. (2003). Powering e-learning in the new millennium: an overview of e-learning and enabling technology. *Information Systems Frontiers*, *5*(2), 207–218. doi:10.1023/A:1022609809036

APPENDIX A

WebCT Evaluation Questionnaire

Dear Respondents,

The purpose of this questionnaire is to collect information on the evaluation of WebCT course content management systems at the University of Botswana. The questionnaire is meant for the students at the University of Botswana. Information provided will be purely meant for research exercise and besides, the information is anonymous. Your responses would be valuable and highly contribute to the success of the research. All information will be treated with utmost confidentiality, and no individual will be identified by name in the final document.

Direction: Please indicate (by ticking) your agreement with the following items on course content management systems.

Strongly Agree = SA

Agree = A

Disagree = D

Strongly Disagree = SD.

Note: Course content management system (CCMS) is defined as the use of series of information communication technology and web-based tools to manage online teaching and learning activities. Example of course content management system used at the University of Botswana is WebCT.

Now respond to the following items:

A. Criterion Measure (Success of CCMS)		SA	A	D	SD
1.	Overall the impact of course content management system on learning at UB has been positive				
2.	Overall the impact of course content management system on me has been positive				
3.	The performance of course management system at UB to me as student is beneficial				
4.	From my own perspective as UB student, use of WebCT CCMS is a success.				
B. Course Content Management System Quality		SA	A	D	SA
5.	Course content management system availability is very high				
6.	Course content management system is easy to use				
7.	Course management system is user-friendly				
8.	Course content management system provides interactive Features between users and system				
9.	Course content management system provides high-speed access to Information.				
C. Content Quality		SA	A	D	SD
10	I think course content is always presented in a useful format				
11.	Course content management system provides up-to-date information				
12.	Course content management system provides course content/information that seems to be exactly what I need.				
13.	Course content management system provides content/information relevant to my discipline.				

	D. Service Quality A		SA	A	D
14.	The CCMS system provides a proper level of on-line assistance and explanation.				
15.	The IT department/e-learning support staff are always available for consultation.				
16.	The IT department/e-learning support staff provide satisfactory support to users using the e-learning course management system at UB.				

	E. Teaching and Learning Quality	A	SA	A	D
17.	Learning through a course management system is stress free.				
18.	Learning through a course content management system is easier.				
19.	Course content management system aides active learning				

	F. Self-regulated learning	SA	A	D	SD
20	CCMS allows me to ask myself questions to make sure I understand the material and courses I have been studying and offered.				
21.	CCMS helps me to practice exercises/answer assignment and quiz questions.				
22.	CCMS helps me decide on the things I will need to do to learn before offering a course.				
23.	CCMS enables me to control my learning progress				

	G. Intention to use/Content Management Usage	SA	A	D	SD
24.	The frequency of my using course content management system is high				
25.	If course content management system were not mandatory, I would still use it.				
26.	I spend many hours per week with course content management system.				
27.	I do not spend long hours per week with course content management system.				
28.	Assuming I have access to CCMS, I intend to use it				

	H. User Satisfaction with CCMS	SA	A	D	SD
29	The course content management system is efficient				
30.	I find the CCM system dependable				
31.	I am satisfied with the accuracy of the system				
32.	The output of the system(content) is presented in a useful format				
33.	The system is adequate to meet the information processing needs of my area of responsibility				
34.	Over-all, I am satisfied with the system				

	I. Net Benefits	SA	A	D	SD
35.	The course content management system helps me improve my learning performance				
36.	The CCMS helps me think through problems.				
37.	The CCMS enables the University to respond more quickly to change regarding teaching and learning.				
38.	The CCMS helps the University to produce better products.				
39.	The course content management system helps the University save cost relating to teaching and learning.				

J. Challenges of using WebCT CCMS

40. Which of these problems and challenges do you face when using the WebCT course content management system?

J. Challenges of using WebCT CCMM		Please Tick
11.	Log on problem	
2.	Loss or forgotten password	
3.	Network/Serve failure	
4.	Access problem	
5.	Long download time for large adobe and PPT files.	
6.	Others please specify…	

Your Faculty…………………………………………………………………………………........................

Your Department……………………………………………………………………………….....................

Year of Study……………………………………………………………………………………...................

Gender……………………………………………………………………………………............................

APPENDIX B

Interview Questions

- Explain how you implemented your course through WebCT course content management system.
- What benefits and advantages have you experience from the use of WebCT course content management system since you have been using it to teach your course?
- What are your general observations about using WebCT CCMs for teaching courses?
- What are the problems you have encountered using WebCT course content management system?
- What solutions would you proffer for the problems identified above?

This work was previously published in International Journal of E-Adoption, Volume 2, Issue 2, edited by Sushil K. Sharma, pp. 48-78, copyright 2010 by IGI Publishing (an imprint of IGI Global).

Chapter 16
E-Assessment as a Driver for Cultural Change in Network-Centric Learning

Henk Eijkman
University of New South Wales at the Australian Defence Force Academy, Australia

Allan Herrmann
Independent Researcher and Consultant, Australia

Kathy Savige
University of New South Wales at the Australian Defence Force Academy, Australia

ABSTRACT

This paper explores the potentially powerful role e-assessment practices can have on culture change in learning and teaching. This paper demonstrates how new e-assessment practices can 'push back' through educational institutions. This is done by applying the work of Gibbs and Simpson (2004/5) to e-assessment practices. To illustrate the practical effects of this evidence-based framework, the authors use UNSW@ADFA to demonstrate the possibilities for new e-assessment practices and their potential to drive systemic change. The authors conclude that the incorporation of these structured, evidence-based e-assessment practices demonstrably improve learning outcomes and student engagement without increasing the workload of staff and students.

INTRODUCTION

The use of Web 2.0 technologies provides higher-education practitioners with the opportunity to engage in new assessment practices. However, practice does not necessarily follow possibility. This is particularly the case in universities in which traditional pedagogic practices dominate. In this paper, we explore the *potentially* powerful role that e-assessment practices can play in driving a culture change in learning and teaching. There is a continuing problem in digital learning and e-assessment of definitional 'fuzziness' or 'slippage', which occurs mainly as a result of the wide range of backgrounds and theoretical positioning of practitioners. Therefore, for the

DOI: 10.4018/978-1-4666-0041-6.ch016

purpose of clarity, and borrowing from a definition attributed to the University of Oregon, we define e-assessment as: the use of digital information and communication technologies to gather and analyse information from multiple and diverse sources to develop a deep understanding of what students know, understand, and can do with their knowledge as a result of their educational experiences.

Our aim is to demonstrate how new e-assessment practices can 'push back' through the organization and its various parts and members (Eijkman, Kayali, & Yeomans, 2009) by highlighting the value of applying Gibbs and Simpson's (2004/5) seminal evidence-based work on conditions under which assessment supports learning to e-assessment practices. Using UNSW@ADFA as a case study in which assessment is framed as an essentially contested practice (Eijkman, 2008) we demonstrate the possibilities for new e-assessment practices and their potential to drive systemic change.

ORGANIZATIONAL CONTEXT

The core mission of the University of New South Wales at the Australian Defence Force Academy (UNSW@ADFA) campus is to provide undergraduate education to officer cadets and midshipmen, designed to fit them for service in increasingly network-centric work environments. Driving cultural change to develop essential graduate attributes in such a 'traditionally oriented' university college proves a formidable challenge for those supporting innovation in learning and teaching practices.

While UNSW@ADFA may not be unique, an overview of its organizational structure and student profile highlights how this environment presents educators with a distinctive space in which to implement new e-assessment practices. We want to highlight how, in traditional contexts such as this, the different, if not at times contradictory, understandings about the meaning, objectives,

and role of assessment can generate significant cultural tensions across an organization.

ADFA (or 'the Academy') provides the Australian Defence Force with a distinctive education-focused environment for officer cadets and midshipmen. This immediately raises tensions between university education and military training in terms of different practices and underpinning general mindsets, and also around differences in the role and application of e-assessment technologies. For example:

- Military training and assessment is focused on competency-based outcomes, while the educational outcomes leading to a degree qualification have a much broader capability focus on a wide range of graduate attributes.
- Competency outcomes are designed to be stored on the Department of Defence (DoD) human resource database (PMKeys), while the attributes and learning outcomes are entered into UNSW@ADFA's learning management system (LMS), also known as Online LIVE or OLIVE, and subsequently officially stored in the university's student administration system.

Significantly, there is also a difference in cultures at a basic level of a digital environment. E-assessment artefacts and records developed in OLIVE and a student administration database, respectively, cannot be directly transferred to the *official* military repository of student training histories. Other issues, relating to differing privacy and security requirements within the two environments, further exacerbate these cultural tensions and make a shared understanding of e-assessment even more problematic.

With respect to the students, ADFA has a recruitment process distinctly different from other universities in Australia. Students are selected on academic achievement, nationally and on the results of a comprehensive battery of tests relating to the applicants' suitability to working in the armed forces. This leads to a distinct cohort of students. Significantly, we were unable to state with any degree of assurance that our student group reflects national and international norms regarding e-skills. This uncertainty led to the use of a survey (based on the EDUCAUSE ECAR survey) to gather an accurate profile (Eijkman & Herrmann, 2009). Indeed, it could be argued that all universities need to understand more specifically, their student e-skills rather than relying on multi-institutional or national information.

LEARNING AND TEACHING CONSIDERATIONS

To date, relatively few empirical research studies have sought to ascertain the actual information and communication technology (ICT) experiences, attitudes, and expectations of these millennials (also known as Generation Y or GEN Y) as they enter higher education. Prominent studies include the EDUCAUSE Center for Applied Research (ECAR) surveys of US universities and colleges (Salaway, Caruso, & Nelson, 2007, 2008); the Joint Information Systems Committee (JISC) research in the UK (Conole, de Laat, Dillon, & Darby, 2006) which drew on Kirkwood and Price (2005); the research-based study of Trinder, Guiller, Margaryan, Littlejohn, and Nicol (2008); and in Australia, the survey of first year University of Melbourne students by Kennedy, Judd, Churchward, Gray, and Krause (2008). Even then, and with the notable exception of the Australian study by Kennedy et al. (2008), all studies have targeted multiple institutions and therefore tend to present broad-brush data. In addition, all are one-off snap-shot studies except for the longitudinal ECAR studies.

In terms of learning and teaching, we highlight two critical cultural-change issues associated with e-assessment. The first focuses on the challenges e-assessment poses to (predominantly

Baby Boomer and Gen X) educators, especially their mental models about assessment and digital learning technologies. The second is about how e-assessment challenges our students particularly in terms of their transfer of skills from social applications to educational applications – regardless of their GEN Y status.

Firstly, a review of the age and background of UNSW@ADFA academic staff has led the authors to the view that staff tend, by and large, to hold a 'traditional' view of teaching and learning in general and assessment in particular. This view is supported by university and faculty policy. To a large extent their educational worldview and concomitant practices focus on their discipline and may not harmonise with the need to develop in students, the knowledge and skills that fit them for work in the increasingly network-centric environment that characterises modern defence establishments. Therefore, the continuing 'roll out' of our digital learning environment itself is a key driver in changing staff attitudes and approaches to teaching, learning in general, and assessment in particular.

Secondly, as some current literature (see above) claims, e-learning approaches may not meet the expectations of incoming and allegedly GEN Y digital native students. By implication, this applies to assessment practices as well. While these students are increasingly digitally aware and adept at a social level, the recent survey of the first-year cohort (Eijkman & Herrmann, 2009) highlighted their discrimination between the use of 'established' (e.g., Web 1.0) technologies and newer social technologies (e.g., Web 2.0) for respectively (a) social purposes, and (b) as mechanisms for teaching, learning and assessment. From this we extrapolated a problematic transfer of digital skills between the two. In every sense, both staff and students are learning about our e-learning environment 'on the job'. We will canvas these issues below.

TECHNICAL CONSIDERATIONS

One of the key reasons for selecting our new LMS was the availability and range of teaching and learning tools, and their ease of use. These tools range from the standard text, discussion and media tools to collaborative tools such as wikis, blogs, debates, rich digital media, and various collaborative and network-conferencing tools, many of which are commonly referred to as 'Web 2.0' tools. However, as alluded to earlier, the availability of such a range of new Web 2.0 tools does not automatically guarantee their appropriate application, let alone usher in a cultural change in learning and teaching (Eijkman, 2008). Moreover, of equal importance is the fact that these tools are available in a manner that is pedagogically agnostic as far as type and quality of assessment is concerned in that, while some of the tools provide more affordances for social-learning approaches, none of the tools specifically privileges any theoretical or pedagogic perspective.

Nevertheless, the underpinning academic staff and student mental models that inform the design and implementation of e-assessments impact on the way in which each participant views the purpose of assessment, and hence the associated teaching and learning practices more broadly. For example, the ease with which multiple-choice questions can be developed, imported or purchased as e-assessments, often leads to their use being over-emphasised. The effort (real or apparent) needed to develop and deploy a much wider range of more current and theoretically informed e-assessment practices, and concomitant learning and teaching practices, in more sophisticated (e.g., Web 2.0) digital environments invites a substantive change, if not revolution, in related mental models, knowledge, skills and workflows.

As indicated above, the design of the LMS used embraces versions of social-networking tools, which would be recognised by instructional designers as Web 2.0. Because these tools provide more options for social interaction, collabora-

tion and cooperation in teaching and learning, they immediately raise the opportunity for the development of a much wider spectrum of more authentic assessment practices (Mills, Glover, & Stevens, 2006). However, as in all cases, the mere use of new tools does not necessarily change the assessment or if it does, it does not guarantee improvements in line with good assessment practices (Boud, 2000).

Should we wish to ensure pedagogy drives technology applications, the technology (e.g., an LMS) must, in turn, have the capacity to enable educators to apply sound assessment principles and practices that support the learning needs of both on-campus undergraduates as well as mature-aged, off-campus postgraduate coursework and research students. In this paper, we argue that to fulfil expectations around good assessment practices, the LMS must be able to support assessment approaches and designs that align with Gibbs and Simpson's (2004/5) 'Eleven conditions under which assessment supports learning'.

RETHINKING THE ASSESSMENT, FEEDBACK, AND LEARNING CULTURE

Changes in assessment practices driven by technological opportunities that offer innovative, relevant and more easily developed materials and processes are also valuable opportunities for both staff and students to reconfigure their mental models about teaching and learning, respectively (Bates, 2000). However, such changes need to be grounded in sound pedagogical principles (Eijkman, 2004; Eijkman, 2008).

In relation to assessment, such a set of sound 'first principles' is provided by Gibbs and Simpson (2004/5). These evidence-based principles, that pertain to the conditions under which assessment (and feedback) supports student learning, are being increasingly adopted or inform assessment projects in various disciplines (e.g., REAP projects:

Nicol & Milligan, 2006; Jordan, Brockbank, & Butcher, 2007; FAST projects: Mills & Glover, 2006). In the case of promoting a cultural shift in assessment, learning and teaching at UNSW@ADFA, Gibbs and Simpson (2005/05) conditions provide a useful theoretical framework to support more engaging and effective forms of e-assessment. As Gibbs and Simpson (2004/5, p. 3) pointed out, "Standards will be raised by improving student learning rather than by better measurement of limited learning".

Arguing for a return of a focus on mutually meaningful formative assessment and useful feedback, Gibbs and Simpson proposed eleven conditions[1] under which assessment and feedback support learning. In brief, they propose that assessment needs:

1. Frequent tasks that capture student study time and effort;
2. Tasks that distribute effort evenly across a course and focus effort on all learning outcomes;
3. Tasks that lead to productive and appropriate (deep) learning activities; and
4. Tasks that communicate clear and high expectations and standards.

In response feedback must also be:

5. Focused on content so as to provide students with options for action;
6. Provided quickly enough to be useful for further learning;
7. Linked to the purpose of the assessment and its criteria for success;
8. Able to make sense to students in terms of the stated assessment expectations;
9. Focused on learning rather than marks so that students are open and attentive to feedback; and
10. Encouraging of students to monitor their own performance and strategically direct further study.

In this paper, due to the constraints of the space rather than an indication of any priority, we focus specifically on the *four conditions*. These conditions focus on what assessment needs to be, based on the underpinning assumption that assessment drives learning. We provide some specific examples of these principles in an e-assessment environment.

ASSESSMENT PRINCIPLES IN A DIGITAL ENVIRONMENT

To put it succinctly, if we are to apply evidence-based principles as proposed by Gibbs and Simpson (2004, 2005) to e-assessment practices, we need to place considerable emphasis on the application of formative assessments. The reasons are because they: focus on key learning outcomes and high standards; lead to productive deep-learning outcomes; distribute effort evenly across the course; and appropriately capture student time and effort. We also acknowledge the objections commonly raised by academics about the workloads associated with formative assessments. However, other than to indicate that there are many effective strategies available (e.g., Race, 2007), a detailed response is out of scope. Can e-assessments meet these four conditions?

In this section we outline the possibilities presented by digital learning and assessment spaces and discuss both opportunities and barriers to their uptake from both educator and student perspectives within the context of UNSW@ADFA.

E-assessment, especially with the proliferation of Web 2.0 tools, provides some increasingly powerful options here. New collaborative tools support students working together and reviewing each others' work, thereby "capturing effort", as Gibbs and Simpson (2004, 2005, p. 14) put it, through social pressure. Within e-learning environments the lecturer has the option of opening up class work to evaluation by others (peer-based

Table 1. Online activity of incoming undergraduate ADFA students (Source: adapted from Eijkman & Herrmann, 2009)

Online activity	Modal number of hours per week (percentage)
Formal education	4 hours (15.1%)
Work-related	2 hours (19.8%)
Social interaction	10 hours (14.6%)
Personal use (individual)	4 hours (12.9%)

assessment) or assistance from others (collaborative activities).

Students need e-skills to work productively (time on task) online. Our recent survey (Eijkman & Herrmann, 2009) of the incoming undergraduate student cohort shows that they may not bring a full range of e-skills with them. Therefore students might need development and practice to enhance the return on investment in terms of time spent learning online, as well as the time learning the necessary online learning and e-assessment skills. All incoming students had ICT experience. However, Table 1 shows that by far the greatest online use was for social interaction, not formal education or work.

While only 22% of respondents had **not** used a social-networking site, the major use (76%) was for staying in touch with friends (as opposed to 14% using it to make new friends not previously met in person). Conversely, only 15% had used such sites to communicate with classmates about course-related topics and 1.9% to communicate with their teachers about course-related topics. (Our suspicion might be that this last figure is related to the lack of skills/use of such sites by the same staff.) One could also postulate that student perceive that e-skills developed in essentially social environments might not transfer easily to more formal educational environments.

Similarly, only 37.6% of respondents to the survey indicated that they had previously used an online learning system. However, the understanding of 'using' an online learning system varies. Downloading a PDF, for example, is less time-consuming than contributing to a wiki or keeping a blog. So, the perception of students as to the amount of time spent on learning and carrying out assessment tasks in an online environment will also vary. While our 'digital natives' (Prensky, 2001) were online-savvy, they may not necessarily be online-learning-savvy and particularly network-centric-learning-savvy (NCL-savvy).

The assumption that they would present with skills appropriate to online learning (including e-assessment) is not well-founded. Therefore, there is a real risk that the greatest percentage of time spent by students in e-assessment initially, would not be an efficient use of study time, but spent familiarising themselves with the interface and the technical 'nuts and bolts' of the assessment tools. Clearly preparatory training is needed.

For collaborative tool use, the feedback from our students is even worse. Fifty-nine point seven percent of respondents believed that they have never used a wiki or Wikipedia; 71.9% believed that they have never used a blog and 57.2% believed that they have never used a photo or video website (e.g., Flickr, YouTube). This led to some discussion during the analysis of data from this survey as to whether our digital natives actually recognised some of the collaborative tools, which were typically adapted in different visual and structural ways for social sites, thus impeding e-skills transfer.

Therefore, to increase the possibility of students attending to more/all/part of the curriculum through the increased use of cooperative or collaborative tools, we needed to focus on staff and student skills development along with e-assessment design. These skills will also be useful in the network-centric environments into which our students will graduate.

Our criteria for effective e-assessment includes identifying tasks that orient students to allocate appropriate amounts of time and effort to the most important parts of the course. The two aspects of this condition are also relevant to the design and development of high-quality e-assessment. The first is engagement. Ongoing formative student feedback collected by Educational Technology Services (ETS) at UNSW@ADFA over a number of years as part of its quality-assurance and continuous-improvement process, reinforces our existing perception that the mere change from one medium to another, or the change to richer digital media, does not automatically increase student engagement. While there may be an initial novelty effect, busy work is busy work, whether online or on paper. Our survey responses indicate that engagement for school-leaver undergraduates can be quite different from engagement for mature-aged postgraduates and hence requires different design approaches. Results over a number of years highlight the importance of *innovation* for undergraduates and *relevance* for postgraduates.

For mature-aged students making assessment more relevant, or more authentic, improves motivation and, through the use of collaborative tools, leads to the development of teamwork skills. E-learning environments support case-study and project-based approaches because of their inherent technical ability to store, and make available in an ordered manner, a great deal of resource and background material. Students can be taught sound research skills in a controlled environment within the system, using the quality materials supplied or developed by staff. Such a well-designed approach can also control or open up the learning pathways the students might follow. One of the great benefits of e-learning identified for students is the possibility of not following a pre-determined sequence (unless demanded by the curriculum).

The corollary is true for e-assessment development. Working in an online environment can allow more flexibility in e-assessment which can be used to encourage changes in the approaches used by staff. Variety, novelty, relevance and authenticity can all be encouraged.

The potential problem is that staff developing the assessment items, whether formative or summative, can skew the student perception of what is important in the curriculum by over-assessing particular parts of the curriculum because they find it easier to develop e-assessment activities for those parts of the curriculum. The classic example is the ready availability of multiple-choice questions and tests and their ease of implementation. Similarly, more collaborative approaches may be more time-consuming for students to undertake and for staff to mark, but there is little evidence backing up the assertion that they necessarily provide better learning outcomes. Equally, an e-assessment framework can also guide and train students to identify and acquire sound time-management and evaluation skills. At the same time, staffs often raise concerns over security and veracity of e-assessment. They believe that e-assessment encourages, or at least allows, cheating and other forms of misconduct – the technology is seen as the problem, as opposed to the assessment design and implementation.

Feedback associated with assessment can improve student time management and assist in directing students to more productive processes. Gibbs highlights the importance of this feedback, which has increased the need to develop staff skills in providing effective and efficient online feedback. Again, this is an opportunity for the use of new technologies to drive changes in approaches that can lead to more appropriate outcomes. UNSW@ADFA provides significant design and development support to staff.

Moreover, given that we need assessment tasks that engage students in productive and appropriate learning activities the critical question that arises is: "How can the application of e-assessment

Table 2. Specific examples of application of the principles

Principle	Examples
Frequent tasks that capture student study time and effort	• student e-journals for summaries of read articles (to be used in assignments and exams); • resource pages where students provide links to other useful digital objects
Tasks that distribute effort evenly across a course and focus effort on all learning outcomes	• topic blogs • personal blogs • focused theme discussions
Tasks that lead to productive and appropriate (deep) learning activities	• topic wikis • project wikis • peer assessment • reflective journal
Tasks that communicate clear and high expectations and standards	• clearly articulated learning outcomes • hyper-linking outcomes to specific content and/or e-activities • providing examples and templates relating to presentation and structure requirements

change the current view of assessment and support the improvement of student learning in a NCL environment?" Making assessment more authentic is fundamental in engaging students with the curriculum and tying this to maximising assessment results for them while addressing staff concerns about student misconduct. What does this mean in a Defence organizational context?

Defence provides a rich source of primary and secondary materials that can be used in designing relevant assessment. Well-designed and implemented LMSs are able to use their repositories to hold the materials to be deployed in ways that, for example, reduce the success of plagiarism, support the transfer of embedded NCL-related skills to work environments and focus student learning on the important aspects of the curriculum. Increasing emphasis on the possibility of the use of these resources in design support provided to academic staff has increased their use over time.

Similarly, the record-keeping facilities of LMS-based e-assessment can identify student activity paths and processes, times and attempts that collectively can become powerful diagnostic tools. Organizational support for enhancing the development of quality e-assessment has been provided through the successful implementation of an enhanced e-learning environment, and

identification and remediation of skill deficits in students and staff, based on evidence from previous approaches taken by staff and students to e-assessment activities (Nicol & Macfarlane-Dick, 2006). Table 2 summarizes the cumulative experience of the last few years. Given the admittedly problematic nature of available evidence we measure success by student use and comments on student feedback surveys.

USING WEB 2.0 FOR SEAMLESS ASSESSMENT AND LEARNING: A CASE STUDY AT ADFA

Earlier this year the authors were invited by a senior lecturer[2] in the School of Aeronautical, Civil and Mechanical Engineering to work with him in designing, at short notice, a very different learning architecture for a course in sustainable and durable concrete structures for fourth-year students who were about to graduate as military engineers. The design parameters were as follows. First, because of military attendance requirements classes need to be face-to-face. Second, the aim was to create as far as possible, a totally learner-centred environment characterised by student-centred authentic learning and assessment.

Together we created a course that replicated a military engineering design office in which the academic facilitator (we banned the word 'lecturer') would act as their 'chief engineer'. As such the chief engineer would be available for consultation and support on a needs to or just-in-time basis. The students (who were referred to *not* as students but as engineers) were divided into two teams (of six members each) and given an authentic task, namely to present a complex set of design specifications for a concrete structure (a headquarters in Basra and a helipad in The Gulf). As engineers in a defence environment, these engineers may actually not share the same physical space but work in very different locations. Therefore to provide for authenticity and to make their research (again we did not use the word 'learning') transparent to all the members of both teams we focused on their use of wikis and blogs for communication and collaborative report-writing. Mindful of the reality that assessment drives learning we specifically designed the research/ learning process around Gibbs and Simpson's 11 conditions. The engineers, on commencement of their project, were asked to write up their research on the team's blog. In this way their work was immediately visible to everyone to enable cross-fertilisation of ideas and sharing of knowledge that was of value to both teams.

To meet university requirements the assessment was formally divided into four elements – three formative assessments of work in progress and a summative assessment by way of their completed written report and verbal presentation (for which they also, unlike most summative assessments, received immediate feedback). In reality however, there was ongoing online and face-to-face informal formative assessment and immediate feedback on their research. Hence, there was a seamless integration between research (learning), its ongoing assessment, and immediate feedback. In fact at one point the student/engineers themselves informed us that they were not interested in grades for formative assessments as

the constant flow of feedback gave them a good sense of where they were going and how well they were doing.

A cursory glance at the course website would immediately convey that in all its simplicity it was radically different. First the usually static 'welcome' page was turned into a dynamic communication tool by using a blog. Thus the 'welcome' page became a very visible and immediately accessible communication medium. Second, the navigation bar, apart from one reference to 'course information' (which linked to requisite, important course information) focused solely on the communication and participation tools – thus immediately signalling that the focus of this website was on communication, participation and sharing of knowledge – and *not* on one-way information transfer. Even more radical for some staff was the linking of the ubiquitous 'Assessment' item with 'Learning' on a single button. This was because the assessments (and feedback) were simply – but effectively, totally integrated into the research/ learning process. Hence, other than in the course outline, there was no need to have a separate assessment button on the navigation bar.

Student outcomes in terms of the assessed final projects were excellent. Student feedback on the experience was also very positive even though there were some technical teething problems. However, given the participatory and collaborative atmosphere in which there was constant negotiation between staff and students, it was the students who (feeling clearly empowered) at least twice came up with excellent suggestions on how to respond to these difficulties. At one point, and unable to immediately solve these technical difficulties, we expected an uprising and a great deal of frustration boiling over into negativity. Instead they responded with positive suggestions and a determination to help make the process work.

This hurriedly designed rupture with old paradigm pedagogic thinking (i.e., an information-driven use of Web 1.0) overall proved rather deceptively simple to implement, yet powerful in its consequences and for future systemic expansion.

DRIVERS FOR CULTURAL CHANGE

Change cannot occur without developing the appropriate expectations and skill set in both students and staff, but also gaining senior management 'buy-in' to champion the cause (Bates, 2000). The implementation of e-assessment processes does not, by itself necessarily change the way in which assessment is used to improve student learning outcomes. However, the opportunity to re-think approaches to assessment can be used as a 'Trojan horse' for introducing change into the teaching and learning environment. As Tony Bates stated in a seminar in 2004 organised for senior UNSW@ ADFA managers, "The opportunities for change which the increasing use of educational technology provide offer a once in a generation chance for change". Change needs to be evidence-based and take into account unintended consequences (Tenner, 1996), which might otherwise derail plans. Merely transferring materials and processes from one environment/media/approach to another will not elicit change. Careful planning has to be undertaken to ensure change and change in the right direction, avoiding insignificant issues. The added complication in the Defence Academy environment is the continuing existence of the (military) training versus. (academic) education dichotomy.

ETS at UNSW@ADFA is responsible for provision of the LMS and, along with the Academic Learning and Teaching Fellow, supports the development of staff skills. Responses from teaching staff to ETS indicate that while some staff are quite sophisticated in their approach to e-learning and e-assessment, many others need considerable skill development in terms of both technical skills and pedagogic knowledge to guide their application especially in e-assessments. Typical questions are:

- How long does it take to develop an e-assessment?
- What form of e-assessment suits?
- How can I avoid plagiarism and cheating?
- What design and technical support is available?
- Does the system enable formative tests to provide efficiencies from automation?
- What item banks are available for quizzes (e.g., pre-tested and normalised)?

As mentioned above, tools need to be agnostic and must support a range of approaches to learning, but the complexity of tools (and related skills) means a change in assessment-development workflow and a related increase in the time to developing high-quality e-assessments. Organizations need to recognise this, and particularly the fact that certain disciplines (involving more abstract subject matter) may need more time to develop sound e-assessments than others.

Technology in and of itself is not a solution or a problem. For example, many of the issues raised in the Futurelab Report: 10 Literature review of e-assessment (Ridgeway, McCusker, & Pead, 2004) are concerned with more than technology. Moreover, while technology may be able to assist with a solution, it often does not solve the problem by itself. Merely increasing the complexity of the process without related efficiency or effectiveness improvements is not sensible. In a small institution, for example, economies of scale may not be available to warrant the development and implementation costs.

CONCLUSION

The options provided by e-learning to re-configure the curriculum, learning and assessment in this e-learning environment, evidence the possibilities that can be applied across all disciplines. However, in a complex organizational environment, evidenced-based principles can help improve the intellectual rigour of actions to drive cultural change in learning and teaching practice. Because e-assessment practices are structured, evidence-based and practical, these practices can being incorporated in courses to demonstrably improve outcomes and engagement, without necessarily increasing the workload of staff and students.

Bull and McKenna (2004) argued that one outcome of establishing good e-assessment practice at an institutional level is that it triggers the re-examination of assessment practice generally. Through the implementation of a new e-learning environment and the encouragement of staff to explore new options, supported by skill analysis and development for both staff and students, we hope to encourage evidence based changes in assessment practice which will drive curriculum and teaching changes.

REFERENCES

Bates, A. (2000). *Managing technological change: Strategies for college and university leaders*. San Francisco, CA: Jossey-Bass.

Boud, D. (2000). Sustainable assessment: rethinking assessment for the learning society. *Studies in Continuing Education, 22*(2), 151–167. doi:10.1080/713695728

Bull, J., & McKenna, C. (2004). *Blueprint for computer-assisted assessment*. London: Routledge Falmer. doi:10.4324/9780203464687

Conole, G., de Laat, M., Dillon, T., & Darby, J. (2006). *JISC LXP: Student experience of technologies*. Retrieved September 6, 2010, from http://jisc.ac.uk/media/documents/programmes/elearning-pedagogy/lxp_project_final_report_nov_06.pdf

Eijkman, H. (2004). The academic divide and curriculum practice in Australian Higher Education: A counternarrative. *New Horizons in Education, 111*, 14–27.

Eijkman, H. (2008). Web 2.0 as a non-foundational network-centric learning space. *Campus-Wide Information Systems, 25*(2), 93–104. doi:10.1108/10650740810866567

Eijkman, H., & Herrmann, A. (2009). Confidential report on the implementation of an adaptation of the EDUCAUSE Center for Applied Research Survey (ECAR). In *Proceedings of the UNSW@ADFA, 2008,* Canberra, University of New South Wales.

Eijkman, H., Kayali, O., & Yeomans, S. (2009). Using soft systems thinking to confront the politics of innovation in engineering education. In Patil, A., & Gray, P. (Eds.), *Engineering education quality assurance: A global perspective* (pp. 223–234). New York: Springer. doi:10.1007/978-1-4419-0555-0_18

Gibbs, G., & Simpson, C. (2004/05). Conditions under which assessment supports students' learning. *Learning and Teaching in Higher Education, 1*, 3–31.

Jordan, S., Brockbank, B., & Butcher, P. (2007). *Extending the pedagogic role of online interactive assessment: Providing feedback on short free-text responses*. Paper presented at the REAP international online conference on assessment design for learner responsibility. Retrieved September 6, 2010, from http://www.reap.ac.uk/reap07/Portals/2/CSL/feast%20of%20case%20studies/Extending_the_pedagogic_role_of_online_interactive_assessment.pdf

Kennedy, G. E., Judd, T. S., Churchward, A., Gray, K., & Krause, K. (2008). First year students' experiences with technology: Are they really digital natives? *Australasian Journal of Educational Technology, 24*(1), 108–122.

Kirkwood, A., & Price, L. (2005). Learners and learning in the twenty-first century: What do we know about students' attitudes towards and experiences of information and communication technologies that will help us design courses? *Studies in Higher Education, 30*(3), 257–274. doi:10.1080/03075070500095689

Mills, J., & Glover, C. (2006). *Who provides the feedback – Self and peer assessment*? Retrieved September 6, 2010, from http://www.open.ac.uk/fast/pdfs/Mills%20and%20Glover.pdf

Mills, J., Glover, C., & Stevens, V. (2006). Using assessment within course structures to drive student engagement with the learning process. In *Proceedings of the 2005 13th International Symposium Improving Students Learning: Improving Student Learning Through Assessment, Refocusing feedback*. Oxford, UK: Alden Press.

Nicol, D. J., & Macfarlane-Dick, D. (2006). Formative assessment and self-regulated learning: A model and seven principles of good feedback practice. *Studies in Higher Education, 31*(2), 199–216. doi:10.1080/03075070600572090

Nicol, D. J., & Milligan, C. (2006). Rethinking technology-supported assessment in terms of the seven principles of good feedback practice. In Bryan, C., & Clegg, K. (Eds.), *Innovative assessment in higher education*. London: Routledge.

Prensky, M. (2001). Digital natives, Digital immigrants. *Horizon, 9*(5), 1–6. doi:10.1108/10748120110424816

Race, P. (2007). *The lecturer's toolkit: A practical guide to assessment, learning and teaching*. Oxon, UK: Routledge.

Ridgeway, J., McCusker, S., & Pead, D. (2004). *Report 10: Literature review of e-assessment*. Bristol, UK: Futurelab Series.

Salaway, G., Caruso, J. B., & Nelson, M. R. (2007). The ECAR study of undergraduate students and information technology, 2007. *ECAR Research Study, 6*.

Salaway, G., Caruso, J. B., & Nelson, M. R. (2008). The ECAR study of undergraduate students and information technology, 2008. *ECAR Research Study, 8*.

Tenner, E. (1996). *Why things bite back: Technology and the revenge of unintended consequences*. New York: Alfred A. Knopf.

Trinder, K., Guiller, J., Margaryan, A., Littlejohn, A., & Nicol, D. (2008). *Learning from digital natives: Bridging formal and informal learning (Research Project Final Report)*. New York: The Higher Education Academy.

ENDNOTES

[1] There are two versions of this paper. One details 11 conditions, the other apparently later version, 10. This paper follows the later paper but retains condition 4 about setting high expectations which is (inexplicably) removed in the later paper.

[2] We gratefully acknowledge the openness and confidence of Dr Obada Kayali to engage in such a brave attempt at innovation with very little lead-up time.

This work was previously published in International Journal of E-Adoption, Volume 2, Issue 3, edited by Sushil K. Sharma, pp. 14-25, copyright 2010 by IGI Publishing (an imprint of IGI Global).

Chapter 17
Impact of E–Adoption on Teaching and Learning in the Context of Teaching French

Christèle Joly
Chinese International School, Hong Kong, China

Nathalie Iseli-Chan
The University of Hong Kong, China

ABSTRACT

Growing use of information technology and communication (ICT) tools in language courses with communication at their core has brought opportunities as well as challenges in the predominantly conventional face-to-face context of the classroom. When the French programme in the Department of Linguistics and Modern Languages at The Chinese University of Hong Kong started to integrate an e-learning platform into all language courses, students as well as teachers showed reservations and even disbelief. However, it was unexpected to observe such an interdependent relationship between new technologies and the conventional teaching approach. In this paper, the broad implications of the e-adoption applied to learning French as a foreign language are investigated to highlight students' learning habits and learning process. The strategies used to make technology act as a facilitator across cultures, and various ways to savoir-faire diffusion are also discussed. The study shows how new technologies modify in-class teaching, while the traditional face-to-face teaching and learning approach can influence choices in the use of different web tools that lead to blended models of education.

TEACHING AND LEARNING FRENCH IN HONG KONG: A CHALLENGING SITUATION

Hong Kong is a territory where East meets West: cultures and languages are embraced, making the former British Colony quite a unique and linguistically complex place to live. Since the handover to the People's Republic of China (PRC), students are expected to become fluent in three languages – English and two Chinese languages, Cantonese (the dominant local dialect) and Putonghua (or Mandarin, the official language of the PRC). Moreover, as part as their school and later university curriculum, students have the option of studying another foreign language.

DOI: 10.4018/978-1-4666-0041-6.ch017

In secondary school in Hong Kong, language learning is traditionally memorization-oriented and focuses on grammar and translation, rather than on communication (Rao, 2001). As a result, when joining a university, local students' learning habits are often challenged, as they have to adapt to new learning and teaching styles. In an attempt to make learning and teaching more efficient, the French programme at The Chinese University of Hong Kong (CUHK) opted for the integration of e-based material and activities into their syllabi in a blended model of learning and teaching. The specific aim of this case study is to analyze the interdependence between the face-to-face teaching and the technologies applied to university education in Hong Kong.

A detailed survey of the whole programme was conducted in January 2008 involving 229 students (Joly, 2009). Responses to questions about learning habits confirmed the conventional notion that East Asian students share common patterns of learning and perception (Worthey, 1987): preference was given to a certain learning modalities. Reading and writing were chosen over listening and speaking although the later were also desired. Emphasis was put on the grammar–translation method, rote memory and repetition – strategies which have been acknowledged as the dominating teaching/ learning style in learning English in most East Asian countries (Liu & Littlewood, 1997; Rao, 2001), along with a detail- and precision-oriented approach that involves dissecting and analyzing the learning material (Oxford & Burry-Stock, 1995). The tendency to learn through reading explains students' request to have visual material (Reid, 1987), as well as their general shyness and low oral participation in the classroom – fewer speaking turns showed by Sato (1981) and lack of taking risk in conversation analyzed by Oxford, Hollaway, and Murillo (1992).

In this regard the French programme's teaching style did not match with CUHK students' predominant learning habits. The programme uses textbooks that are based on the communicative approach and its socio-constructivist framework (Vygotsky, 1934). This teaching methodology relies on the Common European Reference of Framework for languages (CERF), which is action-oriented and task-based (European Council, 2000). It is founded on the belief that learning should no longer be understood as a process of reproduction; it is rather a construction process in which learners build up their knowledge while conducting tasks (Piaget, 1969).

In recent years, the universities in Hong Kong have been focusing on an outcomes-based approach (Carless, Joughin, Liu, & Associates, 2006) and assessing programmes by analyzing their outcomes. This makes sense with the political and ideological leadership of Hong Kong, which bases success on society's efficiency and productivity. In this regard the French programme with its competence-based approach (Gérard, 2003) is certainly consistent with CUHK's policy.

IMPLEMENTATION OF THE FRENCH PLATFORM FRE0000

When implementing the e-learning platform FRE0000, the French programme aimed to support existing face-to-face teaching practice. Support was provided in terms of:

- Reinforcement of language and culture learning;
- Reduction of in-class workload; and
- Extension of face-to-face teaching and learning.

The layout of the platform was organized accordingly, with distinct sections for communication, learning support and course-related activities and projects. The freeware software package Moodle was preferred over WebCT (both platforms are supported at CUHK) or conventional websites as it was seen to offer a wide range of tools, was user-friendly, provided a restricted area with controlled access and provided log reports and statistics that were seen as desirable for monitoring usage and utility.

By integrating the e-learning platform Moodle, where pedagogical reference relies on the socio-constructivist theory, the programme reinforced the belief that students are at the centre of the teaching/ learning process and should be involved in the construction of their knowledge and their savoir-faire (translated literally as knowledge and action – knowing how to do). The web tools have thus been chosen with the aim at helping students develop their language competences, interpersonal skills, sense of autonomy and ability for self-assessment. Tasks were designed with precise objectives related to a real-world context and became "meaning-focused work" by involving students in understanding, producing and interacting in the target language (Nunan, cited by Mangenot & Louveau, 2006, p. 38). Hence, practitioners hoped that ICT could provide tools that will assist in the development of the communicative language competences in linguistics, socio-linguistics and pragmatics referred by the CERF (European Council, 2000, p. 122) as 'savoir-faire'.

When applying ICT to teaching and designing online activities, choices must be made. It consequently leads to reflection about pedagogical beliefs and the applicability of technology for designing online activities for language learning. The success of online activities partially lies in teachers' pedagogical beliefs that affect the uses of technology within institutional contexts (Warschauer, 2000). Such an approach is important to avoid "technology-centered approaches" (Belisle, 1998), keeping in mind that "the integration of ICT means that the web tools efficiently serve learning, which requires examination of the pedagogical and institutional conditions in order to make technology beneficial" (Mangenot, 2000, translated from French).

Communicative Approach

The e-learning platform was implemented with the idea of strengthening the four communicative skills through writing (blog entries and forums), reading (posts of fellow students and interactive exercises), listening (dictation exercises, video and audio clips, music players) and speaking (podcasts). The variety of tools is a response to the need for developing different skills in an environment that is as real as possible. The internet provides hyper-textuality which makes the use of authentic documents possible and easy. Language is thus used in a meaningful and authentic way (Savignon, 1983). These tools also boost students' confidence in using French as a lingua franca and learning more about cultures (Seo, Miller, Schmidt, & Sowa, 2008).

Collaborative Approach

Learning as a social construction process can only happen while being a member of a society in which interactions take place. Interactive tools that allow asynchronous and synchronous communication (discussion forums, instant messaging – IM), and collective cooperation (wiki) were selected and used within group-focused discussion projects that demand collaboration between peers. The use of tools like blogs, which are not considered interactive tools because of the lack of interaction (the comments function is not possible in the Moodle platform), shows that the face-to-face teaching/ learning has a great influence on the designing of online activities. The concept of tandems ("binômes") already applied in class for oral activities were extended to blogs. In the same way, the belief in active learning through engagement in discussions (Hativa, 2000; Hara, Bonk, & Angeli, 1998) led the practitioners to choose the online discussion forums to extend in-class debates.

Intercultural Awareness

The design of online cross-cultural projects was conditioned by the pedagogical belief that cultural competence goes along with communicative language competences in a task-based approach. The French instructors at CUHK believe in the interaction between both cultures – French as the target culture and Hong Kong identity as the students' native culture. We concede there is room for intercultural awareness, defined as the interaction between two identities instead of an ethnology-focused approach of the target culture (Abdallah-Pretceille, 1999). Language acquisition alike, intercultural awareness becomes a construction in which students go from the known (their own culture) to the unknown (the target culture) while making some adjustments of their own personalities in order to accommodate the new culture. The concept of a 'third place' (Kramsh, 1993) led us to create web-based situations where French and Chinese cultures would meet. Within the culture course, blogs were thus used as a tool for recording observations and thoughts while discussion forums, arranged through culture teaching, allowing the sharing of emotions, arguments and opinions which should be arranged in culture teaching (Crawford-Lange & Lange, 1984). Online collaborative learning facilitated reflections on cultural issues and contributed to positive learning outcomes and mutual benefits (Kimber, 1994). It also prepared students for the face-to-face discussions conducted in class with people from the target culture people, making the contact more personal and the ethnographic approach more efficient (Robinson-Stuart & Nocon, 1996).

Student Oriented Approach and Teacher's Monitoring

The student-oriented approach used in class was reflected in the e-learning platform through the designing of a reserved area for students' community building (Dillenbourg, Poirier, & Carles, 2003). The discretion of teachers in specific discussions aimed at making students interact and assist each other. As well, teacher mediation (Larose & Peraya, 2001) with constant technical, methodological and pedagogical support aimed to enable a higher degree of autonomy in students (Van Lier, 1996). Nonetheless, it has been observed that teachers with more traditional teaching habits struggle with some tools such as the use of blogs as a writing practice with communicative purposes that requires collective feedback instead of individual correction about the language accuracy. The technology in effect required and even led teachers to modify their teaching habits.

EVALUATION METHOD

In this case study, learning benefits were assessed online and face-to-face. The following evaluation strategies were used: surveys using a five-point Likert scale; focus-group meetings; statistics provided by Moodle; and feedback from students' term-end evaluations. Whilst conducting the research the practitioners had in mind the following two research objectives (ROs). First, to what extent will e-adoption affect face-to-face teaching/ learning? What will be its implications? Second, what, if any, might be any direct and tangible impacts on learning outcomes and student benefits? This case study highlighted the gap between the conventional teaching/ learning habits in Hong Kong and the CUHK French programme's teaching style, while showing the inter-relationship between the teaching/ learning habits and the use of ICT applied to the acquisition of French language and culture. Study findings are discussed in order of these two identified questions.

Towards a Blended Model of Education

RO 1: Looking first at the extent that e-adoption would affect the face-to-face teaching/ learning and what are any related implications, the study findings are outlined below.

Online Activities Extended in Classroom

Since January 2008, a series of online projects and activities have taken place in different courses including: intercultural awareness in the culture course (Joly, Iseli, & Lam, 2009); cross-cultural exchange with Austrian students (Iseli, Joly, & Lam, 2009) and Chinese students' self-reflection on French learning in advanced courses. These online activities extended the time spent in the classroom and allowed the group of learners to experience something that would have been impossible within the face-to-face class because of the lack of interest for the topic or the lack of preparation for it, and also because of the reluctance to take risks in conversation (see Oxford, Hollaway, & Murillo, 1992). Questions that students would not have asked in public for fear of losing face or embarrassing the teacher (Rao, 2001) could be raised on the e-learning platform and answered online or in class as shown in this student's message posted in French in one of the forums:

Thanks for answering my question in class this morning. I didn't dare to ask in class last time as I thought it wouldn't be relevant and my classmates already knew the answer. It was a good discussion today and I am happy that I wasn't the only one having this problem!

Online debates created more learning opportunities, as students could not have communicated face-to-face with all fellow students in class. Moreover, the online activities provided teachers with valuable personal data about their students, including essential details about learning habits (Holec, 1990).

Individual Needs and Constant Feedback on Students' Progress

Forums with specific purposes were designed for students to ask their questions accordingly. Blog entries are by nature quite intimate because author-oriented (Soubrié, 2006) and students feel free to provide teachers and fellow students with personal information regarding their own personality, their family, their studies and their difficulties in different areas. Their linguistic content is fruitful for feedback on students' progress in learning French, their grasp on the course content, as well as their way of thinking. Thus, teachers had the chance to take into account individual needs when devising their course.

An illustrative comment, as shared in a student's blog, is precious for teachers (translated into English):

I spend quite a lot of time on learning French but not regularly. I often wait till the last moment. I know I should be studying a bit almost every day but I don't know how to organize the notes and prioritize the tasks. The conjugation is the worst; I really don't know how to group the verbs!

Availability, Flexibility and Transparency

We found that the interest of both teachers and students grew through the virtual dimension of the e-learning platform. The platform makes everything (resources) and everyone (learners and tutors) close and available. Time, duration and place are also no longer obstacles, while students' learning pace is respected (Poncet & Régnier, 2003). As Moodle administration reports showed, CUHK students are used to studying at night and are often not aware of teachers' office hours. Hence, the office hours are often perceived as a hindrance to communication. Therefore, the e-learning platform facilitated a drastic change.

Teachers log in every day and when they are not teaching they can be found on the platform. Even part-time teachers whose email addresses were not released in course outlines and who were relatively difficult for students to contact, check the platform almost on a daily basis. These part-time teachers can effectively work from anywhere and get in touch with their group of students or individual members of the class directly, without involving full-time colleagues.

Researchers also observed that students are using the platform not only as a learning tool, but also as a communication tool, just like they would do with MSN or Facebook. The platform also added a sense of transparency and consistency as information was able to be transmitted at the same time to all students at the same course level regardless of who their teacher was, and this information remained available in the forums.

Nature of Exchanges

The flexibility and availability of people through the e-learning platform have a great impact on the nature of exchanges between teachers and students. Beyond personal details available in blogs, profiles and forums, messages sent individually via the IM tool consolidated previously casual student–teacher relationships. Although students and teachers address each other using the formal denominator (second person French pronoun) VOUS, instead of TU in French – with use being explained and practiced in class (Iseli, Joly, & Lam, 2009) – less formal smileys and pictures are common in messages. As a student explained in an instantaneous message:

That's so funny to use smileys and "frenglish" with you ... I couldn't imagine having such a casual conversation with a teacher!! Usually, teachers don't chat online with students ... It is great because I LOVE smileys!!

Informal language with shortcuts and familiar expressions as well as the use of "Frenglish" imply different attitudes and differences in syntax and discourse (Sotillo, 2000). The medium definitely shapes the linguistic content (Thorne, 2003).

Community Building

The researchers observe that blogs and forums greatly extended the learning attitudes of students. The forum postings of projects showed that students broadened their horizons by getting involved in others' contributions and by trying to give advice. As an example, the following post by a student in a forum:

Well, that's not my field and maybe I shouldn't send you a message but I read the messages of you guys and I found your topic very interesting. I searched on the web and lucky me, I discovered a great website about this issue!!! I'd like to share it with you!

Through mutual assistance (Develotte & Mangenot, 2004), students created a real community where all members are acknowledged for their own personalities. Practitioners encouraged this community building by sharing students' talents such as musical gifts: files were uploaded on the main page for students to enjoy pieces of work from their fellow students' pieces of work.

Online forum discussions that are part of projects are the starting points for the construction of a social community in a blended learning environment (Kim, 2000). The transition operated as a "threshold" for students' communication (Wegerif, 1998), showing the beginning of a growing interest in their fellow students. Beyond the learning purpose, students encouraged each other and provided support. This support is visible in the classroom and in extra-curricular activities (Joly, Iseli, & Lam, 2009).

Administrator reports showed that most of the students regularly check the e-learning platform and increase the pace when they are involved in a discussion, whether it was within a project or in another forum. The majority of students who were in advanced level courses became online active learners: they read other students' posts, replied to other's statements and sent thoughts that went beneath the surface of the discussion (Hamann, Pollock III, & Wilson, 2005). This active attitude was also reflected in the class where students often changed seats (Iseli, Joly, & Lam, 2009). Therefore, it does not seem to be exaggerating to say that, in this case study, virtual participation and learning boosted students' real-life engagement. In effect, rather than preventing students from facing reality and communicating with the outside world, ICT got people together and also assisted in improving their face-to-face relationships.

Autonomy Through the Collective

Through the presence of the community, students no longer feel lonely and isolated. They are from now on part of the class community, both online (Kim, 2000) and in the classroom. The face-to-face teaching certainly benefits from this community building, which enhances communication within the class and creates a nice learning atmosphere. Teacher and students can refer to remarks made online outside the classroom and the teaching content was adjusted accordingly. Students are more organized in terms of assignments and deadlines. To a certain extent, they are more autonomous despite the strict framework given to the designed online activities, which might otherwise give the feeling of limiting students' freedom and autonomy. However, it is exactly this strict guidance as well as their involvement in the process (Soubrié, 2005) that assisted students to become more responsible and more autonomous (Portine, 1998).

Mutualization of coursework also contributed to the stimulation of students in performing better (Develotte & Mangenot, 2004). It aroused their motivation and made them more responsible for their own learning. A student comment highlights this outcome:

I wrote in my blog and published the entry, [but] when I looked at my peer's blog entries and I was so ashamed of mine that I decided to change it!!! Actually, it happened a few times. It made me spend more time on my French learning (more than what I wanted first!!) but I don't regret because my efforts paid and eventually it forced me to do better and ... not to miss the deadline too!!

Changes in Learning Habits and CUHK Students' Behavior

ICT certainly modified CUHK students' learning habits and behaviour. The relationships between the e-learning platform and the changes in in-class learning are shown in Table 1.

Changes in Teaching Habits and Teachers' Behaviors

Table 2 summarizes the changes noted in teachers' teaching habits and behaviour.

RO 2: Turning next to the second research objective, about whether there was evidence of a direct and tangible impact on learning outcomes and benefits, study findings are discussed below.

So far, there is no definitive evidence showing the efficiency of the course material on students' learning process. A study about the impact of the dictation exercises on the academic results (Lam, Joly, & Iseli, 2009) tried to examine the relationship between the availability of these resources and students' marks on dictation tests. However, the difference in the marks before and after the use of Moodle does not indicate that the online resource was the determining factor. However,

Table 1. Relationships between the e-learning platform and the changes in in-class learning

Areas of change	Tools/ sections	Results for students	Challenges
Open assignments or discussions	blogs, forums, gong	- More reading practice - More exposure to others - Sense of belonging to a community	- Intimidating vs. protected/ safe (online) - Lack of confidentiality
Conducting individual interactions with teachers/fellow students	chat, messages	- More feedback = more efficient learning - Closer relationships with teachers - Closer relationships with fellow students	- Time-consuming
Providing more personal information	blogs, forums, users' profile	- Closer relationships with teachers - Closer relationships with fellow students	- Require a sense of autonomy and initiatives
Providing inexplicit feedback	users' reports	- Enjoying individual guidance - Increasing sense of responsibility and commitment	- Sense of being controlled
Providing and having portraits and names	users' profiles	- Closer relationships with teachers - Closer relationships with fellow students	- Reluctance to associate online 'life' with real pictures
Frequency (duration and timing) and number of interactions with teachers/fellow students	all	- More efficient learning - Closer relationships with teachers/fellow students - Enjoying answers to questions asked by other students	- Need for constant checks by the teacher on the platform
Experiencing more interactions with fellow students	forum discussions	- Increasing chances for practicing - Increasing sense of autonomy	- Mostly written feedback (lack for oral)
Solving technical and methodological obstacles	all	- Transversal expertise (IT knowledge) - Need to define questions and/or area of the problem before seeking for help and information	- Additional skills required for both students and teachers
Writing assignments without being individually assessed	blog (without comments' function)	- Getting collective comments in class and self-amending assignments (blog entries) - Adapting to new type of exercise (no individual feedback but productions checked by teachers) and of assessment methods	- Require flexibility and an open mind, as well as student autonomy
Being in touch with fellow students from all FRE courses	all	- Increasing attractiveness of learning - Sensing the community's spirit	
Interacting with guest speakers (crosscultural projects)	forums	- Enlarging horizons with exposure to different cultures, mindsets and language levels	- Logistical obstacles and time consuming
Accessing to materials from all levels	course materials section	- More efficient learning = adapting to personal needs and expectations	- Require sense of autonomy and responsibility
Enjoying teaching materials for self-learning/ assessment	audio clips video clips model answers	- Increasing sense of autonomy - More time for interactions and oral activities in classroom	- Require sense of autonomy and responsibility

improvement in the final written exams, as well as enhancement in proficiency in composition and oral exams have led the researchers to think that there is an inter-relationship between the use of online resources and students' learning processes. It is still an open question as to whether this change in students' performance has its roots in the availability of online resources and the design of online activities.

DISCUSSION AND REMARKS

Achievement of the Expected Outcomes

When implementing the e-learning platform and integrating the ICT tools into the syllabi, the practitioners of the French programme had three outcomes in mind, all of which have been fulfilled, based on the observations that:

Table 2. Changes noted in teachers' teaching habits and behaviour

Areas of change	Tools/ sections	Results for teachers	Challenges
Conducting individual interactions with students	chat, messages	- More feedback = more efficient teaching - Closer relationships with students	- Time-consuming
Getting more personal information about students	blogs, forums, users' profile	- Closer relationships with students	- Lots of reading
Getting general feedback	users' reports	- Providing individual guidance	- Time-consuming
Having students' pictures and names	users' profiles	- Closer relationships with students	- Time for reminding students to upload personal pictures
Frequency (of any duration and timing) and number of interactions with students	all	- More efficient teaching - Closer relationships with students - Saving time (no repetitive questions)	- Time-consuming
Experiencing more interactions between students	forum discussions	- Enhancing students' productions - Increasing students' sense of autonomy	- Time-consuming for reading, improving and commenting productions
Providing technical and methodological support	all	- Transversal (IT knowledge) - Emphasis on methodology (help students to first define questions and/or problem area before seeking for help and information)	- Require training and specific skills - Additional work
Requesting writing practice without individual assessment/ feedback	blog (without comments' function)	- Collective comments in class - Change of type of exercise (no individual feedback but production checked by teachers) and of assessment methods	- Change in teaching habits
Providing materials for different levels	course materials section	- More efficient teaching = adapting to students' needs and expectations	
Providing teaching materials for self-learning/ assessment	audio clips video clips model answers	- More time for interactions and oral activities in classroom	- Time-consuming to develop online interactive activities

- Students had a higher proficiency as shown in online forums and by overall better academic results, and had their intercultural competence developed and reinforced.
- Students developed a sense of autonomy in their learning through teachers' monitoring and fellow students' assistance.
- A genuine friendly community was built online and extended to the classroom.

Beyond the Expected Outcomes: Challenges

The practitioners expected that Hong Kong students, even though they were born in the era of the internet and instant communication technologies, would show some reservations towards the adoption of e-based activities. However, these new activities, such as blogs and forum-based discussions, were surprisingly welcomed and accepted. Students' interest and involvement increased as the variety of activities became wider, and even went beyond pedagogical goals (Furstenberg, Levet, English, & Maillet, 2001; Kinginger, Gouvès-Hayward, & Simpson, 1999), evidenced by the following observations:

- A lack of a specific purpose in logging in as students often clicked randomly on various applications;
- A very high participation and personal engagement in forum-based discussion projects;
- A closer relationship with teachers as well as with fellow students; and
- An increasing number of requests to the alumni account from students who com-

pleted all French courses and wish to keep their access to Moodle.

Unexpected outcomes also occurred on the part of the teachers:

- The difference between full-time and part-time teachers softened: this became evident in terms of greater transparency, consistency and sharing between teachers.
- Systematic pedagogical guidelines were adopted.
- There was better understanding and acceptance of students' learning patterns.

ICT's overall positive impact was surprising and partially unexpected. FRE0000 was implemented with the aim of supporting the French programme's teaching approach. Although CUHK student's habits were taken into account when choices about web tools were made, flexibility that made a task-based teaching approach possible without denying a teacher-centred learning approach was an expected outcome.

Researchers were initially concerned over the likely acceptance of ICT by CUHK students, as a mismatch between learning and teaching habits would result in inefficiency in learning French (Rao, 2001) and consequent poor course evaluations for teachers. The University values its course-evaluation system, which is believed to reflect the quality, the accuracy and the suitability of the teaching approach. However, they did not imagine that ICT, which adopts a socio-constructivist approach, could bridge the gap between the outcomes-based teaching approach and the more conventional teacher-centred learning habit by relying on CUHK students' familiarity with computer-mediated communication, with a preference for asynchronous discussion over instant-messaging tools. The e-adoption not only brought an additional dimension to the learning and teaching approach and, as it overlapped with

the French programme's teaching approach and the CUHK students' learning habits, it reconciled both kinds of patterns and made teaching more accepted and efficient.

Nonetheless, obstacles related to time and workload, that are specific to e-adoption still remain. These obstacles do not question whether the e-adoption is meaningful and worthwhile for the French programme since evidence of better efficiency and improved outcomes proved the relevance of such an adoption. However, their existence leads us to reflect on the structure that an application of ICT to education should have and where the limits of its use reside.

CONCLUSION

The integration of ICT into a university course implies drastic changes in the way students build up knowledge, their idea of learning and also the teaching arrangement and the teacher's role (Albero, 2000) extending to other areas that in-class teaching alone does not require (Denis, 2003). However, ICT's impact also depends on the usage of the teaching staff and not just the nature of the web tools themselves. ICT provides education with a lot of possibilities that can only benefit students and teachers if they are carefully thought-out in order to be aligned with the face-to-face in-class teaching. Thus, it is essential to define the in-class teaching/ learning before determining which web tools can be appropriately used. These web tools will in turn modify the traditional face-to-face by extending its limits. This interdependence is inspiring and makes us reflect on the emergence of blended models of education. It reminds us that nowadays ICT cannot be avoided and that the education system should focus on reforming pedagogical approaches rather than integrating ITC (Bibeau, 1998).

REFERENCES

Abdallah-Pretceille, M. (1999). *L'éducation interculturelle*. Paris: Que sais-je? Presses Universitaires de France.

Albero, B. (2000). *L'autoformation en contexte institutionnel: Du paradigme de l'instruction au paradigme de l'autonomie*. Paris: L'Harmattan.

Belisle, C. (1998). Enjeux et limites du multimédia en formation et en éducation. In *Proceedings of the Les Cahiers de l'ASDIFLE* (No. 9, pp. 7-24). Paris: Association de didactique du français langue étrangère.

Bibeau, R. (1998). *L'élève rapaillé – Le Cercle de Recherche et d'Action Pédagogiques et kes Cahie*. Retrieved September 3, 2010, from http://www.cahiers-pedagogiques.com/article.php3?id_article=2603

Carless, D., Joughin, G., & Liu, N. F. (2006). *How assessment supports learning: Learning-oriented assessment in action*. Hong Kong: Hong Kong University Press.

Crawford-Lange, L., & Lange, D. (1984). Doing the unthinkable in the second-language classroom: A process for the integration of language and culture. In Higgs, T. (Ed.), *Teaching for proficiency, the organizing principle* (pp. 139–177). Lincolnwood, IL: National Textbook Company.

Denis, B. (2003). Quels rôles et quelle formation pour les tuteurs intervenant: dans des dispositifs de formation a distance? *Distances et Savoirs*, *1*(1), 19–46. doi:10.3166/ds.1.19-46

Develotte, C., & Mangenot, F. (2004). Tutorat et communauté dans un campus numérique non collaboratif. *Distances et Savoirs*, *2*(2-3), 1–25. doi:10.3166/ds.2.309-333

Dillenbourg, P., Poirier, C., & Carles, L. (2003). Communautés virtuelles d'apprentissage: E-jargon ou nouveau paradigme? In Senteni, A., & Taurisson, A. (Eds.), *Pédagogies.net: L'essor des communautés virtuelles d'apprentissage* (pp. 11–47). Montréal, Canada: Presses de l'Université du Québec.

European Council. (2000). *Common European Framework of Reference for Languages: Learning, teaching, assessment*. Cambridge, UK: Cambridge University Press.

Furstenberg, G., Levet, S., English, K., & Maillet, K. (2001). Giving a virtual voice to the silent language of culture: The cultura project. *Language Learning & Technology*, *5*(1), 55–102.

Gérard, F. M. (2003). Les manuels scolaires d'aujourd'hui, de l'enseignement à l'apprentissage. *Option*, *4*, 27-28. Retrieved September 3, 2010, from http://www.fmgerard.be/textes/option.html

Hamann, K., Pollock, P. H., III, & Wilson, B. M. (2005). *Active learning through reading and writing in online discussion boards: Assessing the effects on learner outcomes*. Paper presented at the annual meeting of The Midwest Political Science Association, Palmer House Hilton, Chicago, IL.

Hara, N., Bonk, C. J., & Angeli, C. (1998). *Content analysis of online discussion in an applied educational psychology course* (CRLT Tech. Rep., pp. 2-98). Bloomington, IN: Indiana University, Center for Research on Learning and Technology.

Hativa, N. (2000). *Teaching for effective learning in higher education*. Dordrecht, The Netherlands: Kluwer.

Holec, H. (1990). Qu'est-ce qu'apprendre à apprendre? *Mélanges pédagogiques*, 82-83.

Iseli, N., Joly, C., & Lam, P. (2009). Use of language beyond the classroom: The outcomes, challenges and success of an e-based cross-cultural project in French class. In F. Salajan (Ed.), *Proceedings of the 4th International Conference on e-Learning* (pp. 214-221). Reading, MA: Academic Publishing Limited.

Joly, C. (2009). *Réforme du système éducatif de 2012 à Hong Kong: Enjeux, Evaluation et Propositions de transformation pour le Programme de Français du Département de Linguistique et des Langues Vivantes de l'Université Chinoise de Hong Kong*. Unpublished master's thesis, Université Stendhal 3, Grenoble, France.

Joly, C., Iseli, I., & Lam, P. (2009). Developing intercultural awareness of Chinese students in online asynchronous discussions and blogs within a French culture course. In F. Salajan (Ed.), *Proceedings of the 4th International Conference on e-Learning* (pp. 228-235). Reading, MA: Academic Publishing Limited.

Kim, A. J. (2000). *Community building on the web*. Berkeley, CA: Peachpit Press.

Kimber, D. (1994). *Collaborative learning in management education: Issues, benefits, problems and solutions: A literature review*. Paper presented in Australian and New Zealand Academy of Management (ANZAM) conference, New Zealand.

Kinginger, C., Gouvès-Hayward, A., & Simpson, V. (1999). A tele-collaborative course on French-American intercultural communication. *French Review*, *72*(5), 853–866.

Kramsh, C. (1993). *Context and culture in language teaching*. New York: Oxford University Press.

Lam, S. L., Lam, P., Joly, C., & Iseli, N. (2009, July). *Study of the effect of providing online dictation exercise on students' dictation mark*. Paper presented at the 2009 International Conference on ICT in Teaching and Learning, Hong Kong.

Larose, F., & Peraya, D. (2001). Fondements épistémologiques et spécificité pédagogique du recours aux environnements virtuels en enseignement: Médiation ou médiatisation? In *Les TIC ... au coeur des pédagogies universitaires* (pp. . 31–68). Québec, Canada: Presses de l'Université du Québec.

Liu, N. F., & Littlewood, W. (1997). Why do many students appear reluctant to participate in classroom learning discourse? *System*, *25*(3), 371–384. doi:10.1016/S0346-251X(97)00029-8

Mangenot, F. (2000). *L'intégration des TICE dans une perspective systémique, Les Langues Modernes. Les nouveaux dispositifs d'apprentissage*. Paris: Association des Professeurs de Langues Vivantes.

Mangenot, F., & Louveau, E. (2006). *Internet et la classe de langue. Techniques et Pratiques de classe*. Paris: CLE international.

Oxford, R. L., & Burry-Stock, J. A. (1995). Assessing the use of language learning strategies worldwide with ESL/EFL version of the Strategy Inventory for Language Learning (SILL). *System*, *23*(2), 153–175.

Oxford, R. L., Hollaway, M. E., & Murillo, D. (1992). Language learning styles: Research and practical considerations for teaching in the multicultural tertiary ESL/EFL classroom. *System*, *20*(4), 439–445. doi:10.1016/0346-251X(92)90057-A

Piaget, J. (1969). *Psychologie et pédagogie*. Paris: Denoël.

Poncet, P., & Régnier, C. (2003). Les TIC: éléments sur leurs usages et sur leurs effets. *Les notes Évaluation*. Retrieved September 3, 2010, from http://trf.education.gouv.fr/pub/edutel/dpd/noteeval/ne0301.pdf

Portine, H. (1998). L'autonomie de l'apprenant en question. *ALSIC*, *1*(1), 73–77.

Rao, Z. H. (2001). Matching teaching styles with learning styles in East Asian contexts. *Internet TESL Journal, 7*(7), Retrieved September 3, 2010, from http://iteslj.org/Techniques/Zhenhui-TeachingStyles.html

Reid, J. (1987). The learning style preferences of ESL students. *TESOL Quarterly, 21*(1), 87–111. doi:10.2307/3586356

Robinson-Stuart, G., & Nocon, H. (1996). Second culture acquisition: Ethnography in the foreign language classroom. *Modern Language Journal, 80*(4), 431–449. doi:10.2307/329724

Sato, C. (1981). Ethnic styles in classroom discourse. In Hines, M., & Rutherford, W. (Eds.), *On TESOL '81* (pp. 11–24). Washington, DC: Teachers of English to Speakers of Other Languages.

Savignon, S. J. (1983). *Communicative competence: Theory and classroom practice*. Reading, MA: Addison-Wesley.

Seo, K. K., Miller, P. C., Schmidt, C., & Sowa, P. (2008). Creating synergy between collectivism and individualism in cyberspace: A Comparison of online communication patterns between Hong Kong and U.S. Students. *Journal of Intercultural Communication, 18*. Retrieved September 3, 2010, from http://www.immi.se/intercultural/

Sotillo, S. M. (2000). Discourse Functions and syntactic complexity in synchronous and asynchronous communication. *Language Learning & Technology, 4*(1), 82–119.

Soubrié, T. (2005). Le présentiel allégé à l'université pour les grands groupes: un dispositif au service de l'autonomisation des apprenants. *Actes du colloque SIF*. Paris: Les institutions éducatives face au numérique. Retrieved September 3, 2010, from http://sif2005.mshparisnord.org/pdf/Soubrier.pdf

Soubrié, T. (2006). *Le Blog: retour en force de la «fonction auteur»*. Paper presented at the Colloque JOCAIR'06, Amiens. Retrieved September 3, 2010, from http://hal.archives-ouvertes.fr/docs/00/13/84/62/PDF/16-_Soubrie.pdf

Thorne, S. L. (2003). Artifacts and cultures-of-use in intercultural communication. *Language Learning & Technology, 7*(2), 38–67.

Van Lier, L. (1996). *Interaction in the language curriculum: Awareness, autonomy, & authenticity*. New York: Longman.

Vygotski, L. S. (1934). *Pensée et langage*. Paris: Éditions Sociales.

Warschauer, M. (2000). Online learning in second language classrooms: An ethnographic study. In Warschauer, M., & Kern, R. (Eds.), *Network-based language teaching: Concepts and practice* (pp. 41–58). New York: Cambridge University Press.

Wegerif, R. (1998). The social dimension of asynchronous learning networks. *Journal of Asynchronous Learning Networks, 2*(1), 34–49.

Worthey, K. M. (1987). *Learning style factors of field dependence/independence and problem-solving strategies of Hmong refugee students*. Unpublished master's thesis, University of Wisconsin, Stout, WI.

This work was previously published in International Journal of E-Adoption, Volume 2, Issue 3, edited by Sushil K. Sharma, pp. 26-38, copyright 2010 by IGI Publishing (an imprint of IGI Global).

Chapter 18
Examining Diffusion and Sustainability of E–Learning Strategies through Weblog Data

Paul Lam
The Chinese University of Hong Kong, China

Judy Lo
The Chinese University of Hong Kong, China

Antony Yeung
The Chinese University of Hong Kong, China

Carmel McNaught
The Chinese University of Hong Kong, China

ABSTRACT

The study focuses on 'horizontal' and 'vertical' adoption of e-learning strategies at The Chinese University of Hong Kong as revealed through computer log records in the centrally supported learning management systems. Horizontal diffusion refers to whether e-learning has spread to influence the practice of more teachers and students. In vertical diffusion, the authors examined whether or not teachers tend to adopt more varied online learning activities in successive years. The overall findings are that, while adoption of simple strategies is increasing, there is little evidence of horizontal and vertical diffusion of more complex strategies. Indeed, the use of some of the more complex strategies, which may relate to greater potential learning benefits, decreased. Results have led to discussions about new focuses and strategies for our institutional eLearning Service.

CONCEPTUAL CHANGE

Adoption of innovations is challenging. Many individual and social factors relate to the acceptance of the use of technology in teaching and learning, including whether teachers have enough motivation and support for the conceptual change involved in new ways of working. The process of conceptual change was studied by Lewin (1952) who looked at how social changes were made possible through group decision-making. Lewin's work was adapted to education by a number of researchers in science education in the 1980s (e.g., Nussbaum & Novick, 1982; Strike & Posner, 1985;

DOI: 10.4018/978-1-4666-0041-6.ch018

West, 1988). In the conceptual change process three stages are involved:

- "A process for diagnosing existing conceptual frameworks and revealing them to those involved;
- A period of disequilibrium and conceptual conflict which makes the subject dissatisfied with existing conceptions; and
- A reforming or reconstruction phase in which a new conceptual framework is formed" (Kember et al., 2006, p. 83).

One way of capturing this challenge is with the J-curve model (Figure 1). The J-curve is a mathematical and economic theorem developed in the early 1900s and has been widely used to study productivity, business value and/or returns on investment arising from changes within organizations over time. It has been widely applied to many contexts – both individual companies and entire nations (Bremmer, 2006). Put simply, things often get worse before they get better because of the expenses and challenges that occur early on in the innovation cycle.

Figure 1. The J-curve challenge (after Cheng, Lam, & McNaught, 2006)

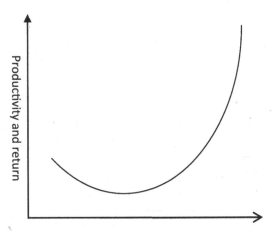

ADOPTION OF E-LEARNING INNOVATIONS

Two possible ways of examining the adoption of e-learning innovations are presented here. First, we may consider a 'horizontal' spread so that more teachers begin to use appropriate e-learning strategies; this is the concept of *diffusion* of innovation. Second, the continuous use of a strategy by the same teachers year after year so that it 'vertically' benefits multiple cohorts of students is the concept of *sustainability*. Adoption of innovations can be studied in either or both of these dimensions.

Horizontal Diffusion

Diffusion is an important process if e-learning strategies are to gain popularity among university teachers and students, and thus have significant impact on the overall institutional learning environment. Thomas, Lam, and Ho (2009) interviewed eight teachers in a Hong Kong university and found that individual teachers who used innovative e-learning strategies did not effectively disseminate their practice. The primary obstacle to uptake of e-learning was the apparent reluctance by other teaching staff to commit any effort because of the perceived time involved. Another social barrier related to senior professors tending to be somewhat removed from the innovative work of more junior teaching staff. We therefore do not expect individual teacher cases to lead to significant conceptual change across an entire institution.

Even if the 'early adopters' (Rogers, 2003) are willing to disseminate their new ideas and methods, there is still the question of whether other teachers will readily accept them. Fitzgibbon and Jones (2004) reflected on their experiences in organizing e-moderating courses for the teaching staff in a UK University and noted that teachers generally did not have the time for the training, many of them lacked the confidence and competence in IT skills, and they were also uncomfortable that they had to adopt new teaching skills for the activities that were conducted online. Scott and Quick (2005) worked with quite robust webcasting platforms and yet failed to get appreciable take-up in two business projects. Once the technical team was gone, no-one had confidence to use webcasting.

Both Friesen (2003) and Parrish (2004) critically examined the phenomena of learning objects. They questioned the feasibility of the idea that teachers will reuse online materials developed by others, often because there is no teaching culture which supports sharing teaching materials. There are also various technical and design problems in most repositories so that, in general, teachers find it difficult to find materials that match their teaching and learning objectives and styles.

Part of the challenge of reuse is that evaluation of e-learning initiatives and resources is often very limited. E-learning developments are often behind schedule and evaluation is often the part that gets sacrificed. Jones and McNaught (2005) reported on a project that supported 36 developments and, at the end, less than half (17) had the evaluation component successfully carried out as planned. Lam and McNaught (2005) explained that e-learning evaluations need to be tailored; therefore, the aggregation of findings at the level of individual courses to make some meaningful input to institutional decision-making is really quite challenging (Ellis et al., 2007).

Sustainability

Costs and challenges met in using an e-learning strategy for the first time can be compensated when it is used repeatedly because 1) developed resources can be reused (and hence the cost per use reduced); and 2) the technical and administrative procedures run more smoothly (Keing, Lo, Lam, & McNaught, 2007). Many of the challenges of e-learning strategies are threshold obstacles and are significant only in the first, or first few, attempts when a great deal of background work is needed and teachers and students are still in a transitional period. Workload and discomfort in changing habits are the initial overheads of the new technology. The situation is depicted in Figure 2 as a model of diminishing effort.

Apart from reusing developed resources, sustainability is also concerned with the reuse of new teaching and learning designs and new strategies. Teaching practice is difficult to change. Often there is no widespread change in pedagogic practice to take advantage of the functionality afforded by learning management systems (LMSs) and other e-learning tools (Becker & Jokivirta, 2007; Collis & van der Wende, 2002). Thus, even if teachers attempt technology-enabled teaching and learning strategies in one year, they may not be successful through not understanding how best to make use of the functionality available to them.

Figure 2. Model of diminishing effort for e-learning

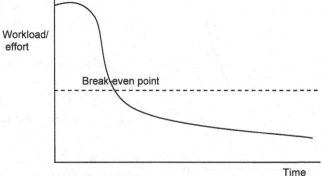

If they achieve little or limited success, there is no certainty that they will maintain the new design; they may shift back to their old practices and design in the following year.

FACTORS IMPINGING ON DIFFUSION AND SUSTAINABILITY

Many factors tend to determine diffusion and sustainability of an e-learning strategy. The innovation itself, first of all, has to have certain characteristics. Rogers (2003) defined five characteristics of innovations that influence adoption of innovations, including:

1. Relative advantage: the degree to which an innovation is perceived as better than the comparable strategies it supersedes.
2. Compatibility: the amount of consistency the innovation has with the existing values and the past habits and experiences of the target recipients of the innovation.
3. Complexity: the degree to which an innovation is perceived as difficult to understand and use.
4. Trialability: the degree to which an innovation may be experimented with on a limited basis.
5. Observability: the degree to which the results of an innovation are visible to others.

The rate of adoption of different e-learning strategies thus can be quite different because they differ in the above characteristics.

Different e-learning strategies (for example, related to administrative information, course content, teacher–student and student–student communications, assessments, etc.) may have different learning benefits. Focusing on interaction may be one way to understand the learning potential of various strategies. Interaction is central to learning in a constructivist model of learning (Lam, Csete, & Hodgson, 2007). Student learning is supported in an interactive learning environment, as feedback and reflection effectively assist knowledge construction (O'Connor, 1998). Interaction comes in different forms. Swan (2003) described e-learning as facilitating at least three main kinds of useful interactions: interaction with content, with instructors, and with peers. There is evidence in Hong Kong universities that interactions that lead to constructive dialogue are more beneficial to learning than students being provided with access to information alone (Kember et al., 2010).

Despite the significant potential benefits to teaching and learning, the more interactive types of e-learning strategies tend to be less used by university teachers. A series of studies at The Chinese University of Hong Kong (CUHK) show that, while the percentage of supplementary online course websites has grown a great deal from ~45% in 2003–04 to over 80% in 2008–09, the Web continues to be mostly seen as a convenient storage house for easy distribution of course materials to students, often using existing basic functions in LMSs, such as WebCT and Moodle. Most communications are done through online forums with simple designs which are not very active; students, on average, post only one to three messages (McNaught, Lam, Keing, & Cheng, 2006; McNaught & Lam, 2009).

One way of understanding this situation is to consider what constitutes a mutual comfort zone for all the stakeholders, including teachers, students, and the technical and pedagogical support staff (McNaught et al., 2009). For an e-learning project to be successful and thus be reused, the e-learning strategies should be situated within this mutual comfort zone; in many universities the mutual comfort zone seems to be quite small. It is therefore easy to see why successful and sustainable cases of complex e-learning are not common and are restricted to highly motivated pioneering teachers who are comfortable with innovative technologies, and may also be in an innovation-friendly environment.

There are also contextual factors that influence the adoption and sustainability of e-learning strategies. A model of drivers that influence the growth of blended learning was described in McNaught (2008), and then extended in McNaught and Lam (2009). The model was used to study both positive and negative contextual factors at a research-intensive, comprehensive university (CUHK), which seem to positively and negatively influence the adoption of innovation.

In this model, the factors of most relevance to the context of the University are commitment of senior management, allocation of time, and a positive cost-benefit decision by teachers that their investment is likely to pay off. These factors can be framed as a set of competing drivers (both internal and external to the University). A summary of the model is in Figure 3. The arrows indicate that there is always a tension between any process of innovation and change, and the maintenance of the status quo.

At CUHK, the University's eLearning Service is a collaboration between colleagues in the Information Technology Services Centre (ITSC) and the Centre for Learning Enhancement And Research (CLEAR). The eLearning Service of the University has implemented a number of strategies to 1) further enhance the positive factors that support the growth of e-learning; and 2) minimize the effect of the negative factors. The weblog data described below is another piece of information we use to continue to refine our service to the University's teachers and students.

LEARNING MANAGEMENT SYSTEM (LMS) LOGS

Effective record-keeping, and extraction and interpretation of e-learning logs can reveal valuable information on at least some standards of design and development, and programme delivery. The

Figure 3. Internal and external drivers impinging on decisions about directions for e-learning (adapted from McNaught & Lam, 2009)

Factor	Coordinated and supported e-learning		Laissez-faire approach	
	←------------------------------------		-----------------------------------→	
	Internal drivers	*External drivers*	*Internal driver*	*External driver*
1. Senior management	Evidence of institutional research	External government quality audits	Culture of a face-to-face university	Good external rankings
	Implementation of a new student information system with concomitant reviews of internal university processes			
	←------------------------------------		-----------------------------------→	
	Internal drivers	*External driver*	*Internal driver*	*External driver*
2. Time	Increased diversity of students' profile	Changing curriculum mandated at government level	Commitment to a university research life	Frenetic city with a just-in-time philosophy
	Students as 'digital natives'			
	←------------------------------------		-----------------------------------→	
3. Teachers' decisions about change	*Internal drivers*	*External driver*	*Internal driver*	*External driver*
	Local support	Strong push for outcomes-based approaches (OBAs) to T&L in HK	Peer groups in departments	Benchmarking within the discipline
	Change in policy for promotion			

logs can reveal information about the magnitude and the nature of the online learning content and the online activities. This strategy is not intended to be a comprehensive solution to all evaluation needs but it is a comparatively easy, automatic, and non-intrusive method to provide relatively quick and accurate data to help answer some questions and concerns. The work is an extension of a 2004 study to monitor e-learning in our University (McNaught et al., 2006; Lam, Keing, McNaught, & Cheng, 2006).

In universities with centralized web-based teaching and learning systems, monitoring the logs can be accomplished because most e-learning platforms have in-built mechanisms to track and record a certain amount of information about online activities occurring within the systems. At CUHK, ITSC is responsible for maintaining the e-learning platforms for teaching staff in the University. ITSC also provides consultation and training for teachers to familiarize them with the functionality of the platforms, and supports the development of simple e-learning materials. At CUHK the majority of the e-learning activities are supported by the central services, though there are non-centrally-hosted course websites in Engineering and parts of Education and Medicine. Our monitoring model concentrates on the learning activities that are recorded in the centralized platforms only.

System logs recorded in centralized e-learning platforms can provide data on the popularity, the nature of the functions/ strategies in use, and engagement of teachers and students. Extraction of system logs is also completely non-intrusive to both teachers and students.

One limitation of this approach is that it monitors only uses of the Web that utilize the central system. Also, it has a bias on quantity rather than quality as logs focus on numbers rather than providing a full picture of the educational quality of the design of course websites. The exact activities that are ongoing are not transparent in a log mechanism for two reasons. Firstly, staff in

central units has no rights to access the content and messages on course websites without proper authorization. Secondly, not all online activities and the engagement of these activities can be effectively recorded by the logs. For example, the availability of course outlines on course websites is an online activity that is of great interest to our University. However, having an online course outline is not an activity separately recorded by the logs of either WebCT or Moodle. It is impossible to identify unless researchers go into the individual websites and examine the documents there. The picture portrayed by the logs is thus only a partial representation of the total learning activities, and the engagement teachers and students have with these activities.

There is a tension between practicality and maximum usefulness that we needed to negotiate, and we have sought a good balance point. Of course, issues of quality and usefulness are vital. The data provided by the log system complements a number of other projects at CUHK which are designed to provide feedback to individual departments and course teachers. In a face-to-face university such as CUHK, weblogs cannot provide information about the plethora of teaching and learning events that occur offline. At CUHK all course websites are part of a blended learning design and there are no totally online courses.

The monitoring mechanism was also restricted by technical limitations. The e-learning platforms do not normally provide institution-level data; they are mainly intended for individual teachers to monitor their students but not for the institution to monitor all courses at the same time. For example, WebCT does not supply detailed documentation on database structure and definitions, making the locations where log records are stored in the system difficult to access outside of the in-built logs display. As a result, considerable time and effort needed to be spent on: 1) allocating information through trial and error; 2) checking whether the data were accurate; and 3) developing software to enable automatic extraction of the information on all courses in the University.

The data for analysis came from the weblog records of our two LMSs (WebCT and Moodle) in two academic years (2007–2008 and 2008–2009). The following measures were taken to refine the data to suit the purposes of our study:

- We included Term 1 and Term 2 programmes in our study as the CUHK academic year is separated into two major semesters. A course (in other contexts, called subject, unit or module) was used as the unit of analysis. Sometimes one course was run in a number of sessions (at different times and even by different teachers). A course was considered e-learning-enabled if at least one of the sessions had an active website on any one of the LMSs.
- In this study, we considered both undergraduate and postgraduate courses.
- We realized that the use of e-learning strategies should be more meaningful to classes that are not too small. In our weblogs study, we limited the study to classes with a class size equal to or larger than 10.
- We also realized that not all websites created on the servers should be considered 'active' websites. For example, some of the websites might have been created by the teachers or the teaching assistants for testing purposes (preparing to be used in the next term perhaps) and there were actually no students active in the site. In our weblog study, an 'active' website needed to have at least one student access during the course period.
- The similar 'active' concept was also applied in the study of all e-learning strategies in our study. A website that had none of these active features could be a site that was used by the teacher for announcing course information such as examination dates or news of events.

  ○ Whether or not a particular course used 'forum' for 'active discussion', for example, was judged not only from the existence of a forum on the site, but rather on whether there was at least one student posting in the forum as well.
  ○ 'Active online quizzes' meant quizzes that had at least one student attempt.
  ○ 'Active assignment submission' meant that at least one student submitted work to the platform.
  ○ Active content meant the website contained at least one document (could be PowerPoint, word documents, pdf or any other multimedia files) for download and there was at least one student download recorded in the logs.

- As noted above some faculties are more dependent on these centrally provided platforms while teachers in some faculties are more inclined to local solutions because of history, or because of their ability to use technology, set up their own servers and use third-party software. These sites, especially in Engineering, Education and Medicine were not considered. In addition, we omitted websites in the central servers that were not associated with a course (e.g., programme websites that provided information about the whole programme).

FINDINGS

Diffusion

In order to consider adoption in the horizontal dimension, we compared and contrasted the existence of active course websites based on the log data in the two consecutive academic years: 2007–2008 and 2008–2009 (Table 1).

Table 1. Courses with active websites (percentages explained in text)

	Undergraduate Term 1	Undergraduate Term 2	Postgraduate Term 1	Postgraduate Term 2	**Overall**
2007–2008	410 (25.8%)	398 (25.1%)	154 (21.0%)	162 (22.1%)	**1124 (48.4%)**
2008–2009	450 (27.6%)	454 (27.8%)	167 (22.7%)	191 (25.9%)	**1262 (53.3%)**

In the year 2007–2008, out of the 2321 courses we studied (courses with 10 or more students), 1124 (48.4%) of them [808 undergraduate + 316 postgraduate courses] had an active website on one or more of our LMSs. Comparatively, a higher percentage of courses in the year 2008–2009 had active websites. Out of the 2369 courses we studied (courses with 10 or more students), 1262 (53.3%) of them [904 undergraduate + 358 postgraduate courses] had an active website on one or more of our LMSs. In-

dependent sample *t*-test runs on these figures showed that the differences (2007–2008 undergraduate compared to 2008–2009 undergraduate courses, 2007–2008 postgraduate compared to 2008–2009 postgraduate courses, 2007–2008 all courses compared to 2008–2009 all courses) were all statistically significant at the $p \leq 0.001$ level, indicating a significant increase in courses with active websites.

Figures 4 and 5 illustrate our findings when we drilled down into four e-learning functions

Figure 4. Usage of functions in undergraduate courses

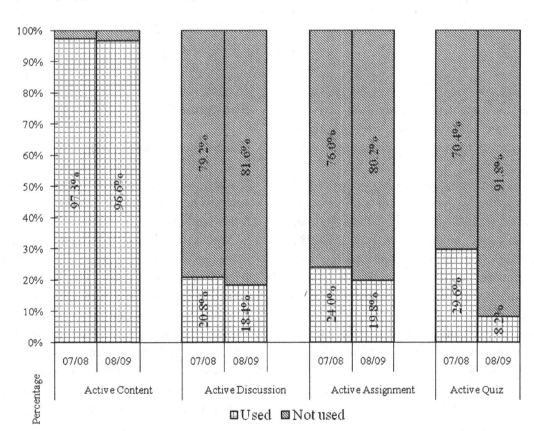

Figure 5. Usage of functions in postgraduate courses

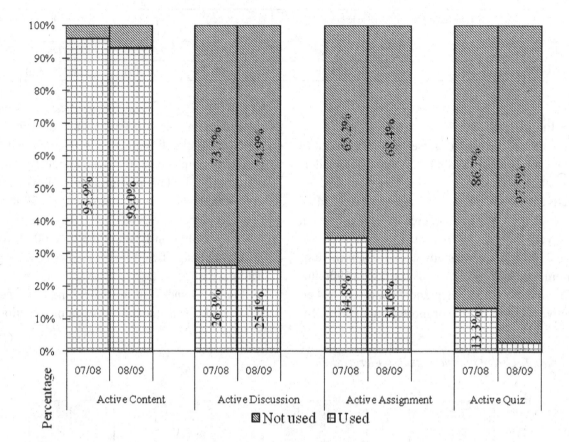

(i.e., active content, active discussion, active assignment and active quiz) that were or were not used in each of these course websites as recorded in the LMS logs.

Unlike the rising trend in the number of websites over the two years, the data on these two graphs showed a slight decline in the use of these online strategies on the sites from 2007–2008 to 2008–2009. Among the possible comparisons, the decreases in the use of active assignment (postgraduate courses and all courses combined) and active quiz (undergraduate courses, postgraduate courses and all courses combined) were statistically significant at the $p \leq 0.05$ level (Figure 4 and Figure 5).

Sustainability

When we looked at the concept of sustainability, we expected teachers who used certain e-learning strategies would keep on using them or could be attracted to using other functions as well in the following years.

We first of all identified courses that were run in the two consecutive years (i.e., 2007–08 Term 1 and then again in 2008–2009 Term 1, and/or 2007–2008 Term 2 and then again in 2008–09 Term 2). If a course used a course website in the first year, we then checked to see whether the website was still available and used in the second year. We also compared what sorts of e-learning strategies were used by the same course in the first year and second year respectively.

Table 2. Use of number of features among courses in two years

	Courses that used more e-features in 2008–2009	Courses that used less e-features in 2008–2009	Total courses
Undergraduate	76 (13.0%)	184 (31.5%)	585 (100.0%)
Postgraduate	31 (13.1%)	62 (30.2%)	205 (100.0%)
Total	**107 (13.5%)**	**246 (31.1%)**	**790 (100.0%)**

The first set of data we collected showed that the use of e-learning was quite versatile. We found 790 courses (585 undergraduate and 205 postgraduate courses) that had a website in both years. However, we also found 82 courses that ceased using the LMSs after using them in 2007–08. At the same time, 158 courses began to have a course website in 2008–09 that had not had a course website in the previous year.

Table 2 shows the use of number of features among the 790 courses which had a course website in both years. If the use of these features was sustainable, we would expect many of the courses to use at least the same number of web functions or more in 2008–2009 compared with 2007–2008.

Quite to our surprise, however, we found that many courses (246; 31.1%) had fewer active features in their course websites in the second year, suggesting that teachers had stopped doing some of the e-learning strategies. Chi-square tests showed that the variations in the features used across the two years were statistically significant at $p \leq 0.001$ level. As Table 3 shows, the features that ceased to be used (thus the less sustainable features) in these 246 courses were mostly forums (discussion), assignment and quiz. The *t*-tests we ran confirmed that the decreases in use of these three features were statistically significant ($p \leq .001$).

DISCUSSION

There are both positive and negative trends in our data concerning adoption of e-learning at CUHK. The overall impression seems to be that more courses have begun to have a Web presence in our LMSs. However, when we looked at these course websites closely, we did not find many functions were being used actively. Most of the websites had content for students to download. There might also be course information and announcements, but the other discussion, assignment and quiz functions were not popular (35% or below). The situation did not improve in the second year of our investigation; indeed the use actually decreased.

Moreover, many of these functions did not seem to be sustainable in the sense that many teachers used particular functions or strategies the first year but did not continue to use them in the second year. In other words, the use of some of the more complex strategies (which are thought to relate to greater potential learning benefits) actually decreased in terms of both horizontal and vertical directions.

Table 3. Features deleted in the 246 courses which used fewer features in the second year

Decrease	Active content	Active discussion	Active assignment	Active quiz
(1) 2007–2008 courses	246	121	156	140
(2) 2008–2009 courses	237	24	33	7
(2) vs (1)	**-9**	**-97**	**-123**	**-133**

Figure 6. Diverse developmental stages of e-learning strategies

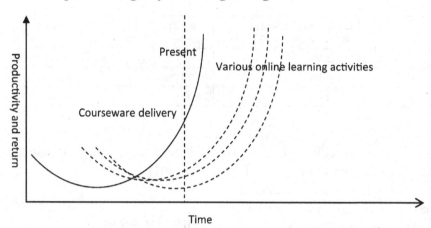

Relating these findings to our discussion about the J-curve of innovation adoption, it seems that multiple J-curves could be used to understand e-learning adoption (Figure 6). The situation at present is that for the use of minimal course websites with simple strategies (content/ courseware delivery), teachers feel comfortable and adoption is readily improving. But for the other e-learning strategies, we are still near the bottom of their J-curves. Adoption is still challenging.

The findings suggest that institutional e-learning support should not merely focus on having a web presence in courses or the courseware delivery usage of the Web. These functions are slowly gaining popularity. The attention needs to be on the diffusion and sustained use of the other online learning activities.

Recalling the factors that influence adoption, the findings seem to lead us to new interpretations of some of them: we should reconsider these factors especially in the view of facilitating the more challenging online learning activities, not only to support more teachers to use them but also to ensure they continue to be used in successive years.

- *Acknowledge the need for appropriate motivation for teachers*: Thomas et al. (2009) discussed how some teachers consider innovative e-learning projects to be lonely and time-consuming. Being self-motivated and intellectually committed is a key factor that sustains teachers and allowed them to stay engaged. Another key factor is the perceived intrinsic return on effort in terms of better teaching practice and students' learning, as well as the expected extrinsic benefit during performance appraisal. One teacher was quoted as saying that after having taught the same course for many years, an e-learning project helped her "regain her enthusiasm for teaching". The experience thus gave the teacher a clear personal reward.

- *Support the departmental context*: The existence of peer groups in departments is important. The existence of a strong emphasis on teaching and learning (e.g., change in policy for promotion) will certainly favour more active use of innovative strategies. Having the support of technical staff is a key advantage, for design and functionality, and consequent extension of project goals, as well as the simple opportunity to delegate tasks. Another structural condition that supports diffusion is the support provided by the department or by the University – in terms of monetary development grants, technical services, and consultative teaching and learning support in terms of e-learning pedagogical design. This support, though somewhat limited, still has significant impact on workload.

- *Use an evidence-based and pragmatic approach*: Strategies that are likely to diffuse and sustain are those that meet the comfort zones of all the involving parties. Another criterion is the willingness to evaluate and then respond to the evaluation data as no strategies can be perfect in the first time. Evaluation should be an integrated feature of all projects. Without evidence, there can be no diagnosis and subsequent discussion about alternatives.

- *Support projects that are most likely to succeed*: At the institutional level, care should be taken in identifying projects and strategies that may be able to sustain and diffuse. In order to do so, according to the discussion above, projects that have the following characteristics seem to be more likely to have good outcomes:

  - Projects that start off with the intention to sustain and diffuse;
  - Projects headed by the 'right' persons (enthusiastic and with leadership qualities);
  - Projects in the 'right' context (collegial, supportive);
  - Projects with the 'right' design (meeting comfort zones of the parties involved); and
  - Projects with a commitment to evaluation.

CONCLUSION

Adoption of innovations in e-learning can be difficult. Many individual and social factors relate to the acceptance of the use of technology in teaching and learning. The study focused on 'horizontal' and 'vertical' adoption of e-learning

strategies at CUHK as revealed through computer log records in the centrally supported LMSs. Horizontal diffusion refers to whether e-learning has spread to influence the practice of more teachers and students. In vertical diffusion we examined whether or not our teachers tend to have richer learning activities conducted online in subsequent years. The overall findings are that while adoption of simple strategies is increasing, there is little evidence of horizontal and vertical diffusion of the more complex strategies. While, on the whole, we found more course websites using simple strategies over the two years, the use of some of the more complex strategies (which are thought to relate to greater potential learning benefits) actually decreased. This is a topic for further investigation.

The results led us to reconsider strategies for supporting e-learning in our institution. Acknowledging the need for reward and motivation, as well as supporting both development and evaluation is important. We have altered our criteria for awarding grants and increased local support to teachers at a departmental level. The use of the weblogs should enable us to continue fine-tuning support for CUHK teachers.

REFERENCES

Becker, R., & Jokivirta, L. (2007). Online learning in universities: Selected data from the 2006 Observatory survey – November 2007. *Observatory on Borderless Higher Education (OBHE) Online*. Retrieved August 10, 2010, from http://www.obhe.ac.uk/documents/view_details?id=15

Bremmer, I. (2006). *The J curve: A new way to understand why nations rise and fall*. New York: Simon & Schuster.

Cheng, K. F., Lam, P., & McNaught, C. (2006, September 7-8). Lessons learnt from two unsuccessful complex web-based teaching and learning development projects. In *Proceedings of the Third International Conference on Educational Technology*, Singapore.

Collis, B., & van der Wende, M. (2002). *Models of technology and change in higher education: An international comparative survey on the current and future use of ICT in higher education*. Retrieved August 10, 2010, from http://doc.utwente.nl/44610/1/ictrapport.pdf

Ellis, R. A., Jarkey, N., Mahony, M. J., Peat, M., & Sheely, S. (2007). Managing quality improvement of e-learning in a large, campus-based university. *Quality Assurance in Education, 15*(1), 9–23. doi:10.1108/09684880710723007

Fitzgibbon, K. M., & Jones, N. (2004). Jumping the hurdles: Challenges of staff development delivered in a blended learning environment. *Journal of Educational Media, 29*(1), 25–35. doi:10.1080/1358165042000186253

Friesen, N. (2003). *Three objections to learning objects and e-learning standards*. Retrieved July 15, 2010, from http://www.learningspaces.org/n/papers/objections.html

Gellman-Danley, B., & Fetzner, M. J. (1998). Asking the really tough questions: Policy issues for distance learning. *Online Journal of Distance Learning Administration, 1*(1). Retrieved July 15, 2010, from http://www.westga.edu/~distance/danley11.html

Hitch, L. P., & MacBrayne, P. (2003, March/April). A model for effectively supporting e-Learning. *The Technology Source Archives*. Retrieved July 15, 2010, from http://technologysource.org/article/model_for_effectively_supporting_elearning/

Hoffman, M. E., & Vance, D. R. (2005). Computer literacy: What students know and from whom they learned it. *ACM SIGCSE Bulletin, 37*(1), 356–360. doi:10.1145/1047124.1047467

Jones, A. J. (2003). ICT and future teachers: Are we preparing for e-learning? In *Proceedings of the 3.1 and 3.3 Working Groups Conference on International Federation for Information Processing: ICT and the Teacher of the Future* (Vol. 23, pp. 67-69). Retrieved July 15, 2010, from http://crpit.com/confpapers/CRPITV23Jones.pdf

Jones, J., & McNaught, C. (2005). Using learning object evaluation: Challenges and lessons learned in the Hong Kong context. In Richards, G., & Kommers, P. (Eds.), *ED-MEDIA 2005* (pp. 3580–3585).

Keing, C., Lo, J., Lam, P., & McNaught, C. (2007). Summative eAssessments: Piloting acceptability, practicality and effectiveness. In C. Montgomerie & J. Seale (Eds.), *Proceedings of the 19th annual World Conference on Educational Multimedia, Hypermedia & Telecommunications (ED-MEDIA 2007)*, Vancouver, Canada (pp. 486-495). Chesapeake, VA: Association for the Advancement of Computers in Education.

Kember, D., Ma, R., McNaught, C., & 18 exemplary teachers (2006). *Excellent university teaching*. Hong Kong, China: Chinese University Press.

Kember, D., McNaught, C., Chong, F. C. Y., Paul Lam, P., & Cheng, K. F. (2010). Understanding the ways in which design features of educational websites impact upon student learning outcomes in blended learning environments. *Computers & Education, 55*, 1183–1192. doi:10.1016/j.compedu.2010.05.015

Lam, P., Csete, J., & Hodgson, P. (2007). Enrichment of interaction in online assessments. In Frankland, S. (Ed.), *Enhancing teaching and learning through assessment* (pp. 392–401). New York: Springer.

Lam, P., Keing, C., McNaught, C., & Cheng, K. F. (2006). Monitoring eLearning environments through analyzing web logs of institution-wide eLearning platforms. In L. Markauskaite, P. Goodyear, & P. Reimann (Eds.), *Proceedings of the Who's learning? Whose technology? 23rd annual Australian Society for Computers in Learning in Tertiary Education 2006 conference*, University of Sydney (pp. 429-440). Retrieved July 15, 2010, from http://www.ascilite.org.au/conferences/sydney06/proceeding/pdf_papers/p62.pdf

Lam, P., & McNaught, C. (2005). Management of an eLearning evaluation project: e3Learning. In G. Richards & P. Kommers (Eds.), *Proceedings of the 17th annual World Conference on Educational Multimedia, Hypermedia & Telecommunications (ED-MEDIA 2005)* Montreal, Canada. Norfolk, VA: Association for the Advancement of Computers in Education.

Lewin, K. (1952). Group decision and social change. In Swanson, G. E., Newcomb, T. M., & Hartley, F. E. (Eds.), *Readings in social psychology* (pp. 459–473). New York: Holt.

McNaught, C., & Lam, P. (2009). Institutional strategies for embedding blended learning in a research-intensive university. In *Proceedings of the Elearn2009 Conference, Bridging the development gap through innovative eLearning environments*, The University of the West Indies, St Augustine, Trinidad and Tobago.

McNaught, C., Lam, P., Cheng, K.-F., Kennedy, D. M., & Mohan, J. B. (2009). Challenges in employing complex eLearning strategies in campus-based universities. *International Journal of Technology Enhanced Learning*, *1*(4), 266–285. doi:10.1504/IJTEL.2009.030778

McNaught, C., Lam, P., Keing, C., & Cheng, K. F. (2006). Improving eLearning support and infrastructure: An evidence-based approach. In O'Donoghue, J. (Ed.), *Technology supported learning and teaching: A staff perspective* (pp. 70–89). Hershey, PA: Information Science Publishing.

Nussbaum, J., & Novick, S. (1982). Alternative frameworks, conceptual conflict and accommodation: Toward a principled teaching strategy. *Instructional Science*, *11*, 183–200. doi:10.1007/BF00414279

O'Connor, M. C. (1998). Can we trace the efficacy of social constructivism? *Review of Educational Research*, *23*, 25–71.

Parrish, P. E. (2004). The trouble with learning objects. *Educational Technology Research and Development*, *52*(1), 49–67. doi:10.1007/BF02504772

Rogers, E. M. (2003). *Diffusion of innovations* (5th ed.). New York: Free Press.

Scott, P. J., & Quick, K. (2005). Heroic failures in disseminating novel e-learning technologies to corporate clients: A case study of interactive webcasting. In *Proceedings of the 4th international symposium on Information and communication technologies*, Cape Town, South Africa (Vol. 92, pp. 26-31). Dublin, Ireland: Trinity College Publisher. Retrieved July 15, 2010, from http://portal.acm.org/citation.cfm?id=1071752.1071758

Strike, K. A., & Posner, G. J. (1985). A conceptual change view of learning and understanding. In West, L. H. T., & Pines, A. L. (Eds.), *Cognitive structure and conceptual change* (pp. 231–240). New York: Academic Press.

Swan, K. (2003). Learning effectiveness online: What the research tells us. In Boume, J., & Moore, J. C. (Eds.), *Elements of quality online education* (*Vol. 4*, pp. 13–46). Needham, MA: Sloan-C, The Sloan Center at Olin and Babson Colleges.

Thomas, K., Lam, P., & Ho, A. (2009). Knowledge diffusion in eLearning: Learner attributes and capabilities in an organization. In G. Siemens & C. Fulford (Eds), *Proceedings of the 21st Annual World Conference on Educational Multimedia, Hypermedia and Telecommunications*, Honolulu, HI (pp. 493-497). Chesapeake, VA: Association for the Advancement of Computers in Education.

West, L. (1988). Implications of recent research for improving secondary school science learning. In Ramsden, P. (Ed.), *Improving learning: New perspectives* (pp. 51–68). London: Kogan Page.

This work was previously published in International Journal of E-Adoption, Volume 2, Issue 3, edited by Sushil K. Sharma, pp. 39-52, copyright 2010 by IGI Publishing (an imprint of IGI Global).

Compilation of References

Abdallah-Pretceille, M. (1999). *L'éducation intercul-turelle*. Paris: Que sais-je? Presses Universitaires de France.

Abernathy, D. J. (1999). A chat with Chris Argyris. *Training & Development, 53*(5), 80–84.

Agarwal, R., & Prasad, J. (1999). Are individual differences germane to the acceptance of new information technologies? *Decision Sciences, 30*, 361–391. doi:10.1111/j.1540-5915.1999.tb01614.x

Ahuja, M., & Carley, K. (1998). Network Structure in Virtual Organizations. *Journal of Computer-Mediated Communication, 3*(4), *10*(6), 741-757.

Aimi, G., & Finley, I. (2007, May/June). SOA: The new value driver. *Supply Chain Management Review, 12-14.*

Ajzen, I. (1985). *From intentions to actions: A theory of planned behavior. Actioncontrol: From cognition to behavior*. Heidelberg, Germany: Springer.

Ajzen, I. (1989). *Attitude, personality, and behavior*. Milton Keynes, UK: Open University Press.

Ajzen, I. (1991). The theory of planned behavior. *Organizational Behavior and Human Decision Processes, 50*(2), 179–211. doi:10.1016/0749-5978(91)90020-T

Ajzen, I., & Fishbein, M. (1980). *Understanding attitudes and predicting social behavior*. Upper Saddle River, NJ: Prentice-Hall.

Akinoglu, O., & Ozkardes Tandogan, R. (2007). The effects of problem-based active learning in science education on students' academic achievement, attitude and concept learning. *Eurasia J. Math. Sci. & Tech. Ed., 3*(1), 71–81.

Al-Ayyat, S., Bali, M., Ellozy, A., Kosheiry, M., Mansour, M., & Pappas, W. (2004). Two years into WebCT: Perceptions of AUC Students. In *Proceedings of the 2nd International E-learning Conference*. Retrieved August 14, 2008, from http://acs.aucegypt.edu/Presentations/studsurvey.pdf

Al-Hammadi, B., & Shahsavari, M. (1999). Certified exchange of electronic mail (CEEM). In [Washington, DC: IEEE.]. *Proceedings of the Southeastcon, 99*, 40–43.

Al-shehry, A., Rogerson, S., Fairweather, N., Prior, M. (2006). *The Motivations for Change towards E-government Adoption: Saudi Arabia as a case Study, eGovernment Workshop*. West London: Brunel University.

Albero, B. (2000). *L'autoformation en contexte institutionnel: Du paradigme de l'instruction au paradigme de l'autonomie*. Paris: L'Harmattan.

Alharbi, S. (2006). *Perceptions of Faculty and Students toward the Obstacles of Implementing E-Government in Educational Institutions in Saudi Arabia (Tech. Rep.)*. Morgantown, West Virginia: West Virginia University.

Allen, D. (1995). Information systems strategy formation in higher education institutions. *Information Research, 1*(1). Retrieved February 28, 2008, from http://informationr.net/ir/ir/1-1/paper3.html

Alshareef, T. (2003). *E-Government in the Kingdom of Saudi Arabia, Applicational Study on the governmental mainframes in Riyadh City*. Riyadh, Saudi Arabia: King Saud University.

AlShihi, H. (2006). *Critical Factors in the Adoption and Diffusion of E-government Initiatives in Oman*. PhD thesis, Victoria University, Australia.

Alsuwail, M. (2001). *Directions and local experiences, Foundations and Requirements of E-Government*. Paper presented at the E-Government Conference, Institute of Public Administration, the Kingdom of Saudi Arabia.

Amin, A., & Roberts, J. (2008). Knowing in action: Beyond communities. *Research Policy*, *37*, 353–369. doi:10.1016/j.respol.2007.11.003

Anakwe, U. (1999). Online learning and Cultural Diversity: Potential Users' Perspective. *The International Journal of Organizational Analysis*, *7*(3), 224. doi:10.1108/eb028901

Anderson, A. (2005). *A comparison of two Privacy Policy Languages: EPAL and XACML* (Sun Microsystems Labs Tech. Rep.). Retrieved from http://research.sun.com/techrep/2005/smli_tr-2005-147/

Ardagna, C., Damiani, E., De Capitani di Vimercati, S., Fugazza, C., & Samarati, P. (2005). *Offline Expansion of XACML Policies Based on P3P Metadata* (. *LNCS*, *3579*, 363–374.

Argyris, C., & Schon, D. (1978). *Organizational learning: A theory of action perspective*. Reading, MA: Addison Wesley.

Arıcı, N., & Kıdıman, E. (2007). Mesleki ve teknik orta öğretimde probleme dayali öğrenme yönteminin akademik başariya ve öğrenmenin kaliciliğina etkisi. *e-Journal of New World Sciences Academy*. Retrieved September 13, 2007, from http://www.newwsa.com/makale_ozet.asp?makale_id=118

Arnab, A., & Hutchison, A. (2007, October 11-13). DRM Use License Negotiation using ODRL v2.0. In *Proceedings 5th International Workshop for Technology, Economy, and Legal Aspects of Virtual Goods and the 3rd International ODRL Workshop*, Koblenz, Germany.

Arney, W. R. (1990). *Understanding statistics in the social sciences*. New York: W.H. Freeman.

Ashbourn, J. (2004). *Practical biometric from aspiration to implementation*. London: Springer.

Augar, N., Raitman, R., & Zhou, W. (2004, December 5-8). Teaching and learning online with wikis. In R. Atkinson, C. McBeath, D. Jonas-Dwyer, & R. Phillips (Eds.), *Beyond the comfort zone: Proceedings of the 21st ASCILITE Conference*, Perth, Australia (pp. 95-104). Retrieved from http://www.ascilite.org.au/conferences/perth04/procs/augar.html

Awad, E. M., & Ghaziri, H. M. (2004). *Knowledge Management*. Upper Saddle River, NJ: Pearson Education.

Aziz, T., Khan, M., & Singh, R. (2010). Effects of Information Technology Usage on Student Learning: An Empirical Study in the United States. *International Journal of Management*, *27*(2), 205–217.

Babbie, E. (1990). *Survey Research Methods*. Belmont, CA: Wadsworth Publishing Company.

Bagozzi, R. P., & Yi, Y. (1988). On the evaluation of structural equation models. *Journal of the Academy of Marketing Science*, *16*(1), 74–94. doi:10.1007/BF02723327

Baker, W. (1992). The network organization in theory and practice. In Nohria, N., & Eccles, R. (Eds.), *Networks and Organizations* (pp. 327–429). Cambridge, MA: Harvard Business School Press.

Barker, B., & Baker, M. (1995). Strategies to ensure interaction in telecommunicated online learning. In *Proceedings of the 11th Annual Conference on Teaching and Learning*, Madison, WI (pp. 17-32).

Barker, R., & Holley, C. (1996). Interactive Online learning: Perspective and Thoughts. *Business Communication Quarterly*, *59*(4), 88–97. doi:10.1177/108056999605900409

Barnatt, C. (1995). Office space, cyberspace and virtual organizations. *Journal of General Management*, *21*(4), 78–91.

Barnes, S., & Scornavacca, E. (2004). Mobile Marketing: The Role of Permission and Acceptance. *International Journal of Mobile Communications*, *2*(2), 128–139. doi:10.1504/IJMC.2004.004663

Barnes, S. J. B. (2003). Known by the Network: The Emergence of Location-Based Mobile Commerce. In Lim, E. S. (Ed.), *Advances in Mobile Commerce Technologies* (pp. 171–189). Hershey, PA: IGI Global.

Barrows, H., & Mayers, A. (1993). *Problem based learning in secondary schools*. Unpublished monography, Springfield, IL.

Barrows, H. S., & Tamblyn, R. M. (1980). *Problem-based learning: an approach to medical education*. New York: Springer Publishing Company. ISBN 0826128416, 9780826128416

Barson, R. J., Foster, G., Struck, T., Ratchev, S., Pawar, K., Weber, F., & Wunram, M. (2000). *Inter and Intra-organizational Barriers to Sharing Knowledge in the Extended Supply Chain*. Retrieved from www.corma.net

Bartlett, J. E., Kotrlik, J. W., & Higgins, C. C. (2001). Organizational research: Determining appropriate sample size in survey research. *Information Technology, Learning and Performance Journal, 19*(1), 43–50.

Bates, A. (2000). *Managing technological change: Strategies for college and university leaders*. San Francisco, CA: Jossey-Bass.

Bauer, H., Reichardt, T., Barnes, S., & Neumann, M. (2005). Driving Consumer Acceptance of Mobile Marketing: A Theoretical Framework and Empirical Study. *Journal of Electronic Commerce Research, 6*(3), 181–192.

Bauman, M. (1997). *Online learning communities*. Retrieved December 2, 2002, from http://www-personal.umd.umich.edu/~marcyb/tcc-l.html

Becker, R., & Jokivirta, L. (2007). Online learning in universities: Selected data from the 2006 Observatory survey – November 2007. *Observatory on Borderless Higher Education (OBHE) Online*. Retrieved August 10, 2010, from http://www.obhe.ac.uk/documents/view_details?id=15

Belisle, C. (1998). Enjeux et limites du multimédia en formation et en éducation. In *Proceedings of the Les Cahiers de l'ASDIFLE* (No. 9, pp. 7-24). Paris: Association de didactique du français langue étrangère.

Bennett, R. E. (2001). How the Internet will help large-scale assessment reinvent itself. *Education Policy Analysis Archives, 9*(5).

Bennett, S., Marton, K., & Kervin, L. (2008). The 'Digital Natives' debate: A critical review of the evidence. *British Journal of Educational Technology, 39*(5), 775–786. doi:10.1111/j.1467-8535.2007.00793.x

Berends, H., Boersma, K., & Weggeman, M. (2003). The structuration of organizational learning. *Human Relations, 56*(9), 1035–1056. doi:10.1177/0018726703569001

Berge, Z. (1999). Interaction in post-secondary web-based learning. *Educational Technology, 39*(1), 5–11.

Beyerlein, M., & Johnson, D. (1994). *Theories of self-managing work teams*. Stamford, CT: JAI Press.

Bhatti, R., Ghafoor, A., Bertino, E., & Joshi, J. B. D. (2005). X-GTRBAC: an XML-based policy specification framework and architecture for enterprise-wide access control. [TISSEC]. *ACM Transactions on Information and System Security, 8*(2), 187–227. doi:10.1145/1065545.1065547

Bibeau, R. (1998). *L'élève rapaillé – Le Cercle de Recherche et d'Action Pédagogiques et kes Cahie*. Retrieved September 3, 2010, from http://www.cahiers-pedagogiques.com/article.php3?id_article=2603

Biggs, J. B. (2003). *Teaching for quality learning at university* (2nd ed.). Buckingham, UK: Society for Research into Higher Education & Open University Press.

Bjørgen, I. A. (1991). *Ansvar for egen læring*. Trondheim, Norway: Tapir.

Black, A. (2005). The use of asynchronous discussion: Creating a text of talk. *Contemporary Issues in Technology & Teacher Education, 5*(1). Retrieved from http://www.citejournal.org/vol5/iss1/languagearts/article1.cfm.

Black, J. A., & Edwards, S. (2000). Emergence of virtual or network organizations: fad or feature? *Journal of Organizational Change Management, 13*(6), 567–576. doi:10.1108/09534810010378588

Blackler, F. (1995). Knowledge, knowledge work and organizations: An overview and interpretation. *Organization Studies, 16*(6), 1021–1046. doi:10.1177/017084069501600605

Blau, A. (2002). Access isn't enough: Merely connecting people and computers won't close the digital divide. *American Libraries, 33*(6), 50–52.

Blau, J. (1997). Global networking process management challenges. *Technology Management, 40*(1), 4–5.

Boerner, S., Eisenbeiss, S., & Griesser, D. (2007). Follower behavior and organizational performance: The impact of transformational leaders. *Journal of Leadership & Organizational Studies*, *13*(3), 15–28. doi:10.1177/10717919070130030201

Bolle, R., Connell, J., Pankanti, S., Ratha, N., & Senior, A. (2004). *Guide to Biometrics*. New York: Springer.

Bonatti, P. A., Duma, C., Fuchs, N., Nejdl, W., Olmedilla, D., Peer, J., & Shahmehri, N. (2006). Semantic Web Policies - A Discussion of Requirements and Research Issues. In *Proceedings of the European Semantic Web Conference (ESWC 2006)* (LNCS 4011, pp. 712-724). New York: Springer.

Boni, A. A., Weingart, L. R., & Evenson, S. (2009). Innovation in an academic setting: Designing and leading a business through market-focused, interdisciplinary teams. *Academy of Management Learning & Education*, *8*(3), 407–417.

Bonsor, K., & Johnson, R. (n.d.). How Facial Recognition Systems Work. *How Stuff Works*. Retrieved October 1, 2007 from http://computer.howstuffworks.com/facial-recognition.htm

Boreham, N., & Morgan, C. (2004). A sociocultural analysis of organisational learning. *Oxford Review of Education*, *30*(3), 307–325. doi:10.1080/0305498042000260467

Borg, W. R., & Gall, M. D. (1989). *Educational Research: An Introduction* (5th ed.). White Plains, NY: Longman.

Bork, A., & Gunnarsdottir, S. (2001). *Tutorial online Learning: Rebuilding our education system*. New York: Klumar Academic/Plenum Publishers.

Borras, J. (2007). *Election Markup Language (EML) Version 5.0. Organization for the Advancement of Structured Information Standards (OASIS)*. Retrieved December 18, 2009 from http://docs.oasis-open.org/election/eml/v5.0/os/EML-Process-Data-Requirements-v5.0.pdf

Boud, D. (2000). Sustainable assessment: rethinking assessment for the learning society. *Studies in Continuing Education*, *22*(2), 151–167. doi:10.1080/713695728

Bremmer, I. (2006). *The J curve: A new way to understand why nations rise and fall*. New York: Simon & Schuster.

British Education Communication and Technology Association (BECTA). (2004). *Self review framework for e-leadership. Coventry: BECTA*. Retrieved August 18, 2010, from http://schools.becta.org.uk/index.php?section=srf

Bruner, C., & Kumar, A. (2007). Attitude toward Location-Based Advertising. *Journal of Interactive Marketing*, *7*(2), 3–15.

Bruner, I., Gordon, C., & Kumar, A. (2007). Gadget Lovers. *Journal of the Academy of Marketing Science*, *35*(2), 329–339. doi:10.1007/s11747-007-0051-3

Bubonic, E. J. (2001). *Improving student learning and attitude throuhg problem–based learning*. Unpublished master's thesis, Ashland University, Ashland, OH.

Bull, J., & McKenna, C. (2004). *Blueprint for computer-assisted assessment*. London: Routledge Falmer. doi:10.4324/9780203464687

Cameron, K. S., & Quinn, R. E. (2006). *Diagnosing and changing organizational culture*. San Francisco, CA: Jossey-Bass.

Camillus, J. (1993). Crafting the competitive corporation: Management systems for future organizations. In Lorange, P., Chakravarthy, B., Roos, J., & Van De Ven, A. (Eds.), *Implementing strategic process: Change, learning, and cooperation* (pp. 313–328). Oxford, UK: Blackwell.

Campbell, D. R., & Fiske, D. W. (1959). Convergent and discriminant validation by multitrait-multimethod matrix. *Psychological Bulletin*, *56*(2), 81–105. doi:10.1037/h0046016

Carless, D., Joughin, G., & Liu, N. F. (2006). *How assessment supports learning: Learning-oriented assessment in action*. Hong Kong: Hong Kong University Press.

Carswell, L. T., Petre, M., Price, B., & Richard, M. (2000). Online education via Internet: the student experience. *British Journal of Educational Technology*, *31*(1), 29–47. doi:10.1111/1467-8535.00133

Casassa-Mont, M., Crosta, S., Kriegelstein, T., & Sommer, D. (2007). *PRIME Architecture V2*. Retrieved March 29, 2007 from https://www.primeproject.eu/prime_products/reports/arch/pub_del_D14.2.c_ec_WP14.2_v1_Final.pdf>

Cascio, W. F. (1999). Virtual work places: Implications for organizational behavior. In Cooper, C. L., & Rousseau, D. M. (Eds.), *The Virtual Organization* (*Vol. 6*, pp. 1–14). Trends in Organizational Behavior.

Central Department of Statistics & Information (CDSI). (2009). Retrieved from http://www.cdsi.gov.sa

Central Intelligence Agency (CIA). The Word Fact Book. (2009). Retrieved from https://www.cia.gov/library/publications/the-world-factbook/

ChanLin. L. J. (2008). Individual Differences in Computer-Mediated Communication Individual Differences in Computer-Mediated Communication. *Journal of Educational Media & Library Sciences, 45*(4), 505-524. Retrieved from http://joemls.dils.tku.edu.tw/45/45-4/505-524.pdf

Chaum, D. (1981). Untraceable electronic mail, return adresses, and digital pseudonyms. *Communications of the ACM, 24*(2), 84–86. doi:10.1145/358549.358563

Chaum, D. (2004). Secret-ballot receipts: True voter-verifiable elections. *Security & Privacy, 2*(1), 38–47. doi:10.1109/MSECP.2004.1264852

Chaum, D., Carback, R., Clark, J., Essex, A., Popoveniuc, S., Rivest, R., Ryan, P., Shen, E., & Sherman, A. (2008, May/June). Scantegrity II: End-to-End Verifiability for Optical Scan Election Systems Using Invisible Ink Confirmation Codes. *Security & Privacy.*

Chaum, D., Essex, A., Carback, R., Clark, J., Popoveniuc, S., Sherman, A., & Vora, P. (2008). Scantegrity: End-to-End Voter-Verifiable Optical- Scan Voting. *Security & Privacy, 6*(3), 40–46. doi:10.1109/MSP.2008.70

Chen, C. C., Chen, X., & Meindl, J. R. (1998). How can cooperation be fostered? The cultural effects of individualism-collectivism. *Academy of Management Review, 23*, 285–304. doi:10.2307/259375

Cheng, K. F., Lam, P., & McNaught, C. (2006, September 7-8). Lessons learnt from two unsuccessful complex web-based teaching and learning development projects. In *Proceedings of the Third International Conference on Educational Technology*, Singapore.

Cheng, T. C. E., Lam, D. Y. C., & Yeung, A. L. C. (2006). Adoption of internet banking: An empirical study in Hong Kong. *Decision Support Systems, 42*(3), 1558–1572. doi:10.1016/j.dss.2006.01.002

Chew, M., Balfanz, D., & Laurie, B. (2008, May 18-21). Mining Privacy in Social Networks. Web 2.0 Security and Privacy. In *Proceedings of the 2008 IEEE Symposium on Security and Privacy*, Oakland, California.

Chia, Y. M., & Koh, H. C. (2007). Organizational culture and the adoption of management accounting practices in the public sector: A Singapore study. *Financial Accountability and Management, 23*(2), 189–213. doi:10.1111/j.1468-0408.2007.00425.x

Cho, T. S., & Hambrick, D. C. (2006). Attention as the mediator between top management team characteristics and strategic change: The case of airline deregulation. *Organization Science, 17*, 453–469. doi:10.1287/orsc.1060.0192

Christie, P. M. J., & Levary, R. R. (1998). Virtual corporations: Recipe for success. *Industrial Management (Des Plaines), 40*(4), 7–11.

Chu, H. C., Chen, T. Y., Lin, C. J., Liao, M. J., & Chen, Y. M. (2009). Development of an adaptive learning case recommendation approach for problem-based e-learning on mathematics teaching for students with mild disabilities. *Expert Systems with Applications, 36*(3), 5456–5468. doi:10.1016/j.eswa.2008.06.140

Çiftçi, S., Meydan, A., & Ektem, I. S. (2007). Sosyal bilgiler öğretiminde probleme dayali öğrenmeyi kullanmanin öğrencilerin başarisina ve tutumlarina etkisi. *Selçuk Üniversitesi Sosyal Bilimler Enstitüsü Dergisi. Sayı, 17*, 179–190.

Clemente, F. J. G., Perez, G. M., & Skarmeta, A. F. G. (2005). *An XML-Seamless Policy Based Management Framework (. LCNS, 3685*, 418–423.

Cohen, D. (2009). The Impact of Wiki-Based Collaborative Environment on Mathematical Dialogue. In *Proceedings of the Learning in the Technological Era, Chais Conference on Instructional Technologies Research* (pp. 64-69).

Cohen, J. (1992). A power primer. *Psychological Bulletin, 112*, 155–159. doi:10.1037/0033-2909.112.1.155

Cohen, J., & Fischer, M. (1985). A robust and verifiable cryptographically secure election scheme. In *Proceedings of the 26th IEEE Symposium on the Foundations of Computer Science (FOCS)* (pp. 372-382). Washington, DC: IEEE.

Cohen, J., & Yung, M. (1986). Distributing the power of government to enhance the privacy of voters. In *Proceedings of 5th ACM Symposium on Principles of Distributed Computing (PODC)*, 52–62. ACM.

Cohen, N. (2007, October 1). Use My Photo? Not Without Permission. *New York Times*. Retrieved from http://www.nytimes.com/2007/10/01/technology/01link.html?ex=1348977600&en=182a46901b23f450&ei=5124&partner=permalink&exprod=permalink

Cohen, W. M., & Levinthal, D. A. (1990). Absorptive capacity: A new perspective on learning and innovation. *Administrative Science Quarterly*, *36*(1), 128–152. doi:10.2307/2393553

Colbert, A. E., Kristof-Brown, A. I., Bradley, B. H., & Barrick, M. R. (2008). CEO transformational leadership: The goal importance congruence in top management teams. *Academy of Management Journal*, *51*(1), 81–96. doi:10.2307/20159495

(1998). *Collins Cobuild English Dictionary*. London: Harper Collins Publishers Ltd.

Collis, B., & van der Wende, M. (2002). *Models of technology and change in higher education: An international comparative survey on the current and future use of ICT in higher education*. Retrieved August 10, 2010, from http://doc.utwente.nl/44610/1/ictrapport.pdf

Conole, G., de Laat, M., Dillon, T., & Darby, J. (2006). *JISC LXP: Student experience of technologies*. Retrieved September 6, 2010, from http://jisc.ac.uk/media/documents/programmes/elearningpedagogy/lxp_project_final_report_nov_06.pdf

Cook, S. D., & Brown, J. S. (1999). Bridging epistemologies: The generative dance between organizational knowledge and organizational knowing. *Organization Science*, *10*(4), 381–400. doi:10.1287/orsc.10.4.381

Cooksey, R. (2003). Learnership in complex organizational textures. *Leadership and Organization Development Journal*, *24*(4), 204–214. doi:10.1108/01437730310478075

Cooper, L. W. (2001). A comparison of online and traditional computer applications classes. *T.H.E. Journal*, *28*(8), 52–56.

Cornell, R., & Martin, B. L. (1997). The role of motivation in web-based instruction. In Khan, B. H. (Ed.), *Web-Based Instruction* (2nd ed., pp. 93–100). Englewood Cliffs, NJ: Educational Technology Publications Inc.

Coulson, K. R., & Kantamneni, S. P. (2000). *Virtual corporations: The promise and the peril*. Retrieved March 23, 2005, from http://www.dcpress.com/jmb/virtual.htm

Council of Europe. (1950). *Convention for the Protection of Human Rights and Fundamental Freedoms*. Paris: Council of Europe.

Council of Europe. (1999). *Directive 1999/93/EC on a Community framework for electronic signatures*.

Council of Europe. (2004a). *Recommendation Rec(2004)11 of the Committee of Ministers to member states on legal, operational and technical standards for e-voting*. Paris: Council of Europe.

Council of Europe. (2004b). *Explanatory Memorandum to the Draft Recommendation Rec(2004) of the Committee of Ministers to member states on legal, operational and technical standards for e-voting*. Paris: Multidisciplinary Ad Hoc Group of Specialists IP1-S-EE, Council of Europe.

Council of Europe. (2006). Directive 2006/123/EC of the European Parliament and of the Council of 12 december 2006 on services in the internal market.

Coutinho, C., & Bottentuit, J., Jr. (2007). Collaborative Learning Using Wiki: A Pilot Study With Master Students In Educational Technology In Portugal. In C. Montgomerie & J. Seale (Eds.), *Proceedings of World Conference on Educational Multimédia, Hypermedia e Telecommunications (ED-MEDIA)*, Vancouver, CA (pp. 1786 -1791). Retrieved from https://repositorium.sdum.uminho.pt/bitstream/1822/6720/1/Edmedia2007.pdf

Coventry, L. (2005). *Usable Biometrics, Security and usability* (pp. 181–204). London: University College London, Human Centered Systems Group.

Cox, J. F., Pearce, C. L., & Perry, M. L. (2003). Toward a model of shared leadership and distributed influence in the innovation process: How shared leadership can enhance new product development, team dynamics and effectiveness. In Pearce, C. L., & Conger, J. A. (Eds.), *Shared leadership: Reframing the hows and whys of leadership*. Thousand Oaks, CA: Sage.

Cox, M., Abbott, C., Blakeley, B., Beauchamp, T., & Rhodes, V. (2004). *ICT and pedagogy. A review of the research literature*. Coventry, UK: British Education Communication and Technology Association (BECTA). Retrieved August 18, 2010, from http://publications.becta.org.uk/download.cfm?resID=25813

Cramer, R., Gennaro, R., & Shoenmakers, B. (1997). A secure and optimally efficient multi-authority election scheme. In *Advances in Cryptology - Eurocrypt 97* (LNCS, pp. 103-118). Berlin: Springer Verlag.

Cramer, S., Havice, W., & Havice, P. (2002) Attitudes toward computer-mediated online training. *The Journal of Technology Studies.*

Crawford-Lange, L., & Lange, D. (1984). Doing the unthinkable in the second-language classroom: A process for the integration of language and culture. In Higgs, T. (Ed.), *Teaching for proficiency, the organizing principle* (pp. 139–177). Lincolnwood, IL: National Textbook Company.

Crook, C., Cummings, J., Fisher, T., Graber, R., Harrison, C., Lewin, C., et al. (2008). *Web 2.0 technologies for learning: The current landscape – opportunities, challenges and tensions*. Coventry, UK: British Education Communication and Technology Association (BECTA). Retrieved August 18, 2010, from http://partners.becta.org.uk/upload-dir/downloads/page_documents/research/web2_technologies_learning.pdf

Crook, C., & Harrison, C. (2008). *Report 5: Web 2.0 technologies for learning at Key Stage 3 and 4: Summary report* (No. 5). Coventry, UK: British Education Communication and Technology Association (BECTA). Retrieved August 19, 2010, from http://research.becta.org.uk/upload-dir/downloads/page_documents/research/web2_ks34_summary.pdf

Cunningham, W. G., & Corderio, P. A. (2000). *Educational administration: A problem-based aproach*. Boston: Allyn & Bacon.

Damiani, E., De Capitani di Vimercati, S., Fugazza, C., & Samarati, P. (2004). *Extending Policy Languages to the Semantic Web* (LNCS 3140, pp. 330-343).

Davidow, W. H., & Malone, M. S. (1992). *The Virtual Corporation: Structuring and Revitalizing the Corporation for the 21st Century*. New York: Harper Collins Publishers.

Davidrajuh, D. (2003). Realizing a new e-commerce tool for formation of a virtual enterprise. *Industrial Management & Data Systems*, *103*(6), 434–445. doi:10.1108/02635570310480006

Davies, F., Goode, M., Mazanec, J., & Moutinho, L. (1999). LISREL and neural networks modeling: Two comparison studies. *Journal of Retailing and Consumer Services*, *6*(4), 249–261. doi:10.1016/S0969-6989(98)00009-5

Davis, F. (1989). Perceived usefulness, perceived ease of use, and user acceptance of information technology. *Management Information Systems Quarterly*, *13*(3), 319–340. doi:10.2307/249008

Davis, F. D., Bagozzi, R. P., & Warshaw, P. R. (1989). User acceptance of computer technology: A comparison of two theoretical models. *Management Science*, *35*(8), 982–1003. doi:10.1287/mnsc.35.8.982

Davis, G., & Olson, M. (1985). *Management information systems: conceptual foundations, structure and development*. New York: McGraw-Hill.

DE-Mail. (2009). *Richtlinie für Bürgerportale (Version 0.98)*. Bonn, Germany: Bundesamt für Sicherheit in der Informationstechnik.

Deal, W. F. III. (2002). Online Learning: Teaching technology online. *Technology Teacher*, *61*(8), 21–27.

Dearstyne, B. (2001). E-business, e-government and information proficiency. *Information Management Journal, 34*(4).

Delcourt, M., & Kinzie, M. (1993). Computer technologies in teacher education: The measurement of attitudes and self-efficacy. *Journal of Research and Development in Education*, *27*, 35–41.

Delone, W. H., & Mclean, E. R. (1992). Information system success: The quest for the dependent variable. *Information Systems Research*, *3*(1), 61–95. doi:10.1287/isre.3.1.60

Delone, W. H., & Mclean, E. R. (2003). The Delone and Mclean information system success: A ten years update. *Journal of Management Information Systems*, *19*(4), 30–36.

Denis, B. (2003). Quels rôles et quelle formation pour les tuteurs intervenant: dans des dispositifs de formation a distance? *Distances et Savoirs*, *1*(1), 19–46. doi:10.3166/ds.1.19-46

Derry, J. S. (2005). eSteps as a case of theory-based web course design. In A. M. O 'Donnell, C. E. Hmelo-Silver, & G. Erkens (Eds.), *Collaborative learning, reasoning, and technology* (pp. 171-197). New York: Routledge.

Desmedt, Y. (1992). Threshold cryptosystems. In J. Seberry & Y. Zheng (Eds.), *Proceedings of Advances in Cryptology - Auscrypt '92* (LNCS 718, pp. 3-14). Berlin: Springer-Verlag.

Desmedt, Y. (1994). Threshold cryptography. In *European Trans. on Telecommunications* (pp. 449-457).

Desmedt, Y., & Frankel, Y. (1989) Threshold cryptosystems. In G. Brassard (Ed.), *Proceedings of Advances in Cryptology - Crypto '89* (LNCS 435, pp. 307-315). Berlin: Springer Verlag.

Deveci, H. (2002). *Sosyal bilgiler dersinde probleme dayali öğrenmenin öğrencilerin derse ilişkin tutumlarina, akademik başarilarina ve hatirlama düzeylerine etkisi.* Unpublished, doctoral dissertation, Eskişehir University, Eğitim Bilimleri Enstitüsü.

Develotte, C., & Mangenot, F. (2004). Tutorat et communauté dans un campus numérique non collaboratif. *Distances et Savoirs*, *2*(2-3), 1–25. doi:10.3166/ds.2.309-333

Dillenbourg, P., Poirier, C., & Carles, L. (2003). Communautés virtuelles d'apprentissage: E-jargon ou nouveau paradigme? In Senteni, A., & Taurisson, A. (Eds.), *Pédagogies.net: L'essor des communautés virtuelles d'apprentissage* (pp. 11–47). Montréal, Canada: Presses de l'Université du Québec.

Diong, A., & Choo, D. (2008). Transformative innovation for growth. *Industrial Management*. Retrieved May 4, 2009, from http://www.allbusiness.com/company-activities-management/company-structures/11463342-1.html

Doherty, F., & Doig, G. (2003). An analysis of the anticipated cultural impacts of the implementation of data warehouses. *IEEE Transactions on Engineering Management*, *5*(1), 78–88. doi:10.1109/TEM.2002.808302

Dolezalek, H. (2003). Online degree. *Training (New York, N.Y.)*, *40*(5), 26–32.

Dombrowski, C., Kim, J. Y., Desouza, K. C., Brganza, A., Papagari, S., Baloh, P., & Jha, S. (2007). Elements of innovative cultures. *Knowledge and Process Management*, *14*(3), 190–202. doi:10.1002/kpm.279

Drury, D. H. (1998). A hierarchical structural model of information systems success. *Infor*, (3). Retrieved January 15, 2008, from http://findarticles.com/p/articles/mi_qa3661/is_199802

Dubinskas, F. A. (1993). Virtual Organizations: Computer Conferencing and Organizational Design. *Journal of Organizational Computing*, *3*(4), 389–416. doi:10.1080/10919399309540210

Duch, B. J. (1995). *What is problem-based learning?* Retrieved October 1, 2007, from http://www.udel.edu/pbl/cte/jan95-what.html

Duch, B. J., Groh, S. E., & Allen, D. E. (2001). *The power of problem-based learning.* Sterling, VA: Stylus Publishing.

Ducoffe, R. (1995). How Consumers Assess the Value of Advertising. *Journal of Current Issues and Research in Advertising*, *17*(1), 1–18.

E-government Program (Yesser). (2009). *The Ministry of Communications and Information Technology.* Retrieved from http://www.yesser.gov.sa

Eastlake D., & Reagle, J. (2002). *XML Signature Syntax and Processing (W3C Recommendation).*

Educause Center for Applied Research ECAR. (2003). Supporting e-learning in higher education. *Educause Report.* Retrieved April 5, 2007, from http://www.educause.edu.ecarl

Edwards, A. L. (1957). *Techniques of Attitude Scale Construction.* Englewood Cliffs, NJ: Prentice Hall Inc.

Eijkman, H. (2004). The academic divide and curriculum practice in Australian Higher Education: A counternarrative. *New Horizons in Education*, *111*, 14–27.

Eijkman, H. (2008). Web 2.0 as a non-foundational network-centric learning space. *Campus-Wide Information Systems*, *25*(2), 93–104. doi:10.1108/10650740810866567

Eijkman, H., & Herrmann, A. (2009). Confidential report on the implementation of an adaptation of the EDUCAUSE Center for Applied Research Survey (ECAR). In *Proceedings of the UNSW@ADFA, 2008,* Canberra, University of New South Wales.

Eijkman, H., Kayali, O., & Yeomans, S. (2009). Using soft systems thinking to confront the politics of innovation in engineering education. In Patil, A., & Gray, P. (Eds.), *Engineering education quality assurance: A global perspective* (pp. 223–234). New York: Springer. doi:10.1007/978-1-4419-0555-0_18

Ellis, R. A., Jarkey, N., Mahony, M. J., Peat, M., & Sheely, S. (2007). Managing quality improvement of e-learning in a large, campus-based university. *Quality Assurance in Education, 15*(1), 9–23. doi:10.1108/09684880710723007

Erl, T. (2008). *SOA Principles of service design.* Upper Saddle River, NJ: Prentice Hall.

Essex., et al. (2007). The Punchscan Voting System: Vo-Comp Competition Submission. *In Proceedings of the 1st Univ. Voting Systems Competition (VoComp).* Retrieved from http://punchscan.org/vocomp/PunchscanVocompSubmission.pdf

Etnon, R. (2008). The use of the world wide web in learning and teaching in higher education: reality and rhetoric. *Innovations in Education and Teaching International, 45*(1), 15–23. doi:10.1080/14703290701757401

ETSI. (2008). [*Electronic Signatures and Infrastructures][ESI][, Registered Electronic Mail][REM]. ETSI TS, 102,* 640.

European Council. (2000). *Common European Framework of Reference for Languages: Learning, teaching, assessment.* Cambridge, UK: Cambridge University Press.

Euzenat, J., & Shvaiko, P. (2007). *Ontology Matching.* Berlin: Springer-Verlag.

Exley, K., & Dennick, R. (2004). *Small group teaching: tutorials, seminars and beyond* (pp. 76–94). New York: Routledge Group.

Eyitayo, O. T. (2005). Experimenting e-learning with a large class. *International Journal of Education and Development using Information and Communication Technology, 1*(3), 160-171.

Federal Election Commision. (2001). *Voting system Standards, Performance Standards, Introduction.* Retrieved from http://www.fec.gov/agenda/agendas2001/mtgdoc01-62/v1/v1s1.htm

Federal Election Commision. (2001a). *Voting System Standard.* Retrieved from http://www.fec.gov/agenda/agendas2001/mtgdoc01-62/overview.htm

Feldman, S. P. (1988). How organizational culture can affect innovation. *Organizational Dynamics, 17*(1), 57–68. doi:10.1016/0090-2616(88)90030-7

Felt, A., & Evans, D. (2008, May 18-21). Privacy Protection for Social Networking Platforms. In *Proceedings of the Web 2.0 Security and Privacy at the 2008 IEEE Symposium on Security and Privacy,* Oakland, California.

Feng, L. (2003). Implementing E-government Strategy is Scotland: Current Situation and Emerging Issues. *Journal of Electronic Commerce in Organizations, 1*(2), 44–65.

Ferguson, S., Hider, P., & Kelly, T. (2005). *Information systems evaluation and the search for success: lessons for LIS research.* Retrieved July 22, 2008, from http://www.alia.org.au/publishing/alj/54.3/full.text/ferguson.hilder.kelly.html

Ferratt, T., & Hall, S. (2009). Extending the Vision of Online learning to Learning via Virtually Being, There and Beyond. *Communications of AIS, 2009*(25), 425-435.

Ferrer-Gomilla, J., Onieva, J., Payeras, M., & Lopez, M. (2009). *Certified electronic mail: Properties revisited. Computers & Security.* Atlanta, GA: Elsevier.

Fishbein, M., & Ajzen, I. (1975). *Belief attitude intention and behavior: An introduction to theory and research.* Reading, MA: Addison-Wesley.

Fisher, D. H., & McKusick, K. B. (1989). An empirical comparison of ID3 and back propagation. In *Proceedings of the Eleventh International Joint Conference on Artificial Intelligence,* Detroit, MI (pp. 788-793).

Fisher, E. A., & Coleman, K. J. (2005). *The Direct Recording Electronic Voting Machine (DRE) Controversy: FAQs and Misperceptions.* Washington, DC: The Library of Congress.

Fitzgibbon, K. M., & Jones, N. (2004). Jumping the hurdles: Challenges of staff development delivered in a blended learning environment. *Journal of Educational Media, 29*(1), 25–35. doi:10.1080/1358165042000186253

Flaig, S. (1992). Virtual enterprise: Your new model for success. *Electronic Business*, 153-155.

Forte, A., & Bruckman, A. (2007). *Constructing text: Wiki as a toolkit for (collaborative?) learning.* Retrieved February 19, 2009, from http://www.wikisym.org/ws2007/_publish/Forte_WikiSym2007_ConstructingText.pdf

Fraenkel, J., & Wallen, N. (2000). *How to design & evaluate research in education.* New York: McGraw-Hill.

Frees, R. (n.d.). Biometric technology improves identification security. *U.S. Air Force.* Retrieved March 3, 2008 from http://www.af.mil/news/story.asp?id=123084564

Friesen, N. (2003). *Three objections to learning objects and e-learning standards.* Retrieved July 15, 2010, from http://www.learningspaces.org/n/papers/objections.html

Fujioka, A., Okamoto, T., & Ohta, K. (1992). A practical secret voting scheme for large scale elections. In *Advances in Cryptology - Auscrypt 92* (pp. 244-251).

Fullan, M., & Stiegelbauer, S. (1991). *The new meaning of educational change* (2nd ed.). New York: Teachers College Press.

Furstenberg, G., Levet, S., English, K., & Maillet, K. (2001). Giving a virtual voice to the silent language of culture: The cultura project. *Language Learning & Technology, 5*(1), 55–102.

Gable, G. G., Sedera, D., & Chan, T. (2003, December 14-17). Enterprise systems success: A measurement model. In *Proceedings of the twenty-fourth international conference on information systems*, Seattle, WA (pp. 576-591).

Gall, M. D., Gall, J. P., & Borg, W. R. (2002). *Educational Research: An Introduction* (7th ed.). Boston: Allyn and Bacon.

García, R., & Gil, R. (2006, November). An OWL Copyright Ontology for Semantic Digital Rights Management. In Proceedings of the *IFIP WG 2.12 & WG 12.4 International Workshop on Web Semantics*, Montpellier, France.

Garera, S., & Rubin, A. D. (2007). An Independent Audit Framework for Software Dependent Voting Systems. *In Proceedings of the 14th ACM Conf. Computer and Comm. Security (CCS 07)* (pp. 256-265). New York: ACM Press.

Gatian, A. W. (1994). Is user satisfaction a valid measure of system effectiveness? *Information & Management, 26*(3), 119–131. doi:10.1016/0378-7206(94)90036-1

Gellman-Danley, B., & Fetzner, M. J. (1998). Asking the really tough questions: Policy issues for distance learning. *Online Journal of Distance Learning Administration, 1*(1). Retrieved July 15, 2010, from http://www.westga.edu/~distance/danley11.html

General Administrative Process Law. (1991). *AVG – Allgemeines Verwaltungsverfahrensgesetz. Bundesgesetzblatt 1991/51 idF Bundesgesetzblatt 2004/10.* Austria.

Gennai, F., Martusciello, L., & Buzzi, M. (2005). A certified email system for the public administration in Italy. In P. Isaías & M. Nunes (Eds.), *IADIS International Conference WWW/Internet 2005* (Vol. 2, pp. 143-147).

Gérard, F. M. (2003). Les manuels scolaires d'aujourd'hui, de l'enseignement à l'apprentissage. *Option, 4*, 27-28. Retrieved September 3, 2010, from http://www.fmgerard.be/textes/option.html

German, B. S. I. (2007). *Basissatz von Sicherheitsanforderungen an Onlinewahlprodukte (Version 0.18)*. Bonn, Germany: Bundesamt für Sicherheit in der Informationstechnik.

German, K. E. (1988). Attitudes toward computer instruction. *Journal of Computers in Mathematics and Science Teaching, 7*(1-2), 22–28.

Gesellschaft für Informatik e. V. (2005). *GI-Anforderungen an Internetbasierte Vereinswahlen.* Germany.

Ghosh, A. (2004). Learning in strategic alliances: A Vygotskian perspective. *The Learning Organization, 11*(4/5), 302–311. doi:10.1108/09696470410538206

Gibbs, G., & Simpson, C. (2004/05). Conditions under which assessment supports students' learning. *Learning and Teaching in Higher Education, 1*, 3–31.

Gibson, C. (Ed.). (1998). *Online Learners in Higher Education.* Madison, WI: Atwood Publishing.

Gibson, C., & Graff, A. (1992). Impact of adults' preferred learning styles and perception of barriers on completions of external baccalaureate degree programs. *Journal of Online Education, 7*(1), 39–51.

Giesing, I. (2003). *User response to biometric* (pp. 95–135). Pretoria, South Africa: University of Pretoria.

Gilley, K. M., Walters, B. A., & Olson, B. J. (2002). Top management team risk taking propensities and firm performance: Direct and moderating effects. *The Journal of Business Strategy, 19*(2), 95–114.

Goldman, S., Nagel, R., & Preiss, K. (1995). *Agile Competitors and Virtual Organizations*. New York: Van Nostrand Reinhold.

Governatori, G., & Iannella, R. (2009, August 31-September 4). Modelling and Reasoning Languages for Social Networks Policies. In *Proceedings of the Thirteenth IEEE International EDOC Conference*, Auckland, New Zealand.

Grabowski, M., & Roberts, K. H. (1998). Risk mitigation in virtual organizations. *Journal of Computer-Mediated Communication, 3*(4), 49–65.

Grandison, T., & Maximilien, E. M. (2008, May 18-21). Towards Privacy Propagation in the Social Web. In *Proceedings of the Web 2.0 Security and Privacy at the 2008 IEEE Symposium on Security and Privacy*, Oakland, California.

Grant, L. (2006). *Using Wikis in Schools: a Case Study*. Retrieved April 5, 2009, from http://www.futurelab. org.uk/resources/documents/discussion_papers/Wikis_in_Schools.pdf

Green, H., & Hannon, C. (2007). *TheirSpace: Education for a digital generation*. London: Demos. Retrieved August 15, 2010, from http://www.demos.co.uk/files/Their%20 space%20-%20web.pdf?1240939425

Green, K., & Inman, R. (2006). Does implementation of a JIT-with-customers strategy change an organization's structure? *Industrial Management & Data Systems, 106*(8), 1077–1094. doi:10.1108/02635570610710764

Green, S. B. (1991). How many subjects does it take to do a regression analysis? *Multivariate Behavioral Research, 26*, 499–510. doi:10.1207/s15327906mbr2603_7

Greening, T. (1998). Scaffolding for success in problem-based learning. *Medical Education Online, 3*(4). Retrieved October 2, 2007, from http://www.med-ed-online.org/f0000012.htm

Greiner, R., & Metes, G. (1995). *Going Virtual: Moving Your Organization into the 21st Century*. Upper Saddle River, NJ: Prentice Hall.

Gronn, P. (2003). *The new work of educational leaders*. London: Sage Publications.

Grunwald Associates. (2007). *Creating and connecting: Research and guidelines on social and educational networking*. Alexandria, VA: National School Boards Association. Retrieved August 15, 2010, from http://nsba. org/site/docs/41400/41340.pdf

Gubernick, L., & Ebeling, A. (1997). I got my degree through E-mail. *Forbes, 159*, 84–92.

Gülseçen, S., & Kubat, A. (2006). Teaching ICT to Teacher Candidates Using PBL: A Qualitative and Quantitative Evaluation. *Journal of Educational Technology & Society, 9*(2), 96–106.

Gülsüm, A., & Sungur, S. (2007). Effectiveness of Problem-Based Learning on Academic Performance in Genetics. *Biochemistry and Molecular Biology Education, 35*(6), 448–451. doi:10.1002/bmb.97

Gunhan, B. C. (2006). *Ilköğretim II. kademede matematik dersinde probleme dayali öğrenmenin uygulanabilirliği üzerine bir araştirma*. Unpublished doctoral dissertation, Dokuz Eylül University, Eğitim Bilimleri Enstitüsü.

Guri-Rosenblit, S. (2005). Distance education' and 'online learning': Not the same thing. *Higher Education, 49*, 467–493. doi:10.1007/s10734-004-0040-0

Gürsul, F., & Altun, A. (2007). okul öncesi öğretmen adaylarinin karma yöntemle yapilan bilgisayar dersine ilişkin görüsleri. *Uluslar Arası Öğretmen Yetiştirme Politikaları ve Sorunları Sempozyumu* (pp. 12-14). Mayıs, Bakü: Azerbaycan

Guth, S., & Iannella, R. (2009, September 25). *ODRL Version 2.0 Common Vocabulary* (Working Draft). Retrieved from http://odrl.net/2.0/WD-ODRL-Vocab.html

Ha, I., Yoon, Y., & Choi, M. (2007). Determinants of adoption of mobile games under mobile broadband wireless access environment. *Information & Management, 44*(3), 276–286. doi:10.1016/j.im.2007.01.001

Haghirian, P., & Madlberger, M. (2005). Consumer Attitude Toward Advertising Via Mobile Devices - An Empirical Investigation Among Austrian Users. In *Proceedings of the European Conference on Information Systems*, Regensburg, Germany (pp. 44-56).

Hamann, K., Pollock, P. H., III, & Wilson, B. M. (2005). *Active learning through reading and writing in online discussion boards: Assessing the effects on learner outcomes.* Paper presented at the annual meeting of The Midwest Political Science Association, Palmer House Hilton, Chicago, IL.

Hambrick, D. C. (2007). Upper echelon's theory: An update. *Academy of Management Review, 32*(2), 334–343. doi:10.2307/20159303

Hambrick, D. C., & Mason, P. (1984). Upper echelons: The organization as a reflection of its top managers. *Academy of Management Review, 9*, 193–206. doi:10.2307/258434

Hammel, J., Royeen, C. H., Bagatell, N., Chandler, B., Jensen, G., Loveland, R., & Stone, G. (1999). Student perspectives on problem-based learning in an occupational therapy curriculum: a multiyear qualitative evaluation. *The American Journal of Occupational Therapy., 53*, 199–206.

Han, B. M., & Anantatmula, V. S. (2007). Knowledge sharing in large IT organizations: A case study. *VINE: The Journal of Information and Knowledge Management Systems, 37*(4), 421–439.

Hannan, M., & Freeman, J. (1984). Structural inertia and organizational change. *American Sociological Review, 49*(2), 149–164. doi:10.2307/2095567

Hara, N., Bonk, C. J., & Angeli, C. (1998). *Content analysis of online discussion in an applied educational psychology course* (CRLT Tech. Rep., pp. 2-98). Bloomington, IN: Indiana University, Center for Research on Learning and Technology.

Harrison, C., Comber, C., Fisher, T., Haw, K., Lewin, C., Lunzer, E., et al. (2002). *ImpacT2: The Impact of Information and Communication Technologies on Pupil Learning and Attainment* (ICT in Schools Research and Evaluation Series, No. 7). London: DfES/BECTa. Retrieved from http://partners.becta.org.uk/index.php?section=rh&rid=13606

Harvey, D., & Brown, D. R. (1996). *An experiential approach to organizational development.* Upper Saddle River, NJ: Prentice Hall.

Hassan, A. M. A., & Shrigley, R. (1984). Designing a likert scale to measure chemistry attitudes. *School Science and Mathematics, 84*(8), 659–669. doi:10.1111/j.1949-8594.1984.tb09581.x

Hativa, N. (2000). *Teaching for effective learning in higher education.* Dordrecht, The Netherlands: Kluwer.

Hayes, D. N. (2007). ICT and learning: Lessons from Australian classrooms. *Computers & Education, 49*(2), 385–395. doi:10.1016/j.compedu.2005.09.003

He, D., & Lu, Y. (2007). Consumers Perceptions and Acceptances towards Mobile Advertising: An Empirical Study in China. In *Proceedings of the International Conference on Wireless Communications, Networking and Mobile Computing*, Shanghai, China (pp. 3775-3778).

Head, A., & Eisenberg, M. (2009). *Finding Context: What Today's College Students Say about Conducting Research in the Digital Age.* Retrieved from [REMOVED HYPERLINK FIELD]http://www.projectinfolit.org/pdfs/PIL_ProgressReport_2_2009.pdf

Hedberg, B., Dahlgren, G., Hansson, J., & Olve, N. (1997). *Virtual Organizations and Beyond.* New York: Wiley.

Heeks, R. (2000). *Reinventing government in information Age.* London: Routledge Press.

Hiltz, S., & Turoff, M. (2005). EDUCATION GOES DIGITAL: The Evolution of Online learning and the Revolution in Higher Education. *Communications of the ACM, 48*(10), 59–64. doi:10.1145/1089107.1089139

Hirt, M., & Sako, K. (2000). Efficient receipt-free voting based on homomorphic encryption. In *Proceedings of the Eurocrypt 2000.*

Hitch, L. P., & MacBrayne, P. (2003, March/April). A model for effectively supporting e-Learning. *The Technology Source Archives*. Retrieved July 15, 2010, from http://technologysource.org/article/model_for_effectively_supporting_elearning/

Hitt, M. A., Hoskisson, R. E., & Harrison, J. S. (1991). Strategic competitiveness in the 1990s: Challenges and opportunities for U.S. executives. *The Academy of Management Executive, 5*(2), 7–24.

Hoffman, D. W. (2002). Internet-Based online learning in higher education. *Tech Directions, 62*(1), 28–33.

Hoffman, M. E., & Vance, D. R. (2005). Computer literacy: What students know and from whom they learned it. *ACM SIGCSE Bulletin, 37*(1), 356–360. doi:10.1145/1047124.1047467

Hofstede, G. (2001). *Culture's consequences: Comparing values, behaviors, institutions, and organizations across nations* (2nd ed.). Thousand Oaks, CA: Sage.

Holec, H. (1990). Qu'est-ce qu'apprendre à apprendre? *Mélanges pédagogiques*, 82-83.

Hollosi, A., & Hörbe, R. (2006). Bildung von Stammzahl und bereichsspezifischem Personenkennzeichen (SZ-bPK-Algo -1.1.1). *Platform Digital Austria, AG Bürgerkarte*. Retrieved May 12, 2007 from http://www.ref.gv.at

Hollosi, A., Karlinger, G., Rössler, T., & Centner, M. (2008). *The Austrian Citizen Card (Specification), Specification of the Austrian Citizen Card version 1.2*. Retrieved November 20, 2009 from http://www.buergerkarte.at/konzept/securitylayer/spezifikation/aktuell/

Hollosi, A., Leitold, H., & Rössler, T. (2007). *Object Identifier der öffentlichen Verwaltung*. Austria.

Hu, Y. J. (2007). Semantic-Driven Enforcement of Rights Delegation Policies via the Combination of Rules and Ontologies. In *Proceedings of the Workshop on Privacy Enforcement and Accountability with Semantics, International Semantic Web Conference*, Busan, Korea.

Huang, J. (2010). Remote health monitoring adoption model based on artificial neural networks. *Expert Systems with Applications, 37*, 307–314. doi:10.1016/j.eswa.2009.05.063

Huang, J. C., Newell, S., Galliers, R., & Pan, S. L. (2003). Dangerous liaisons? Component based development and organizational subcultures. *IEEE Transactions on Engineering Management, 50*(2), 89–99. doi:10.1109/TEM.2002.808297

Huber, G. (2001). Transfer of knowledge in knowledge management systems: Unexplored issues and suggested studies. *European Journal of Information Systems, 10*(2), 72–79. doi:10.1057/palgrave.ejis.3000399

Hussein, R., Abdu-Karim, N. S., Mohamed, N., & Ahlan, A. R. (2007). The influence of organizational factors on information system success in e-government agencies in Malaysia. *Electronic Journal of Information Systems in Developing Countries, 29*(1), 1–17.

Hwang, B., & Liu, Y. (1994). A study of proportional reasoning and self-regulation instruction on students' conceptual change in conceptions of solution.

Hyland, P., Davison, G., & Sloan, T. (2003). Linking team competences to organizational capacity. *Team Performance Management, 9*(5/6), 97–106. doi:10.1108/13527590310493873

Iannella, R. (2002, September 19). *Open Digital Rights Language* (Version 1.1 Specification). Retrieved from http://odrl.net/1.1/ODRL-11.pdf> and <http://www.w3.org/TR/odrl/

Iannella, R. (2009, January 15-16). Industry Challenges for Social and Professional Networks. In *Proceedings of the W3C Workshop on the Future of Social Networking*, Barcelona, Spain. Retrieved from http://www.w3.org/2008/09/msnws/papers/nicta-position-paper.pdf

Iannella, R., Henricksen, K., & Robinson, R. (2006, October 17-18). A Policy Oriented Architecture for the Web: New Infrastructure and New Opportunities. In *Proceedings of the W3C Workshop on Languages for Privacy Policy Negotiation and Semantics-Driven Enforcement*, Ispra, Italy.

Igbaria, M., Guimaraes, T., & Davis, G. B. (1995). Testing the determinants of microcomputer usage via a structural equation model. *Journal of Management Information Systems, 11*(4), 87–14.

Iivari, J., & Huisman, M. (2007). The relationship between organizational culture and the deployment of systems development methodologies. *Management Information Systems Quarterly, 31*(1), 35–58.

Iseli, N., Joly, C., & Lam, P. (2009). Use of language beyond the classroom: The outcomes, challenges and success of an e-based cross-cultural project in French class. In F. Salajan (Ed.), *Proceedings of the 4th International Conference on e-Learning* (pp. 214-221). Reading, MA: Academic Publishing Limited.

ISO/IEC. (1989). ISO/IEC 7498-2:1989. *Information processing systems – Open systems interconnection – Basic Reference Model – Part 2: Security Architecture.*

ISO/IEC. (1996). ISO/IEC 10181:1996. *Information technology – Open systems interconnection – Security framework in open systems.*

ISO/IEC. (1998). ISO/IEC 2788:1998. *Information technology – Security techniques – Non-repudiation.*

Israel, G. D. (2003). *Determining sample size*. Retrieved February 10, 2007, from http://edis.ifas.edu

Ivkovic, M., Leitold, H., & Rössler, T. (2009). Interoperable elektronische Identität in Europa. In *7. Information Security Konferenz (Krems)* (pp. 175-190).

Jaccard, J. (2001). *Interaction effects in logistic regression*. Thousand Oaks, CA: Sage Publications.

Jarvenpaa, S. L., & Leidner, D. E. (1998). Communication and trust in global teams. *Journal of Computer-Mediated Communication, 3*(4), 18–37.

Jaskyte, K., & Dressler, W. W. (2005). Organizational culture and innovation in nonprofit human services organizations. *Administration in Social Work, 29*(2), 23–43. doi:10.1300/J147v29n02_03

Jassawalla, A. R., & Sashittal, H. C. (2002). Cultures that support product-innovation Processes. *The Academy of Management Executive, 16*(3), 42–56.

Jefferies, P., Carsten-Stahl, B., & McRobb, S. (2007). Exploring the relationships between pedagogy, ethics and technology: Building a framework for strategy development. *Technology, Pedagogy and Education, 16*(1), 111–126. doi:10.1080/14759390601168122

Jefferson, D., Rubin, A. D., Simons, B., & Wagner, D. (2004). *A security analysis of the secure electronic registration and voting experiment*. Serve.

Jensen, C., Tullio, J., Potts, C., & Mynatt, E. D. (2005). *STRAP: A Structured Analysis Framework for Privacy* (Tech. Rep. No. GIT-GVU-05-02). Atlanta, GA: Georgia Institute of Technology.

Jeyaraj, A., Rottman, J. W., & Lacity, M. C. (2006). A review of the predictors, linkages, and biases in IT innovation adoption research. [Palgrave Macmillan]. *Journal of Information Technology, 21*(1), 1–23. doi:10.1057/palgrave.jit.2000056

Johnson, J. R. (2002). Leading the learning organization: Portrait of four leaders. *Leadership and Organization Development Journal, 23*(5), 241–249. doi:10.1108/01437730210435956

Joly, C. (2009). *Réforme du système éducatif de 2012 à Hong Kong: Enjeux, Evaluation et Propositions de transformation pour le Programme de Français du Département de Linguistique et des Langues Vivantes de l'Université Chinoise de Hong Kong*. Unpublished master's thesis, Université Stendhal 3, Grenoble, France.

Joly, C., Iseli, I., & Lam, P. (2009). Developing intercultural awareness of Chinese students in online asynchronous discussions and blogs within a French culture course. In F. Salajan (Ed.), *Proceedings of the 4th International Conference on e-Learning* (pp. 228-235). Reading, MA: Academic Publishing Limited.

Jones, A. J. (2003). ICT and future teachers: Are we preparing for e-learning? In *Proceedings of the 3.1 and 3.3 Working Groups Conference on International Federation for Information Processing: ICT and the Teacher of the Future* (Vol. 23, pp. 67-69). Retrieved July 15, 2010, from http://crpit.com/confpapers/CRPITV23Jones.pdf

Jones, J., & McNaught, C. (2005). Using learning object evaluation: Challenges and lessons learned in the Hong Kong context. In Richards, G., & Kommers, P. (Eds.), *ED-MEDIA 2005* (pp. 3580–3585).

Jordan, S., Brockbank, B., & Butcher, P. (2007). *Extending the pedagogic role of online interactive assessment: Providing feedback on short free-text responses.* Paper presented at the REAP international online conference on assessment design for learner responsibility. Retrieved September 6, 2010, from http://www.reap.ac.uk/reap07/Portals/2/CSL/feast%20of%20case%20studies/Extending_the_pedagogic_role_of_online_interactive_assessment.pdf

Juang, W.-S., & Lei, C.-L. (1996). A collision free secret ballot protocol for computerized general elections. *Computers & Security, 15*(4), 339–348. doi:10.1016/0167-4048(96)00011-9

Kagal, L., Finin, T., & Joshi, A. (2003, October 20-23). A Policy Based Approach to Security for the Semantic Web. In *Proceedings of 2nd International Semantic Web Conference (ISWC2003)*, Sanibel Island, Florida.

Kaiser, M. (2007, November). Toward the Realization of Policy-Oriented Enterprise Management. *IEEE Computer*, 57-63.

Kaplan, B., & Duchon, D. (1988). Combining Qualitative and Quantitative Methods information system research; a case study. *Management Information Systems Quarterly, 12*(4), 571–586. doi:10.2307/249133

Kaplan, B., & Maxwell, J. A. (2005). *Evaluating the organizational impact of healthcare information system* (2nd ed.). New York: Springer.

Katwibun, D. (2004). *Middle school students' mathematical dispositions in a problem-based classroom.* Unpublished doctoral dissertation, Oregon State University, OR.

Keing, C., Lo, J., Lam, P., & McNaught, C. (2007). Summative eAssessments: Piloting acceptability, practicality and effectiveness. In C. Montgomerie & J. Seale (Eds.), *Proceedings of the 19th annual World Conference on Educational Multimedia, Hypermedia & Telecommunications (ED-MEDIA 2007)*, Vancouver, Canada (pp. 486-495). Chesapeake, VA: Association for the Advancement of Computers in Education.

Kekkonen-Moneta, S., & Moneta, G. B. (2002). E-learning in Hong Kong: comparing learning outcomes in online multimedia and lecture versions of an introductory computing course. *British Journal of Educational Technology, 33*(4), 423–433. doi:10.1111/1467-8535.00279

Kember, D., Ma, R., McNaught, C., & 18 exemplary teachers (2006). *Excellent university teaching.* Hong Kong, China: Chinese University Press.

Kember, D., McNaught, C., Chong, F. C. Y., Paul Lam, P., & Cheng, K. F. (2010). Understanding the ways in which design features of educational websites impact upon student learning outcomes in blended learning environments. *Computers & Education, 55*, 1183–1192. doi:10.1016/j.compedu.2010.05.015

Kennedy, G. E., Judd, T. S., Churchward, A., Gray, K., & Krause, K. (2008). First year students' experiences with technology: Are they really digital natives? *Australasian Journal of Educational Technology, 24*(1), 108–122.

Kennedy, S. J. (2007). Learning and transfer compared in two teaching methods: online problem-based learning and the traditional lecture method. Unpublished doctoral dissertation, Capella University, MN.

Kerrey, B., & Isakson, J. (2000). The power of the Internet for learning: Moving from promise to practice. *Report of the Web-based education commission to the president and the congress of the United States.* Retrieved July 22, 2008, from http://www.ed.gov/offices/AC/EBEC/FinalReport/WBECReport.pdf

Kessler, G. (2009). Student initiated attention to form in autonomous wiki based collaborative writing. *Language Learning & Technology, 13*(1), 79–94. http://llt.msu.edu/vol13num1/kessler.pdf

Kim, A. J. (2000). *Community building on the web.* Berkeley, CA: Peachpit Press.

Kim, D. H. (1993). The link between individual and organizational learning. *Sloan Management Review, 35*(1), 37–50.

Kim, S., & Ju, B. (2008). An analysis of faculty perceptions: Attitudes toward knowledge sharing and collaboration in an academic institution. *Library & Information Science Research, 30*(4), 282–290. doi:10.1016/j.lisr.2008.04.003

Kimber, D. (1994). *Collaborative learning in management education: Issues, benefits, problems and solutions: A literature review.* Paper presented in Australian and New Zealand Academy of Management (ANZAM) conference, New Zealand.

Kinginger, C., Gouvès-Hayward, A., & Simpson, V. (1999). A tele-collaborative course on French-American intercultural communication. *French Review*, *72*(5), 853–866.

Kinzie, M., Delcourt, M., & Powers, S. (1994). Computer Technologies: Attitudes and self-efficacy across undergraduate disciplines. *Research in Higher Education*, *35*(6), 745–767. doi:10.1007/BF02497085

Kirkwood, A., & Price, L. (2005). Learners and learning in the twenty-first century: What do we know about students' attitudes towards and experiences of information and communication technologies that will help us design courses? *Studies in Higher Education*, *30*(3), 257–274. doi:10.1080/03075070500095689

Kitchell, S. (1995). Corporate culture, environmental adaptation, and innovative adoption: A qualitative/quantitative approach. *Journal of the Academy of Marketing Science*, *23*(3), 195–205. doi:10.1177/0092070395233004

Klueber, R., Alt, R., & Oesterle, H. (1999). Emerging electronic services for virtual organizations - concepts and framework. In P. Sieber & J. Griese (Eds.), *Workshop on Organizational Virtualness and Electronic Commerce* (pp. 183-204). Zurich, Switzerland: Simowa.

Koch, M., & Parisi-Presicce, F. (2006). UML specification of access control policies and their formal verification. *Software and Systems Modeling*, *5*(4), 429–447. doi:10.1007/s10270-006-0030-z

Kohno, T., Stubblefield, A., Rubin, A. D., & Wallach, D. S. (2007). *Analysis of an Electronic Voting System, 2004.* Retrieved from http://avirubin.com/vote.pdf. 21.01.2007

Kolari, P., Ding, L., Shashidhara, G., Joshi, A., Finin, T., & Kagal, L. (2005, June 6-8). Enhancing Web privacy protection through declarative policies. In *Proceedings of the Sixth IEEE International Workshop on Policies for Distributed Systems and Networks* (pp. 57- 66).

Kolari, P., Finin, T., Yesha, Y., Lyons, K., Hawkins, J., & Perelgut, S. (2006). Policy Management of Enterprise Systems: A Requirements Study. In *Proceedings of the Seventh IEEE International Workshop on Policies for Distributed Systems and Networks.*

Kong, S., Ogata, H., Arnseth, H., Chan, C., Hirashima, T., Klett, F., et al. (Eds.). (2009). Factors Influencing Knowledge Sharing Among University Students. In *Proceedings of the 17th International Conference on Computers in Education* (CDROM), Hong Kong, China.

Kotorov, R. P. (2000). Virtual Organization: Conceptual Analysis of the Limits of its Decentralization. *Journal of Modern Business.* Retrieved from http://www.dcpress.com/jmb/jmb.htm

Kramsh, C. (1993). *Context and culture in language teaching.* New York: Oxford University Press.

Kruger, K. (2000). Using Information Technology to Create Communities of Learners. *New Directions for Higher Education*, *109*, 59–70. doi:10.1002/he.10907

Kung, S. (2002). Factors that affect students' decision to take online learning courses: A survey study of technical college students in Taiwan. *Educational Media International*, *39*(3-4), 299–305.

Lam, P., Csete, J., & Hodgson, P. (2007). Enrichment of interaction in online assessments. In Frankland, S. (Ed.), *Enhancing teaching and learning through assessment* (pp. 392–401). New York: Springer.

Lam, P., Keing, C., McNaught, C., & Cheng, K. F. (2006). Monitoring eLearning environments through analyzing web logs of institution-wide eLearning platforms. In L. Markauskaite, P. Goodyear, & P. Reimann (Eds.), *Proceedings of the Who's learning? Whose technology? 23rd annual Australian Society for Computers in Learning in Tertiary Education 2006 conference*, University of Sydney (pp. 429-440). Retrieved July 15, 2010, from http://www.ascilite.org.au/conferences/sydney06/proceeding/pdf_papers/p62.pdf

Lam, P., & McNaught, C. (2005). Management of an eLearning evaluation project: e3Learning. In G. Richards & P. Kommers (Eds.), *Proceedings of the 17th annual World Conference on Educational Multimedia, Hypermedia & Telecommunications (ED-MEDIA 2005)* Montreal, Canada. Norfolk, VA: Association for the Advancement of Computers in Education.

Lam, S. L., Lam, P., Joly, C., & Iseli, N. (2009, July). *Study of the effect of providing online dictation exercise on students' dictation mark*. Paper presented at the 2009 International Conference on ICT in Teaching and Learning, Hong Kong.

Lamparter, S., Ankolekar, A., Studer, R., Oberle, D., & Weinhardt, C. (2006, August 14-16). A policy framework for trading configurable goods and services in open electronic markets. In *Proceedings of the 8th International Conference on Electronic Commerce, Fredericton*, New Brunswick, Canada.

Lane, P. J., Koka, B., & Pathak, S. (2002). A thematic analysis and critical assessment of absorptive capacity research. In *Proceedings of the Academy of Management, BPS: M1, Academy of Management*.

Larose, F., & Peraya, D. (2001). Fondements épistémologiques et spécificité pédagogique du recours aux environnements virtuels en enseignement: Médiation ou médiatisation? In *Les TIC ... au coeur des pédagogies universitaires* (pp. 31–68). Québec, Canada: Presses de l'Université du Québec.

Laurillard, D. (1994). Multimedia and the changing experience of the learner. In M. Ryan (Ed.), *Proceedings of the Asia Pacific Information Technology in Training and Education Conference (APITITE94)* (Vol. 1, pp. 19-24). Brisbane, Australia: APITITE.

Leach, J. (2007). The rise of service-oriented IT and the birth of infrastructure as a service. *CIO Research & Analysis*. Retrieved April 7, 2007, from http://www.cio.com/article/101100/The_Rise_of_Service_Oriented_IT

Lederer, A. L., Maupin, D. J., Sens, M. P., & Zhuang, Y. (2000). The technology acceptance model and the World Wide Web. *Decision Support Systems, 29*, 269–282. doi:10.1016/S0167-9236(00)00076-2

Lee, A. S. (1991). Integrating Positivist and Interpretive Approaches to Organizational Research. *Organization Science*, (2): 342–365. doi:10.1287/orsc.2.4.342

Leem, J., & Lim, B. (2007). The current status of e-learning and strategies to enhance educational competitiveness in Korean Higher education. *International Review of Research in Open and Distance Learning, 8*(1), 1–18.

Lei-da, C. (2008). A model of consumer acceptance of mobile payment. *Int. J. Mobile Communications, 6*(1).

Leidner, D. E., & Kayworth, T. (2006). Review: A review of culture in information systems research: toward a theory of information technology conflict. *Management Information Systems Quarterly, 30*(2), 357–399.

Leitold, H., Hollosi, A., & Posch, R. (2002). Security architecture of the Austrian citizen card concept. In *Proccedings of ACSAC '2002, Las Vegas, 9-13 December 2002* (pp. 391-400). Washington, DC: IEEE Computer Society.

Leuf, B., & Cunningham, W. (2001). *The wiki way: Quick collaboration of the web*. Boston: Addison-Wesley.

Levina, N. (2001). Sharing Knowledge in Heterogenous Environments. *Reflections: The SoL Journal, 2*(2), 32–42. doi:10.1162/15241730051091993

Lewin, K. (1952). Group decision and social change. In Swanson, G. E., Newcomb, T. M., & Hartley, F. E. (Eds.), *Readings in social psychology* (pp. 459–473). New York: Holt.

Li, X. (2007). Intelligent Agent–Supported Online Education. *Decision Sciences Journal of Innovative Education, 5*, 311–331. doi:10.1111/j.1540-4609.2007.00143.x

Liang, H., Sharaf, N., Hu, Q., & Xue, Y. (2007). Assimilation of enterprise systems: The effect of institutional pressures and the mediating role of top management. *Management Information Systems Quarterly, 31*(1), 59–87.

Lincoln, Y. S., & Guba, E. G. (1985). *Naturalistic Inquiry*. Thousand Oaks, CA: Sage.

Ling, Y., Simsek, Z., Lubatkin, M. H., & Veiga, J. F. (2008). Transformational leadership's role in promoting corporate entrepreneurship: Examining the CEO-TMT interface. *Academy of Management Journal, 51*(3), 557–576. doi:10.2307/20159526

Lipnack, J., & Stamps, J. (1997). *Virtual Teams: Reaching Across Space, Time, and Organizations with Technology*. New York: John Wiley & Sons.

Liu, N. F., & Littlewood, W. (1997). Why do many students appear reluctant to participate in classroom learning discourse? *System, 25*(3), 371–384. doi:10.1016/S0346-251X(97)00029-8

Ljoså, E. (1998). *The Role of University Teachers in a Digital Era.* Retrieved from http://www.lnks.no/eurodl/shoen/eden98/Ljosa.html

Lopez-Ortiz, B. I. (n.d.). *Online collaborative problem-based learning: Design, facilitation, student work strategies and supporting technologies.* EdD dissertation, Teachers College, Columbia University, NY.

Love, S., & Kewley, J. (2005). Does Personality Affect Peoples' Attitude Towards Mobile Phone Use in Public Places? In Ling, R., & Pederson, P. E. (Eds.), *Mobile Communications* (pp. 273–284). London: Springer. doi:10.1007/1-84628-248-9_18

Lowe, N. J., & Kaplan, R. (2007, September 5-7). Reflections on the changing use of Web-CT in a business communication course. In *Proceedings of the 9th Annual Conference on World Wide Web Applications*, Johannesburg, South Africa. Retrieved from http://www.zaw3.co.za

Loyd, B., & Loyd, D. (1985). The reliability and validity of an instrument for the assessment of computer attitudes. *Educational and Psychological Measurement, 45,* 903–908. doi:10.1177/0013164485454021

Lu, L., Leung, K., & Koch, P. T. (2006). Managerial knowledge sharing: The role of individual, interpersonal, and organizational factors. *Management and Organization Review, 2*(1), 15–41. doi:10.1111/j.1740-8784.2006.00029.x

Luck, P., & Norton, B. (2004). Problem-based management learning-better online? *The European Journal of Open and Distance Learning (EURODL).* Retrieved October 5, 2007, from http://www.eurodl.org/materials/contrib/2004/Luck_Norton.htm

Luckin, R., Logan, K., Clark, W., Graber, R., Oliver, M., & Mee, A. (2008). *Learners' use of Web 2.0 technologies in and out of school in Key Stages 3 and 4.* Coventry, UK: British Education Communication and Technology Association (BECTA). Retrieved February 27, 2010, from http://partners.becta.org.uk/upload-dir/downloads/page_documents/research/web2_technologies_ks3_4.pdf

Lundvall, B.-A., & Nielsen, P. (2007). Knowledge management and innovation performance. *International Journal of Manpower, 28*(3/4), 207–223. doi:10.1108/01437720710755218

Ma, Q., & Liu, L. (2004). The technology acceptance model: a meta-analysis of empirical findings. *Journal of Organizational and End User Computing, 16*(1), 59–74.

MacFarlane, A. (2007).Online communities of learning: Lessons from the worlds of games and play. In *Proceedings of the Building Learning Communities 2007 Conference.* Retrieved August 18, 2010, from http://novemberlearning.com/professor-angela-mcfarlane-blc07-keynote/

MacKenzie, S., & Lutz, R. (1998). An Empirical Examination of the Structural Antecedents of Attitude Toward the Ad in an Advertising Pretesting Context. *Journal of Marketing, 53*(1), 48–65.

Mägi, T. (2007). *Practical Security Analysis of E-voting Systems.* Master thesis, Tallinn University of Technology, Tallinn, Estonia.

Malopinsky, L., Kirkley, J., Stein, R., & Duffy, T. (2000, October 25-28). An instructional design model for online problem based learning (pbl) environments: The learning to teach with technology studio. In *Proceedings of the selected research and development papers at the 23rd National Convention of the Association for Educational Communications and Technology,* Denver, CO (Vol. 1-2).

Mangenot, F. (2000). *L'intégration des TICE dans une perspective systémique, Les Langues Modernes. Les nouveaux dispositifs d'apprentissage.* Paris: Association des Professeurs de Langues Vivantes.

Mangenot, F., & Louveau, E. (2006). *Internet et la classe de langue. Techniques et Pratiques de classe.* Paris: CLE international.

Martineau, J. (2004). Laying the groundwork: First steps in evaluating leadership development. *Leadership in Action, 23*(6), 3–8. doi:10.1002/lia.1044

Mason, L. (1998). Sharing cognition to construct scientific knowledge in school context: The role of oral and written discourse. *Instructional Science, 26,* 359–389. doi:10.1023/A:1003103213786

Mathieson, K. (1991). Predicting user intention: Comparing the technology acceptance model with the theory of planned behavior. *Information Systems Research, 2,* 173–191. doi:10.1287/isre.2.3.173

Maushak, N. J., & Ellis, K. A. (2003). Attitudes of graduate students toward mixed-medium online education. *The Quarterly Review of online. Education, 4*(2), 129–141.

Maxwell, J. A. (2005). *Qualitative Research Design: An Interactive Approach* (2nd ed.). Thousand Oaks, CA: Sage Publication.

Mayer, C. L. (2004). *An analysis of the dimensions of a Web-delivered problem-based learning environment.* Unpublished doctoral dissertation, University of Missouri, Columbia, MO.

McAfee, A., & Brynjolfsson, E. (2008). Investing in the IT that makes a competitive Difference. *Harvard Business Review, 86*(7/8), 98–107.

McDonough, E. F. III, Kahn, K. B., & Barczak, G. (2001). An investigation of the use of global, virtual, and collocated new product development teams. *Journal of Product Innovation Management, 18*(2), 110–120. doi:10.1016/S0737-6782(00)00073-4

McLean, L. D. (2005). Organizational culture's influence on creativity and innovation: a review of the literature and implications for human resource development. *Advances in Developing Human Resources, 7*(2), 226–246. doi:10.1177/1523422305274528

McLinden, M., McCall, S., Hinton, D., & Weston, A. (2006). Participation in online problem-based learning: insights from postgraduate teachers studying through open and distance education. *Distance Education, 27*(3), 331–353. doi:10.1080/01587910600940422

McLindin, B. (2005). *Improving the Performance of Two Dimensional Facial Recognition Systems.* South Australia, Australia: University of South Australia.

McLoughlin, C., & Lee, M. J. W. (2007). Social software and participatory learning: Pedagogical choices with technology affordances in the Web 2.0 era. In *Proceedings of the Providing choices for learners and learning,* Singapore. Retrieved August 18, 2010, from http://www.ascilite.org.au/conferences/singapore07/procs/mcloughlin.pdf

McLuhan, M. (1964). *Understanding Media.* New York: McGraw-Hill Book Company.

McMurray, A., Pace, R., & Scott, D. (2004). *Research: a commonsense approach.* Melbourne, Australia: Thomson Social Science Press.

McNaught, C., & Lam, P. (2009). Institutional strategies for embedding blended learning in a research-intensive university. In *Proceedings of the Elearn2009 Conference, Bridging the development gap through innovative eLearning environments,* The University of the West Indies, St Augustine, Trinidad and Tobago.

McNaught, C., Lam, P., Cheng, K.-F., Kennedy, D. M., & Mohan, J. B. (2009). Challenges in employing complex eLearning strategies in campus-based universities. *International Journal of Technology Enhanced Learning, 1*(4), 266–285. doi:10.1504/IJTEL.2009.030778

McNaught, C., Lam, P., Keing, C., & Cheng, K. F. (2006). Improving eLearning support and infrastructure: An evidence-based approach. In O'Donoghue, J. (Ed.), *Technology supported learning and teaching: A staff perspective* (pp. 70–89). Hershey, PA: Information Science Publishing.

McNeal, R., Tolbert, C., Mossberger, K., & Dotterweich, L. (2003). Innovating in digital government in the American states. *Social Science Quarterly, 84*(1), 52–70. doi:10.1111/1540-6237.00140

Media Watch, A. B. C. (2007). Filleting Facebook. *Australian Broadcasting Corporation (ABC).* Retrieved October 29, 2007 from http://www.abc.net.au/mediawatch/transcripts/s2074079.htm

Meishar-Tal, H., & Tal-Elhasid, E. (2008). measuring collaboration in educational wikis: a methodological discussion. In *Proceedings of the 6th Meytal conference,* Haifa, Israel.

Meissonier, R., Houzé, E., Benbya, H., & Belbaly, N. (2006). Performance Factors of A "Full Online Learning": The Case of Undergraduate Students in Academic Exchange. *Communications of AIS, 2006*(18), 2-33.

Merisavo, M., Kajalo, S., Karjaluoto, H., Virtanen, V., Salmenkivi, S., & Raulas, M. (2007). An empirical study of the drivers of consumer acceptance of mobile advertising. *Journal of Interactive Advertising, 7*(2), 41–50.

Merisotis, J. P., & Phipps, R. A. (1999). What's the Difference? Outcomes of online vs. traditional classroom-based learning. *Change, 31*(3), 12–18. doi:10.1080/00091389909602685

Merrifield, R., Calhoun, J., & Stevens, D. (2008, June). The next revolution in Productivity. *Harvard Business Review*, 73–80.

Milburn, R. (2009). IT's take on Web 2.0. *Enterprise Innovation, 4*(6), 31.

Mills, J., & Glover, C. (2006). *Who provides the feedback – Self and peer assessment*? Retrieved September 6, 2010, from http://www.open.ac.uk/fast/pdfs/Mills%20 and%20Glover.pdf

Mills, J., Glover, C., & Stevens, V. (2006). Using assessment within course structures to drive student engagement with the learning process. In *Proceedings of the 2005 13th International Symposium Improving Students Learning: Improving Student Learning Through Assessment, Refocusing feedback*. Oxford, UK: Alden Press.

Minbaeva, D., Pedersen, T., Bjorkman, I., Fey, C. F., & Park, H. J. (2002). MNC knowledge transfer, subsidiary absorptive capacity and HRM. In *Proceedings of the Academy of Management*.

Moody, K. W. (2003). New meaning to IT alignment. *Information Systems Management, 20*(3), 30–35. doi:10 .1201/1078/43647.20.4.20030901/77290.5

Moore, M. (1989). Three types of interaction. *The American Journal of Online Education, 3*(2), 1–6.

Moore, M. G., & Thompson, M. M. (1997). *The effects of online learning*. University Park, PA: American Center for the Study of Distance Education, Pennsylvania State University.

Morgan, G. (2003). Faculty use of course management systems. *Educause Research Study, 2*, 45–46.

Morris, M. G., & Dillon, A. (1997). How user perceptions influence software use, decision support systems. *IEEE Software*, 58–65. doi:10.1109/52.595956

Mowshowitz, A. (1986). *Social dimensions of office automation*. In Myovitz (Ed.), *Advances in computers* (pp. 335-404).

Mowshowitz, A. (1994). Virtual Organization: A Vision of Management in the Information Age. *The Information Society, 10*, 267–288. doi:10.1080/01972243.1994.9960172

Mumford, A. (1991). Individual and organizational learning. *Industrial and Commercial Training, 23*(6), 24–31. doi:10.1108/EUM0000000001581

Mumtaz, S. (2000). Factors affecting teachers' use of information and communications technology: a review of the literature. *Journal of Information Technology for Teacher Education, 9*(3), 319–342.

Murray, K. B. (1991). A Test of Service Marketing Theory: Consumer Information Acquisition Activities. *Journal of Marketing, 55*, 10–25. doi:10.2307/1252200

Mysliwiec, T. (2008). Telling, Doing, Making Mistakes, and Learning. *The Teaching Professor*. Retrieved from http://www.facultyfocus.com/articles/effective-teaching-strategies/telling-doing-making-mistakes-and-learning

Nahm, A. Y., Vonderembse, M. A., & Koufteros, X. A. (2004). Impact of organizational culture on time-based manufacturing and performance. *Decision Sciences, 35*(4), 579–607. doi:10.1111/j.1540-5915.2004.02660.x

Naylor, J. C., Prichard, R. D., & Ilgen, D. R. (1980). *A theory of behaviour in organizations*. London: Academic Press.

Nelson, M. M., & Illingworth, W. T. (1994). *Practical guide to neural nets*. Reading, MA: Addison Wesley.

Newkirk, H. E., & Lederer, A. L. (2007). The effectiveness of SISP for technical resources, personnel resources, and data security in environments of heterogeneity and hostility. *Journal of Computer Information Systems*, 34–44.

Ng, K., & Lippmann, R. P. (1990). A comparative study of the practical characteristics of neural networks and conventional pattern classifiers. In *Proceedings of the advances in Neural Information Processing Systems*, Denver, CO (Vol. 3, pp. 970-976). San Francisco, CA: Morgan Kaufman.

Nicol, D. J., & Macfarlane-Dick, D. (2006). Formative assessment and self-regulated learning: A model and seven principles of good feedback practice. *Studies in Higher Education, 31*(2), 199–216. doi:10.1080/03075070600572090

Nicol, D. J., & Milligan, C. (2006). Rethinking technology-supported assessment in terms of the seven principles of good feedback practice. In Bryan, C., & Clegg, K. (Eds.), *Innovative assessment in higher education*. London: Routledge.

Niederhauser, D., & Stoddart, T. (2001). Teacher's instructional perspectives and use of educational software. *Teaching and Teacher Education, 17*, 15–31. doi:10.1016/S0742-051X(00)00036-6

Nonaka, I., & Takeuchi, H. (1995). *The Knowledge-creating company: How Japanese companies create the dynamics of innovation*. New York: Oxford University Press.

Nonaka, I., Toyama, R., & Konno, N. (2000). SECI, Ba and leadership: A unified model of dynamic knowledge creation long range planning. *Long Range Planning, 33*(1), 5–34. doi:10.1016/S0024-6301(99)00115-6

Nor, L. M. N., Mardziah, H., Halilah, H., & Ariffin, S. (2004). *Community acceptance of knowledge sharing system in the travel and tourism websites: an Application of an extension of TAM.*

Northrup, P. T. (2002). Online learners' preferences for interaction. *The Quarterly Review of online. Education, 3*(2), 219–226.

Nussbaum, J., & Novick, S. (1982). Alternative frameworks, conceptual conflict and accommodation: Toward a principled teaching strategy. *Instructional Science, 11*, 183–200. doi:10.1007/BF00414279

Nysveen, H., Pedersen, P., & Thorbjørnsen, H. (2005). Intentions to use Mobile Services: Antecedents and Cross-Service Comparisons. *Journal of the Academy of Marketing Science, 33*(3), 330–346. doi:10.1177/0092070305276149

O'Connor, M. C. (1998). Can we trace the efficacy of social constructivism? *Review of Educational Research, 23*, 25–71.

OASIS. (2005, February 1). *eXtensible Access Control Markup Language (XACML)* (Version 2.0, OASIS Standard). Retrieved from http://docs.oasis-open.org/xacml/2.0/XACML-2.0-OS-NORMATIVE.zip

Oh, W., & Pinsonneault, A. (2007). On the assessment of the strategic value of Information technologies: Conceptual and analytical approaches. *Management Information Systems Quarterly, 31*(2), 239–265.

Okamoto, T. (1997). Receipt free electronic voting schemes for large scale elections. In *Proceedings of Workshop on Security Protocols 97* (LNCS, pp. 25-35). Berlin: Springer Verlag.

Okazaki, S. (2004). How do japanese consumers perceive wireless ads? A multivariate analysis. *International Journal of Advertising, 23*(4), 429–454.

Okazaki, S., & Taylor, C. (2008). What is SMS advertising and why do multinationals adopt it? Answers from an empirical study in European markets. *Journal of Business Research, 61*(8), 4–12. doi:10.1016/j.jbusres.2006.05.003

Oppliger, R. (2004). Certified Mail: The Next Challenge for Secure Messaging. *Communications of the ACM, 47*, 75–79. doi:10.1145/1012037.1012039

Oppliger, R. (2007). Providing Certified Mail Services on the Internet. *Security & Privacy, 5*, 16–22. doi:10.1109/MSP.2007.15

Oppliger, R., & Stadlin, P. (2004). A certified mail system (CMS) for the Internet. *Computer Communications, 27*, 1229–1235. doi:10.1016/j.comcom.2004.04.006

Ornetsmueller, G. (2007). *WEB-ERV ERVService (Version 1.1)*. Austria.

Orrill, C. (2006). What Learner-Centered Professional Development Looks Like: The Pilot Studies of the Inter-Math Professional Development Project. *The Mathematics Educator, 16*(1), 4–13.

Orrill, C. H. (2000, April 24-28). Designing a PBL Experience for online delivery in a six-week course. In *Proceedings of the Annual Meeting of the American Educational Research Association*, New Orleans, LA.

Ortenblad, A. (2002). Organizational learning: A radical perspective. *International Journal of Management Reviews, 4*(1), 87–100. doi:10.1111/1468-2370.00078

Oxford, R. L., & Burry-Stock, J. A. (1995). Assessing the use of language learning strategies worldwide with ESL/EFL version of the Strategy Inventory for Language Learning (SILL). *System, 23*(2), 153–175.

Oxford, R. L., Hollaway, M. E., & Murillo, D. (1992). Language learning styles: Research and practical considerations for teaching in the multicultural tertiary ESL/EFL classroom. *System*, *20*(4), 439–445. doi:10.1016/0346-251X(92)90057-A

Özdemir, S. (2005). *WEB ortamında bireysel ve işbirliğine dayalı problem temelli öğrenmenin eleştirel düşünme becerisi, akademik başarı ve internet kullanımına yönelik tutuma etkileri*. Doctoral dissertation, Gazi University, Eğitim Bilimleri Enstitüsü, Ankara, Turkey.

Özel, M., Timur, E., Özyalın, Ş., & Danışman, M. A. (2005). Modüler tabanlı eğitim programında matematik ve jeofizik bütünleşmesi. *Dokuz Eylül Üniversitesi, Mühendislik Fakültesi. Fen ve Mühendislik Dergisi*, *7*(2), 101–112.

Palmer, J. W., & Speier, C. (1997). A Typology of Virtual Organizations: An Empirical Study. In *Proceedings of the Association for Information Systems 1997 Americas Conference*, Indianapolis, IN.

Pandey, S., & Sharma, R. R. K. (2009). Organizational factors for exploration and exploitation. *Journal of Technology Management and Innovation*, *4*(1), 48–58.

Pang, L. (2001). Understanding Virtual Organizations. *Information Systems Control Journal*, *6*, 42–47.

Park, W. (2005). Mobile Phone Addiction. In Ling, R. (Ed.), *Mobile Communications: Re-negotiation of the Social Sphere* (pp. 253–272). London: Springer.

Parrish, P. E. (2004). The trouble with learning objects. *Educational Technology Research and Development*, *52*(1), 49–67. doi:10.1007/BF02504772

Perreault, H., Waldman, L., & Alexander, M. (2002). Overcoming Barriers to Successful Delivery of Online learning Courses. *Journal of Education for Business*, *77*(6), 313. doi:10.1080/08832320209599681

Piaget, J. (1969). *Psychologie et pédagogie*. Paris: Denoël.

Piccinini, N., & Scollo, G. (2006). Cooperative Project-based Learning in a Web-based Software Engineering Course. *Journal of Educational Technology & Society*, *9*(4), 54–62.

Pollach, I. (2007, September). What's Wrong With Online Privacy Policies? *Communications of the ACM*.

Poncet, P., & Régnier, C. (2003). Les TIC: éléments sur leurs usages et sur leurs effets. *Les notes Évaluation*. Retrieved September 3, 2010, from http://trf.education.gouv.fr/pub/edutel/dpd/noteeval/ne0301.pdf

Pontecorvo, C. (1990). Social context, semiotic mediation, and forms of discourse in constructing knowledge at school. In H. Mandl, E. DeCorte, S. N. Bennett, & H. F. Friedrich (Eds.), *Learning and instruction, European research in an international context Vol. 2:1. Social and cognitive aspects of learning and instruction* (pp. 1-26). Oxford, UK: Pergamon Press.

Porter, M. (1990). *Competitive Advantage of Nations*. New York: Free Press.

Portine, H. (1998). L'autonomie de l'apprenant en question. *ALSIC*, *1*(1), 73–77.

Poskiene, A. (2006). Organizational culture and innovations. *The Engineering Economist*, *1*(26), 45–52.

Potocan, V., & Dabic, M. (2002). The Virtual Organization from the Viewpoint of Informing. In *Proceedings of the Informing Science* (pp. 1267-1275).

Pragnell, M. V., Roselli, T., & Rossano, V. (2006). Can a Hypermedia Cooperative e-learning Environment Stimulate Constructive Collaboration? *Journal of Educational Technology & Society*, *9*(2), 119–132.

Prahalad, C. K., & Krishnan, M. S. (2008). *The new age of innovation*. New York: McGraw-Hill.

Pratt, L. Y., & Kamm, C. A. (1991). Direct transfer of learned information among neural networks. In *Proceedings of the Ninth National Conference on Artificial Intelligence*, Anaheim, CA (pp. 584-589).

Prensky, M. (2001). Digital natives, Digital immigrants. *Horizon*, *9*(5), 1–6. doi:10.1108/10748120110424816

Prensky, M. (2001b). Digital natives, Digital immigrants, Part II: Do they really think differently? *On the Horizon*, *9*(6). Retrieved August 18, 2010, from http://www.marcprensky.com/writing/Prensky%20-%20Digital%20Natives,%20Digital%20Immigrants%20-%20Part2.pdf

Prensky, M. (2007). *How to teach with technology: Keeping both teachers and students comfortable in an era of exponential change*. Coventry, UK: BECTA. Retrieved August 12, 2010, from http://partners.becta.org.uk/page_documents/research/emerging_technologies07_chapter4.pdf

Preston, B. L., & Stafford-Smith, M. (2009). Framing vulnerability and adaptive capacity assessment: Discussion paper. *CSIRO Climate Adaptation Flagship Working paper Number 2*. Retrieved from http://www.csiro.au/org/ClimateAdaptationFlagship.html

Pretschner, A., Hilty, M., & Basin, D. (2006). Distributed usage control. *Communications of the ACM*, 49.

Puigserver, M. M., Gomila, J. L. F., & Rotger, L. H. (2005). Certified e-mail protocol with verifiable third party. In *Proceedings of the 2005 IEEE International Conference on e-Technology, e-Commerce and e-Service* (pp. 548-551).

Pundziene, A., & Duobiene, J. (2006). CEOs' entrepreneurship in relation to reaction to organizational change. *The Engineering Economist*, 2(47), 91–97.

Qingfei, M., Shaobo, J., & Gang, Q. (2008). Mobile Commerce User Acceptance Study in China: A Revised UTAUT Model. *Tsinghua Science and Technology*, 13(3), 257–264. doi:10.1016/S1007-0214(08)70042-7

Qui, X. (2008). Citizen Engagement: Driving Force of E-Society Development. IFIP International Federation for Information Processing. In Wang, W. (Ed.), *Integration and Innovation Orient to E-Society* (Vol. 252, pp. 540–548). New York: Springer.

Quinn, C. N., Alem, L., & Eklund, J. (2005). *A pragmatic evaluation methodology for an assessment of learning effectiveness in instructional system*. Retrieved March 15, 2008, from http://www.testingcentre.com/jeklund/Interact.htm

Race, P. (2007). *The lecturer's toolkit: A practical guide to assessment, learning and teaching*. Oxon, UK: Routledge.

Raman, M., Ryan, T., & Olfman, L. (2005). Designing knowledge management systems for teaching and learning with wiki technology. *Journal of Information Systems Education*, 16(3), 311–321.

Ramdani, B., & Kawalek, P. (2007). SMEs & IS innovations adoption: A review & assessment of previous research. *Academia, Revista. Latino Americana de Administracion*, 39, 47–70.

Ramsden, P. (1992). *Learning to teach in higher education*. London: Routledge. doi:10.4324/9780203413937

Rao, Z. H. (2001). Matching teaching styles with learning styles in East Asian contexts. *Internet TESL Journal*, 7(7), Retrieved September 3, 2010, from http://iteslj.org/Techniques/Zhenhui-TeachingStyles.html

Ravasi, D., & Schultz, M. (2006). Responding to organizational identity threats: Exploring the role of organizational culture. *Academy of Management Journal*, 49(3), 433–458. doi:10.2307/20159775

Reeves, T. C. (2006). Design research from the technology perspective. In Akker, J. V., Gravemeijer, K., McKenney, S., & Nieveen, N. (Eds.), *Educational design research* (pp. 86–109). London: Routledge.

Reid, J. (1987). The learning style preferences of ESL students. *TESOL Quarterly*, 21(1), 87–111. doi:10.2307/3586356

Rettie, R., Grandcolas, U., & Deakins, B. (2005). Text message advertising: response rates and branding effects. *Journal of Targeting. Measurement and Analysis for Marketing*, 13(4), 304–312. doi:10.1057/palgrave.jt.5740158

Reynard, R. (2009). 3 Challenges to Wiki Use in Instruction. *Campus Technology*. Retrieved from http://campustechnology.com/Articles/2009/02/11/3-Challenges-to-Wiki-Use-in-Instruction.aspx?p=1

Ridgeway, J., McCusker, S., & Pead, D. (2004). *Report 10: Literature review of e-assessment*. Bristol, UK: Futurelab Series.

Robinson, M. (2006). Wikis in education: social construction as learning. *Community College Enterprise*. Retrieved from http://findarticles.com/p/articles/mi_qa4057/is_200610/ai_n17191876

Robinson-Stuart, G., & Nocon, H. (1996). Second culture acquisition: Ethnography in the foreign language classroom. *Modern Language Journal*, 80(4), 431–449. doi:10.2307/329724

Rogers, E. M. (2003). *Diffusion of innovations* (5th ed.). New York: Free Press.

Rössler, T. (2007). *Electronic Voting over the Internet – an E-Government Speciality*. Doctoral dissertation, Graz University of Technology, Austria.

Rössler, T. (2009). Empowerment through Electronic Mandates – Best Practice Austria. *Software Services for e-Business and e-Society. IFIP Advances in Information and Communication Technology, 305,* 148–160.

Rössler, T., Hayat, A., Posch, R., & Leitold, H. (2005). Giving an interoperable solution for incorporating foreign eids in austrian e-government. In [Paris: European Commission.]. *Proceedings of IDABC Conference, 2005,* 147–156.

Rumelhart, D., & McClelland, J. (1986). *Parallel Distributed Processing*. Cambridge, MA: MIT Press.

Russell, T. L. (1999). *No significant difference phenomenon*. Raleigh, NC: North Carolina State University.

Ryan, R. (2000). Student assessment comparison of lecture and online construction equipment and methods classes. *T.H.E. Journal, 27*(6), 78–84.

Saarinen, T. (1996). An expanded instrument for evaluating information systems success. *Information & Management, 31*(2), 103–118. doi:10.1016/S0378-7206(96)01075-0

Sabherwal, R., Jeyaraj, A., & Chowa, C. (2006). Information system success: Individual and organizational determinants. *Management Science, 52*(12), 1849–1864. doi:10.1287/mnsc.1060.0583

Salaway, G., Caruso, J. B., & Nelson, M. R. (2007). *The ECAR study of undergraduate students and information technology, 2007* ( ). Washington, DC: EDUCAUSE. *ECAR Research Study, 6,* 2007.

Sammons, M. (2003). Exploring the New Conception of Teaching and Learning in Distance Education. In Moore, M. G., & Anderson, W. G. (Eds.), *Handbook of Distance Education* (pp. 387–400). Mahwah, NJ: Lawrence Erlbaum Associates.

Santhanam, R., Sasidharan, S., & Webster, J. (2008). Using Self-Regulatory Learning to Enhance E Learning-Based Information Technology Training. *Information Systems Research, 19*(1), 26–47. doi:10.1287/isre.1070.0141

Sarker, S., & Wells, J. (2003). Understanding Mobile. *Communications of the ACM, 46*(12), 35–40. doi:10.1145/953460.953484

Sato, C. (1981). Ethnic styles in classroom discourse. In Hines, M., & Rutherford, W. (Eds.), *On TESOL '81* (pp. 11–24). Washington, DC: Teachers of English to Speakers of Other Languages.

Savignon, S. J. (1983). *Communicative competence: Theory and classroom practice*. Reading, MA: Addison-Wesley.

Savin-Baden, M., & Wilkie, K. (2006). *Problem-Based Learning Online*. Berkshire, UK: Open University Press.

Schein, E. H. (2004). *Organizational culture and leadership* (3rd ed.). San Francisco, CA: Jossey-Bass.

Schneier, B., & Riordan, J. (1997). A certified e-mail protocol. In *Proceedings of ACSAC '97: the Annual Computer Security Applications Conference* (pp. 232-238). Washington, DC: IEEE Computer Society Press.

Schoenmakers, W., & Duysters, G. (2006). Learning in strategic technology alliances. *Technology Analysis and Strategic Management, 18*(2), 245–264. doi:10.1080/09537320600624162

Schrader, P. (2008). Learning in Technology: Reconceptualising immersive environments. *Association for the Advancement of Computers in Education Journal, 16*(4), 457–475.

Schunk, D., & Zimmerman, B. (1994). *Self-regulation of learning and performance. Issues and educational applications*. Hillsdale, NJ: Eribaum.

Scott, M. (2005). An assessment of biometric identities as a standard for e-government services. *Services and Standards, 1*(3), 271–286. doi:10.1504/IJSS.2005.005800

Scott, P. J., & Quick, K. (2005). Heroic failures in disseminating novel e-learning technologies to corporate clients: A case study of interactive webcasting. In *Proceedings of the 4th international symposium on Information and communication technologies*, Cape Town, South Africa (Vol. 92, pp. 26-31). Dublin, Ireland: Trinity College Publisher. Retrieved July 15, 2010, from http://portal.acm.org/citation.cfm?id=1071752.1071758

Seddon, P. B. (1997). A Respecification and Extension of the DeLone and McLean Model of IS Success. *Information Systems Research*, 8(3), 240–253. doi:10.1287/isre.8.3.240

Segars, H. A., & Grover, V. (1998). Strategic planning success: an investigation of the construct and its measurement. *Management Information Systems Quarterly*, 22(2), 139–163. doi:10.2307/249393

Sekaran, U. (2003). *Research Methods for Business: A Skill Building Approach* (4th ed.). New York: John Wiley & Sons Inc.

Selwyn, N. (2008). From state-of-the-art to state-of-the-actual? Introduction to a Special Issue. *Technology, Pedagogy and Education*, 17(2), 83–87. doi:10.1080/14759390802098573

Sendag, S., & Odabasi, F. (2009). *Effects of an online problem based learning course on content knowledge acquisition and critical thinking skills*. Computer and Education.

Senge, P. (1995). *The fifth discipline: The art and practice of a learning organization*. Sydney, Australia: Random House.

Senge, P. (1999). Learning leaders. *Executive Excellence*, 16(11), 12.

Seo, K. K., Miller, P. C., Schmidt, C., & Sowa, P. (2008). Creating synergy between collectivism and individualism in cyberspace: A Comparison of online communication patterns between Hong Kong and U.S. Students. *Journal of Intercultural Communication, 18*. Retrieved September 3, 2010, from http://www.immi.se/intercultural/

Serafeimidis, V. (2002). A Review of Research Issues in Evaluation of Information Systems. In van Grembergen, W. (Ed.), *Information Systems Evaluation Management*. Hershey, PA: IRM Press.

Sharma, S. K., Chen, C., & Sundaram, S. (2006). Implementation Problems with ERP Systems in Virtual Enterprises/Virtual Organizations. *International Journal of Management and Enterprise Development*, 3(5), 491–509. doi:10.1504/IJMED.2006.009572

Shavitt, S., Lowrey, P., & Haefner, J. (1998). Public Attitudes Towards Advertising: More Favourable Than You Might Think. *Journal of Advertising Research*, 38(4), 7–22.

Shavlik, J. W., Mooney, R. J., & Towell, G. G. (1991). Symbolic a neural net learning algorithms; an empirical comparison. *Machine Learning*, 6, 111–143. doi:10.1007/BF00114160

Sheppard, B. H., Hartwick, J., & Warshaw, P. R. (1988). The theory of reasoned action: A meta- analysis of past research with recommendations for modifications and future research. *The Journal of Consumer Research*, 15, 325–343. doi:10.1086/209170

Sherry, L. (1996). Issues in online Learning. *International Journal of Educational Telecommunications*, 1(4), 337–365.

Shirey, R. (2000). Internet Security Glossary.

Shulman, A. H., & Sims, R. L. (1999). Learning in an online format versus an in-class format: An experiment study. *T.H.E. Journal*, 26(11), 54–57.

Simsek, Z., Veiga, J. F., Lubatkin, M. H., & Dino, R. N. (2005). Modeling the multilevel determinants of top management team behavioral integration. *Academy of Management Journal*, 48(1), 69–85. doi:10.2307/20159641

Sirdeshmukh, D., Singh, S., & Sabol, B. (2002). Consumer Trust, Value, and Loyalty in Relational Exchanges. *Journal of Marketing*, 66(2), 15–37. doi:10.1509/jmkg.66.1.15.18449

Skyrme, D. (1999). Virtual Teaming and Virtual Organizations: 25 Principles of Proven Practice. In Lloyd, P., & Boyle, P. (Eds.), *Web-Weaving: intranets, extranets and strategic alliances*. Oxford, UK: Butterworth-Heinemann.

Smalley, N., Graff, M., & Saunders, D. (2001). A revised computer attitude scale for secondary students. *Educational and Child Psychology*, 18(3), 47–57.

Smart, K. L., & Cappel, J. J. (2006). Students' Perceptions of Online Learning. *Journal of Information Technology Education*, 5(1), 201–219.

Smirich, L. (1983). Concepts of culture and organizational analysis. *Administrative Science Quarterly*, 28(3), 339–358. doi:10.2307/2392246

Smithson, S., & Hirschheim, R. (1998). Analysing Information Systems Evaluation: Another Look at an Old Problem. *European Journal of Information Systems*, *7*(3), 158–174. doi:10.1057/palgrave.ejis.3000304

Snow, C. C., Lipnack, J., & Stamps, J. (1999). The virtual organization: promises and pay-offs, large and small. In Cooper, C. L., & Rousseau, D. M. (Eds.), *The Virtual Organization* (*Vol. 6*, pp. 15–30). Trends in Organizational Behavior.

Solomon, M. J., & Chowdhury, A. M. R. (2002). Knowledge to action: Evaluation for learning in a multi-organizational global partnership. *Development in Practice*, *12*(3/4), 346–354. doi:10.1080/09614520220149000

Sommer, R. (2009). A planning solution for virtual business relationships. *Industrial Management & Data Systems*, *109*(4), 463–476. doi:10.1108/02635570910948614

Sotillo, S. M. (2000). Discourse Functions and syntactic complexity in synchronous and asynchronous communication. *Language Learning & Technology*, *4*(1), 82–119.

Soubrié, T. (2005). Le présentiel allégé à l'université pour les grands groupes: un dispositif au service de l'autonomisation des apprenants. *Actes du colloque SIF*. Paris: Les institutions éducatives face au numérique. Retrieved September 3, 2010, from http://sif2005.msh-parisnord.org/pdf/Soubrier.pdf

Soubrié, T. (2006). *Le Blog: retour en force de la «fonction auteur»*. Paper presented at the Colloque JOCAIR'06, Amiens. Retrieved September 3, 2010, from http://hal.archives-ouvertes.fr/docs/00/13/84/62/PDF/16-_Soubrie.pdf

Sperlich, A., & Spraul, K. (2007). Students As Active Partners: Higher Education Management in Germany. *Innovation Journal*, *12*(3). Retrieved from http://www.innovation.cc/peer-reviewed/sperlich11final1draft.pdf

Squires, D., & Preece, J. (1999). Predicting quality in educational software: Evaluating for learning, usability and the synergy between them. *Interacting with Computers*, *5*(11), 467–483. doi:10.1016/S0953-5438(98)00063-0

Staber, U., & Sydow, J. (2002). Organizational adaptive capacity. *Journal of Management Inquiry*, *11*(4), 408–424. doi:10.1177/1056492602238848

Stacey, R. (1993). *Strategic management and organizational dynamics*. New York: Pitman Publishing.

Standing, C., Benson, S., & Karjaluoto, H. (2005). Consumer perspectives on mobile advertising and marketing. In *Proceedings of the Australian & New Zealand Marketing Academy Conference (ANZMAC)*, Perth, Australia (pp. 135-141).

Statistik Austria. (2008). *ICT Usage in Households*. Austria: Bundesanstalt Statistik Österreich.

Stevens, E., & Dimitriadis, S. (2002). New service development through the lens of organizational learning: evidence from longititudinal case studies. *Journal of Business Research*, *57*, 1074–1084. doi:10.1016/S0148-2963(03)00003-1

Stonier, T. (1996). Information as a basic property of the universe. *Biosystem*, *38*(2), 135–140. doi:10.1016/0303-2647(96)88368-7

Storey, V. C., Straub, D. W., Stewart, K. A., & Welke, R. J. (2000). A conceptual investigation of the e-commerce industry. *Communications of the ACM*, *43*(7), 117–123. doi:10.1145/341852.341871

Stough, S., Eom, S., & Buckenmyer, J. (2000). Virtual teaming: a strategy for moving your organization into the new millennium. *Industrial Management & Data Systems*, *100*(8), 370–378. doi:10.1108/02635570010353857

Strike, K. A., & Posner, G. J. (1985). A conceptual change view of learning and understanding. In West, L. H. T., & Pines, A. L. (Eds.), *Cognitive structure and conceptual change* (pp. 231–240). New York: Academic Press.

Sullivan, P. (2001). Gender differences and the online classroom: male and female college students evaluate their experiences. *Community College Journal of Research and Practice*, *25*, 805–818. doi:10.1080/106689201753235930

Sullivan, P. (2002). "It's easier to be yourself when you are invisible": Female college students discuss their online classroom experiences. *Innovative Higher Education*, *27*(2), 129–144. doi:10.1023/A:1021109410893

Swan, A. K., & Jackman, D. H. (2000). Comparing the success of students enrolled in online education courses vs. face-to-face classrooms. *The Journal of Technology Studies*, *29*(1), 58–63.

Swan, K. (2003). Learning effectiveness online: What the research tells us. In Boume, J., & Moore, J. C. (Eds.), *Elements of quality online education* (*Vol. 4*, pp. 13–46). Needham, MA: Sloan-C, The Sloan Center at Olin and Babson Colleges.

Swanson, E. B., & Ramiller, N. C. (2004). Innovating mindfully with information Technology. *Management Information Systems Quarterly, 28*(4), 553–583.

Szulanski, G. (1996). Exploring internal stickiness: Impediments to the transfer of best practice within firms. *Strategic Management Journal, 17,* 27–43.

Szulc, P. (1999). Reassessing the assessment of online education courses. *T.H.E. Journal, 27*(2), 70–74.

Tamuz, M. (2001). Learning disabilities for regulators: The perils of organizational learning in the air transportation industry. *Administration & Society, 33*(3), 276–302. doi:10.1177/00953990122019776

Tandoğan, R. Ö. (2006). *Fen eğitiminde probleme dayali aktif öğrenmenin öğrencilerin başarilarina ve kavram öğrenmelerine etkisi.* Unpublished master's thesis, Marmara Üniversitesi, Eğitim Bilimleri Enstitüsü.

Tapscott, D. (1998). *Growing up digital: The rise of the Net generation.* New York: McGraw-Hill.

Tavukçu, K. (2006). *Fen bilgisi dersinde probleme dayali öğrenmenin öğrenme ürünlerine etkisi.* Unpublished master's thesis, Zonguldak Karaelmas University, Sosyal Bilimler Enstitüsü.

Taylor, G. (2006). *The Wiki as a collaborative tool for staff and students in Secondary Schools.* Retrieved from http://www.decs.sa.gov.au/learningtechnologies/files/links/Web_2_tools2006_Taylor.pdf

Taylor, S., & Todd, P. A. (1995). Understanding information technology usage: A test of competing models. *Information Systems Research, 6*(2), 144–176. doi:10.1287/isre.6.2.144

Taylor, W. A., & Wright, G. H. (2004). Organizational readiness for successful knowledge sharing: Challenges for public sector managers. *Information Resources Management Journal, 17*(2), 22–37.

Tellis, G. H., Prabhu, J. C., & Chandy, R. K. (2009). Radical innovation across nations: The preeminence of corporate culture. *Journal of Marketing, 73,* 3–23. doi:10.1509/jmkg.73.1.3

Tenner, E. (1996). *Why things bite back: Technology and the revenge of unintended consequences.* New York: Alfred A. Knopf.

The Annual Report of the Australian Customs Service (ACS). (2005). Retrieved from http://www.customs.gov.au/webdata/resources/files/ACSannualReport0405.pdf

The Saudi Network. (n.d.). Retrieved January 14, 2009 from http://www.the-saudi.net/

Thomas, K., & Bose, S. (2006). The human face to knowledge management: Extending the knowledge spiral. *The International Journal of Knowledge. Culture and Change Management, 6*(9), 33–44.

Thomas, K., Lam, P., & Ho, A. (2009). Knowledge diffusion in eLearning: Learner attributes and capabilities in an organization. In G. Siemens & C. Fulford (Eds), *Proceedings of the 21st Annual World Conference on Educational Multimedia, Hypermedia and Telecommunications,* Honolulu, HI (pp. 493-497). Chesapeake, VA: Association for the Advancement of Computers in Education.

Thomerson, J. D., & Smith, C. L. (1996). Student perceptions of the affective experiences encountered in online learning courses. *The American Journal of Online Education, 10*(3), 37–48.

Thorne, S. L. (2003). Artifacts and cultures-of-use in intercultural communication. *Language Learning & Technology, 7*(2), 38–67.

Thurstone, L., & Chave, E. (1946). *The measurement of attitude.* Chicago: University of Chicago Press.

Todhunter, J. (2008). Fostering innovation culture in an unpredictable economy. *CIO News.* Retrieved December 31, 2009, from http://advice.cio.com/james_todhunter/fostering_innovation_culture_in_an_unpredictable_economy?commentpage=1

Tolsby, J. (1998). Effects of organizational culture on a large scale IT introduction effort: A case study of the Norwegian army's EDBLF Project. *European Journal of Information Systems*, *7*(2), 108–114. doi:10.1057/palgrave.ejis.3000295

Tonkin, E. (2005). Making the Case for a Wiki. *ARIANDE*, *42*. Retrieved from http://www.ariadne.ac.uk/issue42/tonkin

Tonti, G., Bradshaw, J., Jeffers, R., Montanari, R., Suri, N., & Uszok, A. (2003). Semantic Web Languages for Policy Representation and Reasoning: A Comparison of Kaos, Rei, and Ponder. In *Proceedings of the 2nd International Semantic Web Conference (ISWC2003)* (LCNS 2870, pp. 419-437). New York: Springer.

Townsend, A. M., DeMarie, S. M., & Hendrickson, A. R. (1998). Virtual teams: Technology and the workplace of the future. *The Academy of Management Executive*, *12*(3), 17–29.

Trinder, K., Guiller, J., Margaryan, A., Littlejohn, A., & Nicol, D. (2008). *Learning from digital natives: Bridging formal and informal learning (Research Project Final Report)*. New York: The Higher Education Academy.

Tripp-Reimer, T. (1985). Combining qualitative and quantitative methodologies. In Leininger, M. M. (Ed.), *Qualitative research methods in nursing* (pp. 179–194). Orlando, FL: Grune & Stratton.

Tsang, M., Ho, S., & Liang, T. (2004). Consumer Attitudes toward Mobile Advertising: An Empirical Study. *International Journal of Electronic Commerce*, *8*(3), 65–78.

Tseng, K. H., Chiang, F. K., & Hsu, W. H. (2007). Interactive processes and learning attitudes in a web-based problem-based learning (PBL) platform. *Computers in Human Behavior*, *24*(3), 940–955. doi:10.1016/j.chb.2007.02.023

Tsui, L., Chapman, S. A., Schnirer, & Stewart, S. (2006). *A Handbook on Knowledge Sharing: Strategies and Recommendations for Researchers, Policymakers, and Service Providers.*

Universal Postal Union. (2008). *Postal Registered eMail (PReM), Functional Specification (Version 0.52)*.

University of Botswana. (2007). *WebCT Report*. Botswana: University of Botswana: Center for Academic Development.

University of Botswana. (2007). Facts and Figures. In *University Fact Book*. Botswana: University of Botswana.

Unni, R., & Harmon, R. (2007). Perceived effectiveness of push vs. pull mobile location-based advertising. *Journal of Interactive Advertising*, *7*(2), 28–40.

US Department of Education. (2007). *Connecting students to advance courses online: Innovations in Education (WestEd)*. Washington, DC: US Department of Education Office of Innovation and Improvement.

Uslu, G. (2006). *Ortaögretim matematik dersinde probleme dayali öğrenmenin öğrencilerin derse ilişkin tutumlarina, akademik başarilarina ve kalicilik düzeylerine etkisi*. Unpublished master's thesis, Balıkesir University, Fen Bilimleri Enstitüsü.

Vakola, M., & Wilson, I. E. (2004). The Challenge of Virtual Organization: Critical Success Factors in Dealing with Constant Change. *Team Performance Management*, *10*(5-6), 112–120. doi:10.1108/13527590410556836

Valaitis, R. K., Sword, W. A., Jones, B., & Hodges, A. (2005). Problem-based learning online: perceptions of health science students. *Health Sciences Education, 10*(3), 231-252. New York: Springer.

Valenta, A., Therrirault, D., Dieter, M., & Mrtek, R. (2001). Identify student attitudes and learning styles in online education. *Journal of Asynchronous Learning Networks*, *5*(2).

Van den Hooff, B., Elving, W., Meeuwsen, M., & Dumoulin, C. (2003). Knowledge sharing in knowledge communities. In Huysman, M., Wenger, E., & Wulf, V. (Eds.), *Communities and Technologies* (pp. 119–141). Dordrecht, The Netherlands: Kluwer.

Van den Hooff, B., & Huysman, M. (2009). Managing knowledge sharing: Emergent and engineering approaches. *Information & Management, 46*(1), 1–8. doi:10.1016/j.im.2008.09.002

Van Lier, L. (1996). *Interaction in the language curriculum: Awareness, autonomy, & authenticity*. New York: Longman.

Varshney, U., & Vetter, R. (2002). Mobile commerce: framework, applications and networking support. *Journal of Mobile Networks and Applications, 7*(3), 185–198. doi:10.1023/A:1014570512129

Vasarhelyi, M., & Graham, L. (1997). Cybersmart: Education and the Internet. *Management Accounting,* 32-36.

Venice Commission. (2002). *Code of Good Practice in Electoral Matters. European Commission for Democracy through Law*. Council of Europe.

Venkatesh, V., & Morris, M. G. (2000). Why don't men ever stop to ask for directions? Gender, social influence, and their role in technology acceptance and usage behavior. *Management Information Systems Quarterly, 24*, 115–139. doi:10.2307/3250981

Venkatesh, V., Morris, M. G., & Davis, G. B. (2003). User acceptance of information technology: Towards a unified view. *Management Information Systems Quarterly, 27*(3), 425–478.

von Krogh, G., & Roos, J. (1995). A perspective on knowledge competence and strategy. *Personnel Review, 24*(3), 56–76. doi:10.1108/00483489510089650

Von Meier, A. (1999). Occupational cultures as a challenge to technological Innovations. *IEEE Transactions on Engineering Management, 46*(1), 101–114. doi:10.1109/17.740041

Vovides, Y., Sanchez-Alonso, S., & Nickmans, V. M. (2007). The use of e-learning course management system to support learning strategies and to improve self-regulated learning. *Educational Research Review, 2*(1), 64–74. doi:10.1016/j.edurev.2007.02.004

Vygotski, L. S. (1934). *Pensée et langage*. Paris: Éditions Sociales.

Wakefield, R., & Whitten, D. (2006). Mobile computing: a user study on hedonic/utilitarian mobile device usage. *European Journal of Information Systems, 15*(1), 292–300. doi:10.1057/palgrave.ejis.3000619

Walden, E. A., & Browne, G. J. (2009). Sequential adoption theory: A theory for understanding herding behavior in early adoption of novel technologies. *Journal of the Association for Information Systems, 10*(1), 31–62.

Walshe, K. (2003). Understanding and learning from organizational failure. *Quality & Safety in Health Care, 12*(2), 81–82. doi:10.1136/qhc.12.2.81

Wang, P., & Ramiller, N. C. (2009). Community learning in information technology innovation. *Management Information Systems Quarterly, 33*(4), 709–734.

Wang, S., & Tang, T. I. (2003). Assessing customer perceptions of Web sites service quality in digital marketing environments. *Journal of End User Computing, 15*(3), 14–31.

Wang, W., Butler, J. E., Hsieh, J. J. P., & Hsu, S. (2008). Innovate with complex information technologies: A theoretical model and empirical examination. *Journal of Computer Information Systems, 49*(1), 27–36.

Wang, Y. S., Wang, H. Y., & Shee, D. Y. (2007). Measuring e-learning systems success in an organizational context: Scale development and validation. *Computers in Human Behavior, 23*(4), 792–1808. doi:10.1016/j.chb.2005.10.006

Warschauer, M. (2000). Online learning in second language classrooms: An ethnographic study. In Warschauer, M., & Kern, R. (Eds.), *Network-based language teaching: Concepts and practice* (pp. 41–58). New York: Cambridge University Press.

Wayman, J., Jain, D., Maltoni, H., & Maio, D. (2005). *Biometric Systems: Technology, Design and Performance Evaluation*. New York: Springer.

Webster, J., & Hackley, P. (1997). Teaching effectiveness in technology-mediated online learning. *Academy of Management Journal, 40*(6), 1282–1310. doi:10.2307/257034

Wegerif, R. (1998). The social dimension of asynchronous learning networks. *Journal of Asynchronous Learning Networks, 2*(1), 34–49.

Weiss, S. M., & Kapsuleas, I. (1989). An empirical comparison of pattern recognition, neural nets and machine learning classification methods. In *Proceedings of the Eleventh International Joint Conference on Artificial Intelligence*, Detroit, MI (pp. 688-693).

Weitzner, D. J., Abelson, H., Berners-Lee, T., Feigenbaum, J., Hendler, J., & Sus, G. J. (2007, June 13). *Information Accountability* (Tech. Rep. No. MIT-CSAIL-TR-2007-034). MIT Computer Science and Artificial Intelligence Laboratory.

Wenning, R., & Schunter, M. (2006, November 13). *The Platform for Privacy Preferences 1.1 (P3P1.1) Specification* (W3C Working Group Note). Retrieved from http://www.w3.org/TR/P3P11/

West, L. (1988). Implications of recent research for improving secondary school science learning. In Ramsden, P. (Ed.), *Improving learning: New perspectives* (pp. 51–68). London: Kogan Page.

Wheeler, S., Kelly, P., & Gale, K. (2005). Influence of online PBL on teachers. *Research in Learning Technology*, *13*(2), 125–137.

Wildermuth, B. M. (1993). Post-positivist research: two examples of methodological pluralism. *The Library Quarterly*, *63*, 450–467. doi:10.1086/602621

Wilkinson, D. M., & Huberman, B. A. (2007). *Assessing the value of cooperation in wikipedia.* Retrieved from http://arxiv.org/PS_cache/cs/pdf/0702/0702140v1.pdf

Williams, M., Paprock, K., & Convington, B. (1999). *Online Learning: The essential Guide.* Thousand Oaks, CA: Sage.

Wolff, M. (1995). *New Organizational Structures for Engineering Design Commissioned Report.* Retrieved from http://www.worldserver.pipex.com/ki-net/content.html

Working-Group "E-Voting." (2004). *Abschlussbericht zur Vorlage an Dr. Ernst Strasser, Bundesminister für Inneres.* Austrian Federal Ministry for the Interior.

Worthey, K. M. (1987). *Learning style factors of field dependence/independence and problem-solving strategies of Hmong refugee students.* Unpublished master's thesis, University of Wisconsin, Stout, WI.

Wu, J., & Lederer, A. (2009). A meta-analysis of the role of environment-based voluntariness in information technology acceptance. *Management Information Systems Quarterly*, *33*(2), 419–432.

Wu, J.-H., & Wang, Y.-M. (2006). Measuring KMS success: A respecification of the DeLone and McLean's model. *Information & Management*, *43*, 728–739. doi:10.1016/j.im.2006.05.002

Xiaotong, L. (2009). Managerial entrenchment with strategic information technology: A dynamic perspective. *Journal of Management Information Systems*, *25*(4), 183–204. doi:10.2753/MIS0742-1222250406

Yorks, L., Neuman, J. H., Kowalski, D. R., & Kowalski, R. (2007). Lessons learned from a 5-year project within the Department of Veterans Affairs: Applying theories of interpersonal aggression and organizational justice to the development and maintenance of collaborative social space. *The Journal of Applied Behavioral Science*, *43*(3), 352–372. doi:10.1177/0021886307301431

Zacharias, P., Vassilopoulos, K., & Poulymenakou, A. (2002). *Designing online learning courses: Implications for usability.* Retrieved March 15, 2008, from http://wwwjapit.org/zacharias_eta102.pdf

Zemke, R. (1999). Why organizations are still not learning. *Training (New York, N.Y.)*, *36*(9), 40.

Zhang, D., & Nunamaker, J. F. (2003). Powering e-learning in the new millennium: an overview of e-learning and enabling technology. *Information Systems Frontiers*, *5*(2), 207–218. doi:10.1023/A:1022609809036

Zhao, J., Alexander, M., Perreault, H., Waldman, L., & Truell, A. (2009). Faculty and Student Use of Technologies, User Productivity, and User Preference in Online learning. *Journal of Education for Business*, *84*(4), 206–212. doi:10.3200/JOEB.84.4.206-212

Zhao, Y., & Frank, K. A. (2003). Factors affecting technology uses in schools: An ecological perspective. *American Educational Research Journal*, *40*(4), 807–840. doi:10.3102/00028312040004807

Zollo, M., & Winter, S. G. (2002). Deliberate learning and the evolution of dynamic capabilities. *Organization Science*, *13*(3), 339–351. doi:10.1287/orsc.13.3.339.2780

About the Contributors

Sushil Sharma is a Professor of Information Systems at Ball State University, Muncie, Indiana, USA. Co-author of two textbooks and co-editor of six books, Dr. Sharma has authored over 100 refereed research papers in many peer-reviewed national and international MIS and management journals, conferences proceedings and books. His primary teaching and research interests are in e-commerce, computer-mediated communications, community informatics, information systems security, e-government, ERP systems, database management systems, web services and knowledge management. He has a wide consulting experience in information systems and e-commerce and has served as an advisor and consultant to several government and private organizations including projects funded by the World Bank.

* * *

Benjamin Akintayo Agboola is a research student in the Department of Computer Science, University of Agriculture, Abeokuta. His research interest includes Information systems, Social Network Analysis and Knowledge management.

Nazim Ahmed is a professor of operation management. His primary teaching areas are operations management and management information systems. His research interests include total quality management, operations strategy, and environmental management and healthcare management. He has published many journal articles and more than forty articles in the proceedings of international, national and regional conferences. His articles have appeared in *International Journal of Production Research, Journal of Operations Management, International Journal of Production and Operations Management, Production and Inventory Management, Journal of Business Research, Information and Management, International Journal of Policy and Information, Journal of the Academy of Marketing Science, Transportation Research* and other journals. He has been also active in several professional organizations and served on the editorial review board of several journals.

Thamer Alhussain is a lecturer in the College of Computer Sciences and Information Technology at King Faisal University in Saudi Arabia. Thamer is currently a PhD candidate in the School of Information and Communication Technology at Griffith University in Australia. He obtained his Master degree in Information and Communication Technology from Griffith University. His current research interests include information assurance, acceptance and adoption of e-government and m-government.

Rudy Becarelli, graduated in Electronic Engineering in February 2004 at University of Florence with a thesis concerning motion estimation algorithms and their applications. Starting from April 2004 he's a researcher at MICC (Media Integration and Communication Centre) of Florence. His main interest are now design and development of J2EE applications and related data exchange and marshalling with rich client platforms. Other area of interst are OAI-PMH server development and coordination, digital library customization and profiling, MHP application development and optimization. Research activities mostly concern digital watermaking and in particular fragile and reversible techniques applied to medical images.

Roberto Caldelli, graduated cum laude in Electronic Engineering from the University of Florence, in 1997, where he also received the Ph.D degree in Computer Science and Telecommunications Engineering in 2001. He received a 4-years research grant (2001-2005) from the University of Florence to research on digital watermarking techniques for protection of images and videos. He is an Assistant Professor at the Media Integration and Communication Center of the University of Florence. He is a member of CNIT. His main research activities, witnessed by several publications, include digital image sequence processing, image and video digital watermarking, multimedia applications, MPEG-1/2/4, multimedia forensics.

Wajeeh Daher is with at An-Najah National University, Nablus, Palestine, and Al-Qasemi Academic College of Education, Baqa, Israel. He has academic degrees in mathematics, mathematics education, technological education, economics and accounting. His Ph.D. is from Haifa University and is in the field of web based mathematics education. Wajeeh Daher's research interests include technology in mathematics education, alternative teaching methods of mathematics, distance learning, and teachers' education. His articles probe the use of technology in the mathematics classroom, the integration of history in the mathematics classroom and the use of literature and language in mathematics lessons. Some of his latest articles examine the potentialities lying in using web 2.0 applications, as well as the mobile phone in mathematics education.

Steve Drew is a senior lecturer in the School of Information and Communication Technology at Griffith University's Gold Coast campus in South Eastern Queensland. His current research interests include acceptance and adoption of e-commerce, e-government, e-learning and m-government in emerging information economies. He also guides research into the novel use of mobile and Web technologies in collaborative and cooperative teaching and learning environments. Steve's current teaching interests include introducing first-year business students to the use and analysis of information systems in commercial organisations and guiding final year ICT students through their industry based work integrated learning projects.

Henk Eijkman is the Director, Learning & Teaching Development at University of New South Wales at the Australian Defence Force Academy campus. He is a learning solutions specialist for higher education. His academic background is in the social sciences (sociology, political science and social welfare) and in adult learning with a focus on social inclusion and digital technologies, focusing on Web 2.0+. A central theme through his professional career is innovation and organisational culture change in the service of social inclusion. As a learning, teaching, and assessment solutions analyst, Henk has worked in diverse post-school contexts that include South Africa, Malaysia, Palestine, and India. He publishes widely in international journals and serves on a number of conference committees. As well as being editor of 'The Learning Organisation', he is also co-editor of the new International Journal of Quality Assurance in Engineering and Technology Education (IJQAETE).

Francesco Filippini, obtained the degree in Telecommunications Engineering at the University of Florence in November 2003. From July 2000 to june 2002 was technical adviser and computer scientist at UMS (United medical software), a company leader in the production of medical software. From December 2003 to February 2004 obtained a Research Grant at the Images Communications Laboratory (LCI) of the Faculty of Engineering at the University of Florence in the context of a project entitled "Optimisation of an algorithm to authenticate remote sensing near lossless images" for the Italian Space Agency (ASI). From 2005 works at the center of excellence MICC (media integration and Communication Center) of the University of Florence with tasks research in various areas. In particular deals with the development of MHP applications for digital terrestrial television, both as regards to client-side and server-side development.

Olusegun Folorunso is a Senior Lecturer in the Department of Computer Science, University of Agriculture, Abeokuta. He obtained a B.Sc degree in Mathematical Sciences from the University of Agriculture, Abeokuta in 1992, M.Sc in Computer Science from University of Lagos in 1997 and a Ph.D in Computer Science in 2003 from the University of Agriculture, Abeokuta. His research interest includes Adoption of Information Systems strategies, Human Computer Interaction (HCI), Knowledge Management, Image Processing and Computational Intelligence. He is a member of Nigeria Computer Society and Computer Professional Registration Council of Nigeria. He has published in reputable international and local Journals.

Riccardo Giorgetti Degree in Telecommunications Engineering, obtained at the University of Florence in 2006 with a thesis entitled "Study and development of client-server application for managing information for hotels through DTT " 2006 to present: Research and developer at "MICC - Center for Communication and Integration of Media" of MHP/Java applications for "Digital Terrestrial Television", development websites via html, PHP, JavaScript and MySQL database.

Sevinc Gulsecen, is currently a faculty member and chair of Informatics Department and a faculty member of Mathematics Department at Istanbul University, İstanbul, Turkey. She received her PhD and MS degrees on MIS from same university. Currently she is lecturing in undergraduate, graduate and postgraduate courses and supervising research students. S. Gulsecen is the founder, chair and speaker of International Conference on Innovations in Learning for the Future: e-Learning. Dr. Gulsecen's current research is in the field of ICT and e-learning.

Fatih Gursul works as an instructor in the Department of Informatics at Istanbul University. He worked as a research assistant in Education Faculty, the Department of Computer Education and Instruction Technologies at Hacettepe University between 2000 and 2008. He completed his undergraduate education in the Department of Mathematics Education at Education Faculty at Gazi University; completed his graduate education in the institute for graduate studies in science and engineering in masters of Science in Mathematics at Hacettepe University. He completed his PhD in the Department of Computer Education and Instructional Technologies with the thesis entitled "The effects of online and face to face problem based learning approaches on students academic achievement and attitudes towards mathematics" at Ankara University in 2008. Moreover, he studied as a research scholar at University of Cincinnati in the United States of America in 2005 within the scope of his PhD. Problem based learning; mobile learning, on-line learning and mathematics education are in his area of interests.

Allan Herrmann is an online learning and educational technology consultant based in Tasmania, Australia. He worked previously as the Manager of the Educational Technology Services (ETS), Academic Support Group, at the University of New South Wales at the Australian Defence Force Academy campus. His consulting and research interests are in managing educational technology change and in strategic management-related considerations that underpin introducing new educational technology into an organization.

Annisa Ho is a Research Associate and the Evaluation Services Coordinator at the Centre for Learning Enhancement And Research (CLEAR) at The Chinese University of Hong Kong. She is responsible for the provision of evaluation services to all programs in the University, including questionnaire design, data analysis and reporting. Her research interests are in the areas of e-learning, blended learning, curriculum design and capabilities development.

Nathalie Iseli-Chan recently joined The University of Hong Kong in September 2010 as a French Instructor after a period of three years at The Chinese University of Hong Kong in a similar role. She is currently involved in research activities related to language pedagogy, the application of new technologies to learning and teaching French and its influence on second language learners' behavior both in and outside the classroom.

Christèle Joly is the Head of the French and Spanish Department at the Chinese International School in Hong Kong. Earlier, she worked in the Modern Languages Department at The Chinese University of Hong Kong from 2001 to 2009. Her research interests include second language acquisition and pedagogy, e-learning technologies and building virtual classroom communities, as well as development of tailor-made teaching materials for Chinese learners who are learning French.

David M. Kennedy is Associate Professor and Director of the Teaching and Learning Centre at Lingnan University in Hong Kong. He has over 30 years of teaching experience and publishes on the use of learning technologies in education, including pedagogical frameworks to support their use, problem-based learning, visual and information literacies, and evaluation of curriculum innovations in a diverse number of academic domains. His activities include consultations, professional development and seminars related to e-learning and mLearning, curriculum design, information literacy, using free and open source software, and outcomes-based approaches to teaching and learning in Australia, Canada, Finland, Hong Kong, Malaysia, Mauritius, Oman, Russia, South Africa, the UK and Vietnam. He is also a member of the Editorial Boards of the 'Journal of Multimedia and Hypermedia', the 'International Journal of Teaching and Learning in Higher Education (IJTLHE)', and the Journal 'Education as Change'.

Hafize Keser Graduated from Curriculum and Instruction Department of the Faculty of Educational Sciences of Ankara University and received her master degree from Curriculum and Instruction Department of the Institute of Educational Sciences of Ankara University and received her Ph.D. degree from

Educational Technology Department of the same institute. Currently serving as a Head of Computer Education and Instructional Technology Department of the Faculty of Educational Sciences of Ankara University.

Farid Khoshalhan is an assistant professor in Industrial Engineering and Information Technology at Faculty of Industrial Engineering, K.N. Toosi University of Technology, Tehran-IRAN. Currently, Dr. Khoshalhan is the president of faculty of Industrial Engineering. His research and client work has focused on decision making, operations management, evolutionary algorithms, productivity management and ecommerce. Dr. Khoshalhan earned a bachelor's degree in industrial technology from Iran University of Science and Technology, a master's and PhD in industrial engineering from Tarbiat Modarres University. Tell: +9821-88674843 Email: khoshalhan@kntu.ac.ir.

Paul Lam is an Assistant Professor at the Centre for Learning Enhancement And Research (CLEAR) at The Chinese University of Hong Kong. He is involved in many teaching and learning (T&L) research studies and services such as promotion of outcomes-based approaches to T&L, the enhancement of T&L spaces, and the use of technology for T&L. Additional research interests include case-based T&L, learners' characteristics, self and peer assessment, and English language teaching (ELT). Prior to joining CLEAR, he worked in a number of language-education projects in Hong Kong universities, and before that he was a secondary school teacher in Hong Kong.

Judy Lo is an Assistant Computer Officer in the Information Technology Services Centre of The Chinese University of Hong Kong. She is responsible for developing and maintaining e-learning platforms and services for the University. She suggests and implements enhancements to the e-learning platforms and services to cope with new demands. She provides consultation and technical assistance to help faculty members on e-learning course design, courseware development, and the use of new technology for teaching and. She is also responsible for e-learning promotion at the University and has been involved in major projects such as the 'eLearning Service @CUHK', 'Podcast@CUHK' and 'CUHK on iTunes U'.

Carmel McNaught is the Director and Professor of Learning Enhancement in the Centre for Learning Enhancement And Research (CLEAR) at The Chinese University of Hong Kong (CUHK). She has had extensive experience in secondary and higher education in Australasia and southern Africa in chemistry, science education, second language learning, e-learning, and higher-education curriculum and policy matters. She has been involved in numerous design and implementation projects for e-learning and associated systems. She is a well-known international speaker; is actively involved in several e-learning professional organizations, and is a Fellow of the Association for the Advancement of Computers in Education; is on 12 international editorial boards; and has ~300 academic publications. Further details at http://www.cuhk.edu.hk/clear/people/Carmel.html.

Ray Montagno is professor of management and chair of the Department of Marketing and Management at Ball State University. He teaches courses in general management, human resources, and international management. In 1990, he was named the College of Business Professor of the Year. He has written two books and published numerous articles on human resources, competitiveness, and international issues. His main interest is in the area of organizational competitiveness and innovation. Montagno has consulted with many large U.S. and multinational firms on issues relating to productivity and international competitiveness. He has also done considerable corporate training and has custom designed many corporate training programs. He is also a certified trainer for Zinger-Miller, Inc. and holds certification as Senior Professional in Human Resources. His background includes degrees in both engineering and psychology.

Athulang Mutshewa is a senior lecturer in the Department of Library and Information Studies, University of Botswana. He holds a B.Sc. in Physics and Environmental Science, Postgraduate Diploma in Education, Masters in Library and Information Studies from the University of Botswana, and PhD in Information Systems from the University of Cape Town. His research interests are in information behaviour and ICTs for development. Mutshewa@mopipi.ub.bw.

Stephen M. Mutula is the Head, Department of Library and Information Studies, University of Botswana. He is the author of Digital Economies: SMES & E-readiness published. He is also the first co-author of a book titled: *Web information management: A cross disciplinary textbook*. He is the co-editor of Information *and Knowledge Management in the Digital Age: Concepts, Technologies and African Perspectives*. He is the recipient of three professional excellence awards from the Emerald Literati Club (UK) for in 2002 and twice in 2005; IFLA award recipient for a portfolio developed on information literacy in 2007. He was the researcher of the year at the University of Botswana in 2007 and 2008 respectively. He is an Honorary Research Fellow at the Department of Information Science, University of Zululand, South Africa. He researches in the areas of information society, e-government, digital divide, and development informatics. Mutulasm@mopipi.ub.bw.

Adewale Opeoluwa Ogunde is a Lecturer II in the Computer Science Programme of the Department of Mathematical Sciences, Redeemer's University (RUN), P.M.B 3005, Mowe, Ogun State, Nigeria. He holds B.Sc degree in Mathematical Sciences (Computer Science Option) from University of Agriculture, Abeokuta in 1998, M.Sc Computer Science from same University in 2005 and currently a Ph.D (Computer Science) student in the same university. His research interest includes: Data Mining and Knowledge Discovery, Information Systems, Knowledge-based systems, and Agent-based systems. He is a member of Nigeria Computer Society (NCS) and Computer Professional Registration Council of Nigeria(CPRCN). He has publications in both reputable international and local journals.

Francesco Picchioni received from the University of Florence, Italy, the M.Sc. degree (Laurea) in Telecommunications engineering in 2004. He received a 2-years research grant (2004-2006) from the University of Florence to research on Analysis of Spectral/Spatial characteristics and information extraction from Remote Sensing High-Dimensional Image Data. From January 2007 he is with the Media Integration and Communication Center (MICC), University of Florence as Assistant Researcher. His main research activities includes digital forensic and unmixing of hyperspectral remote sensing images.

Mohammad Rabiei is working as a faculty member of Iranian Research Institute for Information Science and Technology (IranDoc). He earned a bachelor's degree in computer engineering from Shahid Bahonar University of Kerman, Kerman-IRAN, a master's in Information Technology –electronic commerce from K.N. Toosi University of Technology, Tehran-IRAN. Currently, He is a member of Iranian Scientific Association of Information Management. His research interests include technology acceptance, e-commerce, mobile advertising and IT project management. He may be reached at M.rabiei@ irandoc.ac.ir.

Zerrin Ayvaz Reis is a faculty member in Computer and Educational Technologies and Department of Hasan Ali Yucel Educational Faculty in Istanbul University. She had received her B.Sc. degree in Mathematics and Astronomy at Istanbul University in 1986. Her M.Sc. degree from Quantitative Methods at Istanbul University in 1990, and PhD degree from Computer Engineering at Istanbul University in 1999. She has been teaching courses on Computer Based Math Teaching, Software Engineering, Databases and UML (Unified Modeling Language), and Quality on Education. Her current research interests include Web based e-Learning, Instructional Design, Computer Based Instruction, and Content Management System and Education for Disabled People.

Thomas Rössler, is a member of the eGovernment unit of the Institute for Applied Information Processing and Communications (IAIK), Graz University of Technology. Having earned a Master's degree in Telematics from Graz University of Technology, he is currently working in the field of IT security with a focus on the Austrian eGovernment initiative. Since September 2005,he is deputy head of the eGovernment Innovation Center (EGIZ) which is a joint initiative of the Austrian Federal Chancellery and the Graz University of Technology. EGIZ supports the Austrian Federal Chancellery in further developing the Austrian ICT-Strategy by research and innovation.

Kathy Savige is a Flexible Learning Designer (Team Leader) in Educational Technology Services (ETS) at the University of New South Wales at the Australian Defence Force Academy campus. Her role in ETS is to bring together services such as flexible learning including off-campus (distance) education, graphic design, document production, central teaching venue support, media development, photography and online learning.

Arne Tauber received his MS in Telecommunications Engineering in 2005, from the Graz University of Technology. He is currently working in the field of IT security with focus on the Austrian eGovernment initiative. Since September 2005, he is a staff member of the eGovernment Innovation Center (EGIZ), which is a joint initiative of the Austrian Federal Chancellery and the Graz University of Technology. EGIZ supports the Austrian Federal Chancellery in further developing the Austrian ICT-Strategy by research and innovation. He is actively involved in the European large scale pilots STORK (Secure IdentTity acrOss boRders linKed) and SPOCS (Simple Procedures Online for Crossborder Services) in the ICT-PSP (Policy Support Programme), co-founded by EU.

Adeyinka Tella is a lecturer at the Department of Library and Information Science, Faculty of Communication and Information Sciences, University of Ilorin. Nigeria. Tella is a commonwealth scholar who finishes his PhD in September 2009 from the Department of Library and Information Studies; University of Botswana under the supervision of Prof. S.M. Mutula. He has written and published articles in local and International refereed journals together with chapters in book. He is one of the contributors to an information science reference "Cases on Successful E-learning Practices in the Developed and Developing World: Methods for the Global Information Economy" Currently, he is the Associate Editor International Journal of Library and Information Science. His research areas include e-learning, information literacy, information communication technology, psychology of information, etc. This paper is one of the summaries of his thesis. tellayinkaedu@yahoo.com.

Keith Thomas is the Associate Director and the Head of Evaluation Services at the Centre for Learning Enhancement And Research (CLEAR) at The Chinese University of Hong Kong. His interests include professional and executive development, facilitating learning and teaching in higher education, and leadership- and management-related topics. He has taught on both undergraduate and postgraduate (MBA & MIB) programs in Australia, China and Vietnam.

Angelina Totolo is a lecturer in the Department of Library and Information Studies at the University of Botswana. She earned a Doctor of Philosophy from Florida State University in the U.S and her areas of interest are information technology adoption, information seeking behaviours and school librarianship. Totoloa@mopipi.ub.bw.

Rebecca O. Vincent is a Lecturer in the Department of Computer Science, University of Agriculture, Abeokuta. She obtained a B.Sc degree in Mathematical Sciences (Computer Science Option), M.Sc and Ph.D in Computer Science from the University of Agriculture, Abeokuta in 2000, 2005 and 2010 respectively. She has being a research Scholar with the Computational Intelligence Group, at the Institute of Informatics, Clausthal University of Technology, Germany; where she carries out research on Mobile Agents for E-Commerce. Her research interest include: Images and Vision, Knowledge Management, Computational Complexity, Ecommerce, Agents and Mobile Agents. She is a member of Nigeria Computer Society and has published in notable International and local Journals.

Peter Woodhead teaches how to use Information and Communication Technologies (ICTs) at the German Swiss International School, Hong Kong. He was formally the ICT advisor for the English Schools Foundation for many years before retiring. He recently returned to the classroom to teach children from Year 1 to 6, a position he describes as the best retirement job ever! Peter has presented at numerous regional conferences about the benefits of using technology in teaching and learning. He completed his MSc in ICT from the University of Hong Kong in 2009, with the dissertation 'Swine Flu v Digital Natives. How adversity can drive change'. Peter writes case studies based on his classroom practice, runs a Saturday ICT Club for students where the focus in on being creative and innovative in learning.

Antony Yeung is a Research Assistant in the Centre for Learning Enhancement and Research at The Chinese University of Hong Kong. He is interested in research on curriculum improvement. He also assists in managing a project that focuses on undergraduate capstone experience.

Kiyana Zolfaghar earned a bachelor's degree in information technology from Amirkabir University of Technology, Tehran-IRAN. She is now working on her thesis in order to earn a master's degree in information technology from K.N. Toosi University of Technology, Tehran-IRAN. Her research has focused on trust and reputation systems in social web applications.She is also interested in the fields of marketing communication, consumer behavior in electronic commerce, e-readiness and IT adoption. She may be reached at kzolfaghar@sina.kntu.ac.ir.

Index